Eastern

Pyrenees

Mary-Ann Gallagher
Andy Symington
Dana Facaros

GW00683787

Credits

Footprint credits
Editorial: Felicity Laughton
Maps: Kevin Feeney
Cover: Pepi Bluck

Publisher: Patrick Dawson
Advertising: Elizabeth Taylor
Sales and marketing: Kirsty Holmes

Photography credits
Front cover: Pecold/Shutterstock.com
Back cover: Aleksandar Todorovic/
Shutterstock.com

Printed in Great Britain by CPI Antony Rowe,
Chippenham, Wiltshire

Every effort has been made to ensure that
the facts in this guidebook are accurate.
However, travellers should still obtain advice
from consulates, airlines etc about travel
and visa requirements before travelling.

Publishing information
Footprint *Focus Eastern Pyrenees*
1st edition
© Footprint Handbooks Ltd
March 2013

ISBN: 978 1 909268 07 4
CIP DATA: A catalogue record for this book
is available from the British Library

® Footprint Handbooks and the Footprint
mark are a registered trademark of Footprint
Handbooks Ltd

Published by Footprint
6 Riverside Court,
Lower Bristol Road, Bath BA2 3DZ, UK
T +44 (0)1225 469141
F +44 (0)1225 469461
www.footprinttravelguides.com

The content of Footprint *Focus Eastern
Pyrenees* has been taken directly from
Footprint's *Spain* and *Northern Spain*
handbooks and Footprint's *Languedoc-
Roussillon* guide, which were researched
and written by Mary-Ann Gallagher,
Andy Symington and Dana Facaros.

Contents

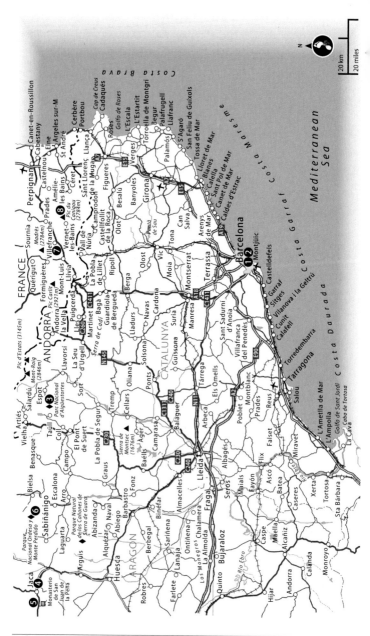

Barcelona, Catalunya's proud, flamboyant capital, really has got it all. Just for starters, there's the location: the city dips its toes in the Mediterranean, leans back against the Pyrenees, and basks in year-round sunshine. Then there is the skyline: this is Gaudí's city after all, and his buildings seem to have erupted magically between Gothic spires and glassy 21st-century design.

Head north from Barcelona to the wild and craggy Catalan Pyrenees, where you can trek across the hauntingly beautiful Parc Nacional Aigüestortes or snowboard at one of a dozen resorts. Further west the rugged Aragonese Pyrenees are mighty impressive too: a formidable barrier between the peninsula and the rest of Europe. Whether you're a serious climber, trekker or skier, or you just enjoy fresh air, picturesque villages and proud granite peaks, the area is deeply satisfying and the awe-inspiring mountainscapes live long in the memory.

Wedged between Spain and France and deep in the Pyrenees, the tiny Principality of Andorra is best known for its duty-free shopping and winter sports. Avoid the brash capital and head into the hills.

Although Roussillon (Pyrénées-Orientales) has been part of France ever since the 1659 Treaty of the Pyrenees, many locals prefer to think of their home as northern Catalunya. Catalan language classes are encouraged, people dance the *sardane*; seafood comes *a la plancha* and the red and yellow Catalan stripes flap from flagpoles.

Catalunya's sacred mountain, the Pic du Canigou, dominates the plains of eastern Roussillon like a benevolent spirit, guarding this lush land of vines, orchards and market gardens. Two valleys, the Conflent and the Vallespir, link to the Pyrenees and offer stunning scenery and a vast range of outdoor activities, plus the chance of a spectacular narrow-gauge train ride. Some of France's greatest Romanesque monuments are here, Renaissance castles (built by Spain, to keep out the French), fortress towns (built by the French, to keep out the Spanish) and the lively capital of Perpignan.

Planning your trip

Best time to visit the Eastern Pyrenees

If you are interested in winter sports, the ski resorts of Catalunya, Aragón and Andorra are best in January and February when the snow can be counted on. In summer the Pyrenees are perfect for walkers and climbers, with plenty of adventure sports on offer from rafting to canyoning. If you want to time your visit to coincide with one of the region's many festivals, see page 13 for a list of the most important ones.

Getting to the Eastern Pyrenees

Air

To reach the Eastern Pyrenees by air from the UK there are two main options: fly to Catalunya and travel north, or fly to the Languedoc-Roussillon region of France and head south. Fares will depend on the season and the kind of ticket you buy. Ticket prices are highest from June to September, and around Christmas and Easter, but it's usually possible to find a reasonably priced ticket at all times of the year thanks to the tight competition. Some useful websites for finding cheap tickets are: www.expedia.co.uk, www.cheapflights.co.uk, wwwlastminute.com, e-bookers.com, www.flynow.com, www.dialaflight.co.uk, www.kelcoo.co.uk and www.opodo.com.

Charter flights can be incredibly cheap, and many also depart from local airports. In the UK, which has the biggest selection of charter flight operators, companies such as Thomson can offer return flights from as little £60.

There are direct flights to **Barcelona** from several UK airports with **Easyjet** and year-round **Ryanair** flights to **Girona** airport.

Languedoc-Roussillon has five regional airports, the closest to the Pyrenees being **Perpignan**, **Bézier-Agde** and **Carcassonne**. These are especially well served in summer from the UK by **Ryanair**. There are also direct flights with **Flybe** and bmibaby to Perpignan. Other flights (also on **British Airways**, **Air France** and **Jet2**) serve **Toulouse** airport (about 150 km from Perpignan).

Frogbus (www.frogbus.com) provides direct links between Girona airport and Perpignan, and between Bacelona and Girona airports and Andorra.

Rail

Travelling from the UK to southern France or Northern Spain by train is unlikely to save either time or money; the only two advantages lie in the pleasure of the journey itself, and the chance to stop along the way. You can take the **Eurostar** ① *www.eurostar.com, T08432 186186,* to Paris, and transfer to a high-speed overnight service to Barcelona. The new high-speed rail link between Paris and Barcelona is due for completion in 2014; for now there are fast trains from Paris to Figueres-Vilafant (5½ hours). There is a high-speed Perpignan–Figueres train connectiong the two cities on a 45-km line which crosses the French–Spanish border via the 8-km Perthus Tunnel. There are also cheaper, slower trains from Paris to Portbou, which connect to Spanish rail services. Contact **Eurostar** and use the TGV website to arrange the journey independently, or contact **European Rail**

Don't miss...

ⓘ *T020-7619 1083, www.europeanrail.com*, and let them do it all. Note that with the TGV's Prem's fares you can get big discounts by booking up to 90 days before you travel.

Road

Car To bring a GB-registered car into France you need your vehicle registration document, full driving licence and insurance papers (or Green Card), which must be carried at all times when driving, along with your passport. You'll need to adjust or tape the headlamps, and carry a warning triangle and safety vest inside the car (not the boot).

Once you get to Paris, the most direct route to Perpignan is the A10 to Orléans, the A71 to Vierzon, the A20 to Toulouse and then the A61. Alternatively, you can continue on the A71/A75 through Clermont-Ferrand to Perpignan.

The main route into Catalunya is the E7, which crosses the Eastern Pyrenees to Barcelona. Although heavily tolled it is worthwhile compared to the slow, traffic-plagued *rutas nacionales* on these sectors. Several more scenic but much slower routes cross the Pyrenees at various points. Motorways charge expensive tolls in France and Spain. Petrol is considerably more expensive than in North America but roughly the same price in France, Spain and the UK.

Coach Eurolines ⓘ *52 Grosvenor Gardens, London SW1, T020-7730 8235, www.goby coach.com*, run several buses from major European cities to destinations in France and Spain, including Girona and Barcelona. Tickets from London–Barcelona cost from £80 (single), £147 (return). Journey times are long and, unless you hate flying, air tickets will often work out cheaper.

Sea

Bear in mind that from the UK it's usually cheaper to fly and hire a car in Northern Spain than to bring the motor across on the ferry. For competitive fares by sea to France and Spain, check with **Ferrysavers** ⓘ *T0844 576 8835, www.ferrysavers.com and www.ferrycheap.com*, which list special offers from various operators. The website www.seat61.com is good for investigating train/ferry combinations. UK to Spain ferry services are run by **Brittany Ferries** ⓘ *T0871 244 0744, www.brittany-ferries.co.uk*, from Plymouth and Portsmouth to Santander and Bilbao. There's one weekly sailing on each route, taking around 24 hours from Portsmouth and 20 hours from Plymouth. Prices are variable but can usually be found for about £70-90 each way in a reclining seat. A car adds about £150 each way, and cabins start from about £80.

Transport in the Eastern Pyrenees

Rail

France's national railway, the SNCF, has a very useful online service (www.voyages-sncf.com) for finding schedules and booking tickets. The website doubles as a tour operator, offering discounts on hotels, ski packages, flights and rental cars, and they'll post tickets to outside France. Regional trains are good for everyday travel: they are cheaper than the high-speed long-distance trains, will carry bicycles for free, and you don't have to book in advance. You can even avoid the queues by buying a ticket with your credit card from a machine in the station. These tickets are valid for two months, but like all train tickets in France you must make sure to date-stamp/validate (*composter*) your ticket in the station before boarding or you will be subject to a fine. Travel from Monday afternoons to Friday mornings (*période bleue*) is cheaper than weekends and holidays (*période blanche*). There are discounts for over 60s, under 26s and under 12s. Frequent trains link Perpignan to Spain. Local trains serve the Côte Vermeille and travel up the Conflent valley to Villefranche and Vernet-les-Bains to link up with the Petit Train Jaune (see box, page 88). This, in turn, goes to Cerdagne, where there are connections to Toulouse, Andorra and Barcelona.

The Spanish national rail network, RENFE, offers a bewildering variety of services. The website, www.renfe.com, has online timetables and ticketing. There are roughly three categories of train in Catalunya. The local trains (*rodalies* in Catalan, *cercanías* in Spanish) are the cheapest and operate for relatively short distances around the main cities. The medium-distance and regional trains may have a few more frills (mainly bathrooms and possibly, although rarely, a trolley service for drinks and snacks). The most luxurious trains are the high-speed services (such as **Euromed** and **Talgo** trains) which will have restaurant cars, films and other perks, but are considerably more expensive and not always much faster over comparatively short distances. For example, a journey between Barcelona and Giron takes 1¼ hours and costs €9.90; a regional train takes 1½ hours and costs €7.40; and a high-speed **Talgo** train takes one hour and costs €20.40.

Road

Bus Roussillon has a network of €1 buses that reach most of the towns in the department. Most branch out from Perpignan's Gare Routière; see www.cg66.fr (T04 68 80 80 80) for routes and schedules.

Buses are the staple of Spanish public transport. Services between major cities are fast, frequent, reliable, and fairly cheap. The bus from Barcelona to Girona takes 90 minutes and costs €6.85. *Express* buses run on some routes; these are more expensive but luxurious and significantly faster.

Rural bus services are slower, less frequent, and more difficult to co-ordinate. They typically run early in the morning and late in the evening; they're designed for villagers who visit the 'big smoke' once a month or so to shop. If you're trying to catch a bus from a small stop, you'll often need to almost jump out under the wheels to get the driver to pull up. The same goes when trying to get off a bus; even if you've asked the driver to let you know when your stop comes up, keep an eye out as they tend to forget. There are hundreds of different bus companies, but most bus stations have an information window and a general inquiry line to help you out. Unfortunately, English is rarely spoken, even in the larger towns. The tourist information offices usually have timetables for bus services to tourist destinations and are a good first port-of-call before you brave the ranks of ticket windows.

All bus services are reduced on Sundays, and many on Saturdays too; some services don't run at all on weekends.

For **Frogbus** services linking the region's airports, see page 6 .

Car Even minor roads in the mountains are well maintained, and most are well signposted, but a good map and/or a Sat Nav are essential. It's always cheapest to fill up with petrol or diesel at supermarkets, many of which now have 24-hour machines that take credit cards. Petrol stations of any kind are few and far between in the mountains. Unless otherwise signposted, the speed limits on autoroutes is 130 kph in France and 120 kph in Spain. On two-lane D (departmental) roads/Rutas nacionales it's 90pm in France, 100 kph in Spain, and in towns it's 50 kph in both countries. Police enforce the limits quite thoroughly and foreign drivers breaking the limit are liable to a hefty on-the-spot fine. Drivers can also be punished for not carrying red warning triangles to place on the road in case of breakdown.

Car hire is almost always cheaper to arrange before you arrive, and it's essential you book in advance in the summer when cars can be in short supply. Compare several car rental websites and then compare them to the fly/drive or rail/drive packages. You'll need to be at least 21 (or 25) and have a credit card with the name of driver matching the name on the card and your passport. Be sure to check the insurance and damage waiver before setting out, and always carry all the papers with you.

Cycling and motorcycling Although the French have great respect for cyclists, it's always best to avoid the busier roads; in Spain there are very few bike lanes, althoughthe Pyrenees are particularly good for cycling. Check out route suggestions and maps on www.bikely.com and www.bikemap.net. Rentals average €10-12 a day, more for a racing or mountain bike. Local tourist offices can advise on hire shops.

Maps
The Michelin series of road maps are by far the most accurate for general navigation, although if you're getting off the beaten track you'll often find a local map handy. Tourist offices provide these, which vary in quality from province to province. The *Everest* series of maps cover provinces and their main towns; they're not bad, although tend to be a bit out of date. The **Instituto Geográfico Nacional** publishes provincial maps, available at bookshops. Good bookshops include the **Librería Quera** ① *C/Petritxol 2, Barcelona, T933 180 743, www.llibreriaquera.com,* or **Altaïr** ① *Gran Vía 616, T933 427 171, www.altair.es,* a large travel bookshop which also has an online shop. Pick up maps in advance from **Stanford**'s at 12 Long Acre, London, WC2, T020-7836 1321, www.stanfords.co.uk.

Where to stay in the Eastern Pyrenees → *See page 11 for price code information.*

All registered accommodations charge 10% value-added tax (IVA); this is often included in the price at cheaper places and may be waived if you pay cash. Outside of the ski areas, the cheapest times to visit are around November to March, although be aware that many hotels and B&Bs outside the cities close down completely. A useful booking website for accommodation is www.booking.com.

In Spain **Hoteles** (marked H or HR) are graded from one to five stars and usually occupy their own building. **Hostales** (marked Hs or HsR) are cheaper guesthouse-style places that go from one to three stars. **Pensiones** (P) are the standard budget option, and are usually family-run flats in an apartment block. Although it's worth looking at a room before taking it, the majority are very acceptable. Spanish traditions of hospitality are alive and well; even the simplest of pensiones will generally provide a towel and soap, and check-out time is almost uniformly a very civilized midday.

Spain's famous chain of state-owned hotels, the **paradors** (www.parador.es) are often set in castles, convents and other historic buildings, although there are plenty of modern ones too. Most are very luxurious, with pools, bars, fine restaurants and other fancy trimmings but standards can vary considerably. They are usually expensive, but they offer all kinds of special deals, including a youth package, which can make them surprisingly affordable.

An excellent option if you've got transport are the network of rural homes, called **casas rurales**, where standards are often as high as any country hotel. The best of them are traditional farmhouses or old village cottages. Rates tend to be excellent compared to hotels, and many offer kitchen facilities and home-cooked meals. The Aragonese regional government publishes its own listings booklet, available at any tourist office in the area; you can also search for them at www.visitaragon.es, www.casasruralesdearagon.es and www.toprural.com.

Hotels in France are also graded from one to five stars according to their amenities. There are several umbrella organizations for hotels that guarantee certain standards. Most rooms now have individual air conditioning and the majority offer free Wi-Fi, or at least internet that guests are welcome to use. That said, the rock-hard sausage pillows still preside over many a rural hotel bed.

Many of Roussillon boutique hotels, guesthouses and B&Bs are located in old stone farmhouses (*mas*), *hôtels particuliers* or châteaux. Some will collect you from the train station or nearest airport. Many (because of French laws limiting B&Bs to five rooms) have self-catering apartments or a mix of rooms, suites, apartments and gîtes. Not all take credit cards, so be sure to ask when you book.

There are a few **albergues/auberges** (youth hostels) around, but the accessible price of *pensiones* rarely makes it worth the trouble except for solo travellers. The exception is in mountain regions, where in Spain there are excellent **refugios**, which are simple hostels for walkers and climbers along the lines of a Scottish bothy. In France, the **gîtes d'étapes** are communal shelters set up along the GR long-distance paths, usually equipped with bunk beds in dorm rooms (bring your own sleeping bag) and basic kitchen facilities; you can pinpoint them at www.gite-etape.com. The mountain **refuges** in the Pyrenees often serve meals; local tourist offices have phone numbers; it's best to ring ahead to make sure there's space.

Price codes

Where to stay

€€€€	over €170	€€€	€110-170
€€	€55-110	€	under €55

Prices include taxes and service charge, but not meals. They are based on a double room, except in the € range, where prices are almost always per person.

Restaurants

€€€ over €20	€€ €10-20	€ under €10

Prices refer to the cost of a two-course meal, without a drink.

Food and drink in the Eastern Pyrenees

Food → *See box, above, for price code information.*

While the regional differences in the cuisine of Spain are important, the basics remain the same. Spanish cooking relies on meat, fish/seafood, beans and potatoes given character by the chef's holy trinity: garlic, peppers and, of course, olive oil. The influence of the colonization of the Americas is evident, and the Moors left a lasting culinary legacy, particularly in the south. The result is a hearty, filling style of meal ideally washed down with some of the nation's excellent wines.

Regional cuisine

The **Catalans** are famous for their cuisine. Seafood from the Mediterranean, rice and vegetables from the plains and meat and game from the mountains are combined in unusual ways; look out for *mandonguilles amb sèpia*, meatballs with cuttlefish, or *gambas con pollastre*, prawns with chicken. The local staple is *pa amb tomàquet*, country bread rubbed with fresh tomatoes, with a little olive oil and salt.

The regional dishes of **Aragón** owe much to the mountains, with hearty stews and game dishes featuring alongside fresh trout from Pyrenean streams. Simple dishes such as *migas* (breadcrumbs fried with garlic, lard and sausage offcuts) are part of an impecunious rural tradition, as are *magras con tomate* (pork strips fried in garlic and tomato). The Ebro valley provides a fertile vegetable-growing area in the heart of the region, whose tomatoes and onions are especially famous. These combine with red peppers and garlic to form the characteristic *chilindrón* sauce used to stew lamb or chicken in. The region's young lamb – called *ternasco* here – has denomination of origin status and is deservedly famous. Game is also widely eaten, and Teruel's ham and other piggy products are renowned nationwide.

Over the border in **Roussillon** you will also find traditional Catalan influences in the fancier restaurants, featuring recipes that combine often unexpected sea and mountain ingredients (*mar i muntanya*), or sweet and savoury. Snails are extremely popular and here they serve them barbecued as a *cargolade* during the wine harvest. In autumn, one of the specialities is a *roussillonnade* – grilled cèpes with sausage. The charcuterie and free-range meats from the Cerdagne are justly renowned. The all-time classic dessert is *crème catalane*, lightly flavoured with cinnamon and anise under a caramel coating.

Wine

In good Catholic fashion, wine is the blood of Spain. It's the standard accompaniment to most meals, but also features prominently in bars, where a glass of cheap *tinto* or *blanco* can cost as little as €0.30, although it's normally a bit more.

A well-regulated system of *Denominaciones de Origen* (DO) is in place. Much of Spain's wine is produced in the north, although Aragón's wines aren't as famous as they deserve to be – the Somontano, Calatayud, Campo de Borja and Cariñena denominations produce some fine reds and good whites from a number of different grape varieties, both traditional and more experimental.

Catalan wines are also gaining increasing recognition. Best known is *cava*, the home-grown bubbly, and a night out in Barcelona should always start with a glass or two of this crisp, sparkling white wine. The largest wine-producing region in Catalunya is Penedés, which produces a vast range of reds, whites and rosés to suit all tastes and pockets, but you'll find other local specialities including the unusual *Paxarete*, a very sweet traditional chocolatey brown wine produced around Tarragona.

One of the joys of Spain, though, is the rest of the wine. Order a *menú del día* at a cheap restaurant and you'll be unceremoniously served a cheap bottle of local red (sometimes without even asking for it). Wine snobbery can leave by the back door at this point: it may be cold, but you'll find it refreshing; it may be acidic, but once the olive-oil laden food arrives, you'll be glad of it. Wine's not a luxury item in Spain, so people add water to it if they feel like it, or lemonade, or *cola* (to make the party drink called *calimocho*).

Languedoc-Roussillon, an enormous patchwork of different types of rocky soils, exposures and microclimates – all the things that make up the French word *terroir* – is divided unevenly into 24 AOC (Appellation d'Origine Contrôlée) growing regions. Combine these AOC wines with the Vins de Pays d'Oc and vins de table, and the region produces more wine than anywhere else in France and, in the past couple of decades, the wine has improved by leaps and bounds.

Restaurants in the Eastern Pyrenees

One of the great pleasures of travelling in Spain is eating out, but it's no fun sitting alone in a restaurant so try and adapt to the local hours as much as you can; it may feel strange leaving dinner until after 2200, but you'll miss out on a lot of atmosphere if you don't.

Lunch is the biggest meal of the day for most people in Spain, and it's also the cheapest time to eat. Just about all restaurants offer a *menú del día*, which is usually a set three-course meal that includes wine or soft drink. There's often a choice of several starters and mains. To make the most of the meal, a handy tip is to order another starter in place of a main; most places are quite happy to do it, and the starters are usually more interesting (and sometimes larger) than the mains, which tend to be slabs of mediocre meat. Most places open for lunch at about 1300, and stop serving at 1500 or 1530, although at weekends this can extend. The quality of *à la carte* is usually higher than the *menú*, and quantities are large.

Most restaurants open for dinner at 2030 or later; any earlier and it's likely a tourist trap. Although some places do offer a cheap set menu, you'll usually have to order *à la carte*. In quiet areas, places stop serving at 2200 on weeknights, but in cities and at weekends people tend to sit down at 2230 or later.

On the French side of the border, Roussillon shuts down for lunch between 1200 and 1400 or 1500. It's wise to get to your restaurant as soon as you can after 1200; to arrive much later, especially in rural areas, is to miss out on the *plat du jour* (dish of the day), or even risk being turned away. Unlike Spain, the dinner witching hour is from 1930 to 2030; if you're going to arrive later, be sure to tell the restaurant when you book.

Festivals in the Eastern Pyrenees

Even the smallest village in Spain has a fiesta, and some have several. Although mostly nominally religious in nature, they usually include the works: a Mass and procession or two to be sure, but also live music, bullfights, competitions, fireworks and copious drinking of *calimocho* a mix of red wine and cola (not as bad as it sounds). A feature of many are the *gigantes y cabezudos*, huge-headed papier-mâché figures based on historical personages who parade the streets. Adding to the sense of fun are *peñas*, boisterous social clubs which patrol the streets making music, get rowdy at the bullfights and drink wine all night and day. Most fiestas are in summer, and if you're spending much time in Spain in that period you're bound to run into one; expect some trouble finding accommodation. Details of the major town fiestas can be found in the travelling text. National holidays can be difficult times to travel; it's important to reserve tickets in advance. If the holiday falls mid-week, it's usual form to take an extra day off, forming a long weekend known as a *puente* (bridge).

Languedoc-Roussillon loves a party too, and puts on a full calendar of festivities and events. Prestigious ballet, music, theatre and film festivals take place in the cities year round. Elsewhere, age-old traditions (among them, the bear festival in Arles-sur-Tech and the Good Friday procession of La Sanch in Perpignan) have survived more or less intact, and where they haven't, the locals love to put on jousts, troubadour singsongs and other events dedicated to evoking the good old pre-Simon de Montfort days. In summer, juices flow at outdoor music festivals and the summer ferias, with their bulls, music, bodegas and general merriment. Check online or with the tourist fices for exact dates and times.

Major fiestas
January/February
5 January Cabalgata de Los Reyes (Three Kings). Throughout Spain. The Three Kings Parade in floats tossing out sweets to kids, who get Christmas presents the next day.

February Fête de l'Ours, Arles-sur-Tech, T04 68 39 11 99, www.ville-arles-sur-tech.fr, and Prats-du-Mollo-la-Preste, T04 68 39 70 83, www.pratsdemollolapreste.com. The Vallespir's 2 festivals of the bear date back to prehistoric times. There's a morning procession, followed in the afternoon by the 'hunting' and 'shaving' of the 'bear' (people in sheepskins and blackened faces) and dances; all good rowdy fun.

March/April
Easter Semana Santa. Easter celebrations are held everywhere in Spain and parades take place in every town, particularly in the south. In Perpignan the **Procession de la Sanch** is a haunting, solemn Good Friday procession of the medieval Brotherhood of the Holy Blood, who were founded by St Vincent Ferrer.

May/June
Feast of Corpus Christi. Held in most towns, it is celebrated with traditional dancing and parades.

21-24 June Fiesta de San Juan, or the **Midsummer's Solstice**. This is celebrated across Spain, often with the strange custom of the 'Burial of the Sardine'. Throughout

Roussillon it is the **Festa Major**, when torches are relayed down from the Pic du Canigou to light a thousand bonfires all across northern and southern Catalunya.

July/August
Festival de la Sardane, Céret, T04 68 87 46 49, www.ceret.fr. A massive Jul celebration of all things Catalan, with costumes and much dancing of the *sardane*, the national circle dance, to the lilting music of the top *coblas* from across Catalunya.

Medieval Festival, Arles-sur-Tech, T04 68 39 11 99, www.ville-arles-sur-tech.fr. Knights, troubadours and ladies fair recapture the spirit of the Middle Ages, culminating in a big medieval banquet in Jul.

Festival Pau Casals, Prades, T04 68 96 33 07, www.prades-festival-casals.com. Founded in 1950 by exiled cellist Pau Casals, this is one of the top chamber music festivals in Europe, featuring performances in St-Michel-de-Cuxa and elsewhere in Jul and Aug.

Course du Canigou, www.coursedu canigou.com, a strenuous 34-km mountain marathon from Vernet-les-Bains to the top of the Pic du Canigou and back that attracts over 800 participants in Aug.

September/October
Barcelona Festes de la Mercé. Huge festival in Barcelona with folkloric parades, fireworks, dragons and giants.

Jazzèbre, Perpignan, T04 68 35 37 46, www.jazzebre.com. Jazz and world music in Perpignan and surrounding towns, from late Sep to Oct.

Visa pour l'Image, Perpignan, T04 68 62 38 00, www.visapourlimage.com. A city-wide celebration of historic and contemporary photojournalism from around the world.

Public holidays
1 Jan New Year's Day.
6 Jan Epiphany (Reyes Magos; Spain), when Christmas presents are given.
Mar/Apr Maundy Thursday, Good Friday, Easter Sunday.
1 May Labour Day.
8 May VE Day (France).
May/Jun Ascension (France).
May/Jun Pentecost (France).
14 Jul Bastille Day (France).
15 Aug Assumption.
12 Oct Columbus Day, Spanish National Day (Día de la Hispanidad; Spain) .
1 Nov All Saints' Day.
11 Nov Armistice Day
6 Dec Constitution Day (Spain; Día de la Constitución Española).
8 Dec Feast of the Immaculate Conception (Spain; Inmaculada Concepción).
24 Dec Christmas Eve (Spain; Noche Buena).
25 Dec Navidad (Christmas Day).

Essentials A-Z

Accident and emergencies
France Fire service T18; **Police** T19;
SAMU (medical emergencies) T15.
Spain Nationwide emergency number for
fire, **police** and **ambulance**: T112.

Electricity
The current in France and Spain is 220V. A
round 2-pin plug is used (European standard).

Embassies and consulates
For embassies and consulates of France and
Spain, see http://embassy.goabroad.com.

Health → *See Directory text throughout the*
book for hospitals and pharmacies.
Comprehensive travel and medical insurance
is recommended. EU citizens should apply for
a free European Health Insurance Card or
EHIC (www.ehic.org), which entitles you to
emergency medical treatment. Note that you
will have to pay all charges and prescriptions
up front and be reimbursed once you return
home. If you develop a minor ailment while
on holiday, a visit to any pharmacy will allow
you to discuss your concerns with staff who
can give medical advice and recommend
treatment (although they don't always speak
English). Outside normal opening hours, the
address of the nearest duty pharmacy is
displayed in the pharmacy window. The out-
of-hours number for a local doctor may also
be listed. In a serious emergency, go to the
accident and emergency department at the
nearest hospital (numbers are listed in the
Directory sections of this book) or call an
ambulance: T15 (France), T112 (Spain).

Insurance
Comprehensive travel and medical insurance
is strongly recommended, as the European
Health Insurance Card (EHIC) does not cover

medical repatriation, ongoing medical treatment or treatment considered to be non-
urgent. Check for exclusions if you mean
to engage in risky sports. Keep all insurance
documents to hand; a good way to keep
track of your policies is to email the details
to yourself.

Make sure you have adequate insurance
when hiring a car and always ask how much
excess you are liable for if the vehicle is
returned with any damage. It is generally
worth paying a little more for a collision
damage waiver. If driving your own vehicle
to the Pyrenees, contact your insurers before
you travel to ensure you are adequately
covered, and keep the documents in your
vehicle in case you need to prove it.

Language
There are 3 official languages in **Catalunya**:
Catalan, Spanish (Castellano) and Aranés
(spoken in the Val d'Aran, high in the
Pyrenees), while in the Pyrenean valleys
of **Aragón** you may come across Aragonés,
still spoken by some 10,000 people. In
Roussillon people are more likely to speak
Catalan or Spanish than French, but you'll
find English translations everywhere.

Most tourist office staff will speak at least
some English, and there's a good range
of translated information available in
many regions.

Money
→ *See www.xe.com for exchange rates.*
The euro (€) is the currency in France and
Spain. There are ATM machines in every
town, and nearly all hotels, restaurants and
shops accept credit cards. Note that many
North American cards lack a chip necessary
for them to work in toll machines or in
24-hour petrol stations, so check with

you bank before you leave. The website www.moneysavingexpert.com has a good rundown on the most economical ways of accessing cash while travelling.

Safety
The Pyrenees are generally a safe region, with considerably less violent crime than many other parts of Europe. However, street crime – bag-snatching and pickpocketing – in the bigger cities is on the rise. Don't invite crime by leaving luggage or cash in cars, and if you are parking in a city or a popular hiking zone, leave the glove box open so that thieves know there is nothing to steal.

In **France** you need to visit the **Gendarmerie** to report lost or stolen possessions. In **Spain** the **Policía Nacional** are the ones to go to if you need to report anything stolen, etc. Police stations are listed in phone books under *comisarías*.

Telephone → *Country code +34.*
France The French have dispensed with area codes, and all numbers dialled within the country are now 10 digits. If a number begins with 06 it's a mobile phone. The country code is 33; when dialling from abroad, leave out the first 0 (T+332). Directory assistance, T118 218.
Spain Domestic landlines have 9-digit numbers beginning with 9 (occasionally with 8). Although the first 3 digits indicate the province, you have to dial the full number from wherever you are calling, including abroad. Mobiles numbers start with 6. Directory enquiries, T11818 for national or T11825 for international numbers. (All these numbers are operated by **Telefónica**; other operators offer the same services.)

Time
Spain and France operate on western European time, ie GMT +1, and change their clocks in line with the rest of the EU.

Tipping
France French bar and restaurant bills nearly always include a 15% service charge so tipping a little extra is discretionary. Taxi drivers appreciate it if you round up the fare or add an extra couple of euros for any help with your bags. Give a guide €1-2 at the end of guided tours.
Spain Tipping in Spain is far from compulsory, but much practised. Around 10% is considered fairly generous in a restaurant; 3-5% is more usual. It's rare for a service charge to be added to a bill. Waiters do not normally expect tips for lunchtime set meals or tapas, but here and in bars and cafés people will often leave small change, especially for table service. Taxi drivers don't expect a tip, but don't expect you to sit around waiting for 20 cents change either. In rural areas, churches will often have a local keyholder who will open it up for you; if there's no admission charge, a tip or donation is appropriate; say €1 per head; more if they've given a detailed tour.

Tourist information → *See individual entries for specific details of tourist offices.*
Aragón www.turismodearagon.com and www.visitaragon.es.
Catalunya www.turismoencatalunya.es.
Roussillon www.cdt-66.com.

Visas and immigration
Entry requirements are subject to change, so always check with the Spanish/French tourist board or an embassy/consulate if you're not an EU citizen. EU citizens and those from countries within the Schengen agreement can enter Spain/France freely. UK/Irish citizens will need to carry a passport, while an identity card suffices for other EU/Schengen nationals. Citizens of Australia, the USA, Canada, New Zealand and Israel can enter without a visa for up to 90 days. Other citizens will require a visa, obtainable from Spanish/French consulates or embassies.

Contents

Barcelona

Arriving in Barcelona → *Population: around 1,625,000.*

Getting there

Barcelona's international **airport** is in El Prat de Llobregat, 12 km to the south of the city. For information on arriving by air, see 6.

If arriving by **car**, the main access road into Barcelona is the A-7 *autopista*, which crosses the Eastern Pyrenees and runs down past Girona and Figueres.

Barcelona's main **bus and coach** station ⓘ *Estació d'Autobuses Barcelona-Nord, C/Ali Bei 80, metro Arc de Triomf, T902 260 606, www.barcelonanord.com*, has services for national and international destinations. Note that the bus station next to Barcelona-Sants train station is a stop on many routes, but it is the final destination for most Eurolines buses.

The main **train** station for international, regional, and local trains is Estació-Sants, metro Sants. Many trains often stop at Passeig de Gràcia station which is more convenient for the city centre. Some trains from France arrive at the Estació de França near the harbour. For RENFE information, see www.renfe.com.

Getting around

The public transport network in Barcelona is excellent: clean, efficient, cheap, safe and easy to use. For maps and information in English, check the website, www.tmb.cat or call the TMB on T902 075 027. ➡ *For further details, see Transport, 35.*

Tourist information

The tourist information services in Barcelona are excellent. The **main tourist office** on the Plaça Catalunya also has a bureau de change, an accommodation-booking service, and a gift shop. You can book tours here and buy the various discount cards (see below). There is plenty of information on the excellent websites www.barcelonaturisme.com and www.bcn.cat. For telephone information, call T906 301 282 within Spain, or T+34 933 689 730 from abroad. **Main office** ⓘ *Plaça Catalunya, daily 0900-2100.* **Centre d'Informació de la Virreina** ⓘ *Palau de la Virreina, La Rambla 99, T933 017 775, Mon-Sat 1000-2000, Sun 1100-1500, ticket sales Tue-Sat 1100-2000, Sun 1100-1430*, is the information service for the Generalitat's culture department, with details of concerts, exhibitions and festivals throughout the city.

La Rambla and down to the sea → *For listings, see pages 32-36.*

Almost inevitably, everyone's first glimpse of Barcelona will be the Rambla, the city's most famous promenade. Caught somewhere between banality and beauty, it's a strange and oddly appealing mixture of the picturesque and the tacky: almost lost among the fleets of 'human statues' are pretty turn-of-the-20th-century kiosks overflowing with flowers, fast-food outlets are squeezed between crumbling theatres and mansions, and banks pop up in whimsical Modernista houses.

Plaça Catalunya

The mouth of the Rambla, and the inevitable starting point for a stroll, is the Plaça Catalunya, a huge square which links the old city with the new, and is the main transport hub of the city, where buses and trains converge, disgorging endless crowds on to the Rambla.

Les Ramblas

The Rambla looks like one street, but in fact it is five, all placed end-to-end in a seamless progress down to the harbour and referred to as La Rambla or Les Ramblas with equal ease by locals. Each section has its own name and its own characteristics. The first stretch of the five adjoining Ramblas is the **Rambla de las Canaletes**, named for the **Font de las Canaletes**, a florid 19th-century fountain which is where fans of **FC Barça** come to celebrate victories. Drink from this fountain, a legend says, and you'll return to Barcelona.

Rambla de las Flores is the prettiest and most sweet-smelling section of the street, with dozens of kiosks spilling over with brightly coloured bouquets. Set back on the right is the elegant **Palau de la Virreina**, which houses the city's cultural information offices and an exhibition space called the **Centre de la Imatge**.

Further down on the right is the famous market, more usually known as **La Boquería**, capped with a lacy wrought-iron roof and a Modernista sign in bright jewel colours in 1914. Inside are piles of gleaming produce and there's a liberal sprinkling of tiny bars for a coffee or some oysters. Dive straight to the back of the market to avoid tourist prices and to enjoy better its unique atmosphere.

Back on the Rambla, there's a large colourful **pavement mosaic** by Miró, overlooked by the delightful **Casa Bruno Quadros**, formerly a Modernista umbrella shop, with a Chinese dragon supporting an umbrella. Stop off for cakes in the Modernista **Antigua Casa Figueres**, now an outpost of the famous **Escribà** patisserie.

Rambla de les Caputxins is named after a Capuchin monastery which was destroyed in 1835. A new opera house, the **Liceu** ① *La Rambla 51-59, T934 859 900, www.liceubarcelona.cat; daily 1000-1300, guided visits at 1000 (buy tickets in L'Espai de Liceu), express non-guided tours at 1130, 1200, 1230 and 1300; Metro Liceu; Bus 14, 38, 51, 59*, was built in its place and has become one of Barcelona's best-loved institutions.

On the left, a pair of tall arches leads into the **Plaça Reial**, a grand 19th-century square with neoclassical arcades and lofty palm trees. The fountain of the Three Graces is flanked by twin lamp posts designed by Gaudí for his first municipal commission.

The last stretch of the Rambla, called the **Rambla de Santa Mònica** is home to a daily craft market. Tucked down an alley off the Rambla is the city's waxwork museum, the **Museu de Cera** ① *Passatge Banca 7, T933 172 649, www.museucerabcn.com, Oct-Jun Mon-Fri 1000-1330 and 1600-1930, weekends and holidays 1100-1930, Jul-Sep daily 1000-2200, €15, children €9; guided night visits by the city executioner daily Jun 2000, Jul-Sep 2100 (over 8s only) €19; Metro Liceu, Bus 14, 36, 38, 57, 59, 64, 91*. The dummies of international criminals have been augmented by Hollywood stars, Royals and the 1992 Olympic mascot, Cobi.

Almost at the harbour, the Rambla opens out into the **Plaça Portal de la Pau** (Gate of Peace), where the **Monument a Colom** ① *Plaça Portal de la Pau (closed temporarily); Metro Drassanes, bus 14, 36, 38, 59, 64, 91*, the world's largest statue of Christopher Columbus, enjoys a bird's eye view of the city.

Barri Gòtic → *For listings, see pages 32-36.*

The Rambla marks the southern boundary of the Barri Gòtic (The Gothic Quarter); the heart of the city for more than 2000 years. It is one of the best preserved Gothic quarters in Europe, a dizzy maze of palaces, squares and churches piled on top of the remnants of the original Roman settlement.

Barcelona

Where to stay 🏨
ABaC 3 A4
Actual 1 A5
Arts Barcelona 2 E6
Casa Fuster 5 A4
Circa 1905 6 B4
Constanza 8 C5
Denit 4 C4
España 7 D3
Montecarlo 9 C4

Restaurants 🍴
Atril 1 D5
Bar Pinotxo 4 C4
Big Fish 2 D5
Bliss 5 D4
Bodega la Plata 8 D4
Café de l'Acadèmia 11 D4
Café de l'Opera 13 D4
Cinc Sentits 3 B4
Kaiku 6 E4

La Paradeta 7 D5
Pla 15 D4
Monvínic 9 B4
Mosquito 10 D5
Suculent 16 D3
Teresa Carles 17 C4
Ticket 12 C2

Bars & clubs 🍸
Be Cool 14 A4
El Mariatchi 18 D4
Jamboree 20 D4
La Macarena 21 D4
Marsella 23 D3
Mirablau 42 A4
Sala Apollo 44 D3

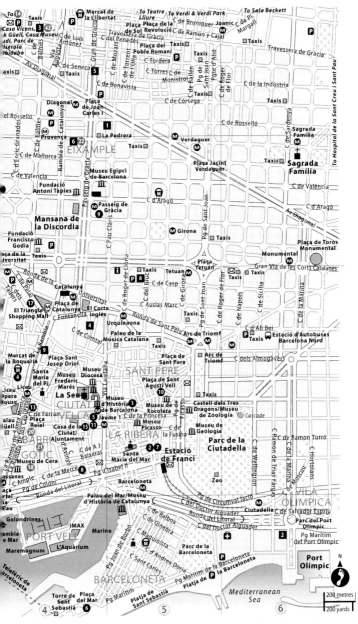

Cathedral of La Seu and around

ⓘ *Pla de la Seu s/n, T933 428 260, www.catedral.bcn.org, cathedral Mon-Fri 0800-1330 and 1600-1930, Sat-Sun 0800-1330 and 1700-1930, free; lift and choir daily 1000-1330 and 1600-1800, €2 each; Museu de la Catedral, T933 102 580, 1000-1300 and 1600-1830 daily, €1, Metro Jaume I, Bus 17, 19, 40, 45.*

The main entrance overlooks the wide Plaça Nova; from here you'll get the full effect of the fairytale façade which was actually stuck on in the 19th century. The main cathedral dates back to the 13th century (some sections survive of the even earlier Romanesque building), and the interior is magnificent, suitably dim and hushed, with soaring naves supported by heavily decorated Gothic cross vaults. Underneath the main altar lie the remains of the city's patron saint, Santa Eulàlia, in a 14th-century alabaster sarcophagus adorned with grisly depictions of her martyrdom. Behind the altar, a lift just off the ambulatory will whip you to the roof for staggering views. The delightful cloister has a lush palm-filled garden in the centre, home to a colony of white geese. They have lived here for so long that no one can remember why. The old tradition of dancing a hollow egg (known as the *l'ou com balla*) on the delicate 15th-century fountain of St George takes place on the feast of Corpus Christi in early June.

Behind the Museu Diocesà is the **Museu Frederic Marés** ⓘ *Plaça Sant Iu (off C/ des Comtes), T932 563 500, www.museumares.bcn.es, Tue-Sat 1000-1900, Sun and hols 1000-2000, €4.20, concessions €2.40, free every Sun 1500-2000 and on 1st Sun of each month 1100-2000*, devoted to the obsessive, patchwork collection of the eccentric sculptor and painter who had obviously never heard the phrase 'less is more'.

Plaça del Rei

Plaça del Rei (King's Square) is a tiny, exquisite square just off the Plaça Sant Jaume. The rulers of Catalunya held court for centuries in the austerely beautiful **Palau Reial Major** which closes off the square, and prayed in the adjoining Royal Chapel with its dainty belltower. Incredibly, the astonishingly intact remnants of the Roman city of Barcino were unearthed beneath this square a century or so ago.

The fascinating **Museu d'Història de Barcelona (MuHBa)** ⓘ *Plaça del Rei s/n, T932 562 100, www.museuhistoria.bcn.es, Tue-Sat 1000-1900, Sun 1000-2000, €7 (includes entry to all of MuHBa's sites, including the Pedralbes Monastery, Metro Jaume I, Bus 16, 17, 19, 40, 45,* reveals the history of the city layer by layer. The deepest layer contains the Roman city of Barcino, established here more than 2000 years ago. Tacked on to it are Visigothic ruins which were built during the 5th and 6th centuries and built on top of the whole lot are the palaces and churches of the middle ages which still enclose the Plaça del Rei.

The echoing throne room, the Saló de Tinell, was built in 1359 and is a masterpiece of Catalan Gothic style. Next to the throne room is the Royal Chapel of Saint Agatha, with a single graceful nave and a dazzling polychrome ceiling supported by diaphragm arches.

Plaça del Pi and around

The pretty Plaça del Pi is named for a glade of pine trees which once stood here, their memory recalled now by a single pine. The hulking 15th-century Gothic church of Santa Maria del Pi is now solely remarkable for its enormous rose window, the biggest in Europe, as looters burnt the interior to a crisp during the Civil War.

El Call

Carrer Banys Nous, off Plaça Sant Josep Oriol, marks the boundary of the old Jewish Quarter, known as El Call from the Hebrew word *quahal*, meaning 'meeting place'. There is virtually no trace of what was once the most important Jewish population in medieval Spain – just a faded stone with a Hebrew inscription from 1314 which was erected at the corner of Carrer Arc de Sant Ramon de Call and Carrer Marlet in the 19th century and the remnants of a medieval **synagogue**.

La Ribera → *For listings, see pages 32-36.*

The old artisans' district of La Ribera is a funky, fashionable neighbourhood with some of the city's trendiest bars, restaurants and shopping, as well as its most popular museum (the Picasso Museum), its most beautiful church, and a string of elegant palaces along the Carrer de Montcada.

Museu Picasso

ⓘ *C/Montcada 15-23, T932 563 000, www.museupicasso.bcn.es, Tue-Sat 1000-2000, Sun 1000-1500, €9 concessions €5, Metro Jaume I, Bus 14, 17, 19, 39, 40, 45, 51, 59.*

The collection includes few of Picasso's most famous paintings, and focuses instead on the early works, particularly those created by the young artist in Barcelona. The early selection of works includes some of the chilly paintings of his Blue Period, like the stricken mother and child of *Desamperados* (The Despairing, 1904), and several works from his Rose Period. There is almost nothing, just a small *Head* (1913), from the Cubist years, and a single *Harlequin* (1917), from the celebrated series. From 1917, there's another leap in time, this time to the extraordinary series of 44 paintings and drawings based on Velázquez's *Las Meninas*, which Picasso painted in a single concentrated burst over six months at the end of 1956, and in which every detail of Velázquez's masterpiece has been picked out, pored over and reinterpreted.

Església de Santa Maria del Mar

ⓘ *Plaça de Santa Mara del Mar, Metro Jaume I, 0900-1330 and 1630-2000, free.*

The loveliest church in all Catalunya sits at the bottom of the Carrer Montcada: the church of Santa Maria del Mar. Construction began in 1329 and was completed in just 54 years – record speed for the era – which meant that other styles and forms couldn't creep in as successive architects took over the job. As a result, the church is considered one of the finest and purest examples of Catalan Gothic.

Parc de la Ciutadella

This is one of Barcelona's most popular parks, a quiet oasis in the heart of the city. The park was originally the site of an enormous star-shaped citadel, built after Barcelona fell to the Bourbon armies in 1714. It became the most hated building in the city, and was torn down in 1869. The park was laid out in the late 19th century by a team which included the young Gaudí, and expanded again for the Universal Exhibition of 1888 – Barcelona's first taste of what an international show could do to change the face of a city.

The **zoo** ① *Parc de la Ciutadella s/n, T932 256 780, daily Nov-Feb 1000-1700, Mar and Oct 1000-1800, Apr and Sep 1000-1900, Jun-Aug 0930-1930, €12.90/8.30 for children aged 3-12, metro Ciutadella*, takes up half of the park, but it's still not enough for the poor animals cramped into small concrete enclosures.

Palau de la Música Catalana

① *Carrer de Sant Francesc de Paula 2, T932 957 200, tickets T902 475 486, www.palaumusica.org, daily 1000-1530, Aug 0900-2000, visits by guided tour only, booking in advance is advisable. Tours depart every 30 mins in English, Castilian, and Catalan and last 50 mins €17, metro Urquinona. The best way to see the Palau is to come for a concert, but tickets are hard to come by.*

The Palau was built between 1905 and 1908 as a new home to the Orfeó Català, the first and biggest of the choral societies which sprang up during Catalunya's *Renaixença* (cultural renaissance) a century ago. It was designed by Domènech i Muntaner, who collaborated with many of Catalunya's most celebrated craftsmen and artists. The main auditorium is spell-binding: rainbow-coloured light streams in through the vast stained glass ceiling of flowers and musical angels.

The Palau won the Building of the Year award in 1908, but just two decades later it was being sneeringly referred to as the 'Palace of Catalan Junk'. After decades of neglect, it was restored in the 1980s was inscribed on UNESCO's list of World Heritage Sites in 1977.

El Raval → *For listings, see pages 32-36.*

Part impoverished ghetto, part boho-chic *barri*, the Raval's fortunes have improved immensely over the last decades, although it remains one of the city's poorest neighbourhoods. The construction of the glossy Museu d'Art Contemporani has brought in trendy new galleries, fashion shops and arty bars, and, with the arrival of immigrants particularly from north Africa and Pakistan, it's also becoming multicultural.

Museu d'Art Contemporani de Barcelona (MACBA)

① *Plaça dels Àngels. T934 120 810. www.macba.cat. Mon, Wed-Fri 1100-1930, Sat 1000-2000, Sun 1000-1500 (open until 2200 on Fri and Sat in summer), €8, concessions €6.60, prices vary for temporary exhibitions. Metro Universitat. Bus 9, 14, 16, 17, 22, 24, 38, 41, 55, 58, 59, 66, 91, 141.*

Richard Meiers' huge, glassy home for MACBA was built in 1995, a symbol of the city's dedication to urban renewal and a monument to its preoccupation with contemporary design. It overlooks a wide, modern square, which has become a huge favourite with skateboarders.

Although the museum's permanent collection officially begins after the Civil War, there are some earlier pieces by Alexander Calder, Paul Klee and Catalan artists like Leandre Cristòfol, Joan Ponç and Àngel Ferrant. Many of the usually excellent temporary exhibitions focus on the latest digital and multi-media works. MACBA has a great bookshop and an attractive café-bar which shares a square with the CCCB (see below) around the corner.

Centre de Cultura Contemporània de Barcelona (CCCB)

ⓘ *Metro Universitat, 9 Sep-May Tue, Thu-Fri 1100-1400 and 1600-2000, Wed and Sat 1100-2000, Sun and holidays 1100-1900, Jun-8 Sep Tue-Sun 1000-2000, €5.50/4.*

The excellent Contemporary Culture Centre (CCCB) sits behind MACBA and is the second prong of the city's institution for contemporary culture. Set in the former Casa de la Caritat, a hospice for pilgrims established in the 16th century, it hosts wide-ranging and eclectic exhibitions on all aspects of contemporary culture not covered by MACBA.

Palau Güell and around

ⓘ *C/Nou de la Rambla 3, T933 173 974, open for guided tours only Mon-Sat 1000-1330 and 1600-1830, tours fill up quickly – book in advance in summer, €2.50, Metro Liceu, bus 14, 38, 51, 59.*

Palau Güell on Carrer Nou de la Rambla was Gaudí's first major commission for the man who was to become his most important patron, Eusebi Güell. Both men were intensely Catalanist and intensely religious, and these themes are replayed throughout the tall, narrow mansion, which recently (2012) emerged from a lengthy and expensive restoration project. The main salon is overwhelming, a lofty hall topped with an arched cosmic dome covered with deep blue honeycombed tiles; thin shafts of light entering through tiny windows symbolise the stars circling the moon. This is the heart of the house, with all the rooms organized around the central hall in the Mediterranean fashion, and surrounded by a series of galleries and miradors. The rooftop boasts a rippling terrace with a playful forest of swirling, *trencadi*-covered chimneys, surrounding a lofty central spire topped with a wrought iron bat, a legendary guardian of Catalan heroes.

Sant Pau del Camp and around

ⓘ *C/Sant Pau s/n. Metro Paral.lel, Wed-Mon 1120-1300 and 1800-1930, Tue 1130-1230, free.*

The Carrer de Sant Pau runs down to the tiny, delightful church of Sant Pau del Camp, the most important surviving Romanesque church in the city. The tranquil cloister has Moorish-inspired arches and simple columns carved with a menagerie of mythical creatures. The modern **Rambla de Raval**, nearby, is lined with terrace cafés and features one of the city's most charming pieces of art: Botero's huge *Fat Cat*.

Museu Marítim (Drassanes Reials)

ⓘ *Av Drassanes s/n, T933 429 920, www.museumaritimbarcelona.com, closed for restoration until late 2013, Metro Drassanes.*

The magnificent Drassanes Reials, the vast medieval shipyards begun in 1243, form the largest and most important civil Gothic structure in the world, and were eventually capable of accommodating 40 galley ships. Now they contain the excellent and entertaining Museu Marítim (Maritime Museum) and the star exhibit is a monstrous galley ship, a replica of the Royal Galley of John of Austria which was built to lead the Holy Alliance against the Turks in the Battle of Lepant in 1571. Down in the Port Vell, a five-minute walk away, the museum has renovated a beautiful turn-of-the-century sailing ship, the *Santa Eulàlia*, which is also part of the visit.

Eixample → *For listings, see pages 32-36.*

The Eixample (pronounced *Ai-sham-play*) is Barcelona's most upmarket neighbourhood, with one of the greatest concentration of Modernista monuments in Europe. Eixample means 'extension' and this elegant gris of wide avenues was laid out in the mid-19th century, when the wealthy escaped the cramped and dirty old city and built themselves lavish new homes.

Passeig de Gràcia
Passeig de Gràcia is the heart of the Eixample, a glossy boulevard of chic boutiques lined with plane trees and twirling wrought-iron lampposts.

The most famous stretch of the Passeig de Gràcia is the block between Carrer Consell de Cent and Carrer d'Aragó, where flamboyant mansions designed by the three most famous Modernista architects – Gaudí, Domènech i Montaner, Puig i Cadafalch – are nudged up against each other. It's known as the **Mançana de la Discòrdia** (Block of Discord), the 'discord' arising from their dramatically different styles. The architects were independently invited by three of the city's most influential families to entirely remodel existing buildings. The first, at the corner of Carrer Consell de Cent, is the **Casa Lleo i Morera**, which was built in 1864, and transformed by Domènech i Montaner in 1902.

Casa Amatller, three doors up at No 41, was designed by Puig i Cadafalch for a wealthy chocolate manufacturer, and looks good enough to eat. The first-floor apartment is currently being restored to its original turn-of-the-20th-century glory and will be opened to the public.

Next door to the Casa Amatller is the fantastical **Casa Batlló** ① *Passeig de Gràcia 43, T934 880 666, www.casabatlloes, daily 0900-2000, €18.15, concessions €14.55; evening concerts are held on the terrace from end Jun to early Sep, €29* (1904-1906), unmistakably the work of Antoni Gaudí. All kinds of theories about the symbolism of the façade have been thrown up, but the story of St George and the dragon seems to fit most neatly. The rippling waves of tiny ceramic tiles and the bone-white pillars which support the balconies evoke the curling dragon, his scaly back formed by the swaying roof ridge. The fibia-like columns of the lower façade gave the building its popular nickname 'the house of the bones'.

One of Gaudí's most famous buildings is a little further up the Passeig de Gracia, the **Casa Milà** ① *C/Provença 261-265, T934 845 980, T902 202 138 (to book tickets), www.caixacatalunya.es, daily Mar-Oct 0900-2000, Nov-Feb 0900-1830; €16.50, concession €14.85, free admission to temporary exhibitions, guided night visits Mar-Oct; rooftop concerts summer only; Metro Diagonal; Bus 7, 16, 17, 22, 24, 28.* Better known as **La Pedrera** ('the stone quarry'), the building rises like a creamy cliff draped with sinuous wrought iron balconies. The first occupants of the apartment building moved in around 1911, and there's a recreation of an apartment from the era on the top floor. There isn't a straight line anywhere, with the walls, ceilings, doorways and windows flowing around the interior patios. A spiral staircase leads up to the climax of the visit, the sinuous rooftop terrace studded with fantastical bulbous crosses, and plump *trencadi*-covered towers, Gaudí's magical response to the building's prosaic need for chimneys, air vents and stairwells. On summer nights, you can enjoy live music on the rooftop (see page 35).

Sagrada Família

ⓘ *C/Mallorca 401, daily Oct-Mar 0900-1800, Apr-Sept 0900-2000, €13, concessions €11 (€15/14 with guided visit), www.sagradafamilia.cat, Metro Sagrada Família, Bus 19, 33, 34, 43, 44, 50, 51.*

Gaudí's unfinished masterpiece, the Templo Expiatorio de la Sagrada Família (Expiatory Temple of the Sagrada Família), is undoubtedly the most emblematic and most controversial monument in Barcelona: Evelyn Waugh found it so depressing he refused to leave his cab to visit it, but Jean Cocteau, like most people, couldn't get his head around it: 'It's not a skyscraper, it's a mindscraper'. Love it or hate it, it's impossible to ignore: the completed towers stand at almost 100 m, and the central spire, when finished, will soar 170 m into the sky. The nave was completed in 2010, and the church was consecrated in November of the same year by Pope Benedict XVI, who elevated the church to the status of basilica.

The temple is supposedly set for completion in 2026, the anniversary of Gaudí's death, but this seems increasingly unlikely in view of the technical problems surrounding the construction of the vast central tower, and delays caused by the controversial construction of a tunnel for the new high-speed rail line beneath the church.

Hospital de la Sant Creu i Sant Pau

ⓘ *C/Sant Antoni Maria Claret 167-171, T933 177 652, www.bcn.cat/visitsantpau, €10, concessions €5; guided tours in English daily at 1000, 1100, 1200, 1300; Metro Hospital Sant Pau.*

The pedestrian Avinguda Gaudí sweeps up to the other enormous Modernista project of this neighbourhood, the Hospital de la Sant Creu i Sant Pau (1926-1930), a fairytale assembly of delightful ceramic-covered pavilions ingeniously linked by underground passages and encrusted with mosaics.

Montjüic → *For listings, see pages 32-36.*

The ancient promontory of Montjüic rises up above the sea to the west of the city. A green, park-filled oasis, it's undergone a series of dramatic face lifts in the last century or so: palaces, museums and gardens were constructed for Barcelona's International Exhibition of 1929, and the upper reaches were entirely revamped to create the Olympic Ring, a string of dazzling sports complexes used during the 1992 Olympics. Despite all the development, in some ways nothing much has changed: it's still a popular weekend destination for locals, who come to wander through the parks and gaze down across the city from the hilltop castle.

Plaça d'Espanya to the Museu Nacional d'Art de Catalunya (MNAC)

The circular **Plaça d'Espanya**, now a busy traffic thoroughfare, was built for the International Exhibition of 1929. The Avinguda Maria Cristina, flanked by a pair of grim towers, leads to the **Font Màgica** ⓘ *shows May-Sep Thu-Sun 2100, 2130, 2200, 22.30 and 23; Oct-Apr Fri and Sat 1900, 1930, 2000, 2030, free; Metro Espanya; Bus Nos 13, 100, 150,* a magical 1920s fountain which is best appreciated during the fabulously kitsch sound and light shows in which jets of fruity-coloured water leap and dance to music.

Close by is the sleek **Pavelló Mies Van der Rohe** ⓘ *www.miesbcn.com, Metro Espanya, Nov-Mar 1000-1830, Apr-Oct 1000-2000, €3,* a cool, glassy reconstruction of Ludwig Mies

Van der Rohe's monument to rationalist architecture which was built for the 1929 International Exhibition.

Just across from the Mies Van der Rohe pavilion is the **Caixa Forum** ① *Av Francesc Ferrer I Guardia, T934 768 600. www.obrasocial.lacaixa.es, Tue-Sun 1000-2000, free; Metro Espanya; Bus 13, 100, 150*, a Modernista textile mill which has been slickly redesigned to house an excellent permanent collection of contemporary art and galleries for temporary exhibitions.

The huge Palau Nacional which looms from the hilltop houses the **Museu Nacional d'Art de Catalunya** ① *Palau Nacional, T936 220 360, www.mnac.es, Tue-Sat 1000-1900, Sun and hols 1000-1430, €10, concessions €7, metro Espanya, bus 9, 13, 30, 50, 55*, which contains a vast collection spanning over 1000 years, and includes everything from Romanesque murals to Modernista furnishings, along with coins, graphics and photography. The utterly spellbinding array of Romanesque murals gathered from the tiny churches of the Catalan hinterlands, is hauntingly lit and displayed on reconstructed church interiors. The Gothic collection is less magical than the Romanesque, but equally magnificent. The 13th to the 15th centuries were Catalunya's glory years, when her ships ruled the seas and the arts flourished. Several galleries are devoted to one of the most brilliant periods in Catalan art and the three outstanding painters of the time: Bernat Martorell, Lluís Dalmau and Jaume Huguet. The museum also includes about 100 paintings, including masterpieces by Fra Angelico, Titian and Tiepolo, from the Thyssen-Bornemisza Collection, as well as more outstanding works from the likes of Fragonard, Cranach and Goya. Some of Gaudí's furnishings for the Casa Batlló have been preserved in the Modern Art collections, and there is also an excellent selection of photography and coins. Note that you don't have to see it all at once: entrance tickets are valid for visits on any two days during one month from the date of purchase.

Poble Espanyol

① *Av Francesc Ferrer i Guàrdia s/n, T935 086 300. Mon 0900-2000, Tue-Thu 0900-0200, Friand Sat 0900-0500. Sun 0900-2300; shops close earlier (1800-2000); €7, concessions €3.90; guided visits in Catalan, Castillian, English and French every hour, €2. Metro Espanya; Bus Nos 13, 100, 150 (take a bus up the hill if you don't want to face a long walk from the metro).*

After all the high art at MNAC, there's the pure kitsch of the Poble Espanyol to look forward to. The 'Spanish Village' was also built for the 1929 Exhibition, a gloriously tacky collection of traditional architectural styles from around the country. Inside, there's an arcaded Plaça Mayor, a pretty little Barrio Andaluz, a Catalan village, and streets copied from villages all over Spain, lined with scores of souvenir and craft shops, cafés, galleries and restaurants.

Fundació Miró

① *Parc de Montjuïc s/n, T934 439 470, www.fundaciomiro-bcn.org, Oct-Jun Tue-Wed and Fri-Sat 1000-1900, Thu 1000-2130, Sun and holidays 1000-1430, Jul-Sep Tue-Wed and Fri-Sat 1000-2000, Thu 1000-2130, Sun and holidays 1000-1430, €10, concessions €7 for permanent and temporary exhibitions; €7, concessions €5 for temporary exhibitions only.*

Further down the Avinguda de l'Estadi is the fabulous Fundació Miró, set in a white, light-drenched building designed by Josep Lluís Sert. The Foundation was established in 1971 and contains the most important and comprehensive gathering of Miró's works in the world. The opening rooms hold some of Miró's huge tapestries, including one created specially for the Foundation (*Tapestry of the Foundation*, 1979), with a huge figure of a woman dancing ecstatically beneath a star and moon.

Castell de Montjüic

① T932 564 445, free admission, daily 0900-1900 (until 2100 in summer).

Just beyond the Fundació Miró is the funicular station which trundles down to the Paral.lel, and which is also the starting point for the cable car ride up to the castle at the top of Montjüic. At the brow of the hill is the Castell de Montjüic, formerly a prison and torture centre, which is now being converted into a peace and reconciliation centre. You can still visit the castle's interior courtyard (with a café) and walk around the ramparts enjoying the spectacular views.

Gràcia and Parc Güell → *For listings, see pages 32-36.*

Gràcia was an independent town until 1897 when it was dragged, under protest, into the burgeoning city of Barcelona. In the 19th century, Gràcia was a hotbed of radicalism, but now it has largely settled down to its role as a mildly bohemian, traditional neighbourhood of narrow streets and charming squares far from the flashiness and pace of the Diagonal which divides it from the Eixample. Gràcia's unique identity is best expressed in the Festa Major (held in August) which turns the streets into a riot of streamers, stars and balloons, as everyone vies for the prize of best-decorated street. On the edge of Gràcia is Gaudí's magical Park Güell.

Squares, markets and Modernista mansions

The centre of Gràcia has no really big sights or monuments; its distinctive charm is best appreciated with a stroll, especially in the evening, when the names of streets and squares – the **Mercat de la Libertat**, the **Plaça de la Revolució** – evoke its fiercely liberal past. **Plaça de Sol** is the hub of the area's nightlife, with dozens of bars and cafés.

Parc Güell

① C/Olot 7, T934 132 400, Nov-Feb 1000-1800, Mar and Oct 1000-1900, Apr and Sep 1000-2000, May to Aug 1000-2100, free, Metro Lesseps, then a 10-min walk, or bus 24 to the gate; Casa Museu Gaudí Oct-Mar 1000-1800, Apr-Sep 1000-1900, €3.

The fabulous *trencadí*-covered creatures and sloping parklands of the Parc Güell are perhaps the most delightful and varied of Gaudí's visionary creations. It wasn't originally designed as a park: it was meant to be an aristocratic housing estate. Gaudí's benefactor and friend, Eusebi Güell, had visions of an exclusive garden city, modelled on the English fashion, but it never took off and the empty grounds passed to the city for use as a public park in 1922.

Two fairy-tale **pavilions**, with their swirling roofs and shimmering coats of *trencadís* guard the entrance to the park. A flight of steps guarded by a multi-coloured **salamander** – one of Barcelona's best-known symbols – culminate in the **Hall of a Hundred Columns**.

More steps lead up from the Hall to the **main square** which offers beautiful views of the city below. The endless **bench** which snakes around the square is thickly encrusted with *trencadís*, which shimmer and change colour in the sunlight.

Just off the main esplanade is the modest, pink Torre Rosa, Gaudí's home for the last 20 years of his life. It's now the **Casa Museu Gaudí**, a delightful little cottage containing a sparse collection of his few personal possessions.

The **Gaudí Experiència** ① *C/Larrard 41, T932 854 440, www.gaudiexperiencia.com, daily 1000-1800 (until 2000 in July and Aug), €9, concessions €7.50*, is a new high-tech museum which provides an overview of the great architect's life and work with a 4D 'experience'.

Port Vell, Barceloneta and Vila Olímpica → *For listings, see pages 32-36.*

The seafront in Barcelona was the main focus for the frenzy of construction and redevelopment which heralded the 1992 Olympic Games. The Port Olímpic was erected in all its towering, neon-lit splendour, and the old port was utterly transformed. Behind the Port Vell sprawls the old fishermen's neighbourhood of Barceloneta, a shabby, old-fashioned district of narrow streets and traditional bars serving fresh seafood tapas. Beyond Barceloneta stretch the city's beaches, not especially lovely, but buzzy and always packed in summer.

Port Vell

The crowds sweep down from the Rambla and across the undulating **Rambla de Mar**, a floating wooden walkway which leads to the Maremagnum shopping centre, the IMAX cinema, and the aquarium. The glassy **Maremagnum** building is stuffed full of shops, bars and restaurants, many with terraces overlooking the yacht-filled harbour. **IMAX** ① *Moll d'Espanya-Port Vell, T932 251 111, open daily (see website for show times); Metro Barceloneta, Bus 14, 17, 19, 36, 40, 45, 57, 59, 64 and 157*, offers everything from dinosaurs to dolphins in 3D and surround sound. Next door at **L'Aquàrium** ① *T932 217 474, Jul and Aug 0930-2300, rest of the year 0930-2100 (2130 at weekends), €11, children €7.70*, the highlight is still the enormous central tank, which you can coast through gently on a conveyor belt to a schmaltzy sound-track as sharks wheel overhead.

The engaging **Museu d'Història de Catalunya** ① *Plaça Pau Vila 3, T932 254 758, www.mac.es, Metro Barceloneta, Tue-Sat 0930-1900, Sun and holidays 1000-1430, €3*, in a renovated warehouse overlooking the marina, is devoted to the story of Catalunya's fortunes from prehistory to the present with plenty of interactive toys and gimmicks. The rooftop café has fantastic harbour views.

Barceloneta

The pre-Olympic reforms only touched the fringes of the old-fashioned Barceloneta neighbourhood, leaving its unassuming, down-to-earth heart largely intact. The best time to appreciate it is during the **Festa Major de Barceloneta**, at the end of September. There are no sights or monuments, but it's a great place for an evening wander when you'll discover scruffy little bars serving up wine from the barrel and freshly fried sardines. There's also a great **market** with a striking contemporary shell, good for picking up picnic supplies.

The **beaches**, which extend for several kilometres, are not the most beautiful nor the cleanest on the Mediterranean, but they are fun, easy to get to, and conveniently lined with cafés and snack bars.

Vila Olímpica and the Port Olímpic

The **Port Olímpic** is the undisputed success of the Olympic Village and encompasses a marina, sailing school and leisure complex stuffed with cafés, restaurants and shops. Above it flaps Frank Gehry's enormous shimmering copper *Fish* and a pair of glassy towers, one of which contains the luxurious **Hotel Arts Barcelona** (see page 32).

Tibidabo and the outlying districts → *For listings, see pages 32-36.*

There are plenty of things to do around the edge of the city centre in Barcelona. Few attractions – besides the giddy peak of Tibidabo with its funfair and the huge Camp Nou stadium in Les Corts – are on the tourist trail and include some lesser known sights, like the quiet monastery of Pedralbes.

Camp Nou and the Camp Nou Experience

ⓘ *Museu FC Barcelona, C/Aristides Maillol 7-9, T934 963 608, www.fcbarcelona.es, Mon-Sat 1000-1830, Sun and hols 1000-1400, €5, €9 with guided tour of stadium. Metro Collblanc. Bus 15, 52, 54, 56, 57, 75.*

The Camp Nou stadium is one of the largest in Europe, built to accommodate 120,000 fans, and yet getting tickets for a match – particularly with arch-rivals Real Madrid – can be unbelievably tough. If you can't get into a game, a visit to the **Camp Nou Experience**, FC Barça's glossy museum, which includes a tour of the legendary stadium, is well worthwhile. The museum displays include the impressive line-up of silverware, including the record six cups earned during a single season in 2009. But the highlight for most fans is the visit to the ground itself; you can go into the changing rooms and walk through the tunnel out onto the fabled pitch itself.

Pedralbes

North of the western end of the Avinguda Diagonal is the affluent suburb of Pedralbes, spilling down the once-wooded slopes of Collserola. Just off the Diagonal is the stately mid-19th-century **Palau Reial de Pedralbes**, originally built for the Güell family, Gaudí's benefactors.

At the top of Avinguda Pedralbes is the lovely 14th-century **Monestir de Santa Maria de Pedralbes**, now the **Museu Monestir Pedralbes** ⓘ *T932 039 282, www.bcn.es/museus, Tue-Sun 1000-1400, €3.50, free first Sun of the month.* Its three-tiered Gothic cloister, one of the best preserved in Europe, is a still, contemplative arcade of slender columns, and the church contains the alabaster tomb of the monastery's founder, Queen Elisende.

Tibidabo

Tibidibo, the highest peak of the Collserola hills which surround Barcelona, is the city's mountain of fun. At the summit, reached by a rickety tram and a funicular railway, is a great old-fashioned funfair, the **Parc d'Atraccions** ⓘ *www.tibidabo.cat, open daily in summer, weekends only in winter (check website for opening hours which change monthly), admission €28.20 for unlimited rides, children under 1.2 m €10.* The ferris wheel, dodgems and other rides are great for little kids, and there is a handful of attractions, including a couple of terrifying rollercoasters, to keep adrenalin kunkies happy. The views across the city can be breathtaking on a clear day.

At the bottom of Tibidabo is the **CosmoCaixa** ① *T932 126 050, www.obra social.lacaixa.es, Tue-Sun and holidays 1000-2000, €3, concessions €2, free for children under 6, free first Sun of the month, bus 17, 22, 58, 60, 73.* This is a big touchy-feely museum and planetarium set in an old Modernista asylum. Most of the descriptions are in Catalan or Castilian, but there are enough gadgets to keep kids occupied for hours.

Barcelona listings

For hotel and restaurant price codes and other relevant information, see pages 10-13.

☺ Where to stay

Most of the cheaper places can be found in the old neighbourhoods in the centre of the city, which are also the noisiest places to stay. The smartest (and quietest) places are generally concentrated in the Eixample. There are relatively few places near the seaside, although Diagonal Mar has a growing number and you might want to think about staying in Gràcia to get a feel for Barcelona without the tourists. There are no campsites close to the city centre – the nearest is 7 km away.

La Rambla *p18, map p20*
€€ **Montecarlo**, La Rambla 124, T934 120 404, www.montecarlobcn.com. With a fantastic location right on the Rambla, this has a lavish turn-of-the-20th-century lobby, and modern, comfortable rooms.

Barri Gòtic *p19, map p20*
€€ **Hotel Denit**, C/Estruc 24-26, T935 454 000, www.hoteldenit.com. A great-value option at the heart of the Gothic Quarter, this has pristine, contemporary rooms and helpful staff.

El Raval *p24, map p20*
€€€ **Hotel España**, C/Sant Pau 9-11, T935 500 000, www.hotelespanya.com. A swirling Modernista dining room and bar designed by Domènech i Montaner greets patrons at this smart hotel, which also boasts a fabulous roof terrace.

Eixample *p26, map p20*
€€€€ **Hotel Casa Fuster**, Passeig de Gràcia 132, T932 553 000, www.barcelonacasa fusterhotel.com. If it's fin-de-siècle opulence you're looking for, this sumptuous Modernista hotel, designed by Domènech i Montaner who created the Palau de la Música, fits the bill perfectly.
€€€ **Constanza**, C/Bruc 33, T932 701 910, www.hotelconstanza.com. Chic and stylish, with very elegant rooms, a great tapas bar, and wonderful views from the roof terrace. The location is ideal too, just a few mins on foot from the Plaça Catalunya, the Gothic Quarter and the Passeig de Gràcia.
€€ **Circa 1905**, C/Provença 286, T935 056 960, www.circa1905.com. A sweet little boutique guesthouse, with just a handful of cosy, antique-filled rooms, and charming staff.
€€-€ **Actual**, C/Rossello 238, T935 520 550, www.hotelactual.com. Trendy hotel, fashionably decorated in the slickest minimalist style, with plenty of white marble and dark wood. Fantastically located and surprisingly affordable.

Port Vell, Barceloneta and Vila Olímpica *p30, map p20*
€€€€ **Arts Barcelona**, C/ Marina 19-21, T932 211 000, www.hotelartsbarcelona.com. Easily the most glamorous hotel in the city, set in one of the enormous glassy towers at the entrance to the Port Olímpic. Inaugurated in 1992, it offers 33 floors of unbridled luxury, including a stunning spa (by **Six Senses Spas**), several excellent eating and drinking options, and the best service in the city.

Tibidabo and the outlying districts *p31*
€€€€ **ABaC**, Av Tibidabo 1, T933 196 600,
www.abacbarcelona.com. The gorgeous
rooms and spa aren't the biggest draw at
this elegant boutique hotel: it's attached
to the city's finest restaurant.

❷ Restaurants

The Catalans are renowned for their cuisine.
The dishes are often simple, and rely on the
freshness of the local ingredients. The Catalan
staple, for example, is *pa amb tomàquet*, bread
rubbed with fresh tomatoes, drizzled with olive
oil and a sprinkling of salt. With extra toppings
(like ham or cheese) it becomes a *torrada*.

Meat and fish are often served simply
grilled, or cooked slowly in the oven (*al forn*)
in a tomato-based sauce. There are some
delicious vegetable dishes – such as the
refreshing *escalivada*, a salad of roasted
aubergine, peppers and onions, or *espinacs
a la catalana*, spinach cooked with pine
nuts and raisins.

Rice dishes are also popular, with variations
on the famous Valencian dish *paella* like *arròs
negre*, rice cooked slowly with squid ink and
shellfish, or *fideuà*, which is made with tiny
noodles cooked in with meat and fish. The
most popular Catalan dessert is *crema
catalana*, a local version of crème brûlée,
or you could finish up with local curd
cheese drizzled with honey, *mel i mató*.

There are plenty of old-fashioned bars
near the harbour which offer fresh seafood
tapas – like *sardines* (grilled sardines) – but
the most common Catalan tapas are *truita*,
thick omelettes (*tortilla*) or platters of
cheeses or *embutits* (charcuterie). Don't
forget to wash them all down in style with
Catalan wine, or the local *Estrella* beer.

La Rambla *p18, map p20*
Tapas bars and cafés
Bar Pinotxo, Mercat de la Boquería 66-67,
T933 171 731, www.pintxobar.com. Mon-Sat
0630-1600. Metro Liceu. The best-known and
most popular counter bar in the market,
serving excellent, freshly prepared food –
don't miss the tortilla with artichokes.
El Café de l'Opéra, La Rambla 74, T933 177
585. Daily 0830-0230. Metro Liceu. Sitting
right on the Rambla opposite the Liceu Opera
house, this is the perfect café for people-
watching. Original Modernista-style fittings
and an Old World ambience add to its charm.

Barri Gòtic *p19, map p20*
€€ **Café de l'Acadèmia**, C/Lledó 1, T933
198 253. Mon-Fri 0900-1200 and 1330-1600
and 2045-1130. Metro Jaume I. An elegant
and romantic restaurant just off the lovely
Plaça Sant Just, with torch-lit tables out on
the square in summer. Classic Catalan cuisine
prepared with a modern twist. There's a
great-value set lunch for around €14.
€€ **Pla**, C/Bellafila 5, T934 126 552,
www.elpla.cat. A stylish restaurant tucked
down a narrow street in the Gothic Quarter,
this serves up delicious and creative dishes,
such as roast lamb with licorice and honey,
or monkfish with artichoke stew.

Tapas bars and cafés
Bliss, Plaça Sants Just i Pastor, T932 681 022.
Mon-Sat 1330-1530, 2030-2315, closed Aug.
metro Jaume I. A small, cosy café, with a
couple of leopard-print sofas to sink into.
Delicious home-made quiches, salads and
cakes. There are tables out on a pretty little
square by the church in summer.
Bodega la Plata, C/Mercé 28, T933 151 009.
This minuscule, prettily tiled *bodega* serves
wine straight from the barrel, and some of
the best, freshly fried sardines in town.

La Ribera and Sant Pere *p23, map p20*
€€ **Big Fish**, Comerç 9, T932 681 728,
www.bigfish.cat. A fashionable address,
this combines retro-chic decor, including
worn Chesterfield sofas and an enormous
mother-of-pearl chandelier, with fabulously
fresh fish, plus an excellent sushi counter.

€€ La Paradeta, C/Comercial 7, T932 681 939, www.laparadeta.com. Cheap and cheerful, it's no wonder that there are always huge queues here. Pick out your fish from the freshly landed selection and then wait for it to be fried up and served. No reservations.

€ Atril, C/Carders 23. T933 101 220, www.atril barcelona.com. There's a great 3-course lunch deal here for about €10, or you could just come for some of the generous portions of tapas. The Sun brunch is a local institution.

Tapas bars and cafés

Mosquito, Carrer Carders 46, T932 687 569. This friendly neigbourhoood bar serves great pan-Asian tapas, including delicious dim sum, and a wide range of international beers, to a relaxed, trendy crowd.

El Raval *p24, map p20*

€ Teresa Carles, C/Jovellanos 2, T933 171 829, www.teresacarles.com. A warm, modern interior and tasty, creative vegetarian cuisine make this a great bet for veggies. It's also good for breakfast or afternoon coffee and cakes.

Tapas bars and cafés

Suculent, Rambla de Raval 43, T934 436 579, www.suculent.com. 3 of Barcelona's best chefs are behind this revamped gastrobar, which peps up classic tapas recipes with unusual ingredients and focuses on superb produce.

Eixample *p26, map p20*

€€€€ Cinc Sentits, C/Aribau 58, T933 239 490, www.cincsentits.com. Canadian-Catalan chef Jordi Artal is at the helm of this charming, Michelin-starred restaurant, where exquisite, imaginative Catalan cuisine is served in a choice of set menus.

€€ Tickets, Paral·lel 164, www.ticketsbar.es. Albert Adrià, brother of Ferran, both formerly of **El Bullí**, are behind this colourful, fun restaurant, currently the hottest ticket in

town. Reserve at least 2 months in advance online (no telephone number).

Tapas bars and cafés

Monvínic, Passeig de Gràcia 38-40, T932 726 187, www.monvinic.com. A huge, glassy wine bar and dining room, serving elegant modern Mediterranean cuisine with an enormous selection of wines.

Port Vell, Barceloneta and Vila Olímpica *p30, map p20*

€€ Kaiku, Plaça del Mar 1. T932 219 082, www.restaurantkaiku.cat. Beautifully fresh Mediterreanean cuisine with the emphasis on seafood and rice dishes is served at this sea-front restaurant. Order the fabulous *arròs del xef* (their own paella, with smoked rice), and settle down on the terrace with some wine.

🎵 Bars and clubs

La Rambla *p18, map p20*

Jamboree, Plaça Reial 17, T933 191 789, www.masimas.com/jamboree. Mon-Sat 2200-0500. Metro Liceu. This jazz club becomes a night club when the sets end: after about 0100, the crowds pour in to enjoy the R&B, soul and funk which plays until dawn.

Barri Gòtic *p19, map p20*

La Macarena, DJ Zone, C/Nou de Sant Francesc 5, T933 175 436, www.macarena club.com. Daily 2300-0400, until 0500 on Fri and Sat. Small, intimate club playing electronica beloved by DJs from around the world. Buzzy, upbeat and very cool.

La Ribera and Sant Pere *p23, map p20*

El Mariatchi, C/Codols 14. Rumour has it that this hard-to-find little bar is owned by singer Manu Chao. True or not, it's still worth tracking down, to enjoy cheap drinks and great (often live) music, in a fun, colourful setting.

El Raval *p24, map p20*
Marsella, C/ Sant Pau 65, T934 427 263.
Mon-Thu 2200-0230. Metro Liceu. The big,
dusty, bottle-lined **Marsella** was started by
a homesick Frenchman more than a century
ago. The smell of absinthe hits you as soon as
you walk in; get there early to grab a battered,
marble-topped table under the lazy paddle
fans and soak up the atmosphere.

Eixample *p26, map p20*
BeCool, Plaça Joan Llongueras. This club
may be small, but it's got a big reputation.
It regularly features some of the hottest DJs
in town, particularly during the **Radar**
mini-festival, held during **Sónar** (mid-Jun).
Nits d'Estiu (Summer Nights) at La Pedrera
(page 26), Pg de Gràcia 92, www.lapedrera.
com. Jul and Aug Thu, Fri and Sat 2100-2400.
Metro Diagonal. Sip a cocktail and check out
the live music and stunning views across the
city from the undulating rooftop of **La Pedrera**.

Montjuic *p27, map p20*
Sala Apolo, C/ Nou de la Rambla 113, T934
414 001, www.sala-apolo.com. Fri-Sat
2430-0600. Metro Paral.lel. This combined
concert hall and nightclub is housed in a
sumptuous old theatre. Now it's one of the
best venues in town – great club nights and
a very varied programme of live music.

Port Vell, Barceloneta and Vila Olímpica
p30, map p20
Razzmatazz/The Loft, C/ Almogàvers 122,
T933 208 200. Fri and Sat 0100-0500. Metro
Bogatell, www.salarazzmatazz.com. Perhaps
the biggest and best nightlife venue in town,
Razzmatazz is both a concert venue and club.
There are 5 spaces, each with a different style.

⊖ Transport

Bus
The main hub for local/city buses is the Plaça
Catalunya. Single tickets cost €2. Most routes
usually run Mon-Sat 0600-2230 (less frequent
on Sun). The night bus (*nit bus*) service runs
2230-0400 daily and covers 18 routes. Most
pass through Plaça Catalunya, and arrive
roughly every half hour. Local bus routes are
clearly marked at bus stops, and the TMB and
tourist offices have a useful transport map (or
see online at www.tmb.cat).

Car
Avis, T902 180 854, www.avis.com.
Europcar, T902 105 030, www.europcar.com.
National (a partner of the Spanish car hire
firm, **Atesa**), T902 100 101, www.national.
com, www.atesa.es.
Vanguard, T934 393 880, C/Villadomat 297,
www.vanguardrent.com. Local car hire firm,
which also rents out motorbikes and scooters.

FGC trains
Some city and suburban destinations are
served by FGC trains (Ferrocarrils de la
Generalitat de Catalunya), which are run
by the Catalan government. They are
mainly useful for getting to the less central
sights like Gràcia or Tibidabo.

Metro
There are 8 metro lines (Mon-Thu 0500-2300,
Fri 0500-0200, Sat 24 hrs, Sun 0600-2400)
identified by number and colour. A single
ticket costs €2 or you can get a T-Dia for €7,
which allows unlimited transport on the bus,
metro and FGC trains for 1 person during 1
day, or a T-10, which offers 10 trips on the bus,
metro and FGC trains for €9.80 and can be
shared. The T-10 is also valid for the airport train.

Taxi

City taxis are yellow and black, and easily available. There's a taxi stand on the Plaça de Catalunya, just across the street from the main tourist information office. To call: **Barnataxi**, T933 222 222; **Fono-Taxi** T933 001 100; **Ràdio Taxi** T933 033 033.

Telefèric/cable cars
Telefèric de Barceloneta (Aeri del Port)

The cable car journey across the bay is one of the most thrilling rides in Barcelona, and definitely not for people suffering from vertigo. It closes intermittently for works. It runs from the Miramar station at the end of Av Miramar on Montjuïc down to Passeig de Joan de Borbo in Barceloneta. Open daily mid-Oct to Feb 1000-1730, Mar to mid-Jun and mid-Sep to mid-Oct 1000-1900, mid-Jun to mid-Sep 1000-2000. Ticket prices are hefty: €10 single €15 return.
Telefèric de Montjuïc The cable car from Av Miramar swings up to the castle at the top of the hill. Daily Jun-Sep 1000-2100; Oct and Mar-May 1000-1900; Nov-Feb 1000-1800. Tickets cost €7 single and €9.80 return.

Tram and funicular
Tramvia Blau/Blue Tram A refurbished antique tram which is the first part of the journey up Tibidabo. It runs every 15-30 mins between from Plaça Kennedy (near FGC train station Av del Tibdabo) to the Plaça Andreu where it joins the funicular (see below). Runs 1000-1800, weekends only in winter (mid-Sep to mid-Jun) and daily in summer and over Easter (€3 single, €4.80 return).
Tibidabo funicular Take the funicular from the Plaça Andreu to the top of Tibidabo (return €7.50, or €4 if you show a park admission ticket). Opening times coincide with those of the Parc d'Atraccions de Tibidabo; generally speaking it's weekends only in winter, daily in summer.

Montjuïc funicular Departs Paral.lel metro station and heads up to Av Miramar, close to the Fundació Miró. Metro tickets and passes are valid, or a single ticket costs €2 (includes a mini-guide. Open spring and summer 0900-2200, autumn and winter 0900-2200. It connects with the telefèric/cable car to the top of Montjuïc (see above).

❶ Directory

Embassies and consulates
See www.embassiesabroad.com.
Emergency numbers Ambulance, fire and police: **T112**. To contact the emergency services directly, call: Ambulance/*Ambulància* T061; Fire service/*Bombers/Bomberos* T080; National Police/*Policia Nacional* T091; Municipal Police/*Policia Municipal* T092.
Medical services Dentist: Dr Nicholas Jones, Av Diagonal 281, T932 658 070. English dentist, trained at London's Royal Dental Hospital. **Hospitals**: CAP 24 hr Perecamps, Av Drassanes 13-15, T934 410 600, metro Drassanes or Paral.lel. This clinic deals with less serious emergencies and injuries. Hospital Clínic, C/ Villarroel 170, T932 275 400, metro Hospital Clinic. **Hospital de la Santa Creu i Sant Pau**, C/ Sant Quintí 89 Sant Antoni María Claret 167, T932 919 000, metro Guinardó-Hospital de Sant Pau or Sant Pau-Dos de Maig. **Pharmacies**: **Farmàcia Clapés**, La Rambla 98, T933 012 843, metro Liceu. 24-hrs. **Farmàcia Torres**, C/ Aribals 62, T934 539 220, metro Universitat 24 hrs.
Police station The most central *comisaría* (police station) is at C/Nou de la Rambla 76-80, T932 904 849.

Contents

Eastern Pyrenees

Catalan Pyrenees

The Catalan Pyrenees cover a vast swathe of the region. The highest and most dramatic peaks are in the northwest corner of Catalunya, near Puigcerdà and La Seu d'Urgell. This is where you'll find the best ski resorts as well as the spectacular National Park of Aigüestortes and the Romanesque churches in the remote Vall de Boí. If you are approaching from the south, the massive Cadí range is not, strictly speaking, part of the Pyrenees proper, but still offers some demanding climbing and hiking in the Cadí-Moixeró Natural Park. One of the most popular sports in the region is whitewater rafting along the powerful Noguera Palleresa river, and you can head also over the border into Andorra for some shopping and magnificent scenery.

Vall de Núria → *For listings, see pages 48-52.*

A tiny rack-and-pinion railway makes the spectacular, vertiginous journey to the Vall de Núria, set more than 2000 m up in the Pyrenees. A low-key ski resort in winter, and hikers' favourite in summer, it's also famous for a miraculous statue of the Madonna in the ugly sanctuary which dominates the valley. Núria is second only to Montserrat as a girl's name in Catalunya. The Vall de Núria can get surprisingly crowded in summer and winter but most people just come for the train ride and a picnic by the lake – so even a 20-minute walk will take you away from the hordes.

La Cremallera
Heading directly north of Ripoll on the N-152 which meanders along the Freser Valley, you'll reach **Ribes de Freser**, a low-key town with a spa (Balneari de Ribes), sheep-trials every September, and a weekly market where you can pick up some of the local farmhouse pâté, *pa de fetge*. This is the departure point for **La Cremallera**, a rack-and-pinion train line, which makes a spectacular and magical journey through the mountains. It makes one stop, at the attractive town of **Queralbs**, a huddle of stone and slate houses with an elegant Romanesque church, which hasn't quite been overwhelmed by the new developments springing up like toadstools on its outskirts. The train continues onwards and upwards across viaducts, through tunnels, past dramatic cliffs, forests and waterfalls, finally disgorging its passengers up at the Vall de Núria, 1000 m above Ribes de Fraser and more than 2000 m above sea level. The lugubrious sanctuary of **La Mare de Deu de Núria** overlooking the valley was built in the late 19th century, and looks more like a prison than a place of worship. Like Montserrat, the valley has long attracted pilgrims, who still come to venerate the 12th-century carved wooden statue of the Madonna, which is almost as famous as Montserrat's La Moreneta. The Madonna is the patron saint of shepherds, but

---

she's also credited with helping women with fertility problems: there's a hole in part of the Choir and anyone hoping to conceive should put their head in it while the bell tolls.

There is a ski station, especially popular with families (11 ski runs, including two black and three red runs), a lake where you can hire boats, horse-riding facilities, and plenty of easy to moderate walking trails; www.valldenuria.com has all the details.

Berga and Parc Natural de Cadí-Moixeró → *For listings, see pages 48-52.*

Berga, on a rocky slope 50 km west of Ripoll, is the capital and main transport hub of the Berguedà *comarca* (county). The old quarter has an old-fashioned faded charm, but the town is best known as a base for the nearby Parc Natural de Cadí-Moixero which offers spectacular hiking and rock-climbing, including the celebrated peak of Pedraforça. If you've got your own transport or plenty of patience with bus schedules, there are some delightful stone villages scattered around the edges of the park which make more attractive bases for exploring.

Berga

Berga doesn't have any particular sights or monuments, and serves mainly as a base for visits to the nearby natural park of Cadí-Moixero. The old town, shabby but still picturesque, is a pleasant place for a stroll. During Corpus Christi, in May or early June, the town explodes with one of Catalunya's most exhilarating festivals, the three-day **Festa de la Patum**, with *gegants* (dragons spitting fire) dancing in the streets to the sounds of strange hornpipes, plenty of carousing by red-capped Catalans, and, for a grand finale, a wild dance by masked men covered in rushes.

Some 14 km west of Berga is the **Rasos De Peguera** ski resort, the closest to Barcelona and a favourite for day-trippers. Small and low key, it's good for families and beginners. For information, see www.rasos.net.

Parc Natural de Cadí-Moixeró

Beyond Berga, the foothills of the Pyrenees loom with startling abruptness, pale and forbiddingly craggy. These dramatic peaks are part of the Sierra Cadí, one of the most spectacular sights in Catalunya, and part of the Parc Natural de Cadí-Moixeró. The sheer Pedraforca ('stone pitchfork') peak is a serious challenge for experienced mountain climbers, who descend in droves during the summer months.

Bagà and around The park information office is in Bagà, a few kilometres further up the C-1411, a tranquil town with another pretty medieval core. From here, a small paved road heads up through a valley of Alpine lushness and beauty, ringing with the soft sounds of cow bells, climbing higher into forested peaks and finally emerging at the heady Coll de l'Escriga. Just beyond it is the attractive hamlet of Gisclareny, a good base for trekking.

Back a mile or two before Bagà is the dreary roadside straggle of **Guardiola de Bergueda**, which hides the elegant Romanesque **Monestir de Sant Llorenç** – get keys from the Ajuntament (Town Hall), mornings only – and is the starting point for the single daily bus which heads west to the more remote, prettier villages of **Saldes** and **Gósol**. Saldes sits right at the foot of Pedraforca and is the usual point of departure for the most difficult routes; lofty Gósol, a dense stone warren of ancient streets, once inspired Picasso who spent the summer of 1906 painting and walking here and is the starting point for a number of easier, if less dramatic, trails up the back of Pedraforca.

La Pobla de Lillet East of Guardiola de Bergueda, a small road follows the thin trickle of the Llobregat to La Pobla de Lillet, with two sturdy stone bridges straddling the river, and an appealing old quarter to wander around. There's also a delightful garden, the Jardí de la Font (Spring Garden) designed by Gaudí on the bank of the river, and a couple of fine Romanesque churches on the outskirts – the **Monestir de Santa Maria**, and the **Santuari de Falgàs**. There are ancient churches tucked into almost every fold of these mountains; one of the loveliest is at **Sant Jaume de Frontanyà**, south of La Pobla de Lillet (get the keys from the tourist office), and there are several within a couple of miles of Berga itself, including **Església de Sant Quirze de Pedret**, a pre-Romanesque church with Moorish sides, and the humble little **Església de Sant Pere de Madrona**, clamped in a little hollow just below the shrine of Queralt.

Castellar de n'Hug and ski resorts Heading north of Pobla de Lillet, the road winds up towards Castellar de n'Hug, an ancient stone sprawl hugging the mountain which has a special place in every Catalan's heart, thanks to the Fonts de Llobregat, a spring which has famously never dried up – it's the source of the great river which meets the sea just south of Barcelona, but here it's a lazy trickle tumbling over stones and overhung with trees. The town makes a good, if touristy, base for walking and isn't too far from the adjoining ski resorts of **La Molina** and **Masella**. La Molina has 53 pistes, with plenty for skiers of all abilities including intermediate and advanced skiers. For information and to book accommodation call T972 892 031 www.lamolina.com. Masella has 37 pistes including six black and 15 red runs. For information and to book accommodation, T972 144 000, www.masella.com. The **tourist office** ⓘ *Castellar de n'Hug's Ajuntament, T938 257 097*, has lists of accommodation.

Toses To the southeast of the ski resorts on the N-152 to Ripoll, Toses stands precariously balanced high on a lofty peak and boasts the enchanting frescoed Romanesque Església de Sant Cristòfol. The original frescoes have been taken to MNAC in Barcelona but copies of the surviving fragments in situ hint at their former splendour.

Cerdanyà Valley → *For listings, see pages 48-52.*

North of Bagà, the mountains are pierced with extraordinary tunnels – including the Tunel de Cadí, Spain's longest – which lead into the lush valley of the Cerdanya, shaped like 'the handprint of God' according to local tradition. The capital of the region is Puigcerdà, jauntily set on a promontory overlooking the valley and surrounded by snow-capped peaks. Most of its monuments were wiped out by bombing during the Civil War, but it's still got a few pretty squares which are the centre of the town's buzzy nightlife. The best times to visit depend on whether you are interested in walking, best in late spring and early autumn, or skiing, you can count on snow in January and February.

Puigcerdà

Puigcerdà was once the capital of the kingdom of Cerdanya which spread across the Pyrenees before being divided between France and Spain in the 17th century. Bombing wiped out most of its ancient monuments during the Civil War, including the Gothic church of Santa Maria on the main square, although its formidable belltower survived, along with the 13th-century church of Sant Domènech on the city's eastern flank. Inside, barely discernible in the gloom, there's a macabre series of murals depicting the saint's head being split in two with a sabre.

A cheerful, appealing town, Puigcerdà has plenty of bars and restaurants, and bustling squares full of outdoor cafés. In summer, you can join in with some typical Catalan sardana dancing on Wednesday afternoons, although check with the tourist office as it takes place on different squares. There are easy strolls down to a lake where you can hire a boat and laze about among the swans and weeping willows, and the town has also got an enormous ice rink (a hangover from the Olympics) and is the capital of Spanish ice hockey.

Llívia

When the former kingdom of Cerdanya was being divided up between the French and Spanish, the French claimed the 33 villages between the Ariège and Roussillon. But after the deal was done, the Spanish triumphantly claimed Llívia by pointing out that it was a town and not a village. As a result, Llívia is now a curious Spanish colony tucked a couple of miles inside the French border. It's a tiny, attractive town, with a twisting medieval hub guarded by a **fortified church** ⓘ *C/dels Forns, Tue-Sat 1000-1300, 1500-1800 (until 2000 in summer)*, and a medieval pharmacy, now part of the **Museu Municipal** ⓘ *C/dels Forns 10, T972 896 313, Apr-Jun Tue-Sun 1000-1800, Jul-Aug daily 1000-1900, Sep Tue-Sun 1000-1900, Oct-Mar Tue-Sun 1000-1630, €1*. The Esteva pharmacy dates back to the 15th-century, and only stopped doling out potions and unguents in 1918 – there's a collection of jars and bizarre apothecary's instruments and some delightful hand-painted herb boxes. The rest of the museum's holdings are a bit musty – Bronze Age relics and old maps – and the entrance ticket also allows admission into the 15th-century Torre Bernat de So next to the church. It's a good place for a stroll and a long, lazy lunch on one of the squares. You can find a **tourist information office** ⓘ *C/Forn 11, www.llivia.org, T972 896 011*, in the town hall.

Bellver de Cerdanya

South of Puigcerdà lie a string of relaxed, country towns: Bellver de Cerdanya, heaped on a hill overlooking the river, is one of the largest, with a handsome porticoed square and pretty, flower-decked balconies strung along the old stone houses. The **Romanesque Església de Santa Eugènia de Nerellà** just south of the town is pierced with a peculiar leaning belltower, and has an ancient polychrome statue of the Madonna. The village is also one of the access points for the Parc Natural de Cadí-Moixeró (see page 39).

Strung along the main road to the west, **Martinet** is less obviously alluring, but has a good reputation for its country cooking and lies just beneath the small ski resort of **Lles**, which also has a lake, the Estany de la Pera, for messing about in boats and kayaks.

La Seu d'Urgell and Castellciutat

At the western end of the valley is La Seu d'Urgell, on the banks of the River Segre, a relaxed market town which was named for its imposing *seu* (cathedral). After mouldering away for years as a remote backwater, La Seu d'Urgell got a new lease of life when the Olympic canoeing events were held here in 1992 and it now has excellent watersports facilities. It's also the main point of access on the Spanish side of the border for Andorra (see page 78).

Fortunately, the new development has left the medieval centre almost untouched, and the cobbled streets linking a chain of little squares are a relaxing place to amble. The **cathedral** ① *T973 353 242, www.museudiocesaurgell.org, Jun-Sep Mon-Sat 1000-1330 and 1600-1930, Sun 1000-1300, Oct-May Mon-Fri 1200-1330, Sat-Sun 1100-1330, €3, concessions €1*, was first established in the eighth century, but completely rebuilt in 1184. There's an elegant cloister with finely sculpted capitals, and the **Museu Diocesana** holds a good collection of ecclesiastical treasures, including an illuminated copy of the *Beato de Liébana*.

La Seu d'Urgell has one odd little curiosity: the **Cloister of Vallira**, in the park of the same name on the edge of town, was designed by Luis Racionera and, instead of the usual saints and beasts, the capitals depict 20th-century icons, from Marilyn Monroe to Picasso.

Castellciutat, up on a rock overlooking the town, is the site of the ancient settlement which was wiped out by the Moors during the eighth century; there are some scenic trails leading along the valley and up to the ruined castle which is all that remains. La Seu d'Urgell's tourist office has a range of leaflets describing walks in some of the surrounding villages, including a particularly beautiful walk to a waterfall near the tiny hamlet of Estana.

Noguera Palleresa Valley and Parc Nacional d'Aigüestortes
→ *For listings, see pages 48-52.*

Heading west of La Seu d'Urgell, the mountains are studded with steep valleys, ancient stone villages of slate-roofed houses and powerful rivers: the most powerful of them all is the Noguera Palleresa, which has become a paradise for rafting and adventure sports. The stunning park of Aigüestortes spreads across this northeastern corner of Catalunya, one of only 14 national parks in Spain, and certainly one of the most enchanting and beautiful regions in the whole country.

Tremp and Talarn
The southernmost large town on the Noguera Palleresa Valley, Tremp is squeezed between two massive hydroelectrical plants which harness the energy of Catalunya's most powerful river. Talarn, tucked behind chunky walls on a hilltop just north of Tremp, makes a much more attractive stopover.

La Pobla de Segur and around
La Pobla de Segur was the final destination for the rafters from the Pyrenees who nudged their loads of felled treetrunks down river to the factories in an epic journey which is re-enacted annually from Sort (see below). A couple of Modernista mansions, including the Casa Mauri (now the Ajuntament, or town hall), are left over from the years of prosperity, but the town is now really a tourist and transport hub for buses into the Pyrenees.

There are some interesting, isolated villages with their own forgotten Romanesque churches nearby; **Ribert** is beautifully set in wooded countryside by the Riu Verde, and **Claverol** is topped by the ruins of an ancient castle. Heading northeast towards Sort, the road passes through a spectacular gorge, the **Congost de Collegats**, pummelled by the Noguera Pallaresa in its rush from the mountains and the inspiration, some say, for Gaudí's La Pedrera. **Gerri de la Sal**, peacefully sitting by the side of the river was, as its name indicates, an important salt-manufacturing village. Salt has been gathered here since Roman times, but a flood wiped out almost all the salt flats in 1982; a small eco-museum describes the process and the history of salt-production. The town is dominated by the 12th-century **Benedictine Monestir de Santa Maria**, with a striking, if shabby, wall of bells looming above the entrance.

Sort

The biggest centre for rafting and adventure sports is Sort, where the pretty old town is rapidly being swallowed up by hasty development. The word *sort* means 'luck' in Catalan, and Sort in fact boasts one of the highest percentages of lottery winners in Spain. The streets are now lined with tour operators and outdoor kit shops, offering an incredible array of activities in the surrounding canyons and valleys. Every year in late June or early July, there's a spectacular festival of **Raiers** (Rafters) who scud down the river on simple rafts made of lashed together branches just as the old timber pilots used to do.

Llavorsí and Port-Ainé

Llavorsí is also full of adventure tour operators offering rafting trips on the Noguera Pallaresa (it's the starting point for many of the trips), and is easily the prettiest town along this stretch. Northeast of Sort is the ski resort of Port-Ainé, a smallish ski station which has a good range of pistes suitable for intermediate and advanced skiiers. For ski information and to book accommodation, T973 621 100, www.skipallars.cat.

Espot and Parc Nacional d'Aigüestortes i Estany de Maurici

Further up the valley, there's another ski resort at Super Espot above the small village of Espot which is the western gateway to the preternaturally beautiful Parc Nacional d'Aigüestortes i Estany de Maurici. This is Catalunya's only national park, a spellbinding landscape of green meadows flecked with scores of crystal-clear lakes and surrounded by jagged, forested peaks. There are hikes for walkers of all fitness levels, and it's also an excellent destination for serious climbers; the **park information office** ⓘ *Casa del Parc, C/Sant Maurici 5, Espot, T973 624 036*, has maps and information on the refuges scattered through the park. These are usually staffed with fulltime wardens during the summer, and it is worth calling in advance to ensure a place. Jeep taxis will drop you off at the park boundaries (or you can avoid the road and walk along the GR11), where you can make the short stroll to the Estany de Maurici, a still, clear lake of hallucinatory beauty, looked over by the strange stone eruptions of Els Encantats (The Enchanted Ones). Legend has it that two hunters and their dog sneaked off one Sunday morning instead of attending mass; they were lured deeper into the mountains by an elusive stag when a bolt of lightning shot down from the heavens and turned them into stone. For experienced walkers, there's a spectacular trek (about 10 hours from Espot to Boí) right through the park from east to west. The park information offices have details. See below for information on Boí, on the western edge of the park.

Vall d'Aran → *For listings, see pages 48-52.*

The lush Vall d'Aran was originally part of the French kingdom Aquitaine, although it joined the kingdom of Catalunya and Aragón in 1389. It was often entirely cut off from the rest of the world during the winter until the massive Vielha tunnel was hammered through the

Maladeta peak by Republican POWs in the 1940s. This is the only Atlantic valley in the Eastern Pyrenees, drained by the River Garonne which meets the sea near Bordeaux; cooler, wetter and altogether neater than the surrounding valleys, it has preserved a distinctly French character audible in the local language, Aranès, a mixture of Gascon French, Catalan and even the odd Basque word thrown in for good measure. The valley's capital, Vielha, is a buzzy mountain town stuffed full of smart boutiques catering to the constant flow of French day-trippers. There are tourist information offices in most of the Aranese villages.

Vielha

The capital of the Vall d'Aran is Vielha, which is prettier when you get off the drab main drag and wander about the narrow streets behind it. Here you'll find the distinctive Aranese stone houses, with their stepped gables, slate roofs, and carved wooden balconies. Vielha is becoming increasingly smart, thanks to the droves of French visitors who have triggered a spate of fashionable shops, galleries and restaurants, and it doesn't hurt that the Spanish royal family traditionally choose this region for their skiing holidays.

In the heart of old Vielha is the 12th-century **Església de Sant Miquèu**, with an octagonal belltower overlooking a little square. The church holds a very beautiful 12th-century sculpture of Christ de Mijaran which is one of the finest examples of Romanesque sculpture in this region. Across the river is the **Museu de la Vall d'Aran** ① *C/Major 10, T973 641 815, Mon-Sat 1000-1300 and 1700-2000, Sun 1000-1300, €2, concessions €1,* in a 17th-century mansion, with a description of the butterflies unique to the valley, and exhibits relating to the history and folklore of the region.

Baqueira-Beret and the Port de la Bonanaigua

At the eastern end of the Vall d'Aran is the ultra-chic ski resort of Baqueira-Beret (www.baqueira.es), where the Spanish royal family like to belt down the pristine slopes. Their patronage has sparked a spate of chi chi development throughout the Vall d'Aran, much of it in harmony with the ancient grey-slated villages (Baqueira-Beret itself being the exception, with some eye-poppingly dreadful modern architecture). Beyond Baqueira-Beret is the dizzying pass of the Port de la Bonanaigua, which at more than 2000 m is one of the most spectacular in the Pyrenees. Shaggy mountain horses daydream in the middle of the road and, with admirable equanimity, refuse to budge for even the biggest lorries. The Port de la Bonanaigua chair lift also runs in summer (usually July to mid-September) and there are some excellent hikes across the top of the mountains.

Salardú and Artíes

Salardú and nearby Artíes make good bases for hiking in the valley, and are delightful crooked old towns of grey stone overlooked by a pair of Romanesque churches. In Salardú, the 13th-century Església de Sant Andreu is set in its own gardens, and has an imposing carved portal; inside, the remnants of its ancient frescoes have been restored revealing a glowing Pantocrater (Christ in Majesty).

Artíes, the most attractive village in the valley, has the Església de Santa Maria, fortified by the Templar knights, and the small Església de Sant Joan, which now holds a small local museum.

Vall de Boí → *For listings, see pages 48-52.*

South of Vielha, the Noguera Ribagorçana River forms a natural boundary between Aragón and Catalunya. Tucked just east of the river is one of Catalunya's greatest treasures, the Vall de Boí, scattered with ancient villages crammed with so many masterpieces of Romanesque art that the whole valley was designated a World Heritage Site in 2000. The finest frescoes have been taken to MNAC in Barcelona, see page 27, in order to safeguard them from rapacious collectors who were snapping them up at an alarming rate at the turn of the last century. They have been replaced by copies, which give a glimmering sense of their original splendour. Thoughtless development and heavy tourism has taken its toll on many of the villages, but the surrounding scenery is spellbinding and the churches themselves can be magical if you get there before the crowds. Most of the villages have several tour operators offering trekking, horse riding and mountain biking in the surrounding hills. The main tourist office for the Boí Valley is in Barruera, one of the first villages along the valley. Stop in at the **Centre d'Interpretació** (**visitor centre**) ① *T973 696 715, www.centreromanic.com*, in Erill la Vall to buy a combination ticket (€9) which allows you to visit all the Romanesque churches.

Coll and Barruera

From El Pont de Suert, a single road winds up through the Vall de Boí, with smaller roads splintering off to the villages; the first of these turnings leads up to **Coll**, often overlooked in the charge towards the biggest prizes at Taüll, but very prettily tucked into a hillside. Its Romanesque **Església de Santa Maria de l'Assumpció** is rarely open, but it is very occasionally possible to arrange guided visits with the valley's main tourist office in **Barruera**, the large town spread along the main road further north. The tourist office is right on the main road and provides plenty of helpful maps, leaflets and accommodation guides. Barruera's Romanesque **Església de Sant Feliu** ① *mid-Sep to mid-Jun 1000-1400, 1600-1900, mid-Jun to mid-Sep 1000-1400, 1600-2000 €2, concessions €1.50*, has a peaceful setting away from the constant whizz of traffic down by the river.

Durro and Erill La Vall

A turning to the right leads to **Durro**, smaller and more peaceful, with the imposing **Església de La Nativitat de la Mare de Déu**, and a humble Romanesque monastery hidden in the mountains beyond. North of Barruera, and just before the turning for Boí, is **Erill La Vall**, a quieter base than Boí or Taüll, with a handful of good restaurants and hotels. The spick-and-span 12th-century **Església de Santa Eulàlia** ① *Tue-Sat 1000-1400 and 1600-1900, Sun 1200-1400 and 1600-1900, €2, concessions €1.50*, has been thoroughly – perhaps too thoroughly – renovated, but still boasts a soaring six-storey belltower, and the town is hoping to build a visitors' centre which will give tourists a glimpse into the Romanesque tradition.

Boí

The tiny medieval centre of Boí is corseted by a grim ring of car parks and modern developments, but it's the closest base for western access to the **Parc Nacional d'Aigüestortes** ① *Estany de Maurici, see page 42*. There's a **park information office** ① *Casa del Parc Nacional d'Aigüestortes i Estany de Sant Maurici, C/de les Graieres 2, Boí, T973 696 189*. The town is surrounded by good walking trails to the other villages of the valley. It's about 3.5 km to the park boundaries, unless you take a jeep taxi (book at the information office), and another 3.5 km to the waterfalls of Aigüestortes ('twisted waters').

Boí's ancient **Església de Sant Joan**, dating back to around 1100, has been extensively renovated and contains a copy of the startling murals which are now in MNAC and are some of the earliest examples of Catalan Romanesque art; there's a vicious depiction of the Stoning of St Stephen, and a lurid Heaven and Hell, in which monsters taunt a soul burning in Hell. The road through the Vall de Boí peters out at the spa complex in **Caldes de Boí**, famous for its waters since Roman times and beautifully set in dense forest.

Taüll and Boí-Taüll ski resort

The road twists upwards through Boí towards the very pretty village of Taüll, which contains the most spectacular church in the valley, the beautiful **Església de Sant Climent de Taüll** ① *summer daily 1030-1400 and 1600-2000, winter Mon-Sat 1030-1400 and 1600-1900, Sun 1030-1400 €3, concessions €2*, with its distinctive soaring belltower. The image of the Pantocrater (Christ in Majesty) is one of the most important elements of Romanesque art, and the Christ which looms from the apse of Sant Climent, fixing the congregation with his limpid terrible gaze, is startling in its intensity. The views from the top of the slim belltower (included in entrance ticket but queues can take forever in summer) are breathtaking.

Taüll is a likeable little town, despite the rash of modern chalets which have sprung up in the wake of the nearby ski resort of **Boí-Taüll**, and another good base for walking in the surrounding hills. At the heart of the oldest part of the town, a stone maze of hunched cottages, is another medieval church, the **Església de Santa María** ① *1000-2000, free*, gently but determinedly subsiding and taking its belltower with it. For ski information and accommodation, T902 406 640, www.boitaullresort.com. The ski resort of Boí-Taüll is relatively new, but unfortunately some thoughtless modern development has already grown up around it. The resort itself has a respectable number of slopes – more than 50, including nine black and 24 red runs – and a wide range of accommodation in all price categories.

Lleida and around → *For listings, see pages 48-52. Phone code: 973. Population: 113,686.*

Cheerful, if rather nondescript, the provincial town of Lleida sits on a bump in the middle of a fertile plain close to the Aragonese border, a strategic location which led to the establishment of a Roman settlement and, later, the capital of a small Moorish kingdom. Nowadays the substantial student population gives Lleida a buzz, particularly around the lively Plaça de Sant Joan, but there are virtually no reminders of its illustrious past. It's the transport hub for bus services to the Pyrenees, with several services a day heading up the Noguera Palleresa valley. With so few monuments or obvious attractions, few visitors bother spending much time in this region, but there are some tiny villages close to Lleida which make excellent bases for some serious walking and are well off the beaten track.

Arriving in Lleida

Getting there There are regular train and bus services from Barcelona to Lleida with connections for the Pyrenees, as well as connections to Madrid and other major cities in

Spain. Lleida is on the high-speed train line between Barcelona and Madrid. Barcelona to Lleida by AVE is 57 minutes; from Lleida to Madrid is around two hours. You'll need your own transport to get to the more remote villages. For general bus information, T973 268 500 (morning only). ▸▸ *For further details, see Transport, page 52.*

Tourist information The **main tourist office** ⓘ *Av Madrid 36, T973 270 997, www.turismedelleida.com.*

Places in Lleida

Lleida was once dominated by the 13th-century fortress of La Zuda, but it was virtually demolished by the Napoleonic armies in 1812, and then given a final battering during the Civil War. The remnants, called the **Castell del Rei**, merit a visit, and shelter Lleida's only remaining 'sight', the old cathedral, la **Seu Vella** ⓘ *T972 230 653, www.turoseuvella.cat, Tue-Sat 1000-1330 and 1600-1930, 1730 in winter, Sun 0930-1330, €5, free Tue*, which can be reached by a rickety lift (€0.50) from Plaça de Sant Joan, or you can make the 20-minute slog up from the centre of town. Begun in 1203, the lofty cathedral is an elegant example of the Transitional style from Romanesque to Gothic, with a sturdy octagonal tower and traces of Mozarabic decoration. The Gothic cloister is particularly charming, with arcades of different sizes and shapes, harmoniously knitted together with delicate stone tracery.

The old cathedral was turned into a military barracks in the 18th century, when a new cathedral, back in town on the Carrer Major, was constructed. It's a dull and uninspiring building, illuminated by narrow stained-glass windows. Around the corner on nearby Carrer Cavallers, there's a collection of art by local artists.

On the other side of the cathedral, the elegant 16th-century Hospital de Santa Maria houses the little-visited **Museo Arqueològic** ⓘ *T972 271 500, Tue-Fri 1200-1400 and 1800-2100, Sat 1100-1400 and 1900-2100, Sun 1100-1400, free*, with a rather tired collection of Roman odds and ends. It's worth a visit for the handsome patio, where you can drowse away an afternoon over a book.

The **Castell de Gardeny** ⓘ *T973 271 942, www.domustemple.com; guided visits Sat 1000, 1200 and 1600, Sun 1000 and 1200*, an impressive castle on a windswept hill overlooking the city, was built by the Templars at the end of the 12th century. Now an interesting museum, it recounts the Templar occupation of the region in the 12th and 13th centuries. This is just one of a string of fortresses constructed by the Templars in what was then the front line of the struggle against the Muslim armies.

Around Lleida

Most of the towns heading towards the Segre Valley are entirely unexceptional, although **Balaguer** is worth a stop for the ruins of its medieval fortress, which was once the castle of the influential Counts of Urgell. There's another beautiful Gothic cloister in the Monestir de Santo Domingo, and the Gothic Església de Santa Maria is very appealing.

A wonderful train line, the Tren dels Laks, trundles between Lleida and La Pobla de Segur, taking in several charming towns and enjoying watery views.

North of Balaguer, a small road peels west off into the hills towards the 12th-century Monestir de Santa Maria de Bellpuig de les Avellanes, which was richly endowed by the Counts of Urgell who were buried here. Their sarcophogi were carried off the Metropolitan museum in New York where they are displayed in a cloister and muttered over by still-furious Catalans. There are wonderful views across the valley and down to the winsome castle-topped village of **Àger**. The original fortress was established by the Romans, then rebuilt by the Moors and finally converted into a church after the Moors were driven out of Catalanya.

Back on the main road north towards **Tremp** (C-147), a tiny road winds eastwards up to the old stone village of **Llimiana**, with another graceful Romanesque church and fine views of the surrounding almond groves, forests and the Sierra de Montsec. Below it is a lake, the **Pantà de Terradets**, where families come to windsurf and picnic at weekends.

Catalan Pyrenees listings

For hotel and restaurant price codes and other relevant information, see pages 10-13.

⊙ Where to stay

Vall de Núria *p38*

€€ Hotel Vall de Nuria, T972 732 030, www.valldenuria.com. The sanctuary only looks like a prison from the outside, and inside you'll find light, attractive rooms and a good restaurant.

€ Els Caçadors, C/Balandrau 24, Ribes de Freser, T972 727 006. This small hotel, close to the Cremallera train station, has a good restaurant dishing up tasty local specialities.

€ Pic de l'Àliga Youth Hostel, Estació de Montaña Vall de Nuria, T972732048, which enjoys a spectacular setting right at the top of the ski-lift.

Camping

Up in the Vall de Núria, you can camp in a small area behind the sanctuary.
Camping Vall de Ribes, Ctra Pardines Km 0.5, T972 728 820. Wonderful, rural campsite with pitches arranged on terraces on the hillside. Few facilities, but fabulous views and lovely staff.

Berga and the Parc Natural de Cadí-Moixeró *p39*

€€ Hotel Les Fonts, Ctra Castellar Km 8, Castellar de n'Hug, T938 257 089, www.hotellesfonts.cat. The largest and best equipped although the decor is high-kitsch with plenty of flounces.

€ Estel, Ctra Sant Fruitós, Berga, T938 213 463, www.hotelestel.com. Modern and accommodating on the edge of town.

€ Hostal Alt Llobregat, C/Portell s/n, Castellar de n'Hug, T938 257 074, www.altllobregat.com. A simple but reasonably priced *pensión* with a café-bar.

€ Hostal La Muntanya, Plaça Major 4, Castellar de n'Hug, T938 257 065, www.hostal lamuntanya.cat. A delightful, cheerful guest-house with a popular restaurant.

€ Hotel La Pineda, C/Raval 50, Bagà, T938 244 515, www.hotelpineda.com. This is the best place to stay in Bagà; a down-to-earth hotel just off the main shopping street.

€ Santuari de Falgars, Poblet de Lillet, T937 441 095, www.falgars.com. A popular *pensión* with wonderful views.

Camping

Càmping Bastareny, Bagà, T938 244 420;
Càmping Cadí at Gósol, T973 370 134 and 2 campsites in Saldes: **Càmping Repòs de Pedraforca**, T938 258 044 and **Càmping Mirador del Pedraforca**, T938 258 062.

Cerdanyà Valley *p40*

Puigcerdà has the best range of accommodation in the Cerdanyà Valley.
€€€€ Torre del Remei, Camí Reial s/n, Bolvir de Cerdanyà, 5 km from Puigcerdà, T972 140 182, www.torredelremei.com. One of the most luxurious hotels in Catalunya. It's spectacularly set in a Modernista palace surrounded by gardens, and rooms are

individually decorated with a stylish mixture of traditional and new fabrics and furniture. The restaurant has a superb reputation.

€€€ El Castell, Ctra N-620, Km 229, Castellciutat, T973 350 000, www.hotel-castell-cintat.com. Tucked next to the ruins of the old castle, **El Castell** is a discreetly elegant modern building with all the luxury trimmings, including a fabulous restaurant.

€€ Del Prado, Ctra de Llívia s/n, Puigcerdà, T972 880 400, www.hoteldelprado.cat. A well-equipped, chalet-style hotel close to the ice-skating rink with a pool and a very good restaurant.

€€ Fonda Biayana, C/Sant Roc 11, Bellver de Cerdanya, T973 510 475. Delightfully rickety with a popular local bar and mid-range restaurant downstairs.

€€ Hostal Rita Belvedere, C/Carmelites 6-8, Puigcerdà, T972 880 356. An old-fashioned *hostal* with some old and some modernized rooms, many with good views.

€€ Hotel La Glorieta, C/Afores s/n, T972351045, www.hotehostallaglorieta.com. A modern hotel just outside town on the way to Castellciutat, with all mod cons including a pool and a good restaurant.

€€ Parador Nacional de la Seu d'Urgell, C/ Sant Domènec 6, La Seu d'Urgell, T973 352 000, www.parador.es. A mix of ancient and modern, this parador is built around a glassed-over Renaissance cloister.

€ Hostal Rusó, C/Frederic Bernades 15, Llivia, T972 146 264, www.hostalruso.es. The best budget option, set around a little courtyard in the town centre and has a decent old-fashioned and cheap restaurant.

Noguera Palleresa Valley and Parc Nacional d'Aigüestortes *p42*

The main access towns for Aigüestortes Park are Espot and Boí.

€€ Hotel Solé, Av Estació 44, La Pobla de Segur, T973 680 452. Conveniently central and perfectly comfortable aparthotel.

€€ Roya, C/Sant Maurici s/n, Espot, T973 624 040, www.hotelroya.net. Simple with an excellent restaurant and close to the park information office and the jeep taxi stand.

€ Pensió del Rey, Llavorsí, T973 622 011. A good budget option.

€ Pensió La Palmira, C/Marineta s/n, Espot, T973 624 072, www.pensiopalmira.com. Also has a cheap restaurant with a good *menú del día* for under €10.

Vall d'Aran *p43*

In Salardú and Artíes there are plenty of places to stay, from super chi chi ski hotels to humble guesthouses.

€€€ Melia Royal Tanau, Ctra de Beret s/n, in Baqueira-Beret, T973 644 446, www.sol melia.com. One of the smartest options, with a fantastic location next to the ski lifts to deliver you straight to the slopes, a heated pool, Turkish baths, gym and a jacuzzi for some post-skiing pampering.

€€€ Parador de Arties, Ctra a Baqueira-Beret s/n, Arties, T973 640 801, www.parador.es. Luxurious, chalet-style parador with all kinds of extras including an outdoor pool.

€€ Besiberri, C/Deth Fòrt 4, Artíes, T973 640 829, www.hotelbesiberri.com. A delightful, family-run chalet-style hotel right by a stream with flower-filled balconies and delicious breakfasts.

€€ Hotel Aran, Av Castiero 5, Vielha, T972 640 050, www.hotelaran.net. Offers pretty wooden rooms, as well as a jacuzzi and sauna to soak tired limbs. Family-run. Prices leap in Aug.

€€ Mont Romies, Plaça Major s/n, Salardú, T973 642 016. This traditional stone hotel is in a perfect location in the heart of the village.

€€ Parador de Vielha, Vielha, T973 640 100, www.parador.es. A modern and slightly soulless place but with great views of the valley.

€ Casa Vicenta, C/ Reiau 7, Vielha, T973 640 819, www.pensioncasavicenta.com. A sweet little *pensión* with simple, but very cheap rooms; those without bathrooms are cheaper.

Vall de Boí *p45*

€€€ Balneari Caldes de Boí, Boí, T973 696 219. A grand spa hotel with all the trimmings in a magnificent location. Closed in winter.

€€ Casa Peiró, La Plaça 7, Coll, T973 297 002, www.hotelcasapeiro.com. A typical 19th-century stone mountain house with a wooden gallery and rustically furnished rooms. The mid-range priced restaurant is particularly good.

€€ Farre d'Avall, C/Major 8, Barruera, T973 694 029. Very comfortable, and has a well-reputed, mid-range restaurant, but traffic noise can be a problem.

€€ Hostal La Plaça, Plaça Església, Erill la Vall, T973 696 026, www.hostal-laplaza.com. Attractive option which overlooks the main square and has another very good restaurant.

€€ Pensió La Coma, C/ Unica s/n, Taüll, T973 696 147. An old favourite with a cosy restaurant much loved by locals.

€ Pensió Pascual, Pont de Boí s/n, T973 696 014. A friendly little place on the outskirts of the village by the bridge. A good budget choice.

Lleida and around *p46*

€€€€ Finca Prats Hotel Golf and Spa, Ctra N240 Km 102.5, T902 445 666, www.fincaprats.com. Ultra-luxurious spa hotel and golf course; one of the best hotels in Catalunya.

€€ Catalonia Transit, Plaza Berenguer s/n, Lleida, T973 230 008, www.hoteles-catalonia.es. Set in a turn-of-the-20th-century building above the train station, the rooms of this historic hotel are surprisingly crisp, modern and very comfortable.

€ Goya, C/ Alcalde Costa 9, Lleida, T973 266 788, www.goyahotel.es. Central budget hotel, with modern en suite rooms.

€ Urgell, C/Urgell 25, Balaguer, T973 445 348. Old-fashioned but impeccably kept.

Berga and the Parc Natural de Cadí-Moixeró *p39*

€€ Balcó de Catalunya, Santuari de Queralt, Berga, T938 213 828. Head up here for a simple lunch enjoying spectacular views; set in the sanctuary of Queralt on a crag overlooking the mountains.

€€ Sala, Paseo de la Paz 27, Berga, T938 211 185, www.restaurantsala.com. The best-known local restaurant run by a welcoming father-and-daughter team, the **Sala** produces excellent regional cuisine with some inspired contemporary touches.

Cerdanyà Valley *p40*

Much of what's on offer in Puigcerdà is geared towards tourists. The cafés set around the two adjoining squares of Santa Maria and Herois at the centre of Puigcerdà are particulary tourist orientated and, consequently, the food here is usually overpriced and very ordinary. Those listed below are exceptions.

€€€ Torre del Remei (see Where to stay, above), Puigcerdà. An award-winning restaurant, for a special treat.

€€ Andria, Passeig Joan Brudeu 24, La Seu d'Urgell, T973 350 300, www.hotelandria.com. This celebrated old restaurant with Modernista decor in the heart of the old town is one of the best in the town. It serves delicious, local dishes. There are a few rooms (**€€**) upstairs.

€€ Can Ventura, Plaça Major 1, Llivia, T972 896 178, www.canventura.com. This delightful restaurant overlooks a lovely square and serves tasty local dishes out on the terrace in summer.

€€ Carlit, Av Catalunya 68, Llivia, T972 896 326. A welcoming restaurant serving unusual Basque specialities.

€€ El Galet, Plaça Santa María 8, Puigcerdà, T972 882 266. A friendly, old-fashioned spot on one of the city's main squares – perfect terrace in summer – offering good Catalan food at good prices.

€ Cal Cofa, C/Frederic Bernades 1, Llivia, T972 896 500. Serves succulent, cheap, grilled meats to a lively, local crowd.

€ Fonda Pluvinet, C/El Segre 13, Martinet, T973 515 075. An appealing stone building in the centre of the village, serving delicious, inexpensive Catalan food.

€ Restaurant Madrigal, C/Alfons I, Puigcerdà. A low-key bar which has freshly made tapas and basic meals at a good price.

Vall d'Aran *p43*

There are great places to eat in the Vall d'Aran; mostly for people with deep pockets.

€€€ Casa Irene, C/Mayor 3, Artíes, T973 644 364. One of the finest restaurants in the whole region, run by the charismatic Irene España, and well worth a splurge.

€€ Era Mola, C/ Marrec 4, Vielha, T973 642 419. A romantic and centrally located restaurant, which offers delicious Aranese specialities, featuring wild mushrooms and very good crêpes.

€€ Urtau, Plaça Artau s/n, Artíes, T973 640 926. Plain but cosy, with wooden beams, whitewashed walls, and a fireplace. Excellent, local dishes, a good wine list and some of the best desserts in the Pyrenees. Next door, they also run a noisy, buzzy bar, where you can find Basque-style tapas (*pintxos*) – slices of bread piled high with all kinds of toppings – which are tasty, filling and very cheap.

€ Nicolas, C/Castèth 10, Vielha, T973 641 820. You'll find more delicious, local specialities and a fantastic array of *pintxos* (Basque-style tapas).

Vall de Boí *p45*

€€ El Caliu, C/Feixanes 11, Taüll, T973 696 212, www.elcaliutaull.com. Serving elegantly prepared dishes and an array of wonderful home-made desserts. One of the best restaurants in these parts.

€€ La Cabana, Ctra de Taüll s/n, midway between Boí and Taüll, T973 696 213, www.lacabanaboi.com. Serves tasty grilled local meat and Catalan mountain dishes.

Lleida and around *p46*

There's lots of choice in Lledia, from good budget places to swish award-winning establishments.

€€ Xaler Suis, C/Rovira Roure 9, T973 235 567. Good local dishes such as roast kid, lobster raviole and tasty stews, and there's a fabulous chocolate fondue for dessert.

€ El Portón, C/Sant Martí 53. Stylish tapas bar with a huge range of tasty snacks.

€ Muixi, Plaça Sant Jaume 4, Balaguer, T973 445 497. Don't miss this award-winning confectioner's shop which makes delicious local cakes and other goodies.

⚛ Festivals

Cerdanyà Valley *p40*

Aug   Festival de l'Estany by Puigcerdà's lake on the last weekend in Aug, which culminates in a spectacular fireworks show.

🏔 What to do

Noguera Palleresa Valley and Parc Nacional d'Aigüestortes *p42*

Tour operators include:

Rafting Llavorsí, Llavorsí, T973 622 158, www.raftingllavorsi.com. Rafting, kayaking and hydro-speed trips are offered.

Yeti Emotions, Llavorsí, T973 622 201, www.yetiemotions.com. For rafting, canyoning, hydrospeed, mountain biking and rock-climbing.

Vall d'Aran *p43*

Vielha tourist office has maps with good suggestions for walking trails close to the town. The town is also stuffed full of tour operators who can organize everything from horse riding and mountain biking to kayaking or heli-skiing.

Deportur, Camí Paisàs s/n, further up the Vall d'Aran in Les, T972 647 045, www.depotur.com.
Escuela de Equitació, Ctra Francia, T973 642 244, www.aranequitacion.es. For horse riding.
Horizontes, Catra Francia 22, T973 642 967, www.horizontesaventura.com.

⊖ Transport

Vall de Núria *p38*
There are regular trains from Barcelona-Sants via Plaça Catalunya to **Ripoll** and **Ribes de Freser**, where you join **La Cremallera**, T972 732 044, up to the Vall de Núria. The rack-and-pinion train runs regularly (usually between 0900 and 1800, although hours are extended in season) daily except in Nov when it is closed (€22.30, children €13.35 for a return ticket from Núria to Ribes).

Berga and the Parc Natural de Cadí-Moixeró *p39*
This region is very difficult to explore without your own car, as buses are infrequent. There are 3 buses a day Mon-Fri, 2 a day Sat and Sun from **Barcelona** to **Berga** with ALSA, T902 422 242; 1 bus a day (except on Sun) to **Castellar de N'Hug** via **La Pobla de Lillet**.

Cerdanyà Valley *p40*
Regular bus services link **La Seu d'Urgell** with **Andorra la Vella** and other towns in Andorra. There are regular trains from **Barcelona-Sants** via Plaça Catalunya to **Puigcerdà** via **Vic** and **Ripoll**. Regular local bus services link **Puigcerdà** with **La Seu d'Urgell** via **Bellver de Cerdanya** with ALSA (T902 422 242) who also run direct services to **La Seu d'Urgell** from the Estació del Nord in **Barcelona**.

Noguera Palleresa Valley and Parc Nacional d'Aigüestortes *p42*
This region is hard to explore fully without your own transport, although all the larger towns are connected by bus.

Bus The bus service is run by **ALSA**, T902 422 242, who run twice-daily buses from **La Seu d'Urgell** for **Sort** and **Llavorsí**, plus a regular bus service to **Llívia**. There are daily buses from **Barcelona** and **Lleida** for **Espot**, but you'll have to ask the bus driver to let you off at the turn-off for the village and walk the last 7 km, or call a **jeep taxi**, T973 696 314, www.taxisvalldeboi.com. There are direct buses from **Barcelona** to **La Pobla de Segur** and **Lleida**, but you'll need your own transport to get to the more remote villages.

Train There are regular trains from **Sants** to **Lleida**, where several buses depart for the Pyrenees, stopping at **Tremp**, **La Pobla de Segur**, **Sort** and **Port de Suert**.

Vall d'Aran *p43*
There are 2 buses from **Barcelona** to **Vielha** which travel via **Port de Suert** from the Estació del Nord with ALSA (T902 422 242).

Vall de Boí *p45*
There's only one bus up the Vall de Boí from **El Pont de Suert** (usually runs Jun-Sep only). El Pont de Suert has twice-daily connections to **Lleida** and **Vielha** with ALSA (T902 422 242) which are timed to connect with the Vall de Boí service.

Lleida and around *p46*
Bus There are direct buses from **Barcelona** to **La Pobla de Segur** and **Lleida**.

Train There are regular services from **Barcelona-Sants** to **Lleida**, where several buses depart for the Pyrenees, stopping at **Tremp**, **La Pobla de Segur**, **Sort** and **El Port de Suert**. The high-speed AVE runs about 8 times a day to Madrid (2 hrs 10 mins) See www.renfe.com for AVE and regional timetables and ticket information.

West to Aragón

The southern part of this zone is an agricultural area at the feet of the soaring Pyrenees, little touched by tourism but boasting some good sights, including the excellent Templar castle of Monzón. Aragón's best wine, Somontano, comes from here, around Barbastro, which is also the spiritual home of the Catholic organization Opus Dei. Nearby is the spectacular canyoning mecca of Alquézar while, further northeast, towards the Pyrenees, is one of Spain's more enchanting villages, Roda de Isábena.

Barbastro and around → *For listings, see pages 57-58.*

After enlisting in Barcelona, to fight alongside the Republican Army in the Spanish Civil War, Barbastro was George Orwell's first stop en route to the front. While things have changed since those dark days, you can see what he was getting at when he referred to Barbastro as "a bleak and chipped town"; he had few good words to say about Aragonese towns in general. The place has taken on new life recently as the centre of the **Somontano** wine region, a small core of producers who have risen to prominence with modern winemaking methods allowing high production and consistent quality.

Barbastro was an important Muslim town in its time, but it's the 16th-century **cathedral** ① *1000-1300, 1800-1930; summer 1000-1330, 1630-1930*, which dominates today. Built between 1517 and 1533, it's an elegant structure with a newer, separate bell tower. Archaeological unearthings have revealed parts of a former church and a mosque alongside the building. The church's pride is the 16th-century *retablo*, sculpted from alabaster and polychrome wood by Damián Forment (whose work is also in Huesca cathedral), an Aragonese of considerable Renaissance kudos. He died before he could complete the work, but you wouldn't know – it's a remarkable piece. **Barbastro's tourist office** ① *T974 308 350, Mon-Sat 1000-1400, 1630-1930, Jul-Aug Mon-Sat 1000-2000, Sun 1000-1400, 1630-1930*, is in the Museo del Vino complex on Avenida de la Merced on the edge of town.

Wineries

The Somontano DO (*denominación de origen*) was approved in principle in 1974 and in practice a decade later. Most of the producers are modern concerns, using up-to-date techniques to produce a range of mid-priced wines from 12 permissible red and white grape varieties, some local, some French. The region's cold winters and hot, dry summers are ideal for ripening wine grapes and production has soared in the bodegas. The **Museo de Vino** ① *above the tourist office, Mon-Sat 1000-1400, 1630-2000, free*, is an arty but not particularly informative display. There's also a shop downstairs and a good restaurant.

Most of the wineries are on the road to Naval relatively close to Barbastro. The best known both inside and outside Spain is **Viñas del Vero** ① *T974 302 216,* *www.vinasdelvero.es, Mon-Fri 1000-1400, 1600-1900, Sat 1000-1400, guided visits last 1 hr and include a tasting*, 3 km from the centre on this road, whose Cabernet Sauvignon- and Merlot-based wines are appealingly good value. Another good producer is **Enate** ① *Av de las Artes, Salas Bajas, 10 km northwest of Barbastro, T974 302 580, www.enate.es, visits Mon-Fri 1030, 1130, 1630, Sat 1000, 1200 (book in advance), €3.*

Monzón

Though seldom visited, Monzón is one of those surprising Spanish towns that has a superb attraction, in this case its relatively unspoiled **castle** ① *Tue-Sat 1000-1300, 1700-2000, Sun 1000-1400, winter Tue-Fri 1130-1300, 1500-1700, Sat 1130-1300, 1700-1900, Sun 1000-1400; €2*, an atmospheric Templar stronghold that feels impregnable, albeit bare. The castle was fought over during the Reconquista, and often changed hands. The mercenary El Cid came here a few times to accept contracts from Muslim governors, while his renowned blade *El Tizón* was later kept here as a relic. Although some reconstruction has been effected, the buildings still preserve the Templar austerity and ambience. There are underground passageways to be explored (take a torch). The **tourist office** is in the bus station, but the admissions booth at the castle also functions as one.

Torreciudad

The holy shrine of **Opus Dei** ① *www.torreciudad.org, daily 0900-1900 (later in summer)*, is worth a visit, but don't expect revelation; it's likely to reinforce anyone's pre-existing love or otherwise of the organization (see box, page 55). In a spectacular setting on a rocky promontory amid craggy hills, it overlooks the Embalse de El Grado and Franco's dam that created it. The main building, once you're past the security guard, is a curious affair. Virtually windowless, the brick design seems to recall the designs of both Oriental temples and Victorian power stations. Inside, the altarpiece is the main attraction, an ornate sculptural relief. In the centre is a Romanesque statue of the Virgin – a passage behind leads to a kissable medallion.

Many Catholic theologians see Opus Dei as an organization looking backwards towards ritual piety rather than a more enlightened spirituality; the complex certainly bears this out – visitors are encouraged to seek God in the rosary and stations of the cross in several admittedly attractive locations. The structure was conceived by Saint Josemaría himself, who was born in nearby Barbastro. He died suddenly in 1975, 11 days before the official opening.

Abizanda

Heading north from Barbastro towards Aínsa, the village of Abizanda is unmissable, with its *atalaya* (defensive tower) looming over the road. The *atalaya* dates from the 11th century but has been recently rebuilt. Typical of the area, it functioned as a watchtower, one of a chain that could relay signals up and down the valley. A series of levels (sometimes spruced up by art exhibitions) leads to a vertiginous wooden platform with views in all directions through narrow wooden slots. Adjacent is the **Museo de Creencias y Religiosidad Popular** ① *tower and museum Jul to mid-Sep daily 1100-1400, 1700-2100; Easter-Jun and mid-Sep to early Dec Sun only 1100-1400, 1600-2000, €1.50*, a small but interesting collection of pieces focusing on the local customs that were (and still are, in some villages) designed to keep evil spirits at bay.

Opus Dei

For this secretive Catholic organization, the stunning success enjoyed by the *The Da Vinci Code*, which portrays it in a distinctly unflattering light, was anathema, and spokesmen reacted angrily to what was, after all, a detective novel that made no claim of objectivity. Whatever the mysteries of Opus, we can be fairly certain that self-mutilating albino monk assassins aren't within their *modus operandi*.

It's ironic that after centuries of severe persecution of Freemasons on the grounds that they were a "secretive, power-hungry cult", Spain should have produced Opus Dei, a Catholic sect with marked similarities to the Lodgemen. It was founded in 1928 by Josemaría de Escrivá, a Barbastro lawyer turned priest appalled at the liberalism prevalent in 1920s Spain. He saw Opus (the name means 'the work of God' as a way for lay people to devote their life to the Lord; one of his favourite phrases was "the sanctity of everyday life". His book *The Way* is the organization's handbook, with 999 instructions and thoughts for achieving greater spirituality in daily matters. Members are both men and women (although The Way has been heavily criticized for its archaic attitude to the latter) and, although some follow a semi-monastic life, the majority continue in their worldly professions.

The organization has members all around the world, but Spain has remained its heartland, where membership in boardrooms, staffrooms and parliament remains high but undisclosed. Politically and religiously conservative, Opus was a powerful peacetime ally of Franco's government. This explains part of the considerable hostility towards the sect, as do its capitalistic ventures; the group is very wealthy and owns numerous newspapers, television channels and companies worldwide. Allegations of secrecy about Opus centre around the lack of transparency in its involvement in these enterprises as much as the private nature of personal participation. More serious, perhaps, is its backward-looking approach to Catholicism, with holiness deemed to derive in a large part from the regular performance of the ritual of the sacraments, and the more recent devotions of the rosary and the stations of the cross, an approach bemoaned by forward-thinking Catholic theologians. The late Pope John Paul II, a devoted admirer of capitalism and conservatism, had a lot of time for Opus, and granted them a privileged status within the Vatican. On 6 October 2002, Escrivá was canonized in Rome as San Josemaría; a controversial event both celebrated and mourned in Spain.

Graus

This small service town doesn't seem much to most who pass through it en route to higher ground. In fact, it's a town with plenty of history, an important bastion of the Reconquista, and long-time marketplace for much of the Eastern Pyrenees.

The **Plaza Mayor** is an extravagant and beautiful square. Surrounded by beautiful mansions, the **Casa de Barrón** stands out for its red colour and two large paintings on its façade. The female forms are depictions of Art and Science, supposedly created to please the owner's Andalucian wife, perhaps longing for a touch of Mediterranean decadence in dusty Aragón. It's also been suggested, though, that there are several symbols of freemasonry in the paintings, an amusing thought in Opus Dei heartland. Another former resident of the square would not have been amused – Tomás de Torquemada, one of the masterminds of the Spanish Inquisition and scourge of the Spanish Jews, who lived here for a period. Not to be outdone, however, the owner of the **Casa de Heredía** did his eaves up with a series of Renaissance female figures. Unable to compete, the **Ayuntamiento** on the square is distinctly restrained by comparison.

Roda de Isábena

One of Aragón's gems is tiny Roda, an unlikely cathedral town with a population of 36 in a valley south of the Pyrenees. Apart from the odd tourist shop, the hilltop settlement preserves a superb medieval atmosphere. The Romans established it as a commanding fortification overlooking the valley, but it owes its current appearance to the powerful counts of Ribagorza, sometime troublemakers who made this a major residence. The town invites wandering around its stone buildings and fortifications; there are several coats-of-arms for heraldists to decipher, and occasional art exhibitions and music recitals.

The **cathedral** ⓘ *admission by guided tour only; €2*, claims to be the smallest in Spain, but it's no chapel. The intricate 12th-century façade (with a later porch) is the portal to several architectural and artistic treasures. It is impressive, with columns crowned with rearing lions around a massive studded door. The delicate crypt has superb Romanesque wall paintings of which the best is a Pantocrator. There are more in a chapel off the cloister. The earthly remains of San Ramón are housed in a carved tomb, while the 350-year-old organ still belts out. The cloister is beautiful, swathed with grass and flowers.

Alquézar and the Guara Canyon → *For listings, see pages 57-58.*

The village of Alquézar, tucked away in the Pyrenean foothills, is one of Aragón's prettiest places, a heavily restored sand-coloured village nestling among crags that makes a great destination in its own right but also happens to be the launchpad for some of Europe's finest canyoning. There are over 200 canyons in the surrounding Sierra de Guara; some can be strolled without equipment, while others require full climbing, abseiling and water gear. Try and avoid going in the height of summer, as the region gets ridiculously crowded, as well as seriously hot. Alquézar is a 45-minute drive from Huesca, signposted off the Barbastro road. There's a **tourist office** ⓘ *C Arrabal, summer daily 0930-1330, 1630-2000, mid-Oct to mid-Jun weekends only*.

The village's twisting medieval streets – no cars – are dominated by a large rock, on which once sat a **Muslim fortress** ⓘ *entrance by guided tour only; Wed-Mon 1100-1330, 1600-1800 (1630-1930 summer), €1.80*, hence the town's name. The foundations and walls are still visible, but following the Christian reconquest of the town in 1067, it was converted into a fortified collegiate church. Although much of it dates from the 16th century, there are some attractive Romanesque elements still present, particularly the irregularly shaped double-columned cloister, which has some capitals carved with Old Testament scenes.

The area's most famous canyon is the **Cañón del Vero**, a popular destination for the tour companies. It's not very difficult, but you'll need to get wet in some parts at most times of year. The canyon is spectacular, wide and deep, with immense numbers of vultures; the rare lammergeyer occasionally puts in an appearance too. Descending the

---

canyon takes about six hours; during summer there's a shuttle bus to the starting point 20 km from Alquézar, otherwise it's about a 4½-hour walk. If you don't fancy doing the whole thing, you can see part of it by walking from Alquézar about an hour to the 'Roman' bridge of Villacantal. ▸▸ See What to do, page 58.

West to Aragón listings

For hotel and restaurant price codes and other relevant information, see pages 10-13.

● Where to stay

Barbastro and around *p53*
Monzón has more charm than Barbastro.
€€ Hotel Clemente, C Corona de Aragón 5, T974 310 186, www.hotelclemente.com. A touch sterile but spacious, modern and friendly, with a/c and a restaurant.

Monzón *p54*
€€ Vianetto, Av de Lérida 25, T974 401 900, www.hotelvianetto.com. The best option in Monzón, with dull but comfortable doubles with a/c. Decent restaurant.

Graus *p55*
€€€ Hotel Palacio del Obispo, Pl Coreche 2, T974 545 900, www.palaciodelobispo graus.com. This excellent hotel occupies a noble 17th-century palace in the heart of the town. Rooms have plenty of historic character, but modern conveniences include a spa complex.

Roda de Isábena *p56*
Roda can get busy in summer at the weekends.
€€ Hospedería Roda de Isábena, Plaza la Catedral s/n, T974 544 554, www.hospederia-rdi.com. Virtually touches the cathedral steps, and garlanded with grapevines. A good, well-priced place. Rooms are comfortable, but more atmospheric is the restaurant in the old refectory of the monks who founded the cathedral, or the patio overlooking the valley.

Alquézar and the Guara Canyon *p56*
€€ Hotel Santa María, C Arrabal s/n, T974 318 436, www.hotel-santamaria.com. Perhaps the nicest place to stay, with some good views over the valley, castle, and village. Attractive rooms. The hotel runs the Avalancha agency (see page 58).
€ Albergue Casa Tintorero, C San Gregorio 18, T974 318 354, www.vertientesaventura. com. A convivial and well-priced hostel in the town centre, with a tour agency.
€ Casa Jabonero, C Mayor s/n, T974 318 908. One of the nicest of the *casas rurales*. Friendly with attractive rooms, some with en suite.

Camping
Camping Alquézar, T974 318 300, www.campingalquezar.com. The closer to town (1 km) of the 2 campsites and open all year.

● Restaurants

Graus *p55*
€€ Itaka, C Joaquín Costa 27, T677 301 601. A good lunch or drink option on the southern edge of Graus, with a very pleasant garden terrace; there's also an internet terminal.

Roda de Isábena *p56*
€€ Hospedería Roda de Isábena, see Where to stay. A good place for an atmospheric bite to eat.
€€ Restaurante Catedral, Plaza Sorolla 2, T974 544 545, set in the cathedral building itself. Closed Nov. Aragonese cuisine with game such as partridge, rabbit and quail, the most unusual being *jabalí al chocolate*

(wild boar with chocolate). There's a reasonable *menú de la casa*.

Barbastro and around *p53*
€€ Europa, C Romero 8, T974 310 350. A fairly upmarket place specializing in gourmet steaks, rabbit and *longaniza* (an Aragonese sausage). The bar serves cheaper *platos combinados*.

€€ Sobrelias, Av de la Merced 64, T974 316 646. A restaurant on the ground floor of the Museo del Vino behind the tourist office. They specialize in typical Aragonese cuisine.

Alquézar and the Guara Canyon *p56*
€€ Casa Gervasio, C Arnal Cavero 13, T974 318 282, www.hotelmaribel.es. In the heart of the village, this offers traditional Aragonese cuisine, including tasty home-made pâtés and cured meats. There's convivial dining inside, and a pretty patio terrace.

⚠ What to do

Alquézar and the Guara Canyon *p56*
There are several companies offering guided descents of canyons. Competition keeps prices very similar, but be sure to check what is offered, as well as insurance; standard travel insurance may not cover this type of activity. The standard day trip costs around €60, usually including a packed lunch.
Avalancha, C Arrabal s/n, T974 318 299, www.avalancha.org. Solid reputation.

⊖ Transport

Barbastro and around *p53*
Bus Barbastro is a major transport junction for the eastern Pyrenean towns. The bus station is near the cathedral.

Buses include **Barcelona** 4 daily (3½ hrs), **Huesca** 11 daily (50 mins); **Benasque** 2 a day (2 hrs), **Lleida** 10 a day, **Monzón** hourly (15 mins), **Aínsa** 1 daily, another on Sun and in summer, **Graus** 3 daily, and 1 to **Alquézar**.

Monzón *p54*
Bus Many daily buses to **Huesca** via **Barbast ro**; 4-6 a day to **Lleida**.

Huesca and around

Huesca is in a slightly strange situation – in spite of being the capital of Aragón's Pyrenean province, it has been eclipsed by Jaca as 'gateway to the mountains'. Its old town, albeit interesting, feels a bit neglected, and although the town has plenty of character, it's hard to pin down. That said, it's far from unpleasant, and has some worthwhile restaurants in the eating zone around Plaza Navarra.

Jaca is a fun-loving outdoorsy place that acts as a supply centre to holiday and ski resorts in the region. Pilgrims on the Camino Aragonés have their first taste of Spain in this area, which also harbours the stunning carved capitals of San Juan de la Peña.

Arriving in Huesca → *Phone code: 974. Population: 52,059.*

Getting there and around Huesca is small and easily traversed on foot. The old town is ringed by a road, which changes name several times; south of here is the main area for bars and restaurants, as well as the combined bus and train station on Calle Zaragoza. There are frequent connections with Zaragoza and regular connections to all major cities in Spain. The new fast train and airport have made Huesca, and the snow beyond, more accessible. ►► *See Transport, page 68.*

Tourist information Huesca's active **tourist office** ⓘ *Plaza López Allué s/n, T974 292 170, www.huescaturismo.com, daily 0900-1400, 1600-2000,* is in the southern part of the old town. As well as being a good source of information, they run guided tours of the city (1100 and 1700 depending on numbers, two hours, €2). An excellent initiative is a vintage bus that has been beautifully restored and runs day trips into the Huescan countryside from Easter to October. It leaves Plaza de Navarra at 0900 daily, returning around 1430. There are dozens of different excursions; it's a great way to reach some hard-to-get-to places. There are details in English on the website; booking is essential. The trip costs €5. There's also a small **information kiosk** on Plaza de Navarra open summer only.

Background

Huesca's history is an interesting one. An important Roman town, it was known as Urbs Victrix Osca and was used by Sertorius as an education centre for Romanizing the sons of local chieftains. Taken by the Muslims, it was known as Al-Wasqa before Pedro I retook it. It became a significant bastion in the continuing Reconquista, a walled town with 90 sturdy towers that was capital of the young Aragonese kingdom for a few years. Its importance declined, along with Aragón's, after union with Castilla. Republicans besieged it for a long period during the Civil War but unsuccessfully; George Orwell tells how an optimistic general's catchcry "Tomorrow we'll have coffee in Huesca" became a bitter, cynical joke in the loyalist lines as the weeks went by.

Huesca

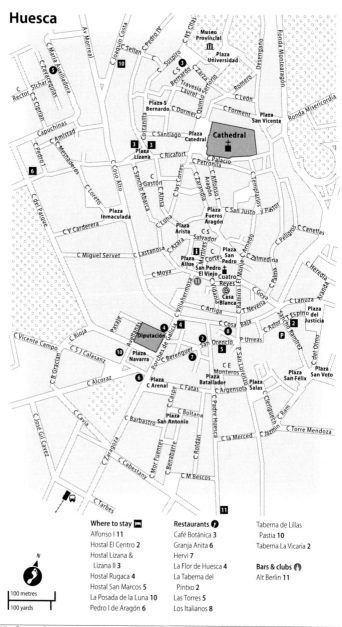

Where to stay 🛏
Alfonso I **11**
Hostal El Centro **2**
Hostal Lizana &
 Lizana II **3**
Hostal Rugaca **4**
Hostal San Marcos **5**
La Posada de la Luna **10**
Pedro I de Aragón **6**

Restaurants 🍴
Café Botánica **3**
Granja Anita **6**
Hervi **7**
La Flor de Huesca **4**
La Taberna del
 Pintxo **2**
Las Torres **5**
Los Italianos **8**

Taberna de Lillas
 Pastia **10**
Taberna La Vicaria **2**

Bars & clubs 🎶
Alt Berlin **11**

Places in Huesca → *For listings, see pages 64-68.*

Cathedral
① *Mon-Fri 1030-1400, 1600-1745, Sat 1030-1400 (cathedral but not museum also open Sat afternoon and Sun), €3.*
The cathedral is a sober Gothic edifice. It has an attractive portal with apostles, and an interesting Diocesan museum, but the highlight is a magnificent alabaster *retablo* sculpted by the Aragonese master Damián Forment. The vivid central pieces depict the crucifixion; the sculpture's beauty makes the gold-painted *retablos* in the side chapels look tawdry.

Museo Provincial
① *Tue-Sat 1000-1400, 1700-2000, Sun 1000-1400, free.*
North of the cathedral, the Provincial Museum houses a varied collection, prettily set around the old royal palace and university buildings. The pieces range from prehistoric finds to Goyas and modern Aragonese art. In one of the rooms of the royal palace the famous incident of 'the bell of Huesca' took place. When his two older brothers died heirless, Ramiro II unwillingly left his monk's cell in France and took the throne. The nobles saw him as a pushover, and he was unable to exercise authority. Desperate, he sent a messenger to the abbot of his old monastery, asking for advice. The abbot said nothing, but led the messenger out to the garden, where he chopped the tops off the tallest plants with a knife. Ramiro got the message, and announced that he was going to forge a bell that would be heard through the kingdom. He summoned the nobles to the palace, and beheaded them as they arrived, making a circle of the heads and hanging one in the centre, thus forming the Bell of Huesca. It was an effective political manoeuvre: Ramiro's difficulties were said to be less from then on.

Iglesia de San Pedro El Viejo
① *Mon-Sat 1000-1330, 1600-1930, Sun 1100-1215, 1300-1345, €2, English tour available.*
In the south of the old town is the church of San Pedro El Viejo, of old stock indeed, as it stands on the location of a Visigothic church, and was the place of worship of the city's Christians during Muslim rule. The current building was constructed in 1117 and features some superb Romanesque capitals in its small cloister. Featuring scenes of the Reconquista and the story of Christ's life, it's thought that the same sculptor was involved both here and at San Juan de la Peña (see page 64). The plain burial chapel off the cloister houses the earthly remains of Alfonso I and Ramiro II (the monk), whose tomb is faced with a panel from a Roman sarcophagus. Inside the church, the soft Romanesque lines are complemented by a number of excellent wall paintings.

The Diputación on Plaza Navarra has an impressive ceiling fresco by Antonio Saura as well as exhibitions of other works. The room is in official use, but is open to the public on weekdays 1800-2100.

Loarre → *For listings, see pages 64-68.*

First recorded in 1033, shortly after it had been built by Sancho the Great of Navarra, the **Castillo de Loarre** ① *www.castillodeloarre.es, Nov-Feb 1100-1730, Mar-Oct daily 1000-1400, 1600-1900 (2000 summer), €3.90,* one of the finest castles in Northern Spain, became an important centre, a monastery, and also briefly a royal residence, before continuing life as a stout frontier post. The design is functional, with few adornments. The towers in the wall are open on the inside, to prevent attacking enemies using them as a refuge once inside the walls. There are some unusual carvings of monkeys above the entrance, while a small dog marks the ascent from the crypt up a narrow staircase that emerges in front of the altar of the church, an unusually high Romanesque structure. The grim dungeons and remains of the royal hall are other highlights, along with the imposing watchtowers. After the early construction used limestone, the masons decided to switch to sandstone, which is much easier to work. This was bad news for the Muslim prisoners, however, who had to drag the blocks from 20 km away. The Castillo de Loarre was also used to film some of Ridley Scott's crusader film, *Kingdom of Heaven*.

Jaca → *For listings, see pages 64-68. Phone code: 974. Population: 13,396. Altitude: 820 m.*

A relaxed spot in northern Aragón, Jaca is far from being a large town but it ranks as a metropolis by the standards of the Pyrenees, for which it functions as a service centre and transport hub. The town has enthusiastically bid for three Winter Olympics, most recently for the 2010 event, but with no luck so far. Most visitors to this part of the Pyrenees are in Jaca at some point, and its also the major stop on the Camino Aragonés pilgrim route, so there's always plenty of bustle about the place.

Jaca's **tourist office** ① *Plaza San Pedro 11, T974 360 098, oficinaturismo@aytojaca.es, Mon-Sat 0900-1330, 1630-1930, mid-Jul to Aug Mon-Sat 0900-2100, Sun 0900-1500*, is down the side of the cathedral in the heart of town.

Background
Jaca was the centre of the Aragonese kingdom in the early Middle Ages under Ramiro I and his son Sancho Ramírez, who established the *fueros*. It was a crucial base in the Reconquista after having been under Moorish control in the eighth century, and a Roman base before that. The city sits on a high plateau above the rivers Aragón and Gállego.

Sights
"It does exist, love for a building, however difficult it may be to talk about. If I had to talk I would have to explain why it should be this particular church that, when I can no longer travel, I will want to have been the last building I have seen." Cees Nooteboom, *Roads to Santiago*.

Jaca's treasure is its delightful Romanesque **cathedral** ① *1130-1330, 1600-2000*, which sits moored like a primitive ship, surrounded not by boats but buildings. Neither majestic nor lofty, it was built in the late 11th and early 12th centuries, although the interior owes more to later periods. The main entrance is a long open portico, which approaches a doorway topped by lions and the Crismon symbol. The idea was perhaps that people had a few paces to meditate on their sins before entering the house of God.

The south door has a wooden porch and fine, carved capitals depicting Abraham and Isaac, and Balaam with the angel. These were beautifully carved by the 'Master of Jaca'. The interior is slightly less charming; the most ornate of the chapels is that of San Miguel, which contains a fanciful 16th-century *retablo* and a carved portal. Next to this is a 12th-century figurine of a wide-hipped virgin and child, dedicated to Zaragoza's Virgin of

Refugios

If you spend time walking in the Pyrenees, you're likely to want to use these comradely places, which are essentially mountain hostels along Scottish 'bothy' lines. The word can mean anything from a one-person lean-to upwards, but the better ones have cosily packed dormitories where wet socks are hung from every nail, and most of the staffed ones offer meals at good rates; the communal atmosphere is usually excellent. It's always worth booking in summer; people aren't usually turned away (at least in remote areas), but you might find yourself on the floor or outside. The staff are usually knowledgeable about the area; it's a good idea to inform them if you're climbing a peak so they can give advice and alert emergency services in case of trouble. Most also have a book where walkers and climbers write hints, describe routes, and give warnings and advice.

the Pillar. The main altar is recessed, with an elaborately painted vaulted ceiling. The cathedral is usually dark; a coinbox just inside the main door takes half-euro pieces, each of which provides light for five minutes.

In the cathedral cloister is the **Diocesan Museum** ① *Tue-Fri 1000-1330, 1600-1900, Sat 1000-1330, 1600-2000, Sun 1000-1330; Jul and Aug Tue-Sun 1000-1330, 1600-2000, €6 (€3 pilgrims)*, which houses a superb collection of Romanesque and Gothic frescoes, taken from other churches in the area and cleverly reconstructed. The best is an awesome 11th-century set from Bagüés, depicting an abbreviated history of the old and new Testaments, comic-strip style. Another highlight is the apse paintings from Riesto, featuring some marvellously self-satisfied 12th-century apostles. Of the paintings, a prim Saint Michael is standing, as is his habit, on a chicken-footed demon who is having a very bad time of it; a wood-carved Renaissance assembly of figures around the body of Christ is also impressive.

Jaca's **citadel** ① *www.ciudadeladejaca.es, guided visits only, Wed-Mon 1100-1400, 1600-1900 (1700-2000 summer); wait at the red line for a guide to arrive, €10*, is still in use by the military. A low but impressively large star-shaped structure, it was constructed during Felipe II's reign. The garrison here rose against the monarchy in 1930, before the rest of the Republican movement was ready for action: two young officers who decided to march on Zaragoza were arrested and executed. Their deaths were not in vain, though, as the indignation caused boosted feeling against the monarchy – the Republic was proclaimed shortly afterwards, and the king went into exile. The tour takes about an hour (including a museum of lead soldiers); it's only €6 to enter if you bypass this and the temporary exhibitions.

Built over the foundations of the old Royal Palace is the **Torre del Reloj**, an attractive Gothic affair that is now HQ to a Pyrenean taskforce. It sits in Plaza Lacadena, an attractive spot at night, with several bars and a floodlit fountain.

Worthy of a quick peek is the **Iglesia del Carmen**, with its interesting façade and scaly columns and a Virgin seemingly flanked by a pair of mandarins.

Walking down **Paseo de la Constitución**, the town comes to an abrupt end in a slope down to the **Río Aragón**. A path leads to the river, a bathing spot, which is traversed by a medieval bridge.

Monasterio de San Juan de la Peña

ⓘ *Mid-Oct to Feb 1000-1530, Mar to May and Sep to mid-Oct 1000-1400, 1530-1900, Jun to mid-Jul 1000-1400, 1500-2000, mid-July to Aug 1000-2000, €7 old monastery only, €8.50 including one of the exhibitions in the new monastery, €11 including both. All tickets include entry to the monastery at Santa Cruz de la Serós, 6 km further north.*

The monastery is difficult to reach without a car, although you can walk the whole way from Jaca on the GR65.3.12 path, part of the Camino de Santiago; otherwise jump off a Pamplona-bound bus at the cruce for Santa Cruz de la Serós; the monastery is just under a two-hour walk from here.

This famous monastery allegedly came into being when a noble named Voto was chasing a deer on horseback. The despairing creature took the Roman option and leaped to its death over a cliff. Voto's horse was unable to stop itself from following. Still in the saddle, Voto launched a quick prayer to John the Baptist and, to his amazement, landed safely outside a small cave. Investigating, he found the body of a hermit and a small shrine to the saint. He was so moved by his salvation that he decided to continue the hermitage and settled here with his brother, who was equally impressed by the tale. The monastery became an important centre on the Pilgrim Route to Santiago in the Middle Ages and today constitutes two separate buildings.

The new monastery is an impressive brick baroque structure which houses a hotel as well as two modern displays, one on the kingdom of Aragón, another on the history and architecture of the old monastery.

It's the older monastery that draws visitors, spectacularly wedged into the cliff 1 km down the hill. Built around bedrock, the lower part consists of a spooky 11th-century church and dormitory, with fragmentary wall paintings and the tombs of several early abbots. Upstairs is a pantheon, where nobles could (with a hefty donation) be buried; it's decorated with the characteristic *ajedrezado jaqués* chessboard pattern that originated in these parts.

The high church features three apses, one of which holds a replica of the Holy Grail and a martial funerary chapel that holds the remains of the Aragonese kings Pedro I and Ramiro I. It's the open remains of the cloister that inspire most awe; the columns are decorated with superbly carved Romanesque capitals under the conglomerate cliff. Scenes from the life of Christ and the book of Genesis are superbly portrayed; Cain takes on Abel with a particularly fearsome sledgehammer.

Huesca and around listings

For hotel and restaurant price codes and other relevant information, see pages 10-13.

🛏 Where to stay

Huesca *p59, map p60*

€€€ La Posada de la Luna, C Joaquín Costa 10, T974 240 857, www.posadadela luna.com. An unusual and offbeat small hotel, set in a sensitively and handsomely renovated Aragonese mansion with mystic and astrological decor. The a/c rooms have all the facilities of a business hotel, including Wi-Fi, flatscreen TV and safe, but it still feels intimate, if overpriced. The location on the edge of town is the only other downside.

€€€ Pedro I de Aragón, C del Parque 34, T974 220 300, www.gargallo-hotels.com. This is a typical modern Spanish hotel, with quiet and cool but vaguely dull rooms and an unremarkable exterior. There are special offers and a large outdoor swimming pool.

€€ **Hostal Lizana** and **Lizana II**, Plaza Lizana 6/8, T974 220 776, www.hostal-lizana.com. These 2 neighbouring places offer good value. The smallish rooms come with or without bathroom and are clean and comfortable. **Lizana II** is a bit more modern.

€€ **Hostal Rugaca**, Porches de Galicia 1, T974 226 449, www.hostalrugaca.com. Right in the heart of things above a popular café, the rooms are simple and smallish but have a/c, TV and en suite bathrooms. Parking is available.

€€ **Hostal San Marcos**, C San Orencio 10, T974 222 931, www.hostalsanmarcos.es. A friendly spot in the café/bar zone, with clean rooms and attractive new wooden furniture. Breakfast served and parking available at €6.

€€-€ **Hostal El Centro**, C Sancho Ramírez 3, T974 226 823, www.hostalelcentrohuesca.es. An old-fashioned establishment with decent rooms with bathroom and TV. It's near the cafés and restaurants, but can be noisy at weekends if you face the street. Free Wi-Fi.

€ **Alfonso I**, C Padre Huesca 67, T974 245 454, www.hostalalfonsohuesca.com. Small but pleasant rooms with and without bathroom. Hospitable management.

Loarre *p61*

€€ **Hospedería de Loarre**, Plaza Miguel Moya 7, T974 382 706, www.hospederiade loarre.com. A beautiful place to stay, in a big stone building with commodious rooms. The major attraction lies 6 km above, on a rocky outcrop. There's a decent restaurant, and breakfast is included.

Jaca *p62*

It's worth booking accommodation ahead here in both high summer and high winter.

€€€ **Hotel Reina Felicia**, Paseo Camino de Santiago 16, T974 365 333, www.proni hoteles.com. This hotel in a new suburb a couple of kilometres from the centre stands out for its avant-garde modern design. Rooms are comfortable, with dark chocolate colours and swish bathrooms. Facilities include a spa and pool complex, but it's a little disappointing that they cost extra. There's a good breakfast buffet.

€€ **Hotel Conde Aznar**, Paseo de la Constitución 3, T974 361 050, www.conde aznar.com. A charming hotel whose rooms show their age but offer significant value. The doubles vary substantially in size; some are quite small. For a little more money, you can procure one with a hydromassage unit, or a 'special', which is part way to being a suite. At peak times, they may only take bookings on a half-board basis; no hardship, as the restaurant is the best in town. Excellent service. Recommended.

€€ **Hotel La Paz**, C Mayor 41, T974 360 700, www.alojamientosaran.com. A very decent place run by decent folk. The rooms are standard modern Spanish, with TV, tiled floors and bathrooms. Some have balconies. Various apartments are also available.

€€ **Hotel Mur**, C Santa Orosia 1, T974 360 100, www.hotelmur.com. This is a historic Jaca hotel with a good feeling about it. Bedrooms are airy and have full facilities; the best overlook the citadel, so you can watch the top-secret manoeuvres of the Spanish army.

€€ **Ramiro I**, C del Carmen 23, T974 361 367, www.hotelramirojaca.es. Closed Nov. Middle-of-the-road hotel with courteous management and fairly simple but spacious enough rooms. The restaurant is uninspiring but decent value.

€ **Hostal París**, Plaza San Pedro 5, T974 361 020, www.hostalparisjaca.com. A good option near the cathedral with clean doubles with excellent modern shared bathrooms. The doors are locked at night until about 0700, so be sure to make some arrangement if you've got an early start.

€ Skipass Hostal, C Mayor 57, T974 363 954, www.skipasshostal.com. Good-value place with unadorned but comfortable rooms at a low price. Rates include Wi-Fi and breakfast.

Camping
Camping Victoria, Ctra Jaca–Pamplona, T974 357 008, www.campingvictoria.es. A year-round site with bungalows that's got less campervan traffic than many, and is only 15 mins' walk from town.

Monasterio de San Juan de la Peña p64
€€ Hospedería San Juan de la Peña, T974 374 422, www.touractive.com. This hotel occupies the southern wing of the upper monastery and adds plenty of modern comforts to the historic building. The rooms are attractive and spacious, with polished wooden floors; some are appealing duplexes that cost some €35 more. Wi-Fi, gym, and other business-standard facilities are present, but the isolated location and short wander down the path to the ancient cloister under the overhang are the real reasons to stay here. The restaurant isn't up to much.

❷ Restaurants

Huesca p59, map p60
Most eating options are south of the old town, around Plaza Navarra.
€€€ Las Torres, C María Auxiliadora 3, T974 228 213, www.lastorres-restaurante.com. In rather uninspiring residential surrounds, this place fights it out with the **Lillas Pastia** for the title of Huesca's best restaurant. Solid Aragonese produce with a gourmet touch is the key to its success.
€€€ Taberna de Lillas Pastia, Plaza Navarra 4, T974 211 691, www.lillaspastia.es. A classy, slightly snooty restaurant in the old casino with undeniably good rich fare served in exquisitely presented small portions. Expect to pay around €50-60 a head à la carte. House speciality is *revuelto de trufas*, a combination of truffles and scrambled eggs.

€€ Hervi, C Santa Paciencia 2, T974 240 333, www.restaurantehervihuesca.com. A popular spot with an outdoor terrace and some excellent fish dishes. Its calamari tapas are particularly highly regarded hereabouts.
€€ La Flor de Huesca, C Porches de Galicia 4, T974 240 402. In the Diputación (provincial government) building, this excellent spot is a favoured lunching place for the not-too-hard-working *funcionarios* tucked under the colonnade on this central street. Modern lines, a high ceiling, and colourful contemporary art on the walls are complemented by good service and plenty of value for a short menu that includes great grilled meats. Lunch *menú* for €17.20. Recommended.
€ La Taberna del Pintxo, C San Orencio 7, T974 226 063. This place specializes in *pinchos*; just help yourself from the little boxes that line the bar. It's an honesty system whereby you leave the toothpicks on your plate and get charged accordingly. The service is excellent, and you can also enjoy *raciones*, or a reasonably priced *menú del día* at the small wooden tables.
€ Taberna La Vicaria, C San Orencio 9, T974 225 195, www.lavicariahuesca.com. With stained glass out front, and some pew-like seats at the tables, this has a churchy theme but is far more about earthly indulgence. A fine range of *pinchos* and tapas are complemented by a selection of meat and seafood *raciones*. The €10 *menú del día* is great, but there are very few tables.

Cafés
Café Botánica, Plaza Universidad 4, T974 240 401. A popular and attractive spot next to the museum. It's a student favourite and offers a huge range of teas, and usually has some relaxing world music on the stereo.
Granja Anita, Plaza Navarra 5, T974 215 712. A smart coffee spot opposite the Diputación, with an ornate façade and huge doors. It's popular with Huesca's parliamentarians and as a smart stop on the evening *paseo*.

Los Italianos, Cosa Baja 18, T974 224 539. An excellent ice cream parlour with tempting pastries and coffee. Try a *pastel ruso*, a traditional confection of almonds, meringue, and hazelnut paste. The sign outside made our day on last visit.

Jaca *p62*

€€€ El Portón, Pl Marqués de la Cadena 1, T974 355 854. This elegant rustic restaurant sits in Jaca's most attractive square. Quality ingredients are prepared and served with style, and the waiting staff are polite and helpful. They're at their best here with traditional Aragonese plates given modern flair.

€€€ La Cocina Aragonesa, Paseo de la Constitución 3, T974 361 050, www.conde aznar.com. Jaca's best, a friendly spot serving up classy Aragonese cuisine with a distinctly French touch. Part of the **Hotel Conde Aznar**. There's a *menú del día*, but it's not really representative of the quality on offer. There's a lovely covered and heated terrace.

€€€ Mesón Cobarcho, C Ramiro I 2, T974 363 643. There are several spots in town that specialize in grilled and roast meats, but this spacious and inviting restaurant might just be the best. Truly excellent ox *entrecots* come sizzling, juicy, tasty and sizeable, and salads or grilled vegetable platters balance out the meal. Recommended.

€€ Gastón, Av Primer Viernes de Mayo 14, T974 361 719. This upstairs establishment offers a €18 set menu that features good home-style cooking. On the main menu, the *lenguado* (sole) in cava is excellent.

€€ La Fragua, C Gil Berges 4, T974 360 618. A good hearty *asador*, popular with locals at weekends for its excellent *chuletón de buey* (ox steaks) and other hearty meat dishes. All portions are enormous.

€€ Mesón Serrablo, C Obispo 3, T974 362 418. An attractive and delicious restaurant in an antique-style stone building. 2 levels, and a good weekend *menú* for €18. The value-for-money is high here.

€ Casa Fau, Plaza de la Catedral 3, T974 361 594. This is a great place by the cathedral, with a homely wooden atmosphere perfect after a day on the slopes; or a sunny terrace for warmer weather. The bar proudly displays an array of tasty *pinchos*, including a tasty terrine from across the border, and the service comes with a smile. Recommended.

€ El Rincón de la Catedral, Plaza de la Catedral 4, T974 355 920. The place to sit and admire the soft Romanesque lines of the cathedral. Large range of French-style meals, salads, and gourmet *montaditos* costing around €2.

€ El Tizón, Av Primer Viernes de Mayo 14, T974 362 780. Gregarious and hospitable, this restaurant is a family favourite after a day on the slopes or walking in the hills. There's something for everyone in the ample menu, from pizzas (€5-9) to a huge range of tasty salads, steaks and game. There's also a decent wine list and helpful service.

€ La Tasca de Ana, C Ramiro I 3, T974 364 726. An indispensable stop on the Jaca food trail with a very large variety of quality hot and cold tapas, great salads, good wine and more. The only problem is that it's so good, it can be tough to get in the door.

Bars and clubs

Huesca *p59, map p60*
The main bar zone is around C Sancho Ramírez and C Padre Huesca, where you can pick and choose the most inviting option.

Alt Berlin, Plaza de López Allue 8, T974 230 429. This bar is one of Huesca's best. It offers good beer on an attractive plaza that comes to life during San Lorenzo. Some German food is available in the evening.

Jaca *p62*
Café, Plaza de Lacadena s/n. Unremarkable-looking spot, this is actually one of Jaca's best bars, with a great collection of vinyl and a good vibe to boot.

Viviana , Plaza de Lacadena s/n. With a mixed selection of Asian prints on the walls, a pool table, and drum 'n bass sounds, this is one of Jaca's most frequented bars. Stick to beer here though: the mixed drinks aren't great.

❀ Festivals

Huesca *p59, map p60*

9 Aug San Lorenzo, a week-long festival, with processions of giants, bullfights, cow-dodging in the ring and partying.

⛰ What to do

Jaca *p62*
Jaca has several tour operators who offer activities throughout the Aragonese Pyrenees.

Alcorce Pirineos Aventura, Av Regimiento Galicia 1, T974 356 437, www.alcorcea ventura.com. Specialize in mountains, particularly skiing, trekking, climbing and caving.

Aragón Aventura, C Pablo Iglesias 12, T974 362 996, www.aragonaventura.es. Experts in canyoning and skiing, but also offer other activities.

Deportes Goyo, Av Juan XXIII 17, T974 360 413, www.deportesgoyo.com. Hire mountain bikes.

Ur Pirineos, Av Premier Viernes de Mayo 14, T974 356 788, www.urpirineos.es. Primarily a summer operator, running, climbing, canyoning, canoeing trips and more.

⊖ Transport

Huesca *p59, map p60*
Air The Huesca-Pirineos airport, 10 km from town, works with **Pyrenair** (www.pyrenair.es), which offers winter budget flights operated by other airlines from **Madrid** among other cities. Their website has offers that include transport to the ski fields and lift passes.

Bus Buses run from Huesca to **Zaragoza** more than hourly (55 mins, €7). Other destinations include **Barcelona** (4 a day), **Pamplona** (5 a day) and **Lleida** (6 a day). Several buses go to **Jaca** (€7.50, 1 hr), **Barbastro** and **Monzón**. 1-2 buses daily to **Loarre**, leaving at 0825 (Mon-Sat) and 1330 (Mon-Fri).

Train 6-8 trains daily to **Zaragoza** (40-60 mins, from €7-16), 3 slow trains to **Jaca** (2 hrs, €8.60) and a fast train to **Madrid** (2 hrs 20 mins, €64.20).

Jaca *p62*
Bus Jaca's bus station is conveniently located on Plaza Biscos in the centre of town. 5-10 daily buses run between Jaca and **Huesca** (1 hr, €7.30). These connect in Huesca with buses to **Zaragoza**. There are 2 buses daily to **Pamplona** (1 hr 40 mins, €8.60).

Alosa run buses from Jaca via **Sabiñánigo** up the Valle de Tena as far as **Sallent de Gállego** and **Formigal**, detouring to **Panticosa** on the way.

There are 5 daily buses from Jaca up the **Canfranc Valley**.

For **France**, get a bus or train to Canfranc, and change there for a French rail bus, which runs 3-5 times daily to Oloron-Sainte-Mairie, from where you can connect by train to Pau and beyond.

For the **Echó** and **Ansó** Valley, there is 1 daily bus from Jaca, leaving Mon-Sat at 1850. The return leaves Ansó at 0630.

Train The trains are neither as handy nor as useful as the buses and the station is to the east of town. A shuttle bus links to it from outside the bus station. 2 daily trains head down to **Huesca** and on to **Zaragoza**. There are also trains to Canfranc.

Pyrenean valleys of Aragón

The eastern section of the Aragonese Pyrenees contains some of Spain's most spectacular scenery: towering mountainscapes that loom large over delightful grey stone villages. This is walking and climbing country par excellence, with favourites being the Ordesa National Park, demesne of the mighty lammergeyer, and Maladeta, where the range's highest peaks cluster. There is activity for any ability, from leisurely flower-filled valley strolls to high-altitude traverses and assisted climbs. A network of hospitable mountain *refugios* (see box, page 63) and hearty alpine cuisine adds to the appeal. Most of the eastern region is deserted in winter, with most services closed until March.

Torla and around → *For listings, see pages 73-77.*

Although heavily visited in summer, there's still something magical about Torla, the base most people use to reach the Parque Nacional Ordesa. Torla's sober square grey belltower stands proud in front of the soaring background massif of **Mondarruego** (2848 m); this imposing wall of rock looks like a citadel built by titans. The village is well equipped with places to stay, eat and stock up on supplies and gear for trekking. The beautiful church houses a small ethnographic museum with a small display of traditional working and domestic life – apart from that it's the great outdoors that beckons. There are several banks in town. Torla's summer-only **tourist office** ① *1000-1400, 1700-2000*, is on the Plaza Mayor.

Further down the valley, **Broto** and **Sarvisé** are pleasant villages with a good range of facilities, handy for Torla and the national park shuttle bus if you've got transport. Broto's star attraction is its amazingly muscular and bulky church; there's plenty of accommodation here. Even better is the tiny village of **Oto**, a 10-minute walk from Broto, and featuring some excellent medieval buildings; there's also a good campsite here and a couple of *casas rurales*.

The area isn't one for winter sports; indeed, nearly everything is closed between November and March. You'll find more action in the Tena Valley to the west, around Biescas and Sallent de Gállego, or to the east around Benasque.

Aínsa → *For listings, see pages 73-77.*

Characterized by its hilltop location and spectacular mountainous backdrop, Aínsa (L'Aínsa) is a remarkably attractive town as well as being an important service centre and transport hub for some of the high Pyrenean villages. Unfortunately, this has its downside in the heart of summer, when the medieval quarter can feel a little like a theme park with hundreds of day trippers. Come the evening, though, you'll have a freer run, and the sleeping and eating options are good; even the plentiful gift shops are fairly tasteful.

The 12th- to 13th-century **old town** stands proud high above the gravelly junction of the Cinca and Ara rivers. From the entrance portal, two narrow streets lead past beautifully preserved houses to the massive cobbled main square, lined with arcades. Every odd year on 14 September there's a play performed here, with most of the town participating – it tells of the defeat of the Moors in AD 724. Legend has it that García Jiménez, attacking the Muslim town with 300 men, was facing defeat. He called on God, and a glowing red cross appeared on a holm oak tree; heartened by this, the Christians won. The top left corner of the Aragonese coat of arms actually refers to this event.

At the other end of the square is what's left of the **castle** ① *mid-Mar to Dec Wed-Sun, Jul-Aug daily, €4,* basically just the still-impressive walls and a reconstructed tower, home to an exhibition of Pyrenean ecology, with a fiendishly complex opening schedule. Back in the narrow streets, there's a better **museum** ① *Plaza San Salvador 5, T974 510 075, summer 1000-1400, 1600-2100, €2.50,* devoted to traditional Pyrenean art. The Romanesque church is Aínsa's other highlight. There's a strangely shaped cobbled cloister, frequently hung with the work of local artists. The semi-crypt behind the altar has a small view out of the window, while the tower offers excellent vistas. Arrive stocked with €1 coins to switch on the lights; this also activates a jukebox-style Gregorian chant. The **tourist office** ① *Mon-Sat 1000-1400, 1600-1930 (1700-2000 summer, plus Sun 1000-1400),* is on the main crossroads below the old town; guided tours of the town run in summer.

There are several marked walking routes radiating out from Aínsa, which are marked on maps supplied by the tourist office but also illustrated on boards near the castle at the top of town (where the tourist parking area is). They range from jaunts of a couple of hours to serious up-hill down-dale treks to other towns and villages in the area.

Parque Nacional Ordesa y Monte Perdido → *For listings, see pages 73-77.*

① *Access to the park is usually confined to the shuttle bus from Torla in summer, see Transport, page 77. There's also a very pleasant 2-hr walk starting from the bridge on the main road in town. Most trails start from La Pradera car park where the bus stops. There's a bar/restaurant here, as well as meteorological information (an important consideration for longer walks even in summer).*

From Torla you can spot the beginning of the Ordesa Valley, taking a sharp right in front of the bulk of Mondarruego. It's the most popular summer destination in the Aragonese Pyrenees, and understandably so, with its dramatic sheer limestone walls, pretty waterfalls, and good selection of walking trails. The valley was formed by a glacier, which chopped through the limestone like feta cheese, albeit over many thousands of years. Beyond the end of the valley looms **Monte Perdido** (Lost Mountain, 3355 m); it's not recorded who managed to lose it, but it must have been a misty day.

The valley and national park is an important haven for flora and fauna – the latter have retreated further into the hills as the stream of visitors became a torrent. You're likely to spot griffon vultures, choughs and wild irises even from the most-used trails, and you may see isard (Pyrenean chamois) and the massive lammergeyer (bearded vulture).

Hiking in the park

The most popular route is an easy four-hour return up and down the valley, passing the pretty waterfalls of **El Estrecho** and **Gradas de Soaso** before arriving at the aptly named **Cola de Caballo** (Horse's Tail). It climbs gently most of the way before levelling and widening out above the Gradas. Hit the ground running when you get off the bus to avoid the crowds on this popular trail.

A much better option, if more strenuous, is to head across the bridge from the car park, following signs for the **Senda de los Cazadores**. As long as the weather is clear you needn't be fazed by the danger sign – the trail has been much improved, although it's not recommended if you don't have a head for heights. After crossing the bridge, you're led straight into a steep ascent 650 m up the valley walls to the small shelter of **Calcilarruego**, where there's a viewing platform. The worst is now over; it's flat and gentle downhill from here on in. The path spectacularly follows the *faja* (limestone shelf) along the southern edge of the valley, with great views north to the **Brecha de Roldán**, a square-shaped pass on the French border. If you think it looks man-made, you may well be right – Charlemagne's knight Roland is said to have cleared the breach with one blow of his sword. The path continues through beautiful beech and pine forest until you slowly descend to the Cola de Caballo waterfall (three to 3½ hours after starting). From here it's a two-hour stroll back down the valley floor. There are several *refugios* in the area, some unmanned.

For attempts on **Monte Perdido** (hard on the thighs but no technical experience required in summer), continue up another hour or two to the **Refugio de Góriz** (see Where to stay, page 73), usually quite full. From here, you can continue east towards the Pineta Valley and Bielsa, or northwest towards France.

Bielsa and around → *For listings, see pages 73-77.*

One of the most peaceful centres in the Aragonese Pyrenees, Bielsa sees most action during the day at weekends, when French Pyreneans nip over the border to secure stashes of cheap whisky and cigarettes. Although the setting isn't as dramatic as Benasque or Torla, it's beautiful here, and the rather unspoiled village atmosphere makes this one of the nicest places to hang out in the area, which is useful as you may end up staying longer than you meant to – it's easy to miss the only bus out at 0645.

Bielsa was mostly destroyed in the Civil War; a posse of determined Republicans held the town against the Nationalist advance before finally retreating up the valley and across the border. The artillery in the car park, however, is used for a less destructive purpose, to trigger avalanches in controlled conditions. The **Plaza Mayor** houses the helpful **national park office** and a small ethnographic exhibition; nearby is the simple but attractive 15th-century church.

Valle de Pineta

Beyond Bielsa the main road makes its way into France via a long tunnel. Above the town, a side road winds over a hill and into the Valle de Pineta, a 15-km stretch of road that admits defeat when confronted with the imposing bulk of Monte Perdido. The car park at the road's end is the start or finish for a number of trails, one heading across the Ordesa National Park towards Torla. There's also a parador here, and the Ronatiza *refugio*, as well as a small chapel with a local Virgin. An information kiosk will give you a map of the trails.

Some 2.5 km short of the car park, you'll see a sign to **Collado de Añisclo**, a tiring but spectacular ascent of the mountain across the valley. Allow eight to nine hours for a return trip in summer – at other times you'll need snow gear to reach the top.

Cañón de Añisclo

South and west of Bielsa, a small, slow and spectacular route links the village of **Escalona** with **Sarvisé** near Torla (there's a quicker way through Aínsa). The road snakes along a pretty gorge before arriving at a car park, about 12 km from the main Bielsa–Aínsa road. This is the head of the Cañón de Añisclo, a small-scale but beautiful gorge with a popular path running down it. Some sections wind easily through oak and beech forest, but other sections are slightly precipitous on one side, although the path isn't steep. Most day trippers walk as far as **La Ripareta**, a level grassy plain about three hours from the car park (the return is slightly quicker), but you can continue to the Fuen Blanca waterfall, about 5½ hour's walk from the car park. From Fuen Blanca it's possible to continue to the Góriz *refugio* and thence to the Ordesa valley and Torla, or to continue to the Pineta valley over the Collado de Añisclo. It's difficult to get to the canyon without your own transport or a tour from Bielsa or Torla, but it's possible to walk in on the GR15 path, staying at one of the two good *refugios* in tiny **Nerín**, a hamlet with a view. If you're in a car, the return road to Bielsa takes you back a different way, over the top of the hills, while the other option is to continue on to Sarvisé.

Benasque and around → *For listings, see pages 73-77.*

One of the major towns of the Aragonese Pyrenees, Benasque is a relaxed resort dedicated to outdoor pursuits. Although some of the modern development is reasonably tasteful, it has buried the old centre, which was outgrown by the massive surge in Pyrenean tourism in the years since Spain's return to democracy. It's a good base – there's plenty of accommodation (though few beds come cheap) several restaurants and bars, and resources for guides, tours, information and equipment.

The intelligent and helpful **tourist office** ① *C Sebastián 5, T974 551 289, www.turismobenasque.com, Sat-Wed 1000-1400, 1700-2100, Thu-Fri 1700-2100*, in Benasque is just off the main road. It's more than adequate for most needs, but for more detailed information about the park there's a **visitor centre** ① *daily in summer from 1000-1400, 1600-2100 and weekends only the rest of the year*, about 1 km from Benasque off the road to Anciles, and also a small exhibition.

The main attraction in the area is the **Parque Nacional Posets Maladeta**, named after the two highest summits in the Pyrenees, which it encompasses. It's a terrain of valleys gouged by glaciers that extends well into Catalunya. Wild and high, the park includes seven summits over 3000 m. The Maladeta's highest peak, **Aneto**, is the Pyrenees' highest at 3404 m – it's climbable from the **Refugio de la Renclusa** (T974 552 106, 45 minutes beyond the bus stop at La Besurta, see Transport, page 77), but come fully equipped, even in summer: not for nothing is the chain known as the 'Cursed Mountains'. On the other side of the main road, to the east, the dark summit of **Posets** is a similarly difficult climb. There are several marked trails and *refugios* around it – one of the most used is the **Refugio Angel Oíns in Eriste** (T974 344 044). It's worth checking out some of the area's glaciers, the southernmost in Europe, sadly rapidly diminishing; some estimates give them less than 30 years of life. There are summer restrictions on vehicles entering the park; you're better off using the bus services provided from Benasque.

There's much scope for shorter walks in the area, around the **Hospital**, **La Besurta** and the **Vallibierna Valley** (also accessible by bus), which is traversed by the GR11 long-distance path. There are several mountain biking routes recommended by the Benasque tourist office.

Some 6 km above Benasque stands the village of **Cerler**, which purports to be the highest place in Aragón to be inhabited year round. It's dominated by a ski resort of average quality but with plenty of runs. There's no shortage of sleeping and eating options, although it lacks the atmosphere of Benasque.

Further up the valley, **Baños de Benasque** is another example of the enduring popularity of spa towns in Spain; there's a hotel here with various regimes targeted at any number of ailments – the spectacularly beautiful location contributes greatly to the healing and relaxation potential.

Pyrenean valleys of Aragón listings

For hotel and restaurant price codes and other relevant information, see pages 10-13.

⊙ Where to stay

Torla and around *p69*
€€€ Hotel Villa Russell, C Ruata s/n, T974 486 770, www.hotelvillarussell.com. This modern hotel is right in the centre of Torla but has stayed true to the attractive stone look of the place. Inside, it's a gem too, with luxurious rustic decoration. The rooms are well equipped, with DVD player, internet access, fridge and microwave; and they are handsome too – some have a terrace but all are of high comfort.

€€ Casa Frauca, Ctra de Ordesa s/n, Sarvisé, T974 486 182, www.casafrauca.com. Closed Jan/Feb. A faded but charming old inn, with characterful and unusual bedrooms with bathroom. Decent restaurant. Great views.

€€ Edelweiss, Ctra Ordesa s/n, T974 486 168, www.edelweisshotelordesa.es. The best of the cluster of main road hotels, with good, simple en suite rooms, many with pretty wooden balconies and views.

€ Villa de Torla, Plaza Nueva 1, T974 486 156, www.hotelvilladetorla.com. Another excellent place to stay in Torla; although the rooms are nothing to write home about, there's a terrace with great views, a swimming pool, good eating and it's in the heart of town.

€ Casa Lali, C Fatas s/n, T974 486 168. A welcoming and well-priced *casa rural* in the heart of Torla. The rooms can be a bit noisy with pub-bound revellers passing under the windows, but it's still a very good option, cosy and homely.

€ Refugio Lucien Briet, C Ruata s/n, T974 486 221, www.refugiolucienbriet.com. The roomier of the 2 *refugios* in town, with a couple of doubles too. Good restaurant, and board rates offered.

Camping and out-of-town refugios
Camping Río Ara, T974 486 248, www.campingrioara.com. A peaceful campsite in the river valley below Torla. Access by car is 1.5 km beyond town, but there's a quicker footpath.

Refugio de Góriz, T974 341 201, www.goriz.es. A crucial *refugio* (see page 63) despite frequent shortages of beds. Book ahead if you don't want to camp out. Meals provided.

Refugio Valle de Bujaruelo, T974 486 412, www.refugiodebujaruelo.com. Open Apr–Oct. A well-equipped and beautiful site further up the valley. Camping and restaurant as well as good accommodation..

Aínsa *p69*

Many of Aínsa's hotels are unattractive options in the new town and budget accommodation is in short supply in the summer months.

€€€ Monasterio de Boltaña, www.monasteriodeboltana.es. A couple of miles down the road from Aínsa near the town of Boltaña, this luxurious spa hotel is partly set in a historic monastery, which the modern additions have tried to remain faithful to. It makes a fine base for exploring the Pyrenees, with a good restaurant, and comfortable, light rooms, many of which offer spectacular views. The decor is artistic in an offbeat way, with period features alongside tribal art and modern designer flourishes. Off-season there are some appealingly discounted prices (**€€**) on their website.

€€€-€€ Hotel Posada Real, C de las Escaleretas s/n, T974 500 977, www.posada real.com. An establishment run out of the Bodegón de Mallacán restaurant, this stately place has an odd mixture of the old and new, with 4-poster beds side by side with modern tiling and art. Still, it's a very comfortable place to stay just off the plaza.

€€ Casa El Hospital, C Santa Cruz 3, T974 500 750, www.casadelhospital.com. A good *casa rural* in a stone house next to the church, with charming doubles at a good price.

€ Albergue Mora de Nuei, Portal de Abajo 2, T974 510 614, www.alberguemorade nuei.com. Just above the lower entrance to the old town, this attractively refurbished stone townhouse is a rather charming walkers' hostel with comfortable bunks and a welcoming atmosphere. There are also doubles available (**€€**).

Bielsa and around *p71*

€€ Parador de Bielsa, Valle de Pineta, T974 501 011, www.parador.es. At the end of the Valle de Pineta road, under looming Monte Perdido, this makes an excellent base for walks in the area. Modern but sensitive construction, recently renovated. It's basically just you and the Pyrenees out here; it feels like a last outpost.

€€ Valle de Pineta, C Los Ciervos s/n, T974 501 010, www.hotelvalledepineta.com. Reasonably priced rooms, some overlooking the river valley. There's also a swimming pool and a pleasant restaurant.

€ Vidaller, C Calvario 4, T974 501 004, www.vidaller.com. One of the best places to stay in Bielsa, with pleasant top-value rooms with and without bathroom above a small and friendly shop. Simple but comfortable for this price, which includes a simple breakfast.

Refugios

€ Añisclo Albergue, Nerín, T974 489 008, www.nerinrural.com. A good place to stop if you're heading for the Cañón de Añisclo on foot. A top situation, with great valley views, dorm beds (€15 per person), and simple but happy meals.

Benasque and around *p72*

€€€ Gran Hotel Benasque, Ctra Anciles s/n, T974 551 011, www.hotelesvalero.com. This large, comfortable hotel is built in modern rustic style and is conveniently close to the centre of town. There's an excellent swimming pool and spa facilities (which cost extra). Rooms are spacious and light, and there's a relaxing mountain retreat feel to the whole place.

€€ Hospital de Benasque Hospedería, Llanos de Hospital, T974 552 012, www.llanosdelhospital.com. With a variety of rooms, this remote inn offers every comfort. There's a very welcoming bar and restaurant, but come prepared to stay a while in winter – every now and then it gets cut off by snow.

€€ **Hostal Solana**, Plaza Mayor 5, T974 551
019, www.hotelsolanabenas.com. Good
clean rooms above an unmemorable but
bustling bar/restaurant. There are 2 separate
sections, a *hostal* and a hotel – both are
decent value and recently refurbished, but
make sure they charge according to the
rate sheet.

€€ **Hotel Avenida**, Av Los Tilos 14, T974
551 126, www.h-avenida.com. A friendly
family-run concern in the heart of Benasque,
with spotless rooms overlooking the main
street and a pleasant terrace restaurant.

€€ **Hotel Ciria**, Av Los Tilos s/n, T974 551
612, www.hotelciria.com. Very nice balconied
rooms on the main street with cheerful
fittings and many facilities. There are also
suites with hydromassage units to soothe
those muscles ailing from hiking or skiing.

€€ **Hotel San Marsial**, Av Francia 77,
T974 551 616, www.hotelsanmarsial.com.
One of the classier options in Benasque,
although often booked out by package
tourists. They organize several activities.
Elegant hunting lodge-style decor.
There's a range of apartment-style
rooms available also.

€ **Casa Mariano**, C Unica s/n, Eresué,
T974 553 034. A top spot for people who
want a base in the great outdoors in a village
10 km southeast of Benasque. This *casa rural*
is very homely, with 2 large bedrooms and
excellent home-cooked meals. One of the
owners is a mountain guide and will happily
help organize activities and give advice.

Camping and refugios

Camping Aneto, Ctra Francia, Km 100,
T974 551 141, www.campinganeto.com.
Several facilities as well as some
simple bungalows.

Refugio La Renclusa, T974 344 646.
High above Hospital de Benasque, this is
the best base for climbing Aneto.

Torla and around *p69*

€€ **El Rebeco**, Plaza Mayor s/n, T974 486
068. Not the friendliest of places, but there's
a good restaurant upstairs, as well as 2
terraces, 1 shady, 1 sunny. It's named after
the isard/Pyrenean chamois, which thank-
fully doesn't feature on the menu, although
it is a traditional local dish.

€€ **L'Atalaya**, C Ruata 1, T974 486 022.
Funky bar and restaurant doing a range of
quality dishes in a colourful atmosphere.
Cheap *menú del día*, and a good evening
menú for €20. The bar does tapas and
platos combinados.

€ **A'Borda Samper**, C Travecinal s/n, T974
486 231. One of the nicest places to eat in
Torla – a great range of simple tapas in a
welcoming family atmosphere, and a good
upstairs restaurant.

€ **El Taillón**, C Ruata s/n, T974 486 304.
A no-nonsense bar featuring a lawn terrace
with superb views of Mondarruego. The
good-value restaurant upstairs does cheap
and filling *menús*.

Aínsa *p69*

€€€ **Bodegas del Sobrarbe**, Plaza Mayor 2,
T974 500 237, www.bodegasdelsobrarbe.com.
A high-class restaurant with traditional
Pyrenean cuisine, based around game.
Last count featured 11 different land-based
creatures on the menu, but vegetarians
can be consoled by the excellent wild
mushrooms. There's a *menú* for €22.50,
but it doesn't feature the best on show.

€€€ **Callizo**, Plaza Mayor, T974 500 385.
Innovative, playful cuisine can be enjoyed
here at comparatively moderate prices.
Their tasting menu is full of unusual
touches; it doesn't all work, but enough
does that you'll leave satisfied.

€€ **El Portal**, C Portal Bajo 5, T974 500 138.
Just about the first building you pass
climbing up into the old town, this restaurant

has some great views over the rivers below and a *menú* for €15.

Bielsa and around *p71*

€€ La Terrazeta, C Baja s/n, T974 501 158. Well set with a dining room overlooking the valley, this is one of Bielsa's better options in summer or winter. There's a cheap *menú* (excluding drinks), but à la carte isn't too pricey either.

€ El Chinchecle, www.elchinchecle.com. An excellent place in a small courtyard serving home-made liqueurs to the sound of traditional music. Also serves some very nice *cecina de ciervo* (cured venison), and put on 1 or 2 nightly dishes for some excellent simple eating.

Benasque and around *p72*

€€ El Pesebre, C Mayor 45, T974 551 507. A dark stony traditional restaurant with a small terrace, serving traditional Aragonese food, with plenty of lamb and game.

€€ La Sidrería, C Los Huertos s/n, T974 551 292, www.lasidreriabenasque.com. An excellent restaurant run by welcoming Asturians. Cider is the obvious choice but there are several good wines to accompany the delicious food. If there's some home-made cheesecake around, grab a slice – it's a short-priced favourite for the best dessert in Aragón.

€€ Restaurant La Parrilla, C Francia s/n, T974 551 134. A spacious and smartish restaurant dealing in well-prepared steaks – eat 'em rare if you want to do as the Aragonese do. There's a *menú del día* for €15.

€ Hostal Pirineos, Ctra Benasque s/n, T974 551 307. A couple of kilometres back down the valley on the main road, this terrace is a nice place to sit and enjoy simple but well-done food and wine. There are good rooms available too.

▲ What to do

Torla and around *p69*

See also Jaca, page 68, for activities in the Aragonese Pyrenees.

Casa Blas, Sarvisé, T974 486 041, www.caballoscasablas.com. All manner of equine activities.

Center Aventura, Av Ordesa s/n, T974 486 337. Has a good supply of trekking equipment and maps.

Compañía Guías de Torla, C Ruata s/n, T974 486 422, www.guiasdetorla.com. The other major operator in Torla for excursions in the area.

Aínsa *p69*

Aguas Blancas, Av Sobrarbe 11, T974 510 008, www.aguasblancas.com. Run white-water rafting and canoeing expeditions.

Benasque and around *p72*

Barrabés, C Francia s/n, T974 551 056, www.barrabes.com. Run a series of alpine, rock climbing, rafting and canyoning activities for all levels. Their massive shop is full of equipment and maps.

Centro Ecuestre Casa Paulo, C La Fuente 14, Cerler, T974 551 092. Horse-riding trips into the valleys.

Compañía de Guías de Benasque, Av de Luchón 19, T974 551 336, www.guias benasque.com. Organizes all sorts of mountainous activities in the area.

Escuela Español de Esquí, Centro Cerler, Cerler, T974 551 553, www.escuela esquicerler.com. Run skiing and snowboarding courses.

Escuela Montaña de Benasque, Campalet s/n, T974 552 019, www.prames.com. Serious mountaineering, canyoning and skiing courses throughout the year; lasting from 3-5 days, book well in advance. It's part of the *Escuela Española de Alta Montaña*, which has a reputation for excellence.

Torla and around *p69*

Bus Torla is accessed by bus from **Aínsa** daily at 1415 (1215 on Sat), 1 hr, €5. There's an extra service at 1815 on Tue and Thu. Return buses leave Torla Mon, Wed, Fri, Sun at 1155, Tue and Thu at 0650, Sat at 1020. See www.alosa.es. 1-2 buses a day arrive from **Sabiñánigo**.

From Jul-Oct (and Easter) a shuttle bus runs from the parking lot at Torla to **La Pradera**, in the valley of Ordesa. Leaving every 15-20 mins 0600-1900, the last return bus leaves the park at 2200. A return trip costs €4.50; outgoing buses stop at the park's visitor centre El Parador. This bus is often the only way to reach the park by road, as private vehicle access tends to be cut off.

Aínsa *p69*

Bus A bus line runs between Barbastro and Aínsa, leaving **Barbastro** Mon-Fri 1715, Sat 1115, Sun 1940, and leaving Aínsa Mon-Fri 0745, Sat 1215, Sun 1815 (1 hr). A daily bus runs to **Sabiñánigo** via **Torla** and **Biescas**.

Bielsa and around *p71*

Bus Services run from Bielsa to **Aínsa** at 0645 Mon, Wed, Fri (Mon-Sat in Jul and Aug), with a connection to **Barbastro**. The bus into town leaves **Aínsa** at 1830 (Sat 1225, Sun 2045).

Benasque and around *p72*

Bicycle hire El Baúl, C Francia s/n, hire bikes from €15 a day, as do **Ciclos A Sánchez**, Av del Luchón.

Bus

There are buses departing Benasque for **Barbastro** at 0630 and 1500 (2 hrs), which connect directly with buses to **Huesca**, **Lleida** and **Zaragoza** (on Sun only the afternoon bus runs). For **Parque Nacional Maladeta**, a bus runs from Benasque to the trailhead of **La Besurta**, leaving at 0430, 0900 and 1300, returning at 1400, 1830 and 2130. The bus also runs to **Vallibierna** and shuttles between La Besurta and the Hospital de Benasque.

Andorra

Andorra gets a bad press, and it's sometimes hard to find reasons to defend it, particularly during the high season and at weekends, when a stream of traffic pours in to the principality to stack up on cheap goods at the ranks of hideous hypermarkets. In the unrelenting drive to plonk a resort on every mountainside, few regions have been left untouched. To find an unspoiled corner takes serious effort; you'll have to tramp your way to tranquillity whenever you come, but it's easiest during the early summer and autumn.

Background

The Principality of Andorra has been squabbled over by the Counts of Foix and the Archbishops of Seu d'Urgell for centuries; a treaty signed in 1278 allowed the Andorrans some autonomy but the community was obliged to pay tribute to the rulers on either side of their borders in alternate years. The remoteness of the region meant that in practice it was difficult for anyone to intervene in local affairs, and the Andorrans zealously protected their rights and privileges, even managing to maintain neutrality during the Civil War and the Second World War. Smuggling was big business during the wars, and was the basis for the legitimate tax-free business which grew up in the 1940s and 1950s. Money also began to roll in from the increasingly popular sport of downhill skiing, opening up new transport connections and allowing an alarming rate of development. Andorra was getting richer and richer and no longer needed the help or patronage of its neighbours. Finally, in 1993, the locals voted overwhelmingly for independence and a democratic constitution to replace their ancient feudal obligations.

Andorra la Vella and around → *For listings, see pages 80-81. Phone code: outside Andorra 00 376. Population: 22,200. Altitude: 1029 m.*

The capital of Andorra, Andorra La Vella, enjoys a spectacular setting but is an ugly modern city lined with hideous, shoddy architecture and neon-lit shopping malls. The city's raison d'être is shopping, and there's virtually nothing else to do. Head for the hills and escape to some of the surrounding hiking trails where you can put all crowds and neon behind you.

The old quarter (Barri Antic) is worth a visit for the **Casa de la Vall** ① *Carrer de la Vall, T829129, Mon-Sat 1000-1400 and 1500-1800, Sun 1000-1400 (closed Sun between Nov and May), admission by guided tour only, reserve in advance, free,* which was the seat of the Counsell de la Tera, the representatives of Andorra's seven valleys who ruled the country until 1993, and is now the seat of the national parliament.

Slope facts

Check out the comprehensive website www.skiandorra.ad for weather reports, links, and information on all the resorts.

There are two enormous ski resorts in Andorra, which each encompass several villages: **Grandvalira**, www.grandvalira.com) is the largest, with 205 km of pistes (118 in total). It includes villages and towns such as Soldeu and Pas de la Casa. **Vallnord** has more than 70 pistes, and includes the villages of Arcalís, Arinsal and Pal.

Almost all the Barcelona travel agencies offer skiing packages, which include transport, lift passes and accommodation. The website www.skiandorra.ad offers great deals and packages too.

Heading northeast of Andorra la Vella, there's some gentle walking around the **Estany d'Engolasters**, overlooked by the Romanesque Església de Sant Miquel with a statuesque belltower. It's a suitably picture-book setting for a handful of old legends including one which states that all the stars of the sky will be so entranced by the beauty of the lake that they will fall to the bottom and stay there until the end of time.

Northeast to Pas de la Casa → *For listings, see pages 80-81.*

The road wiggles along to the French border at **Pas de la Casa**, a hideous high-rise conglomeration of duty-free shops with another big ski-resort, but passes some prettier stopping points along the way. **Canillo** has not managed to survive unscarred, but the old quarter with its balconied houses is quietly attractive with its fine old Romanesque church and characteristic lofty Andorran belltower. On the outskirts of the town is one of the best Romanesque churches in Andorra, Sant Joan de Caselles, with a glittering Gothic retablo and a richly decorated wooden ceiling. **Soldeu**, a popular ski town, is surprisingly small and unassuming, and the villages have some fantastic walking in the surrounding forests during the summer.

Northwest to Ordino → *For listings, see pages 80-81.*

Northwest of Andorra La Vella, the other main route through the principality heads up the Ordino valley. **Ordino** is another good base for hiking, with some handsome old stone buildings still holding their own among the ring of modern apartments. It's also got a pair of small museums on the Carrer Major: one is devoted to a history of Andorra's postal service and the other is the **Areny-Plandolit House Museum** ① *T836908, visits on request*, which carefully recreates the life of a 19th-century Andorran merchant's family with exhibits and original furnishings.

There's also a **Nature Interpretation Centre** ① *on the outskirts of Ordino in La Cortinada, call T849849 for opening hours*, which aims to show the effect mankind has on nature (you'll never forget your litter again). It's very child-friendly with plenty of touchy-feely exhibits and clever multi-media exhibits. Almost opposite is a big, modern sports' centre which has everything you can think of from a pool, gym, and squash courts to a Turkish bath and jacuzzi. There's a **tourist information office** ① *Traviessa d'Ordino 7, T878173, www.ordino.ad*.

Villages north of Ordino → *For listings, see pages 80-81.*

The string of villages which unfurls along the river further north includes **La Cortinada** and **Llorts**, which are sleepier but less over-developed. There are two more ski resorts at **Arsinal** and **Pal** to the west of Ordino; Arsinal is bigger and more dynamic, but Pal, huddled around another Romanesque church, is smaller and prettier thanks to local planning laws which have banned ugly ferro-concrete developments. Up near the border with France, **El Serrat** sits near the Tristaina lakes and is surrounded by waterfalls; beyond it is the ski resort of **Arcalís**, which is a big favourite with British snow boarders and probably Andorra's most attractive resort.

Andorra listings

For hotel and restaurant price codes and other relevant information, see pages 10-13.

⬤ Where to stay

Andorra la Vella *p78*
Only serious shopaholics will want to use Andorra la Vella as a base, but if you get caught overnight, there are dozens of places to stay.
€€€ Husa Cèntric, Av Meritxell 87, T877500, www.husa.es. Modern, very well-equipped hotel with spa, restaurant and a roaring fire in the lounge.
€€ Hotel de l'Isard, Av Meritxell 36, T876800, www.hotelisard.com. A charming stone-built hotel with bright modern rooms.
€€ Hotel Plaza, C/Maria Pla 19-21, T879444. With gym, jacuzzi, sauna and beauty centre. One of the plushest.
€ Hotel Cisco de Sans, C/Anna Maria Janer 4, T863188. A simple spot in the historic quarter, family-run and friendly.

Northeast to Pas de la Casa *p79*
€€ Hotel Roc Sant Miquel, Ctra General s/n, Soldeu, T851079, www.hotel-roc.com. Has a good little restaurant and there's a great bar area where the local ski-instructors play in a band. Warm and friendly.
€€ Petit Hotel, C/Sant Jordi 18. Comfortable little hotel in the centre, with friendly staff and tasty breakfasts.

€€ Sport, Ctra General s/n, Soldeu, T870500, www.sporthotels.ad. The best-equipped hotel in Soldeu and the closest to the ski-lifts. Views of the slopes, a pool, sauna and gym.

Northwest to Ordino *p79*
€€ Hotel Santa Barbara, Ordino, T837100, www.hotelstabarbara.com. Has spacious, immaculate rooms, some of which look out over the main square. There's a good restaurant (**€€**) too.

🍴 Restaurants

Andorra la Vella *p78*
€€ Bodega Poblet, Carrer de l'Alzinaret 6, T376 862 722. Chic and sophisticated, serving some of the best and most creative tapas in town.
€€ Borda Estevet, Ctra de la Comella 2, T864026. A good choice, this traditional, Pyrenean restaurant specializes in delicious grilled local meat and fish – famous all over Andorra.
€€-€ Don Denis, C/Isabel Sandy 3, T820692, off the main shopping drag. An old favourite with locals which does a good- value set lunch at €15, but also serves some of the finest and freshest seafood in the area. Highly recommended.

Northeast to Pas de la Casa _p79_

€€ Cort del Popaire, Plaça de Poble, Soldeu, T851211. One of the town's best restaurants, set in a old stone barn offering friendly service and roaring fires in winter.

€ Molí del Peano, Crtra General, Canillo, T851258, offers local specialities like rabbit and home-made desserts. Friendly, cheap and cosy.

Northwest to Ordino _p79_

€€-€ Topic, Ctra General s/n, Ordino, T736102, www.topicordino.com. An enormously popular restaurant and bar, which offers good regional specialities, as well as fondues and a huge range of international beers spread over 4 levels.

Transport

Andorra la Vella _p78_

Bus There are regular buses to Andorra La Vella with **ALSA** (www.alsa.com) from Estació del Nord bus station, Barcelona, and buses with **Julià** (www.autocaresjulia.es) from Estació de Sants, Barcelona. **Novatel** (www.andorrabybus.com) offer a minibus service from Barcelona airport if you can't wait to get on the slopes. Within Andorra, there are local bus services to **Pas de la Casa** with La **Hispano Andorrana** (www.andorrabybus.com).

Train You can also take the train from Barcelona-Sants to **Puigcerdà** and get a bus from there (services are run by **ALSA**).

Roussillon

Framed by the Pyrenees and the sea, Roussillon (the Pyrénées-Orientales) was part of Catalunya until 1669, and the cultural links are still strong. Most of Roussillon's monuments date from its pre-French days, beginning with the cathedral and royal palace in the sunny capital Perpignan; the Renaissance Fortress at Salses; and a bevy of stunning Romanesque churches, including St-Michel-de-Cuxa and Serrabonne. The Conflent, the main valley into the Pyrenees, is guarded by Louis XIV's fortified town of Villefranche-de-Conflent. Near here you can climb the iconic Pic du Canigou, go canyoning or caving, or take one of the most exciting train journeys in Europe to the magnificent sun-drenched plateau of the Cerdagne, home to the region's top ski resorts and the world's biggest solar furnace. Alternatively, visit Tautavel and see relics of some of the earliest Europeans, or charming Céret, once a favourite resort of the Cubists, with a museum to prove it.

Perpignan → *For listings, see pages 94-100.*

Perpignan has a convivial medieval core, ringed by elegant boulevards. It's home to a cosmopolitan population – Catalan and French but also Romany and North Africans – who add an exotic buzz that may tempt you to linger after doing the sights. Winning the French national rugby title in 2009 (for the first time in 50 years) has put a bounce in Perpignan's step, and the new TGV line from Paris to Barcelona (due for completion in 2014) will make 'southern' Catalunya more accessible than ever.

Arriving in Perpignan
Getting there The **bus station** ① *Av du Général-Leclerc, T04 68 35 29 02*, serves much of the department. The **train station** ① *Place Salvador Dalí*, is just west of the historic centre.

Getting around The historic centre of Perpignan is compact and surrounded by car parks. **City bus 1** (www.ctpmperpignan.com) goes to the nearest beach, Canet-Plage. **Route 66** (www.route66000.free.fr) provides transport between Perpignan and Canet's clubs on Saturday nights from 2330-0600.

Tourist information ① *Palais des Congrès, Place Armand Lanoux, T04 68 66 30 30, perpignantourisme.com. Mid-Jun to mid-Sep Mon-Sat 0900-1900, Sun and national holidays 1000-1600, mid-Sep to mid-Jun Mon-Sat 0900-1800, Sun and national holidays 1000-1300.* You can save money in Roussillon by picking up a free **Pass inter-sites** of the Réseau Culturel Terre Catalan, available at all participating sites. Discounts begin after your first visit.

Palais des Rois de Majorque
① *Rue des Archers, T04 68 34 48 29. Oct-May 0900-1700, Jun-Sep 1000-1800. €4, €2 concession/young person (12-18), under 12s free.*
This, the oldest royal palace on French soil, was begun when the Kingdom of Mallorca was established in 1276 by Jaume I the Conqueror, king of Aragón, for his second son Jaume II. The new kingdom included the Balearic Islands, Roussillon and Montpellier, and only lasted until 1349 when Montpellier was sold to the king of France and Roussillon was re-absorbed by Barcelona. Yet the three kings of Mallorca lived here in style, with an exotic menagerie in the moat and gardens ded as a 'Paradise'. From the 16th century onwards, it was used as a military citadel – the sturdy outer walls were built by Philippe II.

Bits of decoration recall its former glory, notably in the Cour d'Honneur and in the central Donjon, which houses two flamboyant chapels. The upper one, for the royal family, has a lovely Romanesque portal, a vaulted ceiling and Kufic inscription that announces in Arabic that "Only God is God", a lasting witness to the syncretism of the ephemeral Mallorcan court. The tower offers commanding views over Perpignan.

Le Castillet: Casa Pairal Musée des Arts et Traditions Populaires
① *Place de Verdun, T04 68 35 42 05. Oct-Apr Wed-Mon 1100-1730, May-Sep Wed-Mon 1000-1830. €4, €2 student, under 18s free.*
This crenellated red-brick symbol of Perpignan, with its gate and two fat towers, was built around 1368 by the king of Aragón to reinforce the palace's defences from the north. Under the French it became a prison, and today stands as a last vestige of the city walls. Inside, displays recount the history of Roussillon from antiquity until modern times; the former ethnographic exhibits are currently being restored to reside in a new museum.

Place de la Loge
This narrow square paved in pink marble was the hub of old Perpignan, all streets converging here in front of the striking 14th-century Gothic **Loge de Mer**. This was the stock exchange and seat of the Consolat de Mer (a branch of Barcelona's famous maritime council); today it's a restaurant. Look up to see the sailing ship weathervane sticking out of the corner.

Next door, the 13th-century **Hôtel de Ville** has its distinctive symbol as well: three bronze arms sticking out of the wall, symbolizing the three estates of the nobility, the bourgeois and the guilds. Duck inside to the patio to see the elaborately sculpted beams and Aristide Maillol's sculpture, *La Méditerranée*. To its right, the 15th-century **Palais de la Députation** is a masterpiece of Catalan Renaissance civil architecture.

Cathédrale St-Jean

ⓘ *Place Gambetta, T04 68 51 33 72. Open 0730-1800.*

Catalan Gothic is notable for width rather than the verticals of northern Gothic, and this is no exception. Planned as a church with three naves in 1324, St-Jean was daringly reworked in 1433 by architect Guillem Sagrera (builder of the cathedral in Palma de Mallorca) into a single nave supported by immense piers. The exterior wears an attractive pattern of brick and river stones; the white marble porch is all that survives of a more elaborate entrance of 1631. The city is especially proud of the rare 19th-century four-octave carillon in the bell tower.

Elegant 16th- to 18th-century Catalan retables fill the interior and there's a medieval baptismal font bearing a Latin inscription: "The wave of the sacred fountain smothers the hiss of the guilty Snake". The sculpted Moor's head under the superb late 15th-century organ case once had an articulated jaw that could be manipulated by the organist to stick out its tongue or vomit sweets for the children. A leather-covered door on the right aisle leads to the **Chapelle du Dévôt Christ**, with its strikingly realistic, painful figure of crucified Christ sculpted in Cologne in 1307. His head droops towards his chest and according to legend, the world will end when it actually touches.

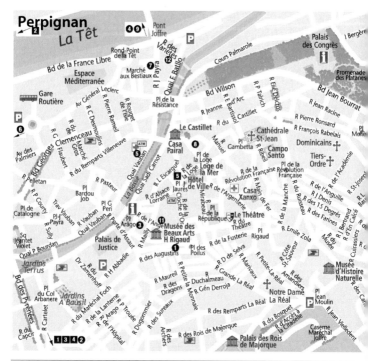

Campo Santo

ⓘ *Behind the Cathedral, Oct-Apr Tue-Sun 1100-1730, closed May-early Oct, free.*

For centuries the Perpignais buried their dead in the white marble Campo Santo (1300-1330), the only surviving enclosed cloister cemetery in France. Amid the arcades, each wealthy and bourgeois family had its own Gothic niche, or *enfeu*, while the poor were buried in the centre.Following the Revolution, the Campo Santo was closed down and, after undergoing several other uses, it's now the perfect venue for summer concerts.

Musée des Beaux Arts Hyacinthe Rigaud

ⓘ *16 rue de l'Ange, T04 68 35 43 40, Tue-Sun 1030-1800, €4, under 26s free.*

Located since 1979 in the Hôtel Lazerme, this recently refurbished museum is named after Louis XIV's Perpignan-born portrait painter, Hyacinthe Rigaud (1659-1743). Among key early works, there's a meticulous *Retable de la Trinité* (1489), showing a fanciful view of Perpignan with the Loge de Mer by the sea, and the 17th-century triptych of *St Vincent Ferrer*. From the 20th century, there are works by Maillol and Picasso, and powerful works on Spanish Civil War exiles by Catalan-American artist Pierre Daura.

The most remarkable works, however, are by Hyacinthe himself. He was much more than your run-of-the-mill Versailles sycophant, evident especially in his self-portraits with their knowing look and five o'clock shadow. Then there's the sumptuous exhibitionist *Portrait of Cardinal Bouillon* (1709), portraying all his pomp and honours: from his cash box (he had been Grand Almoner of France) and cardinal's biretta to the golden hammer showing that he had been in charge of opening the Holy Door at St Peter's for the 1700 Jubilee. His expression is jovial, amid stormy weather and two gesturing children (one representing his younger self, the other his nephew). Because Rigaud showed his squint, however, the cardinal refused to pay for the picture, so Rigaud refused to return the golden hammer.

Where to stay 🛏
Bastide Le Petit Clos **1**
Château La Tour Apollinaire **2**
Hôtel Aragon **4**
Hôtel de la Loge **5**
La Villa Duflot **3**
Park Hotel **6**

Restaurants 🍴
Al Tres **1**
Brasserie L'Aragó **3**
Café de la Loge **4**
Espi **5**
La Galinette **7**
Le Clos de Lys **2**
Le Grain de Folie **6**
Le Rocher des Pirates **9**
Le V.I.P. **8**
Paradis Fouillis **11**
Spaghetteria al Dente **12**

St-Jacques and around

ⓘ *Rue de la Miranda, T04 68 34 74 62, winter 1430-1730; summer 1500-1900.*

Founded around 1245 by Jaume I the Conqueror, St-Jacques stands on **Puig des Lépreux** (Lepers' Hill), on top of the city's Jewish quarter. It's the local hotbed of Catholic tradition, and one of the very few churches in France that celebrates Mass in Latin (OK'd by the Pope in 2007). Inside the 14th-century marble portal, a lavish Catalan interior awaits. Note the 'Cross of Insults' with symbols of all the afflictions suffered by Christ, and a Pregnant Virgin – similar to the one in Cucugnan. The Confraternity of the Holy Blood (*de la Sanch*) was founded here in 1416 by St Vincent Ferrer, the self-styled 'Angel of the Apocalypse', to give comfort to condemned prisoners; on Good Friday they don black and red hoods and robes and go on a procession through Perpignan, bearing the *misteri* (symbols and statues of the Passion), silent except for the sound of tambourines and mournful *goigs*.

The **Quartier St-Jacques** is currently Perpignan's colourful and piquant Romany and North African quarter, and a good place to find a kebab or a tagine. There's been some friction over the years, and it's best to stay away after dark, but during the day it's lively and authentic, full of mums, kids and laundry and the Gypsy Kings (who are really Catalan, too).

Musée d'Histoire Naturelle

ⓘ *12 rue Fontaine-Neuve, T04 68 66 33 68. Mon-Fri 1030-1800, closed holidays, €2, under 26s free.*

Founded in 1770 as a cabinet of curiosities, this museum in the 18th-century Hôtel Cagarriga has handsomely displayed exhibits on the flora, fauna and geology of the Pyrenees and south of France, as well as a room dedicated to Egypt. The mummy was donated in 1847 by Ibrahim Pasha, after he took the cure at Vernet-les-Bains.

Casa Xanxo

ⓘ *8 rue de la Main de Fer, T04 68 62 37 98 Oct-Apr Tue-Sun 1100-1730, May-Sep Tue-Sun 1200-1900, free.*

This elegant residence of 1507 (pronounced 'Sancho') is one of the few left from the period in Perpignan. Built by parvenu cloth merchant Bernat Xanxo (his and his wife's portraits decorate one of the doors), its façade is notable for its fascinating narrow stone frieze representing the *Seven Deadly Sins*, apparently as a warning to passers-by. The house has an enormous dining room on the first floor, where they entertained, and a sumptuous red marble fireplace, but unfortunately little else has survived. On the first floor there's a 3D model of Perpignan in 1686, with its fortifications planned by Vauban for Louis XIV; the rest of the building is used for exhibitions.

Gare de Perpignan

Perpignan's train station is a handsome but unexceptional building, at least in the eye of the average beholder. But by any measure, Salvador Dalí was not average. While sitting at the station one day he had "an example of a cosmogonic ecstasy" and stated "I had a precise vision of the constitution of the Universe." Later, on 19 September 1963, while he was riding past the station in a taxi: "It all became clear in a flash: there, right before me, was the centre of the universe."

Dalí, who lived just south of the border in Cadaqués, was no stranger to Perpignan's *gare*, as he used to send his canvases from there, and claimed that his very best inspirations came while sitting in the waiting room. He painted his taxi vision, the *Mystique de la gare de Perpignan* (Museum Ludwig, Cologne) in 1965, a work now recalled by the station's luminous column topped by a laser beam.

As this is Dalí, the story gets even stranger. After the death of his beloved wife Gala in 1982, he spent a lot of time hallucinating from drugs and dehydration. During these moments he often saw the French mathematician René Thom, the founder of catastrophe theory, who convinced him that Europe would soon vanish, or be 'abducted', beginning in a spot near Salses. This was the subject of Dalí's strange 1983 drawing, the *Topological Abduction of Europe – Homage to René Thom*.

A new Dalí business centre is in the works by the new TGV station.

Centre de Sculpture Romane Maître de Cabestany

① *Parc Guilhem, Cabestany, T04 68 08 15 31, www.maitre-de-cabestany.com. Oct-Apr Tue-Sun 1000-1230 and 1330-1800, May, Jun and Sep Tue-Sun 1000-1230 and 1330-1830; Jul and Aug daily same hours. €3, €1 young person (12-18).*

Cabestany is now a suburb of Perpignan, but in art it's been synonymous with a brilliant 12th-century sculptor known as the Master of Cabestany ever since the tympanum of the church of **Notre Dame des Anges** was rediscovered during restoration work in 1930. Currently displayed in the transept of the church, the tympanum's originality and masterful style created a sensation. Subsequent studies found that the same hand was behind some 121 surviving capitals, tombs and other works around Languedoc, Catalunya and even Tuscany. The centre has casts of over 60 of the sculptor's works and explores just who this master might have been.

Around Perpignan → *For listings, see pages 94-100.*

Forteresse de Salses

① *Salses-le-Château, T04 68 38 60 13, salses.monuments- nationaux.fr. Apr-Sep 1000-1830, Oct-Mar 1000-1215 and 1400-1700. Last tour 1 hr before closing. €7.50, €4.50 concession, under 18s free.*

This late 15th-century Renaissance citadel built by Ferdinand and Isabella of Spain is the most visited sight in Roussillon. Originally, the Salses lagoon came further inland, so the fortress occupied a narrow strip of land between the water and mountains, along the same road used by Hannibal and his elephants in 218 BC.

The French had long coveted Roussillon and had taken an older fort on this site, so Ferdinand ordered Aragón's top military architect, Ramiro López, to build a stronger state-of-the-art defence. López came up with an immense 110- by 90-m stone and red-brick bunker, capable of holding 1500 men. It lay low as a defence against the artillery of the day, and was surrounded by dry moats that held stables for 300 horses. The surrounding walls were 10-12 m thick. If the enemy breeched them and survived the rows of canon facing the inner courtyard, a whole range of defences and tricks were in store in the confusion of corridors. Although the life of the typical soldier would have been grim, officers enjoyed some surprising perks, such as indoor toilets, central heating and hot baths. The bill for the final product was said to be 20% of Aragón's annual budget.

For all that, the French captured it twice, in 1639 and 1640 (both times Spain managed to grab it back), before it became redundant with the Treaty of the Pyrenees in 1659. Louis XIV's own military genius Vauban wanted to demolish it (from jealousy, perhaps?), but to save the expense it was allowed to stand and be used for storage. In 1886, it was declared a *Monument Historique*.

Le Petit Train Jaune

In 2010, this jaunty, 62.5-km narrow-gauge cog railway celebrateD the centenary of its beginnings. Designed to inject new life into Roussillon's mountain villages, the project of running a train up the wildest reaches of the Têt valley to the Cerdagne was so daunting it took until 1927 to complete, at a rate of less than 4 km of track per year. It's an engineering marvel and, unlike many heritage trains, is also a useful way to travel. It runs year round; summer is a lovely time to visit, when the journey is made in open-top cars (although the new cars, with big picture windows, have views that are nearly as grand).

Villefranche-Vernet-les-Bains is the base for the Little Yellow Train. From here, it makes a breathtakingly steep ascent, mostly on a narrow ledge carved into the side of the mountains that make it look like a toy; a couple of times it sails high over gorges on France's highest railway bridges. At the final station, Latour-de-Carol (three hours from Villefranche) you can either carry on to Toulouse or Barcelona, catch a bus to Andorra or do what most people do – catch the next train down.

Musée de Préhistoire, Tautavel

ⓘ *Av Léon-Jean Grégory, T04 68 29 07 76, www.450000ans.com. Sep-Jun 1000-1230 and 1400-1800, Jul-Aug 1000-1900, €8, €4 child (7-14).*
Northwest of Perpignan, where the Corbières meet the foothills of the Pyrenees, pre-Neanderthal *Homo erectus* made their home in an enormous karstic cave in 690,000-300,000 BC. Fossils of these nomadic hunters were first discovered in 1971, and since then over 100 have come to light. They hadn't yet discovered fire, so Tautavel Man and Woman ate their deer, rhinoceri and bison *tartare*.

Conflent and the Cerdagne → For listings, see pages 94-100.

The River Têt is the main artery of Roussillon, and its valley, the Conflent, is as varied and full of interest as any in the Pyrenees. It offers the chance to climb the Pic du Canigou and ride the Petit Train Jaune into the high plateau of the Cerdagne.

Ille-sur-Têt and around

Ille-sur-Têt (pronounced 'Eeya'), 25 km west of Perpignan, is the first large town you come to, with an intricate medieval core and a rare geological treat.

Les Orgues ⓘ *North of Ille-sur-Têt on the D21, T04 68 84 13 13, Nov-Mar 0900-1700, Apr, Sep and Oct 0900-1900, May and Jun 0900-2000, Jul and Aug 0900-2100; the Maison de site visitor centre closes for lunch and on Tue Nov-Mar, €3.50, under 10s free; last tickets 45 mins before closing.* The site, a 30-minute walk from the car park, is where Mother Nature, over the past five million years, sculpted the clay away to leave spectacular walls of tall chimneys and organ pipes in a natural amphitheatre, like an abandoned dream city.

Hospici d'Illa ⓘ *Ille-sur-Têt, T04 68 84 83 96, Feb, Mar, Oct and Nov Mon and Wed to Sat 1400-1800, Apr to mid-Jun Wed to Mon 1400-1900, mid-Jun to Sep Mon to Fri 1000-1200 and*

1400-1900, Sat and Sun 1400-1900, closed Dec to Jan; €3.50, €2.50 concession, under 13s free. Illa's 17th-century Hospice de St-Jacques, houses a fine collection of sacred art from the Romanesque (notably, detached 12th-century frescoes from Casesnoves) to the baroque.

Le Prieuré de Serrabonne ① *South of Ille-sur-Têt, Boule-d'Amont, T04 68 84 09 30, open 1000-1800. €1.50.* It's a long winding road south of Ille-sur-Têt but the remote little Priory of Serrabonne (the 'Good Mountain'), founded in the 12th century, is worth the drive. Its dark schist façade is austere but rose-coloured wonders, sculpted from the local marble, wait inside. There's a cloister gallery decorated with four pairs of columns and marble capitals and an even more elaborate tribune, resembling an interior cloister, decorated with a medieval bestiary, monsters, symbols of the Evangelists, St Michael and the dragon, and a worried-looking fellow blowing a horn.

Prades and around

Although it was a refuge of the famous Catalan cellist, Casals, after the Spanish Civil War and has proudly held the Pau Casals Chamber Music Festival since 1951, Prades has an alternative buzz. The main vortex is the Place de la République, where the church of **St-Pierre** contains a wonderful over-the-top baroque retable (1699) by Josep Sunyer. There's also a small **Musée Pau Casals** ① *next to the tourist office, 4 rue Victor Hugo, T04 68 05 41 02, Apr-Sep Mon-Fri 0900-1200 and 1400-1800, Oct-Mar 0900-1200 and 1400-1700).*

Eus, 5 km northeast, is strikingly piled on its hill, crowned by a 17th-century church built into the walls of a medieval castle. **Moltig-les-Bains**, 7 km north of Prades, is a sweet little spa amid the forests, famous since Roman times for skin treatments. A couple of kilometres further up, **Mosset** takes pride in being 'the world's smallest ski resort' (it has three runs); it also has a pine tree growing out of its bell tower.

St-Michel-de-Cuxa ① *3 km south of Prades, T04 68 96 15 35, http://abbaye.cuixa. monsite-orange.fr, Oct-Apr 0930-1150 and 1400-1700, May-Sep 0930-1150 and 1400-1800, €5, 12-18 €3, under 12s free.* With its tower rising 40 m above the orchards, St-Michel-de-Cuxa was one of the most important religious houses in Catalunya. It was founded in 840 and placed under the protection of Wilfred the Hairy, the first Count of Barcelona. By 978 it was important enough for Doge Pietro Orseolo to come all the way from Venice to retire and die here 'in the odour of sanctity', and it reached its peak of prominence in 1008 when the brilliant multi-lingual Oliba, like Wilifred a descendant of the Counts of Cerdagne, became abbot. By then much of the abbey's building was completed except for its chief glory, the cloister, with its superb capitals sculpted from the local pink marble in the 12th century.

The monks left during the Revolution and over the years the monastery decayed; one of the bell towers collapsed in 1829 and the cloister capitals were sold off to collectors (most were re-used in a bathing house in Prades). In 1913 the remaining dozen capitals were sold to the Cloisters Museum in New York City, mobilizing the locals at long last to protect and reinstall the remaining ones.

The oldest section of the abbey is the slightly uncanny 11th-century circular crypt with a central column known as the 'Crèche' or nativity scene, which is unique in medieval architecture. The nave is remarkable for its rounded Visigothic arches, and the half a cloister that remains in situ is delightful, its columns decorated with imaginary beings, lions and monsters.

Since 1965, St-Michel has been home to a small community of Benedictines from Montserrat who make sheep cheeses (on sale in the shop) and tend the **iris garden**, which explodes into colour in late May/early June.

Villefranche-de-Conflent

Squeezed in its long, narrow walls between the river and road, Villefranche was founded in 1092 by Count Guillaume-Raymond de Cerdagne. He granted it tax advantages in order to attract settlers to defend this strategic neck of the valley, and also built the church of **St-Jacques** with its ornate pink marble portal. In the 1680s, the great engineer Vauban doubled the height of the walls and in 2008 UNESCO included Villefranche in its list of Vauban World Heritage Sites. Its vocation these days is tourism and its two long narrow streets, which are filled with boutiques, can seem like a mini-Carcassonne in season.

Les Remparts ① *32 bis rue St-Jean, T04 68 96 22 96, www.villefranchedeconflent.fr, Feb and Nov 1030-1230 and 1400-1700; Mar-May and Oct 1030-1230 1400-1800; Jun and Sep 1000-1900; Jul and Aug 1000-2000; Dec 1400-1700; €4, €3 concession, under 12s free; audio guide €3.* You can retrace the steps of the guards patrolling Vauban's walls and bastions; many of the walkways are covered because of the danger of attacks from the mountains. Note the inward-facing loopholes – a precaution after the Catalan revolt in the 'Conspiracy of Villefranche' (1674).

Château-Fort Libéria ① *T04 68 96 34 01, www.fort-liberia.com, Jul-Aug 0900-2000, May-Jun 1000-1900, Sep-Apr 1000-1800, €7, €3.80 child (5-11); visit with shuttle €10, €5.10 (5-11).* Vauban added this fort in 1681 to defend the heights, and Napoleon III modernized its fortifications. It is linked to Villefranche by a path and a '1000-step' (actually 734) subterranean staircase (if you don't want to use the shuttle bus). The fort has grand views, cannons and prisons. Eight women accused of poisoning and witchcraft in Versailles were detained here at the time of Louis XIV; one spent 44 years chained to the wall.

La Cova Bastera ① *N11, opposite Villefranche's public gardens, T04 68 05 20 20, www.3grottes.com, Jun, Sep 1400-1700, Jul-Aug 1100-1900. €7, €5 child (5-12).* The smallest of Villefranche's caves, was used by the rebels before Vauban incorporated it into the defences, building a casemate gallery to defend the road. There's no guided tour, but a film and models tell the history of Villefranche – starting with scale models of dinosaurs and cave men.

Grotte des Grandes Canalettes ① *Rte de Vernet, 300 m from Villefranche, T04 68 05 20 20, www.grotte-grandes-canalettes.com, Apr-Jun daily 1000-1800, Jul-Aug daily 1000-1930 (1900 son et lumière), Sep-Nov daily 1000-1730, Dec-Mar Sat-Sun 1100-1700, French school holidays 1100-1700, €10, €6 child (5-12) discounts for visits to 2 or more caves.* Discovered in the 1980s, the Grandes Canalettes is known as the subterranean Versailles of Roussillon. It boasts spectacular formations, including a magical white chamber; 'Angkor Wat'; a ceiling of eccentric formations; a bottomless pit; a subterranean lake and more.

Grotte des Canalettes ① *Rte de Vernet, near the Grandes Canalettes, www.3grottes.com. Jul-Aug visits on the hour 1100-1800, 1130-1730. €9, €5 child (5-12).* Discovered in 1951, this family-run stalactite cave has draperies and pretty formations, although if you only have time for one, the Grandes Canalettes is admittedly more spectacular.

Notre Dame de Corneilla-de-Conflent ① *On the road to Vernet-les-Bains, T04 68 05 63 98 (mairie). Generally open Jun-Sep Mon-Sat 1000-1300 and 1500-1800, but best to ring the mairie to check; €2.50.* This 11th-century priory with a red marble tympanum of the Virgin in Majesty. It is full of art: there's a white marble retable from 1345, beautiful polychrome statues, a 15th-century Déposition and a gorgeous carved walnut wardrobe from the 14th century.

Vernet-les-Bains and around

Further up the road from Notre Dame de Corneilla-de-Conflent is this charming little spa town. It attracted a following of well-to-do Brits in the 1800s and included Rudyard Kipling among its regular visitors. The British gave their name to a beautiful waterfall, the **Cascade des Anglais**, which is a three-hour hike from town and back.

The **tourist office** ① *2 rue de la Chapelle, T04 68 05 55 35, vernet-les-bains.fr,* has a brochure in English on the several routes to the summit of Le Canigou, most of which involve a night in a mountain gîte. Whenever you go, check the weather before setting out.

Le Pic du Canigou At 2784 m it's not the tallest, but the Pic du Canigou, the national symbol and *Montanya Regalada* (fortunate mountain) of the Catalans, stands out as prominently as Mount Fiji. The first recorded climber, King Pere III of Aragón in 1285, found a dragon at the top and some believe it shelters the Holy Grail. On 23 June, the eve of St John's Day (the Festa Major), a flame lit on Canigou at midnight is conveyed down by torches and a relay of runners to light 30,000 bonfires all across French and Spanish Catalunya.

Reaching the summit of the Pic du Canigou isn't difficult. The ideal time is September, when the skies are usually clear. You can drive up in a jeep by way of the Llech forest road as far as the **Chalet des Cortalets** ① *T04 68 96 36 19, open mid-May to early Oct,* but you'll need to set off before 0800, when the road closes to private vehicles; allow 90 minutes by road, followed by two hours of walking to reach the summit. Alternatively, take a jeep taxi from Prades or Vernet-les-Bains (€30, based on six passengers); contact **Garage Villacèque** (T04 68 95 51 14) or **Les Jeeps du Canigou** (T04 68 05 99 89). From the chalet, it takes about two hours to reach the top. Check weather before setting out, and bring sturdy shoes, a pullover, a windcheater (it can get very gusty up there), water, sun block and binoculars. For more information, visit the **Maison du Patrimoine** ① *2 Rue de la Chapelle, Vernet-les-Bains, T04 86 05 55 35, www.vernet-les-bains.fr.*

Abbaye Saint-Martin de Canigou ① *Casteil, above Vernet-les-Bains, T04 68 05 50 03, www.stmartinducanigou.org; guided tours Jun-Sep Mon-Sat 1000, 1100, 1200, 1400, 1500, 1600 and 1700, Sun 1000 and 1230; Oct-May Tue-Sat 1000, 1100, 1400, 1500 and 1600, Sun 1000 and 1230; closed Jan. €5, €3.50 child (12-18); under 12s free. If you can't walk, book a lift with a 4WD through Taxis Montagne et Transport, T04 68 30 02 82 or T06 10 19 60 85, www.montagne-transport.com/fr.* It's a steep 30- to 45-minute walk from the car park (bring water and a hat), but St-Martin's setting under the Pic du Canigou couldn't be more stunning, isolated amid the mountains and forests. Founded in 1009 by Giufré, the Count of Cerdagne and brother of the famous Catalan churchman Oliba, the last five monks left in

1768, and St-Martin gradually became a picturesque ruin. In 1902 it was purchased by the bishop of Perpignan and gradually restored, and since 1988 it's been home to a community of Béatitudes (men and women) devoted to prayer.

Mont-Louis and Le Capcir Guarding the pass into the Cerdagne, Mont-Louis (1580 m) is the highest fortified town in France and one of the few built from scratch by Vauban, in 1679. Named after Louis XIV, it has few of the tourist trappings of Villefranche-de-Conflent, and in fact still houses a garrison and commando training centre in its citadel.

The French army also financed its claim to fame with the 50 kW **Four Solaire** ① *T04 68 04 14 89, www.four-solaire.fr, guided tours on the hour Sep-Jun 1000-1200 and 1400-1800, Jul-Aug 1000-1130 and 1400-1800, winter 1000, 1100, 1400, 1500 and 1600, €6.50, €5 young people (7-17), under 7s free*, the first solar furnace in the world. It was built in 1949 under the supervision of its inventor Félix Trombe for high-temperature experiments in physics and chemistry. Most of these experiments now take place in the bigger model at Odeillo (see page 93).

Le Capcir, the pine-wooded plateau north of Mont-Louis, is a seductive detour, where tiny stone-built villages and glacier lakes were only linked by road to the outside world in the 19th century. The medieval kings of Mallorca used to come up to the atmospheric little capital **Formiguères** for their asthma. It's a favourite spot for winter sports (**Les Angles**), but also for the magnificent hiking around the sapphire lakes at **Lac des Bouillouses**.

The Cerdagne

At 1200 m, the high plateau of the Cerdagne occupies the bed of a prehistoric lake surrounded by high mountains and forests. Royal eagles circle high in soft blue skies over green meadows that are bathed in sunshine for 3000 hours a year; in winter the slopes become a popular playground. The 1659 Treaty of the Pyrenees divided the Cerdagne equally between Spain and France, but on both sides roots lie deep in Catalan culture: in the cuisine, language and in the little Romanesque chapels.

From **Mont-Louis**, the N116 swoops in grand loops down to the market town of **Saillagouse**, with its playful statues and murals in the main square. By-roads lead up to bijou hamlets: **Eyne**, where the valley is a nature reserve, filled with wild flowers in May and June; and **Llô**, at the base of the pretty **Gorges de Sègre**, which has a Romanesque church and **hot springs** ① *T04 68 04 74 55, www.bains-de-llo.com, Mon-Sat 1000-1930, mid-Jul to Aug 1000-2000, €11; €9 child (3-11)*, that fill an outdoor pool and jacuzzi. **Ste-Léocadie**, further along, claims to have the highest vineyards in Europe. Tiny **Hix**, once the seat of the Catalan counts of Cerdagne, has a good Romanesque church from 1177, containing a superb statue of the Virgin; the Romanesque church at neighbouring **Caldégas** has frescoes of hunting scenes.

Bourg Madame sits on the busy frontier, sandwiched between Spain and Llivia. **Llívia** is an enclave of Spain 6 km from the rest of the country, an anomaly left over from the treaty of the Pyrenees that gave France 33 'villages' in the upper Cerdagne – but not the 'town', a status little Llivia was proud to hold. In a ring of sprawl, Llivia's pretty medieval core surrounds a huge 16th-century church, **Nostra Senyora dels Angels**, containing a beautiful 13th-century statue of Christ (ask the sacristan to see it); and a pharmacy that opened in 1415, one of the oldest in the world and now part of the municipal museum.

To the west lies **Ur** with another fine church and tiny **Latour-de-Carol**, the end of the line on the **Petit Train Jaune** and legendary among trainspotters as the only place where three lines with three different gauges meet: the Petit Train Jaune's narrow gauge (see page 88), standard European (French) gauge and Spain's wider RENFE gauge.

From here, the D618 circles back east, where you might be tempted into a side trip up to Dorres, for a hot soak at the open-air granite basins at the **Bains de Dorres** ① *T04 68 04 66 87, www.bains-romains.dorres.eu, open summer 0845-2010; winter 0900-1945, E4; under 5s free*. The main D618 crosses the striking **Taragosse Chaos**, where the hills are strewn with boulders left behind by an ancient glacier. Amid the rock formations at Odeillo towers the strikingly incongruous glimmering concave mirror of the 1000 kW **Le Grand Four Solaire Odeillo-Héliodyssée** ① *T04 68 30 77 66, www.foursolaire-fontromeu.fr , Sep-Jun 1000-1230 and 1400-1800, Jul-Aug 0930-1900, €7, €3.50 young person/child, under 7s free*. Put into use in 1969, this solar furnace is the biggest in the world and is used for experiments and research – the fascinating tour explains all. Just above, brash and modern Font-Romeu and Bolquère are the biggest winter/summer sports resorts in the Eastern Pyrenees, and a favourite destination for French athletes training to compete at high altitude.

The Vallespir → *For listings, see pages 94-100.*

The River Tech flows down this wooded valley from the Spanish border to just north of Argèles-sur-Mer. Its medieval capital, up in the hills to the north, was Castelnou (a member of the 'Most beautiful villages in France' association), built in 990 around a lofty pentagonal castle of the Vicomte de Vallespir.

The current capital of Vallespir, Céret resembles an inland Collioure – a laid-back, quintessentially Mediterranean town of winding lanes set around a medieval core. There are buildings with leopard façades of dappled shade, pretty squares filled with cafés, and, *de rigueur*, a stunning bridge – the 14th-century Pont du Diable, with an arch spanning 45 m. Just like Collioure, Céret was discovered by artists in the early 20th century, this time by the Cubists. Céret is also proud of being France's cherry capital and, May to early June, when the roadside stands do a brisk business, is a luscious time to visit.

Céret and around

The **Musée d'Art Moderne de Céret** ① *8 bd du Maréchal-Joffre, T04 68 87 27 76, www.musee-ceret.com, Jul to mid-Sep daily 1000-1900, mid-Sep to mid-Oct and May to Jun, daily 1000-1800; mid-Oct to Apr Wed-Mon 1000-1800, €5.50, €3.50 concessions (during special exhibitions €8, €6 concessions), under 12s free*, was founded in 1950 when Matisse donated 14 of his sketches from Collioure, and Picasso contributed 53 works – mostly scenes of a *corrida* that he created in an intense five-day period. A good number of the other paintings, by Braque, Gris, Soutine, Marquet, Lhote, Kissling and Manolo, are of Céret itself. As in Collioure, plaques with copies of paintings in key locations tell where artist and easel stood.

East of Céret, **Le Boulou** may be best known as the last stop in France on the *autoroute*, but Romanesque lovers will want to have a look at the marble lintel on its church, sculpted by the Master of Cabestany. Just south, near the hamlet of **Maureillas-las-Illas**, the chapel of **St-Martin-de-Fenollar** ① *T04 68 87 73 82, Jul and Aug daily 1030-1200 and 1530-1900, Sep to Jun Wed-Mon 1400-1700, €3, under 12s free*, as rare 11th-century frescoes in the apse, painted by the monks of Arles-sur-Tech and studied by Braque and Picasso. They are colourful, primitive but heart-felt scenes showing the Nativity story, Christ in Majesty and the 24 Elders of the Apocalypse.

Arles-sur-Tech

The medieval capital of the Vallespir, Arles-sur-Tech is an introspective old place; most of the tourist amenities in the area are concentrated in the old spa of **Amélie-les-Bains**, 4 km downriver.

Abbaye Ste-Marie ① *entrance via the tourist office, T04 68 83 90 66, open Nov-Mar Mon-Sat 0900-1200, 1400-1800, Apr-Jun and Sep-Oct Mon-Sat 0900-1200, 1400-1800, Sun 1400-1800; Jul-Aug Mon-Sat 0900-1900, Sun 1200-1900, €4, €3 concessions*, was founded on the ruins of Roman baths in Amélie during the late eighth century. It was built by Sunifred, brother of Wilifred the Hairy, not long after Charlemagne conquered the area from the Moors, but it was relocated to Arles in the ninth century for safety reasons. It was famous for an unusual relic, which can still be seen today: an empty late-Roman sarcophagus known simply as Ste Tombe, which miraculously fills up with water from an unknown source.

Enter through the late 13th-century cloister into the massive Romanesque church that's so old it's aligned to the west, and corrected by a 'counter apse' in the east with a frescoed upper chapel dedicated to St Michael. In the 10th century, the chronicles tell how Arles was invaded by ape-like 'Simiots', and to counter them the abbot went to Rome for some proper relics. He brought back the bones of two obscure Persian martyrs, SS Abdon and Sennen, and installed them in cupboards high up in the pillars, which solved the Simiot problem; the 17th-century retable in the saints' chapel tells the story. Note the rare 18th-century Schmidt organ.

The tower-framed façade has an austere beauty, while tucked on the side is the famous Sainte Tombe. On 30 July, its 500 litres of pure water are siphoned out and distributed to the faithful.

Gorges de la Fou

① *D115, T04 68 39 16 21, Apr-Nov 1000-1800, €9.50, €5.50 child (5-12).*
This Dante-esque crack in the limestone (deliciously translated in a brochure as 'the throats of the insane') is said to be the narrowest gorge in the world, so narrow that you can often touch both walls with your outstretched hands. A metal walkway wends through and visitors must wear hard hats.

Roussillon listings

⬤ Where to stay

For hotel and restaurant price codes and other relevant information, see pages 10-13.

Perpignan *p82, map p84*
€€€€-€€€ La Villa Duflot, Rond-point Albert Donnezan, T04 68 56 67 67, www.villa-duflot.com. This beautiful art deco-style boutique hotel, located just outside Perpignan and filled with contemporary art, offers 24 spacious and luminous rooms and suites, many over-looking the Mediterranean patio or the pool set in the large park. Known for its exceptional detail and services, it has a gastronomic restaurant, fitness room, and offers Pilates and yoga classes.

€€€ Château La Tour Apollinaire, 15 rue Guillaume Apollinaire, T06 30 89 11 02, www.latourapollinaire.com. Only 10 mins' walk from the centre, this boutique hotel is in a baronial mansion dating from the belle époque (the baron was a cousin of the French-Russian poet Apollinaire). It offers 11 very stylish rooms, and 7 well-equipped 1- to 3-bedroom apartments with optional home cinema and a massive DVD library. The walled subtropical garden has 'Zen cascades' and a heated pool is open Apr-Oct. Free Wi-Fi. 2-night minimum stay in high season.

€€ Park Hotel, 18 bd Jean Bourrat, T04 68 35 14 14, www.parkhotel-fr.com. A 5-min stroll from the centre, this traditional 67-room hotel is Perpignan's best-known lodging. Rooms vary in size, but are all well equipped and soundproofed. There's Wi-Fi and a parking garage.

€ Hotel Aragon, 17 av Gilbert Brutus, T04 68 54 04 46, www.aragon-hotel.com. This welcoming little hotel on the edge of the centre, just off boulevard F Mercador, has 30 homey, immaculate en suite rooms with a/c, Wi-Fi and satellite TV. The helpful owners speak English and there is nearby free parking or a paid lot 300 m away. The €7 breakfast is good value.

€ Hotel de la Loge, 1 rue des Fabriques Nabot, T04 68 34 41 02, www.hoteldela loge.fr. Located a stone's throw from the Place de la Loge (if you're driving, the République and Wilson garages are closest), this is a delightful, good-value hotel with en suite rooms and a/c. Furnishings are charmingly old-fashioned and a bit faded, but comfortable.

Self-catering
Bastide Le Petit Clos, Catalunya, 34 rue de Sitges, T04 68 85 54 60, www.bastide-lepetit clos.com. It's a bit hard to find, south of the centre off the D900, but it's very peaceful once you arrive. The 3 lodgings (sleeping 4, 8 and 14) in this 19th-century house combine traditional features such as wooden floors and tiles with luxury high-tech design. Non-smokers only. Prices start at €430 per week.

Conflent and the Cerdagne p88
€€€€ Château de Riell, Moltig-les-Bains, T04 68 05 04 40, www.chateauderiell.com. This 19th-century baroque folly is a magical oasis in the woods. The 19 stylish rooms (in the château or surrounding houses, some of which have private terraces) are richly decorated in shades of ochre. There's a spa (the waters are rich in freshwater plankton), a garden, a pool and an excellent restaurant open to non-guests; you can even sip your cocktails in the dungeon.

€€ Hôtel Restaurant Planes, Place de Cerdagne, Saillagouse, T04 68 04 72 08, www.planotel.fr. For over a century the Planes family has been running this inn at one of the Cerdagne's main crossroads. The 19 rooms are nicely decorated, equipped with Wi-Fi, and most have views over the mountains. The **Planes** also own the **Planotel**, 150 m away, which has a heated covered pool and sauna that guests can use. The restaurant is excellent, and the *demi-pension* option is good value.

€€ Villa Lafabrègue, 15 av Louis Prat, Prades, T04 68 96 29 90, www.villafrench.com. English Kate and Nick Wilcock are welcoming and knowledgeable hosts, and their B&B in a luxurious Florentine-style villa (1870) makes a great base. Each of the 5 rooms has its own character and stunning mountain views. There's Wi-Fi and a sunny walled garden with a pool, and the delicious breakfast is included in the price.

€ Auberge La Chouette, 2 rue de la Liberté, Font-Romeu, T04 68 30 42 93, www.chouette.fr. An old stone inn by the church at Odeillo, this has 14 basic en suite rooms (sleeping up to 4) for old-fashioned mountain holiday fun. Half-board mandatory; bring your own towel.

€ Cal Xandera, 49 rte de Font-Romeu (D618), Angoustrine, T04 68 04 61 67, www.calxandera.com. This cosy, famil-run inn offers 5 charming rustic rooms equipped with Wi-Fi in an 18th-century farmhouse with grand views, not far from all the activities at Font-Romeu. The excellent restaurant serves seasonal dishes (foie gras with roast figs or pheasant terrine) either on the terrace in summer or by an open fire on cold evenings; the prices are reasonable. Closed Oct.

Self-catering

Mas d'en Roca, Los Masos, T04 68 05 25 59, www.giteking.com. Just 3 km from Prades, this is a stone barn converted by its British owners into a very attractive beam-ceilinged gîte sleeping 8, plus an apartment sleeping 4. Prices for 4 start at €300 per week.

The Vallespir *p93*

€€€ La Mas Trilles, Le Pont de Reynes, Céret, T04 68 87 38 37, www.le-mas-trilles.com. This traditional stone farmhouse from 1631 has been restored by its French and Hungarian owners into a delicious 10-room hotel. Set by the river in a pretty garden with a heated pool, it has well-appointed rooms (the ones in the main house have the most character). Most sleep up to 4 and prices include breakfast.

€€ Relais des Chartreuses, 106 av d'en Carbonner, Le Boulou, T04 68 83 15 88, www.relais-des-chartreuses.fr. There are 12 beauiful rooms in this 17th-century Catalan *mas* located between Céret and Collioure. It's far enough from the crowds to offer a peaceful stay and there's a garden and a welcoming outdoor pool. They have family rooms available, and a range of special offers on their website.

€ Hôtel des Arcades, 1 place Picasso, Céret, T04 68 87 12 30, www.hotel-arcades-ceret.com. Over the years a score of artists have checked into this spotless, family-run hotel in the centre of Céret, many of whom have left paintings on the walls. There are 30 rooms; 22 are en suite (some with a/c) and sleep up to 3 people, whereas 8 have kitchenettes and are rented out by the week.

❼ Restaurants

Perpignan *p82, map p84*

€€€ La Galinette, 23 rue Jean Payra, T04 68 35 00 90. Tue-Sat for lunch and dinner. Chef and owner Christophe Comes is obsessed with vegetables, often seeking out rare varieties for his *potager*. In his cuisine, they share top billing with the seafood, his other great passion – try the saint-pierre (John Dory) *a la plancha* with the best carrots you've ever tasted. The bright dining room and white linen is smart, casual and fashionable, so be sure to book. Menus from €19-62.

€€ Al Tres, 3 rue de la Poissonnerie, T04 68 34 88 39, www.altres.mobi. Tue-Sat for lunch and dinner. On a quiet little lane, this restaurant serves elegant Mediterranean cuisine with a Catalan flair in a stylish contemporary dining room. The menu changes with the season and market availability; try the grilled squid with vegetables and preserved lemon. It also has an exception wine list. 2-course lunch menu €14, 3 courses €18.

€€ Le Clos de Lys, 660 Chemin de la Fauceille, T04 68 56 75 00, www.closdeslys.com. Tue-Sun 1200-1430, Tue, Thu-Sun 1930-2200. Sit out in the charming shady garden, or in the recently remodelled dining room with views into the kitchen, where the chefs prepare a wide range of Catalan and traditional dishes, prepared on a wood fire, or *a la plancha*; check the website for the daily changing market menu. Lovely dessert buffet. Menus from €18.50-39.

€€ Le Grain de Folie, 71 av du Général Leclerc, T0 468 51 00 50. Tue-Sat 1200-1400, 1930-2130; Sun 1200-1400. This informal little restaurant, located in a rather funky area of town by the bus station, is deservedly popular for its light, contemporary cuisine, beautifully served; the ingredients are carefully chosen from the beef to the wild mushrooms, and prepared with just the right knack. Even the children's menu is exceptionally nice. Save room for the superb desserts. Menus from €18-33.

€€ Le V.I.P., 4 rue Grande des Fabriques, T04 68 51 02 30, Mon 1200-1400; Tue-Fri 1200-1400, 1930-2200, Sat 193-2300. Be sure to book for this fashionable, laid-back little restaurant near the canal, offering a delicious chalkboard menu, exquisitely cooked seafood and one of the best value-for-money lunch menus in Perpignan. Reasonably priced wine list, too. Menus from €12.50-25.

€ Brasserie L'Aragó, 1 place Aragó, T04 68 51 81 96. Daily 0900-0200. The typical brasserie menu (mussels, grilled fish and steaks, pizza, pasta, salads) is nothing special, but the balcony and terrace are great for people-watching and soaking up the sun, or sitting out in the evening. Menus from €15-30.

€ Café de la Loge, 38 av Xavier-Llobères, Salses-le-Château, T04 68 38 62 86. http://lalogesalses.com/don-site. Open daily 1200-1400, also Fri and Sat 1900-2100. This café first opened its doors in 1825 and is still decorated with fancy 19th-century ceiling mouldings. Catalan dishes dominate, including the house speciality, *rap y galtes* (monkfish sautéed with prawns and pork cheeks, *déglacé* with Rivesaltes and served with salsify).

€ Le Rocher des Pirates, Rue Georges Méliès, just north of Perpignan, Rivesaltes, T04 68 57 15 84, http://rocherdespirates.com. Daily 1200-1400 and 1900-2200. This family restaurant is disguised as a Caribbean pirates' den and serves pizza, pasta, salads, grilled meats and seafood *a la plancha*. Waiting staff are dressed as pirates, and on most evenings there are various animations (cannon fire, volcanic eruptions, etc).

€ Spaghetteria al Dente, 1 place Variétés, T04 68 61 11 47. Mon-Sat 1200-1500 and 1900-2200. This Italian restaurant with Aldo tending the pots (and often popping out for a chat) offers a huge menu of pasta dishes – the sun-dried tomatoes, goat's cheese, basil and olive oil is delicious.

Cafés and bars

Espi, 43 bis quai Vauban, T04 68 85 39 38, www.maison-espi.fr. Mon-Sat 0730-1930, Sun 0730-1300 and 1530-1930. In business for decades, this café serves the best ice cream in Perpignan, as well as breakfast and home-made pastries.

Paradis Fouillis, 17 rue de l'Ange, T04 68 34 66 32. Mon 1400-1900, Tue-Sat 1100-2000. This fun *salon de thé* serves tea and coffee in the middle of a *brocante* (junk) shop, so you can sip and browse at the same time.

Conflent and the Cerdagne *p88*

€€€ Auberge Saint-Paul, 7 place de l'Eglise, Villefranche-de-Conflent, T04 68 96 30 95, http://auberge.stpaul.pagesperso-orange.fr. Easter-Sep Tue-Sat for lunch and dinner, Sun for lunch, Oct-Easter Wed-Sat for lunch and dinner, Sun for lunch. *The* place for a blow-out dinner in the Conflent: Patricia Gomez serves gourmet delights (breast of pigeon with onion confit and coriander, pigeon thigh with foie gras, or grilled prawns and ravioli stuffed with greens) in the lovely courtyard or 13th-century chapel dining room. Excellent cheese and wines, too. Book in advance. Lunch menus start at €19.50.

€ Le Canigou, Place du Génie, Villefranche-de-Conflent, www.bistrot-villefranche.com, T04 68 96 12 19. Mar-Oct daily 0700-0200, Nov-Feb daily 0800-2200. A popular bistro with a shady terrace, **Le Canigou** serves its Catalan specialities such as *escalivada* (mixed grilled vegetables), hams and charcuterie whenever you're feeling peckish. Owner Joël Méné is a volunteer fireman; don't miss his collection of firefighter memorabilia.

Cafés

Café de l'Union, Rue de l'Eglise, Fillols,
T04 68 05 63 06. Open summer 0800-late.
This tiny village south of Villefranche-
de-Conflent is one of the liveliest in the
valley. The **Café de l'Union** serves food from
Tue-Sat, including its famous *magret* and
morels, and hosts concerts and jam sessions
throughout the year. The nearby **Café de
Canigou** is usually buzzing, too.

Entertainment

Perpignan *p82, map p84*

Clubs and music bars

ABC Dancing, 56 Rue de Dombasle, T04 68
56 90 60, www.abc-dancing.com. Thu-Sun
2100-0500. Long-standing disco club located
in the outskirts of Perpignan, with a variety
of theme nights, including salsa on Thu,
and retro on Fri.

El Che, Rue Fabrique d'En Nadal, T04 68 64 97
63. Tue-Sat 1900-0200. Popular tapas and
music bar in the centre of Perpignan.

La Habana Bodéguita, 5 rue Grande-des-
Fabriques, T04 68 34 11 00. Mon-Sat
1800-0200. A popular music bar serving
excellent *mojitos*, with a restaurant upstairs.
There's great salsa music on Wed nights.

Le Corsair, 6 rue des Abreuvoirs. Wed-Sat
1900-0200. This lively music bar with a
great atmosphere specializes in Carribbean
rum cocktails.

Uba Club, 5 bd Mercader, T04 68 34 06 70,
www.soonnight.com. Wed-Sun 2300-0600.
Gay, lesbian and straight disco playing a mix
of old and new. It's especially popular with
those in their 20s and 30s, and there's no
cover charge.

Shopping

Perpignan *p82, map p84*
Art

Galerie de L'Olympe, 8 rue de la Cloche
d'Or, T04 68 34 65 75. Tue-Sat 1400-1900.
Contemporary art gallery in the pedestrian zone.

Food and drink

Escargots de Roussillon, 9 place de la
République, T04 68 34 47 65. Tue-Sun
0730-1230, closed Jan. More than fresh
snails (a huge local favourite), this shop sells
a wide range of specialities and is handy
for picnic supplies.

Fromagerie du Mas, 9 av André Ampère,
Cabestany, T04 68 34 89 43. Tue-Sat 0900-
1900. Over 80 kinds of (mostly farm-made)
cheese from across Europe. They also do
charcuterie and cheesy lunches.

Marché, Place Cassanyes. Open 0700-1330.
Perpignan doesn't have a covered *halles*,
but you'll find luscious fruit, veg, cheeses
and more in this daily market.

Interior design

Sant Vicens, 40 rue Sant Vicens, T04 68 50 02
18, www.santvicens.fr. Jan and Feb Tue-Sun
1430-1800, Mar-Dec Tue-Sat 1000-1200,
1430-1900, Sun 1430-1830. East of the centre
in an old farmhouse, **Sant Vicens** sells items
and antiques for the home and garden.

Miscellaneous

Maison Quinta, 3 rue Grande des Fabriques,
T04 68 34 41 62, www.maison-quinta.com.
Tue-Sat 0945-1200 and 1415-1900. 'L'Art de
vivre catalan' is the motto, and they have it
all – food, furnishings, fabrics, tableware,
cookware and toys.

Conflent and the Cerdagne p88
Food and drink
Bernard Bonzom, Rte 116, Saillagouse, T04 68 30 14 27, http://confit-canard-charcuterie-artisanale-pyrenees.bernard-bonzom.com. Easter-Sep Tue-Sun 0800-1230 and 1500-1930, Oct-Easter Tue, Thu-Sun 0800-1230 and 1500-1930. Bernard Bonzom and family win awards for their exquisite charcuterie made in the Cerdagne. Their shop also sells a huge range of cheeses, breads and other goodies.

Jewellery
Casa Perez, Place de l'Eglise, Prades, T04 68 96 21 03, www.joyaux-catalans.fr. Mid-Sep to Jun Tue-Sat 0900-1200 and 1430-1900, Jul to mid-Sep Mon-Sat 0900-1200 and 1430-1900. **Casa Perez** makes jewellery in Catalan colours, blood red garnets and gold. Tours of the *atelier* are offered at 1000, 1100, 1430, 1530, 1630 and 1730.

⚠ What to do

Conflent and the Cerdagne p88

Donkey trekking
Les Ânes de la Licorne, Moli d'Oli, Mosset, T04 68 05 03 83, www.altipyr.com. Half-day treks to 15-day excursions.

Golf
Golf de Font-Romeu, Espace Sportif Colette Besson, Font-Romeu, T04 68 30 10 78, www.golf-font-romeu.fr. Mid-May to mid-Nov. A 9-hole par 36 course, high in the Pyrenees.

Mountain sports
Aventure Grotte et Canyon, 24 rue St-Jean, Villefranche-de-Conflent, T04 68 05 51 98, www.aventuregrottecanyon.com. Trained guides for caving, canyoning, rock climbing and Via Ferrata.
Exploration Pyrénéenne, 73 rue St-Jean, Villefranche-de-Conflent, T06-22 45 82 02,

www.ex-pyr.com. Year-round canyoning trips (in winter in natural hot springs), as well as caving, adventure walking and Via Ferrata.
Ozone 3, 40 av Brousse, Font-Romeu, T04 68 30 36 09, www.ozone3-montagne.com, www.ozone3.fr. Adventures include canyoning, rafting, kite flying and kite 'mountain board', fishing, rock climbing, Via Ferrata, treks and ballooning over the Cerdagne.
Têt Aventure, Base Eau Vive, Marquixanes, T04 68 05 72 12, www.exterieur-nature.com. Near Prades, an adventure park for ages 3 and up. Also offers canyoning, tubbing, hydrospeed, whitewater rafting, rock climbing, mountain biking, sea kayaking, diving, and off-piste and helicopter skiing.
Trans Pyr 66, T06 11 87 85 12, www.transpyr66.com. Summer and winter activities in the Cerdagne, including dog sledding, sleeping in igloos, rock climbing and rafting.

Skiing/wintersports
Font-Romeu/Bolquère-Pyrénées 2000, Font-Romeu, T04 68 30 68 30, www.font-romeu.fr. Well-equipped station with 40 pistes, including 8 black and 8 red. Also offers snow shoeing, a surf park, ice skating, dog-sledding and a children's snow park.
Les Angles, T04 68 04 32 76, www.les-angles.com. 2 black, 16 red, 6 blue and 7 green pistes, and rarely any queues. There's also cross-country skiing, snowboarding and equipment and training for disabled skiers.

Wellbeing
Bains de St Thomas, Fontpédrouse, T04 68 97 03 13, www.bains-saint-thomas.fr. Hot spring a 30-min walk from a station on the Petit Train Jaune: hammam, jacuzzi, exterior hot pools, and a choice of treatments including being coated in chocolate. Children welcome. No credit cards.

The Vallespir *p93*
Golf
Golf du Domaine de Falgos, St-Laurent-de-Cerdans, T04 68 39 51 42, www.falgos.com. Beautiful 18-hole par 70 course in the foothills of the Pyrenees.

☻ Transport

Rail
Trains link Narbonne with Perpignan and frequent trains link Perpignan to Spain. Local trains serve the Côte Vermeille and travel up the Conflent valley to Villefranche/Vernet-les-Bains to link up with the Petit Train Jaune (see box, page 88). This, in turn, goes to Cerdagne, where there are connections to Toulouse, Andorra and Barcelona.

Road
Bicycle
Although the French have great respect for cyclists, it's always best to avoid the busier roads. Check out route suggestions and maps on www.bikely.com and www.bikemap.net. Rentals average €10-12 a day, more for a racing or mountain bike. Local tourist offices can advise on hire shops' alternatively check out holiday-bikes.com/fr.

Bus/coach
Roussillon stands out in the region for its network of €1 buses that reach most of the towns in the department. Most branch out from Perpignan's Gare Routière; see www.cg66.fr (T04 68 80 80 80) for routes and schedules.

Car
Motoring in Languedoc-Roussillon presents no great difficulties. Even minor roads in the mountains are well maintained, and most are well signposted, but a good map and/or a Sat Nav are essential. Petrol stations are few and far between in the mountains.

❶ Directory

Perpignan *p82, map p84*
Medical services Hospital 20 av du Languedoc, T04 68 61 66 33. **Pharmacy** Ollet, 3 rue Argenterie, T04 68 34 20 72; Vauban, 23 quai Vauban, T04 68 34 44 24.

Contents

Footnotes

Index

Titles available in the Footprint *Focus* range

Latin America	UK RRP	US RRP
Bahia & Salvador	£7.99	$11.95
Brazilian Amazon	£7.99	$11.95
Brazilian Pantanal	£6.99	$9.95
Buenos Aires & Pampas	£7.99	$11.95
Cartagena & Caribbean Coast	£7.99	$11.95
Costa Rica	£8.99	$12.95
Cuzco, La Paz & Lake Titicaca	£8.99	$12.95
El Salvador	£5.99	$8.95
Guadalajara & Pacific Coast	£6.99	$9.95
Guatemala	£8.99	$12.95
Guyana, Guyane & Suriname	£5.99	$8.95
Havana	£6.99	$9.95
Honduras	£7.99	$11.95
Nicaragua	£7.99	$11.95
Northeast Argentina & Uruguay	£8.99	$12.95
Paraguay	£5.99	$8.95
Quito & Galápagos Islands	£7.99	$11.95
Recife & Northeast Brazil	£7.99	$11.95
Rio de Janeiro	£8.99	$12.95
São Paulo	£5.99	$8.95
Uruguay	£6.99	$9.95
Venezuela	£8.99	$12.95
Yucatán Peninsula	£6.99	$9.95

Asia	UK RRP	US RRP
Angkor Wat	£5.99	$8.95
Bali & Lombok	£8.99	$12.95
Chennai & Tamil Nadu	£8.99	$12.95
Chiang Mai & Northern Thailand	£7.99	$11.95
Goa	£6.99	$9.95
Gulf of Thailand	£8.99	$12.95
Hanoi & Northern Vietnam	£8.99	$12.95
Ho Chi Minh City & Mekong Delta	£7.99	$11.95
Java	£7.99	$11.95
Kerala	£7.99	$11.95
Kolkata & West Bengal	£5.99	$8.95
Mumbai & Gujarat	£8.99	$12.95

Africa & Middle East	UK RRP	US RRP
Beirut	£6.99	$9.95
Cairo & Nile Delta	£8.99	$12.95
Damascus	£5.99	$8.95
Durban & KwaZulu Natal	£8.99	$12.95
Fès & Northern Morocco	£8.99	$12.95
Jerusalem	£8.99	$12.95
Johannesburg & Kruger National Park	£7.99	$11.95
Kenya's Beaches	£8.99	$12.95
Kilimanjaro & Northern Tanzania	£8.99	$12.95
Luxor to Aswan	£8.99	$12.95
Nairobi & Rift Valley	£7.99	$11.95
Red Sea & Sinai	£7.99	$11.95
Zanzibar & Pemba	£7.99	$11.95

Europe	UK RRP	US RRP
Bilbao & Basque Region	£6.99	$9.95
Brittany West Coast	£7.99	$11.95
Cádiz & Costa de la Luz	£6.99	$9.95
Granada & Sierra Nevada	£6.99	$9.95
Languedoc: Carcassonne to Montpellier	£7.99	$11.95
Málaga	£5.99	$8.95
Marseille & Western Provence	£7.99	$11.95
Orkney & Shetland Islands	£5.99	$8.95
Santander & Picos de Europa	£7.99	$11.95
Sardinia: Alghero & the North	£7.99	$11.95
Sardinia: Cagliari & the South	£7.99	$11.95
Seville	£5.99	$8.95
Sicily: Palermo & the Northwest	£7.99	$11.95
Sicily: Catania & the Southeast	£7.99	$11.95
Siena & Southern Tuscany	£7.99	$11.95
Sorrento, Capri & Amalfi Coast	£6.99	$9.95
Skye & Outer Hebrides	£6.99	$9.95
Verona & Lake Garda	£7.99	$11.95

North America	UK RRP	US RRP
Vancouver & Rockies	£8.99	$12.95

Australasia	UK RRP	US RRP
Brisbane & Queensland	£8.99	$12.95
Perth	£7.99	$11.95

For the latest books, e-books and a wealth of travel information, visit us at: www.footprinttravelguides.com.

 footprint travel guides.com

 Join us on facebook for the latest travel news, product releases, offers and amazing competitions: www.facebook.com/footprintbooks.

MINISTRY OF DEFENCE

FIELD SURGERY POCKET BOOK

Edited by
Major General Norman G Kirby OBE QHS FRCS FRCS(Ed)
Guy Blackburn MBE MA(Cantab) MChir FRCS

LONDON HER MAJESTY'S STATIONERY OFFICE

© *Crown copyright 1981*
   First published 1944
   New edition 1981

This publication supersedes
A Field Surgery Pocket Book 1962
(WO Code No 12552)

HER MAJESTY'S STATIONERY OFFICE

Government Bookshops

49 High Holborn, London WC1V 6HB
13a Castle Street, Edinburgh EH2 3AR
41 The Hayes, Cardiff CF1 1JW
Brazennose Street, Manchester M60 8AS
Southey House, Wine Street, Bristol BS1 2BQ
258 Broad Street, Birmingham B1 2HE
80 Chichester Street, Belfast BT1 4JY

Government publications are also avaiable
through booksellers

ISBN 0 11 772360 6

This publication is the United
Kingdom implementation of:
STANAG No 2068

FOREWORD

This new edition of the Field Surgery Pocket Book has returned to its original size in an attempt to make it practical and accessible, however small the pocket, however strange the field.

It has been brought up to date as far as possible by a group of consultants with personal experience and a surgical background, both military and civilian, that covers the whole range of trauma in peace and war.

I gladly commend it to the attention of surgeons both in military and civilian practice.

Richard Bradshaw

Lieutenant General,
Director General, Army Medical
Services

List of contributors

W F Belsham   FFARCS
Brigadier, Consultant Adviser in Anaesthetics

G Blackburn   MBE MChir FRCS
Consultant Surgeon Emeritus, Guy's Hospital, London
Formerly Honorary Civilian Consultant Surgeon to the Army

T. B. Boulton ERD MA FFARCS
Consultant in Anaesthetics, Royal Berkshire Hospital and RAMC TA

N A Boyd   OBE FRCS
Lieutenant Colonel, Consultant in Orthopaedic Surgery

A T Cook QHP FRCP FRCP(Ed)
Major General, Director of Army Medicine

J T Coull FRCS(Ed)
Lieutenant Colonel, Consultant Adviser in Orthopaedic Surgery

A P Dignan CB MD FRCS FRCS(I)
Major General, formerly Director of Army Surgery

C E Drew MVO VRD FRCS
Consultant Thoracic Surgeon, Westminster Hospital and St. George's
Hospital, London. Honorary Civilian Consultant in Thoracic Surgery to
the Army

B Hopkisson FRCS DO
Major, Consultant in Ophthalmology

N G Kirby OBE QHS FRCS FRCS(Ed)
Major General, Director of Army Surgery

I Lister FRCS
Colonel, Consultant Adviser in Urology

B. Livesey FRCS DLO
Brigadier, Consultant Adviser in Otorhinolaryngology

N F Jones MD FRCP
Consultant Physician, St. Thomas Hospital, London

C. MacFarlane FRCS(Ed)
Lieutenant Colonel, Consultant in Surgery

K. Milne FRCS DO
Brigadier, Consultant Adviser in Ophthalmology

W C Moffat OBE FRCS
Colonel, Consultant in Surgery. Formerly Professor of Military Surgery, Royal College of Surgeons of England and Royal Army Medical College, Millbank.

R Myles Gibson TD MD FRCS FRCS(Ed)
Consultant in Neurosurgery, General Infirmary, Leeds. Honorary Civilian Consultant in Neurosurgery to the Army.

M S Owen Smith MS FRCS
Lieutenant Colonel, Professor of Military Surgery, Royal College of Surgeons of England and Royal Army Medical College, Millbank.

M. Payne FRCS(Ed)
Major, Consultant in Surgery.

W J Pryn OBE FRCS
Brigadier, Consulting Surgeon, BAOR.

A P Robinson MRCP D Phys Med
Colonel, Consultant in Rheumatology and Rehabilitation.

C D Sanders FFARCS DA
Brigadier, formerly Consultant Adviser in Anaesthetics.

G Smith FDS RCS D Orth
Brigadier, Consultant Adviser in Dental Surgery.

D G Stock FRCS
Lieutenant Colonel, Consultant in Orthopaedic Surgery.

P H Swinhoe OBE MFCM DRCOG DTM & H
Colonel, CRAMC 3 Division.

G W Taylor MS FRCS
Professor of Surgery, St. Bartholomew's Hospital, London. Honorary Civilian Consultant in Vascular Surgery to the Army.

W G Thomson FRCS(Ed)
Colonel, Consultant in Plastic Surgery.

H H Wandall MD(Copenhagen)
Professor, Institute of Experimental Research in Surgery, Copenhagen.

Contents

List of Illustrations

Abbreviations

BSA	Body Surface Area.
CCRAMC	Corps Commander RAMC (Corps Surgeon).
CRAMC	Commander Royal Army Medical Corps (Divisional Surgeon).
CTAP	Combat Team Aid Post.
DMS	Director of Medical Services.
DPS	Delayed Primary Suture.
Fd Amb	Field Ambulance (Medical Battalion).
FST	Field Surgical Team.
OTT	Operating Theatre Technician.
QARANC	Queen Alexandra's Royal Army Nursing Corps.
RAMC	Royal Army Medical Corps.
RAP	Regimental Aid Post (Battalion Aid Post).
RCT	Royal Corps of Transport.
RMA	Regimental Medical Assistant (Corpsman).
RMO	Regimental Medical Officer (Battalion MO).

INTRODUCTION

This pocket book should be regarded as a directive from the Consulting Surgeon to the Army on surgery in the field in war. It recommends the lines on which casualties should be treated. The advice offered and the methods described are those which Surgical Consultants and Advisers of the Army, past and present, consider most likely to produce the best results in the light of our present knowledge and experience. Written to instruct the young military surgeon it will be as useful to the consultant dealing with missile injuries for the first time in peace as in war. Medical officers isolated due to misfortunes of war will find it of value.

The early and adequate surgical treatment of the wounded constitutes one of the most potent factors in preserving the fighting morale of the troops and in maintaining an Army up to strength. Wounds that are treated promptly and efficiently heal more quickly and leave a minimum of residual disability.

The work of a surgeon in the field is difficult, often exhausting, and calls for considerable surgical skill, experience and the finest judgement. This is not the place for an inexperienced surgeon. Periods of hectic activity produce severe physical and mental strain. This calls for a considerable degree of physical fitness and stamina. Even with extensive experience of civilian surgery, a surgeon may make costly mistakes under field conditions. His new and strange circumstances may cause him to forget basic surgical principles. In war conditions unorthodox individual techniques, and indeed many accepted procedures and techniques, which worked well in civilian practice, may jeopardize the patients' chances of survival. Patients will never remain under an individual surgeon's personal care in the forward area but must be evacuated. They will then come under the care of many surgeons in the evacuation chain. For this reason surgery should be simple and standardized.

When a surgeon joins the Army he will have to accustom himself to working with the minimum of essential items. His equipment includes everything that is really necessary but simplicity of design, general practicability and standardization are essential in the interests of supply and efficiency. It is a matter of common knowledge that the greater the experience of the surgeon in this type of work the fewer items of equipment he will require, particularly as in parachute operations he may have to carry it.

Missile wounds require the removal of all devitalized tissue. Ideally, this is done within a period of six to eight hours after the wound has been sustained and before organisms contaminating it invade deeper tissues. Antibiotics have no effect on dead tissue nor on the absorption of noxious metabolites. Although they are valuable adjuncts and may hold infection at bay for varying periods up to eighteen hours, they are not substitutes for surgery.

The fate of the injured man depends upon carefully planned treatment and evacuation from the time of injury until surgery is available. This implies excellent first aid at the time of the injury, with provision of treatment facilities and resuscitation under medical supervision at each echelon in the speedy evacuation to a surgical centre. The journey from battlefield to hospital may be very short by air or very long by road or even uncharted track.

The fate of the injured depends largely on the adequacy of the surgical service provided. The unit of this service is the surgical team operating in a surgical centre. The surgical potential of any centre depends therefore on the number of teams working there. The work of the teams must be well organized, with time for the members to eat and sleep as well as operate or the standard of work will deteriorate from sheer fatigue in times of stress.

The siting of a surgical centre in a forward area is decided by the tactical administrative staff, taking into account the terrain, roads, state of the battle and the condition of the wounded on arrival at the various stages of their evacuation. The cardinal surgical guide to the siting of surgical centres is not miles but hours on the chain of evacuation. Few severely wounded patients will survive unless resuscitated and operated upon within six hours. Many will not survive casevac as long as that in spite of skilled first aid and resuscitation during evacuation. Larger surgical centres are much more efficient from every point of view, although small scattered centres must be used occasionally.

Definitions

Surgical teams   Surgical teams may be integrated with field and general hospitals or established as independent field surgical teams.
A team consists of: Surgeon, anaesthetist, resuscitation officer, QARANC theatre sister (or OTT, warrant officer), three operating theatre technicians, clerk RAMC, medical assistant resuscitation orderly.

Parachute field surgical teams have a similar organization and capability but their equipment is specially modified for the parachute role. They are supported by parachute nursing facilities and can therefore retain patients until link up with the ground forces occurs.

Field surgical team   A mobile surgical team which is fully equipped to set up its operating theatre, carries sufficient medical equipment and resuscitation fluids for fifty operations. It is used as a surgical support team either to reinforce the surgical centre of a field or general hospital, to replace casualties, or establish an advanced surgical centre in the MDS of a field ambulance. Teams will be resupplied by a system of standard packs.

The ordnance equipment includes overalls with detachable sleeves, caps, masks, rubber boots and linen overboots. The surgeon should be prepared, in emergency, to work in a clean mackintosh overall, and if necessary without gloves.

Specialist teams   In addition to the general teams independent specialist teams are available in the order of battle. They have a capability of forming advanced and rear sections, but are usually attached to general hospitals to form combined 'trinity' head injury centres.

a Maxillo-facial team.
b Neuro-surgical team.
c Ophthalmic team.

Advanced surgical centre   Circumstances may arise in which it is not possible for wounded to reach the surgical centre of a field hospital within an acceptable time because of the casualty overload and/or evacuation difficulties. In these circumstances an independent field surgical team may be moved forward and attached to a field ambulance to form an advanced surgical centre. This deployment must be regarded only as a temporary expedient because the field ambulance is not staffed or equipped to provide adequate post-operative nursing care. This in fact necessitates replacement by a fifty-bed element of a field hospital to provide the nursing care in the centre.

Field and general hospitals The basic requirements for all hospitals are:
a Triage.
b Resuscitation for casualties requiring resuscitation before surgery or before further evacuation.
c Surgery for casualties who would seriously deteriorate or die if they were evacuated prior to surgery.
d Post-operative nursing.
e Sustaining treatment for other casualties 'in transit' to a more rearward hospital.

To meet these requirements, hospitals must have the following departments: Reception, Resuscitation/pre-op, Surgical centre, Wards, Evacuation, Minor treatment, X-ray, Pathology, Administration.

Advanced surgical hospital Is the new field hospital. This is a semi-mobile unit of 400 beds with eight integral surgical teams. It is a corps unit normally provided on a scale of one per division and is deployed as far forward in support of the division as the tactical situation permits.

In deployment a fine balance must be made between reducing evacuation time to a minimum and ensuring that the hospital does not have to move too soon from the chosen location. The role of the unit is primarily surgical although it is staffed and equipped to hold medical cases and minor sick in quiet periods. Under normal circumstances it is at this unit that the wounded man first receives surgical care and can be retained until he is fit to move after operation.

The general hospital This is an Army unit with a capacity of 800 beds. As its name implies it is capable of the full range of surgical and medical treatment of the sick and wounded. Each hospital has integral surgical teams and many have special centres for the treatment of head injuries, chest injuries and/or burns.

Reception of wounded   Triage is the initial classification by priorities of casualties at the reception area of a surgical centre. Casualties fit for further evacuation are sorted from those:

a Who require resuscitation alone or

b Who require resuscitation and immediate surgery before evacuation.

The decision to evacuate or not must depend on the response of the casualty to resuscitation. Only casualties whose vital signs do not stabilize should be operated on at this level.

These patients may have:

(1) Severe haemorrhage from limb wounds or in the abdomen, chest, skull or

(2) Multiple severe wounds of limbs, or

(3) Injuries of face or chest endangering the upper airways and require urgent life saving surgery as Priority One cases. The triage of the wounded should be done by an experienced medical officer possessing not only sound clinical judgement but also an appreciation of the tactical situation and the efficiency of the evacuation system. He should have a knowledge of the medical units in front of and behind his own unit, including the pressure being extended on them by the inflow of casualties. It is upon these facts that decisions regarding disposal depend. An advanced surgical centre or field hospital dealing with a heavy casualty load must evacuate all cases except Priority One. The temptation to retain less seriously ill patients must be resisted. The fresh arrival of more top priority cases inevitably leads to postponement of treatment until long after it could have been given in a less busy surgical centre at the rear. Less urgent cases can be dealt with only during quiet periods.

The majority of the battle wounded probably have had an exhausting journey before reaching the centre. Some will be dehydrated, most will need rest, fluids and quiet. Overheating must be avoided.

In the resuscitation department of the surgical centre casualties who require surgery before further evacuation must be arranged in the order that they are to be sent to the operating theatre. This order depends on the severity of the wounds and actual fitness for operation. A patient with a chest wound may be more seriously ill than an abdominal case, yet because the latter has responded earlier to resuscitation he is fit for operation first. The timing of the patient's operation requires good judgement. Severe haemorrhage requires urgent surgery, as do major muscle wounds failing to respond to resuscitation. There is an optimum time to operate and once past, it never returns.

The average time taken for operation on a top priority case is one hour and one team can not be expected to deal with more than 10–12 heavy cases in 24 hours. Experience has shown that if more is undertaken judgement is liable to be faulty and the standard of work will fall. Exhaustion and sound work are incompatible. The herculean surgeon must remember that other members of the team may not possess similar stamina.

The average stay of surgical patients in a field hospital should be in the region of 48 hours. Within this average is the short stay of only several hours after limb wound excision, the majority of cases, and, at the other extreme, the long term stay of 7–10 days for abdominal injuries.

Consulting surgeon Early in the planning phase of any military operation a consulting surgeon must be appointed who is responsible directly to the Director of Medical Services (DMS) for formulating surgical policy. He is responsible for the supervision of the surgical treatment of all casualties, surgical equipment, surgical training and the co-ordination of surgeons. He must have independent transport, access to all surgical units and the DMS. It is through the consulting surgeon that the highest level of surgical efficiency can be attained. The consulting surgeon, in addition to his staff and administrative duties, visits the various surgical centres observing the state of the wounded as they arrive at dressing stations and surgical centres forward or rear. By correlating reports from surgeons and resuscitation officers, particularly with regard to the time lag after wounding, he can do much with regular liaison visits to obtain the best results in difficult situations. The effects of treatment can be assessed and regular clinical discussion carried out.

The administration of forward surgical units Administration of these units will depend on a variety of factors – whether the warfare is static or one of movement; whether desert, open fertile country or mountainous; and finally whether in advance or retreat. The medical objective is to bring surgical aid to battle casualties in accordance with fundamental principles. This will not always be easy. The tactical situation, enemy shell fire, temporary road blocks, blackouts, etc, will complicate the problem of evacuation.

When the fighting is straggling and mobile columns are skirmishing over tracts of flat country, or desert, multiple mobile centres may be the only answer; but small scattered centres are not economical, are difficult to service, and to clear. From the administrative point of view, the fewer the centres the better. A large medical unit makes a good centre because accommodation is good, nursing more adequate and the equipment available on a more lavish scale. A centre at a field hospital for instance, will have the advantage of an X-ray service, more ample sterilizing and laundry facilities, etc, and here in most circumstances, skilled nursing is provided by officers of the QARANC.

In static warfare surgical centres have the opportunity of becoming settled in and well established, and can deal with convoys of wounded without difficulty; in a war of movement, however, a centre may be called upon to close down, move at short notice, and open up on arrival at a site thirty miles distant. During a rapid advance, surgical teams may have to leapfrog each other, working for two to three days and then moving on again.

CHAPTER 1

War surgery

THE WOUNDING EFFECTS OF WAR MISSILES

When the body is struck by a missile, damage is inflicted which depends on the size, shape, stability and velocity of the missile and on the structures with which it comes in contact. Wounding missiles include bullets, fragments of shells, grenades, bombs and mines and such secondary missiles as building materials, glass, rock splinters, wood and fragments of equipment and clothing.

The study of missile wounds requires knowledge of the physical properties of the missile in flight and the effect it has on the tissues it penetrates.

A wound results from the absorption of kinetic energy (KE) imparted by a missile when it strikes and penetrates tissues. Its available kinetic energy is calculated by the formula:

$$KE = \frac{MV^2}{2}$$

where M represents the mass and V the velocity. When a missile is stopped by the tissues it penetrates, the energy liberated to cause damage must be equal to the total KE of the missile. If it passes through the tissues it has a remaining velocity from which can be calculated the energy released during wounding:

$$E\ Exch = \frac{M(V_1^2 - V_2^2)}{2}$$

where V_1 = strike velocity, V_2 = remaining velocity. The lower this remaining velocity the greater the energy liberated to the tissues.

The retardation of the missile is an important factor in the creation of the wound, for the more rapidly a missile is retarded the greater will be the energy release and consequent tissue damage. Retardation depends upon missile factors such as shape, stability and composition and upon tissue factors such as density and elasticity. The shape of the missile is important, for the more irregular the shape of the missile the more liable it is to tumble in the air with consequent loss of range and accuracy. Some

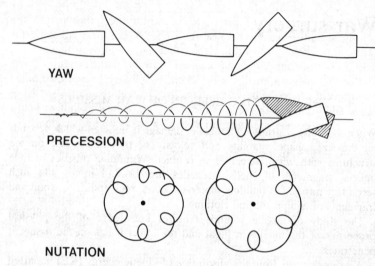

YAW

PRECESSION

NUTATION

Figure 1 Yaw/precession/nutation

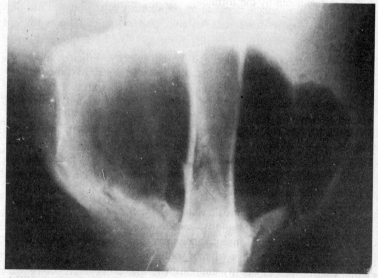

Figure 2 Microsecond radiograph of a sheep's thigh showing temporary cavity caused by a rifle bullet.

missiles like arrows and darts are inherently stable but bullets are aerodynamically unstable because the centre of the mass is behind the centre of resistance to flight, thus the bullet tends to move around its long axis. This important deviation is known as **yaw** and in the extremes of this motion the bullet will tumble end over end (see Fig 1). Spinning the bullet by means of rifling the barrel of a gun gives it stability and this increases range and accuracy; this spin induces other variations in motion of the bullet, eg **precession** and **nutation,** so that it performs a fairly complicated pattern of deviation from the line of its long axis (Fig 1). Irregular movements are rapidly damped by the gyroscopic action of spin at up to 3500 revolutions per second and this action tends to stabilize the bullet after 50–100 metres. This effect is inadequate to maintain stability in media that are denser than air. The soft tissues of the body and water are 800–900 times as dense as air and when a bullet hits these tissues it always becomes unstable. Any angle of yaw that is present will be greatly increased, sometimes to the point of tumbling.

The energy available and the retardation are both proportional to the square of the velocity of the missile. This accounts for the tremendous damage that is caused by high velocity missiles. The variation in the amount of tissue damage depends on the stability of the missile and the density of the tissues traversed. A stable, perforating bullet may use up only 10–20 per cent of its available strike energy in creating a wound, whereas an unstable bullet of the same mass and velocity will always give up much more of its energy, thereby creating a more severe wound.

A missile can cause injury in the following three ways depending on its velocity:

a *Laceration and crushing* As the missile penetrates the tissues, they are crushed and forced apart. This is the principal effect of low velocity missiles travelling at up to 350 metres per second (1100 ft per second). The crushing and laceration caused solely by the passage of the missile are not serious unless vital organs or major blood vessels are injured directly. Only those tissues that come into immediate contact with the missile are damaged, and the wound is comparable to those caused by hand held weapons. No significant energy is transmitted to the tissues surrounding the wound track and therefore minimal excision of damaged tissues is necessary.

b *Shock wave* Whilst forcing a track through solid tissues the missile compresses the medium in front of it and this region of compression moves away as a shock wave of spherical form. Its velocity is approximately that of the velocity of sound in water, 1500 metres per second (4800 feet per second), and although the changes of pressure due to shock waves are of short duration they may reach peak values of up to 100 atmospheres or 1500 pounds per square inch.

c *Temporary cavitation*   This phenomenon is encountered only with high velocity missiles and is the main factor in their highly destructive effects. As the penetrating missile releases its energy it is absorbed by the local tissues which are accelerated violently forwards and outwards. Due to their imparted velocity and the momentum, the tissues continue to move after the passage of the missile, thus creating a large cavity approximately 30–40 times the diameter of the missile (Fig 2). This cavity, containing bacteria from the outside, has a sub-atmospheric pressure with the result that clothing and debris are sucked into its depths through the entry and exit wounds. The cavity reaches a maximum size in a few milliseconds and then collapses in pulsatile fashion leaving a narrow permanent cavity. The high velocity missile neatly shears the tissues involved. It is the cavitation effect, resulting from the rapid transfer of energy from the missile to the tissues, which is the mechanism whereby severe wounds result. It takes place mainly after the passage of the missile, and accounts for the 'explosive' nature of high velocity missile wounds. The greater the energy that is imparted to the tissues, the greater is the size of the temporary cavity and the more extensive the damage. Soft tissues will be pulped, small vessels will be disrupted and bone may be shattered. The larger blood vessels and nerves, being more elastic, may be pushed aside, but the vessels may well suffer damage of the intima at a distance from the wound. Thrombosis and stasis in vessels in the hours following the cavitation further increase the volume of dead tissue. Plasma leaks from the damaged vessels causing tense oedema and further ischaemia. This large amount of dead tissue inoculated with bacteria and debris actively sucked in from the environment is the specific pathological feature of the high velocity missile injury.

The cavitation phenomenon takes place in all tissues whether they be the limbs, abdomen, chest or head. Some tissues such as muscle, liver, brain and the more solid homogenous organs in general are very susceptible to damage by this mechanism, whereas others such as lung tissue which is of lesser density than these is far more resistant to such damage.

Whereas ballistically stable bullets may produce small external wounds in contrast to the large wounds typical of ballistically unstable fragments of shells, grenades and bombs, the actual damage done by the former may be far greater because of their higher velocity. First appearances may, therefore, be deceptive. Missiles tend to be diverted in direction by the resistance offered by tissues of different density, particularly fascia and bone and bizarre tracks may therefore result. It is important when trying to interpret the significance of entrance and exit wounds to determine whenever possible the position of the soldier at the time of wounding.

Mechanism of infection Clostridia spores are carried on the skin and clothing and most infections from these organisms are autogenous. Clostridial contamination of a wound is not in itself significant. Normally only a small proportion go on to develop clostridial cellulitis.

Table 1 Distribution of missile wounds (per cent)

Locations	World War I	World War II	Korea	Vietnam	Borneo	Northern Ireland
Head and Neck	17	4	17	14	12	20
Chest	4	8	7	7	12	15
Abdomen	2	4	7	5	20	15
Limbs	70	75	67	54	56	50
Others	7	9	2	20	–	–

Regional distribution of missile wounds The proportion of wounds that occur in the various regions of the body is different from the calculated areas exposed to the possibility of damage.

There is however a striking preponderance of wounds of the extremities and these, of course, are associated with a very low mortality compared with the other regions of the body.

The proportion of wounds of different areas varies in different wars, and this is virtually a reflection of the type of warfare, the terrain and the weapons available. For example, wounds of abdomen and chest formed a higher than usual proportion of the wounds in the Borneo campaign. There, most skirmishes took place at very close range in the dense tropical rain forest using personal small arms.

Table 2 Wounding missiles (per cent)

	World War I	World War II	Korea	Vietnam	Borneo	Northern Ireland
Bullets	39	10	7	52	90	55
HE fragments	61	85	92	44	9	25
Others	–	5	1	4	1	20

Wounding missiles Wounds are caused by different missiles according to the nature of the campaign. Fragment wounds form a far higher proportion than do bullet wounds in most wars. In some conditions such as in the jungles of Borneo or in the urban terrorist conflict in Northern Ireland the reverse ratio occurs.

PRINCIPLES IN WAR SURGERY

The essentials

Experience in many wars has shown the following principles to be fundamental:

a *The surgical treatment of a war wound is a two stage operation* The first is concerned with the saving of life and limb and the prevention of serious sepsis by primary wound excision. The second, the closure of the wound, is carried out four or five days later, often after evacuation, and aims to procure sound initial soft tissue healing.

b *Every war wound is contaminated* Infection remains latent and superficial for about six hours, after which it becomes established and invasive.

c *If a wounded man needs an operation, he needs it at the earliest suitable moment.*

d *The value of resuscitation before anaesthesia and operation must always be considered.*

e *Shock follows failure of vital capillary perfusion due to loss of blood volume* The most important factor in its production is loss of whole blood by bleeding externally, into body cavities or into tissues, but aggravating factors are pain, anxiety, exposure, dehydration and infection.

f *Frequent inspection of wounds at staging posts is meddlesome and adds greatly to the risk of infection* The wound should not normally be exposed outside the operating theatre or other special dressing area.

g *Gas gangrene is a specific anaerobic infection of skeletal muscle* It commences in ischaemic muscle and is a life threatening disease. Anything that embarrasses the circulation of a limb, such as tight bandaging or badly applied splints, will encourage its development.

h *The adequate treatment of a missile wound consists in the proper and thorough performance of primary wound excision* – see below. Antibiotics, although valuable adjuncts, are not substitutes for surgery.

j *Abdominal casualties tend to deteriorate in noisy, insecure surroundings* It is better, if possible, to treat them in quiet areas even though evacuation may mean some delay before operation. Following operation they travel badly and cannot be further evacuated in under seven days without incurring grave risks of sepsis, ileus and wound disruption.

k *X-ray examination is often advisable in chest and abdominal wounds* and may be helpful in the pre-operative assessment of limb wounds. The presence of metallic or other foreign bodies, including air, may give valuable information about the extent and direction of a wound. Where a foreign body lies, there are likely to be pieces of in-driven clothing or other debris.

l *Triage is the process where casualties are sorted* into groups according to the urgency of their need for treatment. It is not a simple once-only procedure but a continuing process calling for careful observation, critical judgement and wide experience. It is not well to embark on a lengthy and complicated operation with a poor chance of success if by so doing other cases are denied surgery at the optimum time. Triage is difficult and the job should not be given to those ill-equipped to deal with it.

Resuscitation

The treatment of shock and resuscitation is covered in Chapter 3.

Technique of wound excision

Cleansing the wound area Bear in mind that generous wound extension, and possibly counter-incisions, may be required. A large area surrounding the wound including the whole circumference of a limb should be cleaned with soap and water or a detergent and shaved if necessary. The wound itself should be covered with a large sterile pad to avoid contaminating it further. The cleansed area should then be dried and painted with a suitable antiseptic such as chlorhexidine or povidone iodine. Drapes should be placed with regard to the needs of wound extension, eg the abdomen may well have to be opened in wounds of the chest or upper thighs. In the case of multiple wounds, those on the back should be dealt with first to minimize turning the patient. Turning a wounded anaesthetized patient is often associated with circulatory collapse and the procedure should always be done with great care.

Incision Skin is very valuable and remarkably viable. It should be conserved as far as possible and only that which is clearly irreparably damaged should be excised. Generous incision is often required to gain access to the depths of a wound. Such incision should be made in the long axis of a limb but using a tight 'S' to avoid cutting across joint flexures. Subcutaneous fat has a poor blood supply and should be widely excised. It is often easier and quicker from this stage onwards to use sharp curved scissors instead of a knife.

Retraction All damaged deep fascia is excised and intact deep fascia incised throughout the length of the incision. This is an essential step, releasing tension on damaged muscle and allows wide and deep retraction. It may be necessary to add transverse cuts in the deep fascia to improve access and allow the depths of the wound to be clearly seen.

Excision of muscle Dead muscle is a pabulum for the organisms of gas gangrene. Excision of dead and damaged muscle must be thorough and complete. All muscle which is of a mushy consistency, which does not contract when pinched or bleed when cut must be excised. Muscle which has a poor colour should be removed although the presence of interstitial bruising may be compatible with viability. At the conclusion of this stage, the wound should be lined with healthy bleeding contractile muscle.

Foreign bodies
Blood clot, indriven dirt or clothing, missiles or pieces of missile, will be removed as muscle excision proceeds. Irrigation with saline is helpful in washing out the smaller fragments. No prolonged search for foreign bodies should be made beyond the confines of the wound since this is

likely to open up healthy tissue spaces. A foreign body remote from the immediate wound and localized clinically or radiologically may be approached through a separate incision. Small unattached pieces of bone act as foreign bodies and should be removed but all possibly viable bone must be preserved.

Haemostasis
This must be as complete as possible. Large vessels should be secured with thread ligatures and small bleeding points with fine catgut or diathermy if available. Ligatures should be cut short to leave as little foreign material as possible in the wound. Firm pressure with warm packs should control surface oozing.

Limitations of closure   The deep fascia, already widely incised, is left fully open to prevent post-operative oedema causing tension which might prejudice blood supply, and to allow free drainage from all parts of the wound. The skin is also left fully open and without suture. If there is any doubt that drainage is not free dependent counterincisions, also left fully open, may be made.
There are some exceptions to the rule of non-closure:
a   Wounds of the face and head should be carefully excised and closed primarily. See Chapters 16 and 22.
b   Wounds of the chest and abdomen, other than thoracotomy or laparotomy incisions which need careful closure, require closure of pleura or peritoneum reinforced by the muscle layer if possible. The skin related to a muscle wound may be left open. See Chapters 19 and 20.
c   Wounds involving joints require closure of the synovium and capsule. See Chapter 13.
d   In hand injuries it may be necessary to suture skin flaps over exposed tendon, nerve or bone. See Chapter 10.
e   Where a major vessel repair or graft has been done, some muscle cover at least is necessary. See Chapter 11.

Dressings   The wound should be covered by fine mesh gauze and ample absorbent material placed over it. Do not use tulle gras which often impedes drainage. The dressing should be held in place by adhesive strapping applied longitudinally or spirally. Under no circumstances should strapping encircle a limb since it will cause constriction when swelling occurs. If bandage is used, it should be of stretchable material and loosely applied.

Splintage   In all cases where there is an extensive soft tissue wound, even in the absence of fracture, the limb as a whole should be splinted. This is often best done by applying a well padded plaster cast, but this must be split immediately on application. Brief details and a diagram of the injury should be drawn on the plaster using an indelible marker pen.

YOU MUST NOT:

Excise skin unnecessarily
Waste time searching for unimportant foreign bodies
Insert gauze wicks – they come to act as plugs
Use tulle gras – it impedes drainage
Use circular strapping or firm bandaging.

YOU MUST:

Incise constricting fascia freely, both proximally and distally
Leave the wound widely open – except in the special circumstances noted above
Use plenty of absorbent fluffed gauze or wool
Split plasters immediately
Excise dead and damaged muscle thoroughly under direct vision.

Records

Concise notes should be legibly written on the Field Medical Cards. Other surgeons in the evacuation chain must know what was found and what was done. Accuracy and legibility are vital and all essential information must be included. The surgeon should print his name in BLOCK CAPITALS and initial the notes. He must state:

a   The missile if known – and whether removed.
b   The time lapse between wounding and operation.
c   Resuscitation given.
d   Operation findings and procedure. The condition of major vessels and nerves should especially be noted.
e   Any drugs given – especially antibiotics.
f   Brief postoperative directions and warnings, eg:
Arterial graft – watch circulation.
Sciatic palsy – watch skin.
Care with T-tube.
Watch the foot – ? amputation.

Postoperative care

After operation a limb should be comfortably elevated and maintained thus even in the course of evacuation. Distal limb circulation should be repeatedly checked where plaster is used. Any intravenous infusion should be carefully attended and this is particularly so if antibiotics are being given by the intravenous route.

Checks should be made that the urine output is satisfactory. Initial antibiotics should be continued for five days but not longer in the absence of laboratory or clear clinical indication of their continued effectiveness. It should be confirmed that tetanus vaccination has been boosted.

The most likely complications are haemorrhage and sepsis. Haemorrhage occurring within the first twenty four hours is usually due to inadequate primary haemostasis or slippage of a ligature (reactionary haemorrhage). Haemorrhage occurring later (secondary haemorrhage) is usually part of a septic process and due to erosion of a vessel. Other complications likely in the severely wounded are deep vein thrombosis, renal failure and pulmonary insufficiency due to micro-embolization.

Evacuation management

Provided the general condition does not contra-indicate it, and the patient is clinically stable, he may be further evacuated within a few hours of operation. Medical attendants en route and at staging areas must continue the postoperative care and observations, and the patient must have food, drink and analgesics as necessary. While it may be justifiable to replace outer dressings, the main dressing should not be disturbed unless there is an undeniable need due to haemorrhage or grave suspicion of gas gangrene. Splints may well need adjustments or plasters may need to be eased. An unconscious patient needs all the usual attention including two-hourly turning day and night.

AIR TRANSPORTATION OF PATIENTS – LIMITING FACTORS

1 Contra - indications to the carriage of certain patients by air depend on four factors:

a *Reduction in atmospheric pressure* During an ascent there is an expansion of any enclosed gases, and by the time that 18 000 feet is reached such gases – if not forcibly restrained – will occupy twice the volume that they did at sea level. Clinical conditions in which air is trapped in an enclosed space are unsuitable for evacuation at high altitude, and height limitations of, for example, 3000 or 5000 feet may have to be imposed. The exact limiting height will depend on the amount of enclosed air, and on its location within the body. Examples of the types of case in which this point must be borne in mind are:

(1) Pneumothorax.

(2) Any conditions liable to deteriorate should the pressure of intestinal gas be increased. This includes all recent (less than seven days) wounds and injuries and operations on the gastro - intestinal tract.

(3) Head injuries in which air has entered the skull.

(4) Patients encased in plaster jackets.

(5) Obstruction of eustachian tubes. Sinusitis. Acute otitis media.

b *Reduced air density*   This factor makes coughing less effective as a means of removing debris from the respiratory tract. Continued ineffectual coughing is also exhausting, and as the partial pressure of oxygen in the surrounding air is low (see c below), considerable distress may be caused to the following types of patient:

(1) Acute bronchitis, especially with impaired cardiac function.

(2) Patients suffering from conditions in which there is increased liability to aspiration of food and drink.

c *Reduction in oxygen tension*   This may adversely affect the following patients:

(1) Those with marked impairment of cardio-respiratory function.

(2) Patients whose haemoglobin level is down to 7g/100 ml.

(3) Severe chest injuries.

(4) Concussion with raised cerebro spinal fluid (CSF) pressure.

(5) Facial injuries (ie such as to prevent satisfactory administration of additional oxygen).

d *General*   The available space in an aircraft is necessarily limited and medical attendants much handicapped by having to cope with patients while wearing oxygen apparatus. The following types of patient are, on general grounds, unsuitable for air evacuation:

(1) Those in whom the risk of respiratory obstruction is real enough to require that provision be made for emergency tracheostomy.

(2) Patients liable to internal haemorrhage.

(3) Patients requiring a great deal of nursing during transit.

(4) Patients whose carriage or treatment necessitates the use of bulky or awkward equipment which cannot be satisfactorily accommodated on a stretcher or a turning frame.

2   The case of pressurized aircraft has not been taken into account in sub-paragraphs a, b, and c above, and when such machines are available it is normal practice to judge suitability for transfer in relation to the equivalent cabin altitude, and not to the actual altitude of the aircraft. Even then it is necessary to give some consideration to the possibility of failure of the pressurized system, and, should this occur, to the provision of additional oxygen through face masks.

3   The lists of types of clinical condition given are not comprehensive so much as illustrative, and in any given case the decision whether or not to evacuate by air may be far from simple. This decision ultimately falls to the RAF medical officer responsible for emplaning patients, and in giving his judgement he must take into account:

a Advice from specialists who have been responsible for treating the patient – particularly with regard to such matters as immediate prognosis, treatment requirements in flight, possible clinical crises in transit, and the ultimate prognosis should the patient not be evacuated by air.

b The patient's general condition immediately prior to the time of emplanement.

c The availability of specialist escort facilities appropriate to the patient's particular needs.

d The duration of the flight.

e The altitude at which the flight is to take place.

f The staging post medical services existing along the route of the flight.

g The relative priorities of patients awaiting evacuation.

CASUALTY EVACUATION (UK FORCES)

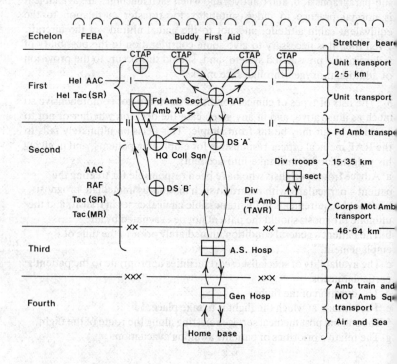

Figure 3 Casualty evacuation (United Kingdom forces)

CHAPTER 2

Initial care of the wounded

Introduction

If units of the combat arms are to retain their mobility and capability to fight, casualties must be cleared from them as quickly as possible. This process of casualty evacuation and treatment is the major role of medical units in war.

In order to achieve this objective, medical resources are organized and deployed as echelons of medical support in the combat and communication zones, in the same manner as the other logistic services. The echelons of medical care are as follows:

First echelon   That support integral to the unit or battle group which is provided by the regimental medical officer (RMO), and regimental medical assistants (RMAs).

Second echelon   The medical unit providing medical support within the division is the field ambulance.

Third echelon   The field hospital sited in the corps area, at which initial wound surgery is carried out.

Fourth echelon   General hospitals situated in the communication zone, at which the full range of surgical and medical treatment of the wounded and sick is provided.

Whilst most casualties will pass through each medical echelon in turn, it is important to appreciate that not all casualties will do this, since those with less serious wounds may be returned to duty and when aeromedical evacuation is possible, patients may overfly a particular echelon and be transferred directly to a surgeon.

The deployment of medical units to cope with the casualty load is affected by the tactical situation and all medical units, at least those within the Combat Zone, must hold themselves in readiness to move. Whilst it is important to the survival of the casualty that he should be operated upon as soon as possible after wounding, the requirement for a relatively stable atmosphere in which to undertake surgery, dictates to a large extent the siting of surgical facilities. In this respect, a compromise may be necessary; nevertheless surgical facilities should be so sited that the seriously wounded patient can reach the surgeon within six hours of wounding.

First aid training
The quality and quantity of the initial first aid given to the casualty may determine whether he survives to reach the surgeon or not. For this reason, the importance attached to all ranks in the Army being skilled in practical emergency first aid procedures cannot be over-estimated.

The standard to be achieved and maintained by annual testing, is contained in the First Aid Training Objectives (All Arms), Objectives 1–10, laid down in Army Training Directive No 11. These objectives cover the following:
Clearing the airway.
Care of the unconscious casualty including the use of the three quarters prone (recovery or coma) position.
Artificial respiration (Exhaled Air and Holger Nielsen methods).
Arrest of haemorrhage and the dressing of wounds.
Simple improvised limb splintage.
Treatment of burns.
Use of a morphine syrette.

CASUALTY CARE WITHIN FIRST ECHELON

At the point of wounding

At the point of wounding, the casualty is entirely dependent upon self administered first aid or that given by his comrade 'Buddy First Aid', for which purpose all ranks carry a first field dressing.

The minor casualty   The minor casualty, having had his wound dressed, will fight on until the immediate battle is over and will then make his own way to the Regimental Aid Post (RAP), for further treatment.

The serious casualty   The serious casualty, having received first aid treatment, will either make his own way to the squadron, company or combat team aid post, be collected by regimental stretcher bearers or be conveyed there by regimental stretcher bearers and by returning unit transport or the ambulance vehicle.

At the Squadron Company or Combat Team Aid Post

At this medical post, which may be mobile, the casualty receives attention from the regimental medical assistant (RMA). The RMA takes the necessary steps to ensure the maintenance of the casualty's airway, arrests uncontrolled haemorrhage and adjusts and applies dressings and simple splintage as may be necessary.

As rapidly as possible, the casualty is transferred to the RAP by ambulance vehicle where the RMO and RAP staff are available to administer full optimum first aid measures and initiate resuscitation.

At the Regimental or Battle Group Aid Post (RAP)

It is at the RAP that the casualty first receives attention from a doctor. His aim is to provide essential life saving measures and to prepare the casualty for rearward evacuation in accordance with a system of priorities based on the requirement for surgery and resuscitation.

Having searched the casualty in order to recover and make safe any weapons which he may be carrying, attention is immediately directed towards ensuring that he has an adequate airway and that haemorrhage is controlled. A thorough evaluation of his condition is then undertaken, including a record of blood pressure, pulse and respiration rate, with the level of consciousness where appropriate.

The scope of treatment available at the RAP is necessarily limited, but includes the following:

a Maintenance of the airway.
b Stabilization of pulmonary ventilation.
c Arrest of haemorrhage.
d Treatment of shock.
e Splinting of fractures and major soft tissue wounds.
f Initial care of burns injuries.
g Control of infection.
h Relief of pain.
j Correction of dehydration.

Maintenance of the airway   Respiratory obstruction is an emergency requiring immediate and urgent correction if the casualty's life is to be saved. The commonest causes are obstruction of the airway by the tongue, blood clot, vomit, foreign bodies such as dentures, or by oedema of the upper respiratory tract as a result of inhalation following burns about the face.

Respiratory obstruction is particularly hazardous in the unconscious casualty, who requires constant supervision and in whom posture is of vital importance. After aspiration of vomitus or blood using a mechanical

Figure 4 Three quarter prone position

sucker, the positioning of an oropharyngeal airway or endotracheal tube may be necessary to maintain an effective airway. The casualty should then be placed in the three quarter prone (recovery or coma) position and the airway and posture checked frequently.

Three quarter prone position   The casualty is placed on his side with his thorax at an angle of 45 degrees to the horizontal, midway between the prone and lateral positions. The chest may be supported by a pillow, but care should be taken to avoid undue pressure on the chest wall which might interfere with breathing. The head is extended to provide a free airway and the uppermost arm is flexed in front of the trunk, with the hand under the jaw, to provide additional support. The under arm is placed behind the back. To maintain the position and to prevent the patient from rolling onto his face or back, either lower limb is flexed at the hip and knee whilst the other limb remains extended. The choice of which leg to flex may be determined by the casualty's wounds. The position is more stable when the under leg is flexed, but when the casualty is placed on a stretcher, pressure on the lateral popliteal nerve may later result in foot drop.

Prone position   In the case of maxillo-facial wounds, the prone position may be valuable in maintaining the airway. It allows blood and secretions to drain from the mouth and prevents the tongue from falling back too far. The casualty is placed on a stretcher with his face projecting beyond the canvas, the forehead being supported by bandages secured between the stretcher handles. In any case where difficulty is experienced in maintaining a clear airway, consideration should be given to performing a tracheostomy or cricothyroidotomy, procedures which may be life saving.

Stabilization of pulmonary ventilation   Chest wounds may interfere seriously with respiration. A sucking chest wound implies an **open pneumothorax.** Air entering or being expelled through the penetrating wound gives rise to a characteristic sucking noise. Because the chest is open, the normal negative intrathoracic pressure becomes equal to the atmospheric pressure. The equalization of the intrapleural and atmospheric pressure results in alteration of pulmonary physiology. Therefore the wound must be sealed immediately by an airtight occlusive dressing. It should be closed by a sterile gauze dressing secured by tight adhesive strapping or on occasion by the insertion of a few temporary sutures. All penetrating wounds of the chest wall must be considered as sucking wounds and treated in this way.

A **tension pneumothorax** exists when the intrapleural pressure exceeds the atmospheric pressure and may occur in penetrating wounds of the chest of the so-called ball valve type in which air may enter but not escape from the chest. However, it is more often seen in lacerations of the lung or bronchus when the chest wall is intact. Tension pneumothorax is a true emergency which requires immediate treatment. It can be recognized by the normal signs of pneumothorax combined with displacement of the trachea and apex beat of the heart to the opposite side. It is treated by the insertion of a large bore chest tube with a one-way (Heimlich) valve through the second or third intercostal space in the mid-clavicular line. A penetrating wound, if present, requires to be treated in the manner already described.

Flail chest is the result of a crush injury to the chest producing double fractures of one or more ribs. The mobilized part of the chest wall moves paradoxically, being drawn inwards in inspiration and blown outwards in expiration. This results in to and fro movement of the mediastinum and transference of air from lung to lung across the carina. The unstable chest wall must be splinted by firmly strapping the affected area.

Arrest of haemorrhage   Virtually all wounds bleed to some extent, either internally or externally, but major haemorrhage endangering life normally results from the laceration of a major vessel.

Severe internal bleeding can only be controlled by surgery and until this can be undertaken, transfusions with plasma substitute and/or crystalloid solutions will be necessary to keep the patient alive. Whole blood is not available at RAP level and is not normally held forward of a field hospital. Such cases require urgent and speedy evacuation.

External haemorrhage will usually cease after firm application of a field dressing together with direct manual pressure over the wound for five minutes. If bleeding continues after this a major vessel is probably involved and special measures are necessary to stop it. Continued bleeding is usually, but not always, arterial and commonly results from a laceration of a large vessel which, being incomplete, prevents vessel retraction. When the vessel is completely divided, bleeding usually ceases.

The following methods are available for controlling haemorrhage:
Direct pressure on the vessel within the wound   In the majority of cases, bleeding can be effectively controlled by applying direct pressure to the wound over a pad such as a field dressing. The pad is then bound firmly into place, taking care not to impede the circulation. It should be

remembered that this method of controlling haemorrhage is not always immediately effective and therefore more heroic measures should not be undertaken until direct pressure has obviously failed to stop the bleeding.
Securing the bleeding vessel with a haemostat   If pressure dressings fail to control haemorrhage from a wound, the bleeding vessel may be secured using a haemostat. In this case, the vessel must be clearly visible and proximal control over the pressure point is essential before clamping of the vessel can be attempted. Blind jabbing with a haemostat in a pool of blood is invariably unsuccessful and will cause damage. Once in position, the haemostat should be left in situ and incorporated in the dressing, no attempt being made to ligate the vessel at this stage.
Packing the wound   When other measures fail, deep inaccessible bleeding may be controlled by packing the wound with broad strips of folded gauze. The pack can be held in position, if necessary, by deep through and through sutures which take in a bite of uninjured tissue, well wide of the wound edges. Often such sutures alone will control deep bleeding. It should be noted that these measures are only used when simpler means fail and may avoid the use of a tourniquet.
Use of a tourniquet   Tourniquets are rarely required for the control of bleeding and should only be used when all other methods fail, the severity of the haemorrhage is considered to be a danger to life and the risk of loss of the limb concerned is accepted. Correctly applied, a tourniquet will save life; improperly applied it may increase bleeding and hasten death by restricting venous return from the limb without occluding its arterial supply. The application of a tourniquet is strictly a first aid measure to enable a casualty to reach the RAP alive. Evacuation rearward of the RAP with a tourniquet in place may seriously imperil the limb. The RMO must carefully assess the need for it, balancing the risk of torrential bleeding following its removal, against the risk of losing the limb if it remains in place. In the event of the casualty being evacuated from the RAP with a tourniquet in place, details of the time of application and site of the tourniquet must be recorded on the field medical card, the casualty must be marked with a 'T' on his forehead and be evacuated by fastest means.

Treatment of shock   It is of great importance that wound shock should be recognized quickly and that measures be instituted to combat it as soon as possible. Whilst blood is not available at RAP level and it maybe unwise to delay the evacuation of casualties unduly in order to resuscitate them, intravenous (N) fluids can be life saving.

Whilst crystalloid solutions remain only temporarily in the circulation after rapid absorption, 1 to 2 litres of Hartmann's solution given rapidly before evacuation will materially improve the casualty's condition, particularly when dehydration is evident, as is frequently the case.

Ideally, resuscitative measures should be continued during evacuation and the casualty transported with the foot of the stretcher raised. Peripheral vasodilatation caused by overheating the casualty should be avoided, but the patient needs protection from the elements.

Splinting of fractures and of major soft tissue wounds Dressings and splints which have been applied previously and appear satisfactory should not be disturbed. All fractures and major soft tissue wounds must be adequately splinted and supported before the casualty is evacuated, taking care to avoid interfering with the circulation to the limb. This prevents undue movement at the fracture site and reduces the damage done to surrounding tissues by sharp bone fragments.

Thomas splints and Cramer wire splintage are available at the RAP along with plaster of Paris pre-cast slabs. Care should be taken to ensure that all splintage applied is adequately padded.

Thomas splint Fractures of the femoral shaft, those around the knee joint and of the upper two thirds of the tibia, as well as massive soft tissue wounds of the leg, should be immobilized using the Thomas splint. Traction should not be excessive and the leg inspected frequently to check the circulation and to make necessary adjustments. The limb must be adequately supported and fixed within the splint and the latter fixed to the stretcher for transportation.

Cramer wire splintage Cramer wire splints are useful for the support of fractures of the upper limb and should be well padded before application. In the absence of splints, an injured arm can be effectively supported by bandaging it to the side of the chest and supporting the forearm in a sling.

Plaster of Paris splints The following points should be noted:
a Plaster slabs must not encircle more than three quarters of the limb circumference.
b Slabs should be applied to the sides of the limb.
c Care should be taken to avoid ridging of the inner surfaces of the plaster.
d Support bandages must exert only gentle, uniform pressure along the full length of the slab.

e All supporting bandages must be cut through along the whole length of the limb before evacuation.

f The slab should be covered with cotton wool before rebandaging.

g The slab may be reinforced by raising a longitudinal ridge on the outside by pinching up the bandage with the fingers.

Inflatable splints   Inflatable splints are not issued at RAP level and are suitable only for short evacuation journeys.

Burn wounds

a *First aid*   In general, clothing should not be removed unless it is smouldering or soaked in chemical agents. The Roehampton Burns Dressing should be applied to cover the burned area. If the hands are burned the best cover is a simple polythene bag closed at the wrist by the patient's own shirt sleeve or by a non constricting bandage. No other local treatment should be attempted.

b *Airway*   In all cases of burns involving the face, inhalation burns must be suspected and the patency of the airway should be assessed.

c *Resuscitation*

(1) Oral fluids for burns less than 15 per cent body surface area (BSA). Fluids should be given frequently by mouth. The ideal oral fluid is water to which has been added common salt and sodium bicarbonate – 5 grams salt and 4 grams bicarbonate per litre. (Moyer's solution.) Tablets are available for the simple production of this solution in the field.

(2) IV fluids for burns over 15 per cent BSA. Severely and extensively burned patients must be evacuated with all haste before shock becomes established. Once shock sets in they travel badly. Resuscitation with IV Hartmann's solution should be commenced at this echelon prior to evacuation.

d *Sedation*   Where the burn is essentially epidermal, pain can be very severe and morphine intravenously is the drug of choice. In deeper burns anxiety and restlessness are more common, and Valium given intravenously may be of great value.

e *Antibiotics*   Penicillin therapy should be commenced in the larger burns.

f *Anti tetanus prophylaxis*   Tetanus toxoid to boost immunity, as in any other wound, should be administered routinely.

Control of infection   All battle wounds are considered to be infected from the outset and antibiotics administered as a therapeutic measure. Tetanus toxoid is given routinely to prevent the development of tetanus. All drugs given to the casualty must be recorded on the Field Medical Card, together with the dose given and the time administered.

Penicillin   Crystalline long acting benethamine penicillin is the antibiotic of choice to be given in doses of 1.5 mega units six hourly. In the case of abdominal wounding, ampicillin is given in addition, using an initial loading dose of 1 g intramuscularly (IM).

Tetracycline   Penicillin sensitive individuals should be treated with tetracycline, the initial dosage to be used being 1 g IM.

Sulphadimidine   Head injuries are given sulphadimidine 1 g IM in addition to penicillin.

Tetanus toxoid   All soldiers have been actively immunized against tetanus and 0.5 ml of tetanus toxoid is given routinely at the RAP to boost their immunity. Tenanus antitoxin (ATS) is not to be used.

Relief of pain   Pain may be alleviated by the use of analgesic and narcotic drugs, by effective immobilization of the injured part and by gentle handling of the casualty at all stages during evacuation.

Careful assessment should be made of the casualty's requirement for pain relieving drugs and unnecessary medication avoided. Morphine remains a most effective drug for the relief of severe pain, but should not be given routinely to all wounded and should be avoided in cases with diminished level of consciousness or in the presence of respiratory embarrassment.

Morphine is normally administered in 15 mg doses and care should be taken to ensure that it is given intramuscularly and not subcutaneously. In the latter case, absorption is slow in the shocked individual and there is a danger of overdosage resulting from the later rapid absorption of repeated subcutaneous doses when resuscitation restores the circulation. Intravenous morphine may be preferable in the severely shocked individual where a rapid effect is required. Caution is necessary to avoid respiratory centre depression and the first dose should not exceed 10 mg.

The dosage of all drugs and the time administered must be recorded on the field medical card and in the case of morphine the casualty's forehead should be clearly marked with an 'M' using a skin pencil.

Combat of dehydration

Casualties are frequently dehydrated on arrival at the RAP, especially in hot weather or in the tropics. This can be serious and add to the circulatory problems resulting from shock. Fluid by mouth is the ideal way of rehydration provided it is not contraindicated, as in the case of abdominal wounds or severe shock which interferes with gastro-intestinal absorption. Intravenous Hartmann's Solution should be given in these cases.

Medical documentation

Medical documentation is initiated at the RAP using the field medical card F Med 26. The fact that the casualty, in the course of his evacuation, passes through several medical posts emphasizes the need for accurate, clear and concise recording of information.

The field medical card, which is securely attached to the casualty, records his administrative details, the date and time of wounding, location and nature of the injury, and essential clinical information, including drugs administered with timing and dosage.

Assessment of priorities for evacuation

The rapid evacuation of casualties who require surgical treatment is vital in reducing the mortality of the wounded. However, not all casualties need to be evacuated and a proportion, after receiving treatment at the RAP, will be fit to return to their units for duty.

Those casualties who require to be evacuated must be sorted into priorities based on their need for surgery and/or resuscitation. The following classification is used, priority one cases being regarded as those requiring most urgent evacuation:

Priority one   Cases requiring resuscitation and early surgery:
a Respiratory emergencies:
   (1) Asphyxia due to respiratory obstruction.
   (2) Maxillo-facial wounds with established or imminent asphyxia.
   (3) Sucking wounds of chest.
   (4) Tension pneumothorax.
b Shock due to:
   (1) Major haemorrhage from visceral injuries, cardio-pericardial injuries or wounds with massive muscle damage.
   (2) Multiple wounds and major fractures;
   (3) Severe burns over 20 per cent BSA.

Priority two   Cases requiring early surgery and possible resuscitation:
a Visceral injuries including perforations of the gastro-intestinal tract; wounds of the genito - urinary tract and thoracic injuries without asphyxia.
b Major vessel injuries requiring repair.
c Brain and spinal injuries, open or closed, requiring decompression.
d Burns under 20 per cent BSA of certain locations, eg face, hands, feet, genitalia and perineum.

Priority three
a All other brain and spinal injuries.
b Soft tissue injuries requiring wound toilet.
c Lesser fractures and dislocations.
d Eye injuries.
e Maxillo - facial injuries without asphyxia.
f Burns of other locations under 20 per cent BSA.

Air evacuation   The availability of helicopters for air evacuation is a major factor in determining their utilization for the evacuation of casualties from forward areas. In addition, their use will be governed by the tactical situation, air superiority, weather and serviceability factors. Direct evacuation from RAP to field hospital for surgery, overflying the divisional field ambulance medical facility, represents the ideal situation for priority one cases.

Treatment of specific injuries

Chest wounds   (See under stabilization of pulmonary ventilation.) Penetrating wounds of the chest, particularly those associated with a tension pneumothorax, can provide a serious emergency requiring urgent treatment to prevent a fatal outcome. In contrast, penetrating chest wounds, without complication, have a good prognosis and often require simple treatment only with a wound dressing held in position with adhesive strapping.

Sucking wounds of chest   This injury implies an open pneumothorax which requires to be sealed immediately by means of an airtight occlusive dressing to prevent the occurrence of paradoxical respiration. The wound is best dealt with by means of a paraffin gauze dressing held in place by a pack secured by adhesive strapping. Occasionally, the wound requires closing by means of a few temporary sutures.

Tension pneumothorax   Tension pneumothorax may occur with penetrating wounds of the chest, and when the chest wound is valvular. Under these circumstances, air becomes trapped in the pleural space and as the pneumothorax increases the lung becomes compressed and mediastinal shift occurs. Having sealed the chest wound, it is necessary to reduce the pressure in the pleural space by introducing a wide bore needle with Heimlich or flutter valve attached.

Flail chest   This condition results when the rigidity of the chest wall is lost as a result of multiple fractures of the ribs. Paradoxical respiration ensues. The chest wall must be splinted by adhesive strapping applied to the affected area.

Abdominal wounds   It is important to recognize the occurrence of abdominal wounding, particularly when injury to adjacent areas occurs which may involve the abdominal cavity. Wounds of the chest and buttocks may extend into the abdomen.

After controlling any gross bleeding from the abdominal wall, the wound should be covered with a large, dry, sterile dressing. If evisceration has occurred, the dressing used should be moistened with sterile normal saline, but no attempt made to return eviscerated gut or omentum to the abdomen. No fluid should be given by mouth. A nasogastric tube should be passed and an indwelling catheter placed in the bladder. Intravenous fluid therapy with Hartmann's Solution should be commenced. Most patients require narcotics in adequate dosage together with appropriate antibiotic therapy, benzyl penicillin supplemented by ampicillin and metronidazole 500 mg given eight hourly intravenously for two days followed by 1 g by suppository or tablet eight hourly for three days.

Patients with abdominal wounds have a high priority for evacuation and if there is evidence of intra - abdominal bleeding, the urgency is increased. Helicopter evacuation is ideal for these casualties who, when possible, should be evacuated direct to surgical facilities.

Head injuries   All casualties with head injuries require careful assessment in order to determine the degree of neurological involvement. It is essential to maintain accurate records of the level of consciousness and of the neurological signs. These will materially assist in the later management of the case. Head injury cases should be told to avoid blowing the nose, especially in naso-maxillary injuries, owing to the risk of aerocele and spread of infection. Morphine should not be given because of its depressant action and the patient should be evacuated in the three quarter prone position and care taken to ensure that the head is not positioned lower than the rest of the body.

Spinal injuries   The casualty with a spinal injury should be placed in a supine position on a stretcher and an attempt made, with suitable padding, to maintain the normal spinal curves. The patient must be warned not to attempt to move himself and if it is found necessary to move him, this should be done with a minimum of two attendants carrying out the lift 'in one piece'. In the case of cervical spine injuries, moderate neck traction should be maintained during lifting and the head immobilized on the stretcher using sandbags. Hard objects liable to produce pressure sores should be removed from the casualty's clothing.

Maxillo-facial injuries   Maxillo-facial injuries are prone to excessive bleeding and this fact adds to the major problem of securing and maintaining a clear airway. The mouth and pharynx must be cleared of clot, loose fragments and foreign bodies, with a swab wrapped around the finger, and use made of a mechanical sucker to remove secretions, blood and vomitus. If the tongue is floating it must be kept well forward by means of traction on a suture inserted through its dorsum. A nasopharyngeal or an endotracheal tube or tracheostomy may be necessary and particular attention must be given to the position of the patient during evacuation. The sitting, three quarter prone or prone position with the face projecting beyond the stretcher canvas and forehead supported by bandages between the handles may be used according to the circumstances and the casualty's state of consciousness. Firm pressure over a pad will normally stop bleeding and care should be taken to preserve tissue, replace detached skin flaps in an anatomical position and avoid twisting and pressure on pedicles. Dressings should fit snugly into the wound and should extend beyond it. Supporting bandages or strapping should be arranged so that pressure on the symphysis menti is upwards and not backwards.

Hand injuries   Apart from obtaining haemostasis, as little as possible should be done to hand wounds at RAP level and no tissue should be trimmed away. With the hand elevated, a sterile first field dressing is applied firmly to the wound and held there until bleeding stops. This dressing is then secured in position by a firm bandage whilst the limb is still elevated. The hand is supported in the position of function using a plaster gutter or Cramer wire padded splint, with the wrist moderately dorsi flexed and the fingers supported in flexion over a rolled bandage or suitable pad. The hand is kept elevated during evacuation by means of an arm sling.

Traumatic amputations The main concern in the treatment of a traumatic amputation is the control of haemorrhage which should be achieved by means of a pressure dressing. A tourniquet should only be used as a last resort and in this case, should be applied as low as possible. In the case of incomplete severance of the limb, completion of the amputation may be necessary. The limb should be immobilized on a splint.

Injuries to the genito-urinary tract External genitalia are frequently involved in wounds of the lower part of the genito-urinary tract. Haemorrhage is controlled by pressure dressings, but occasionally it will be found necessary to insert temporary sutures to assist in stopping bleeding. Tissues should be carefully preserved. In all cases, an indwelling catheter should be inserted into the bladder. When this is found impossible and the bladder is or becomes distended, a suprapubic cannula should be inserted.

Major ear and eye injuries Major ear and eye injuries should be evacuated with the least possible interference at this level. When the eyeball has been perforated, both eyes must be covered with suitable dressings and the casualty evacuated as a stretcher case. The ears should never be syringed and installation of drops and powders should be avoided. Ear injuries should be treated by the application of an external sterile dressing only.

CASUALTY MANAGEMENT WITHIN SECOND ECHELON

The second echelon medical unit is the field ambulance and treatment is afforded to the casualty at the two Dressing Stations of this unit. Since surgery is not normally available at this level, all treatment is directed to continuing and reinforcing, if necessary, the first aid and resuscitative measures already commenced at the RAP. The casualty is prepared for evacuation and priorities are re-assessed with the aim of ensuring that those cases requiring urgent surgery reach the field hospital as soon as possible.

The casualty clearing element of the field ambulance is organized into three departments, Reception, Treatment and Evacuation:

a *Reception department* Immediately on arrival, the casualty's condition is checked and emergency life saving procedures instituted to make sure that his airway is clear and major haemorrhage is being controlled. A more detailed assessment determines the requirement for further resuscitative measures and priorities are allocated for treatment and evacuation. Essential and mainly clinical documentation is recorded on the field medical card.

b *Treatment department* The treatment afforded to the casualty complements that instituted at the RAP and the principles outlined above are unchanged. Adequate and satisfactory dressings should not be disturbed and every effort made to avoid delay in evacuating surgical casualties.

(1) *Management of asphyxia* A clear airway must be maintained and this is of particular importance in the unconscious casualty. Reconsideration should be given to the need for intubation and for tracheostomy. Perforating wounds of the chest wall require special assessment to ascertain that the wound is adequately sealed and that tension pneumothorax is avoided. Chest drains and one way air valves require checking.

(2) *Arrest of haemorrhage* Inadequately controlled bleeding requires further treatment: pressure dressings may need adjustment, lacerated vessels may need securing and the requirement to pack and/or insert deep sutures to secure haemostasis considered. Blood is not available at field ambulance level, but here the casualty may receive dextran infusion in addition to Hartmann's Solution.

(3) *Fracture and major soft tissue wounds* These injuries will already have received first aid splinting at the RAP, but this may only have been of a temporary nature. Further adjustment and improvement may be necessary to ensure immobilization in order to maintain shock during evacuation. This may require the use of plaster of Paris combined with other forms of splinting. Plaster of Paris splints must never be applied skin tight, adequate padding is necessary and valving of the plaster is essential.

(4) *Control of infection* The field medical card should be checked in order to determine what treatment has been given to the casualty. Active immunization against tetanus will be given and antibiotics commenced if this has not already been done.

(5) *Relief of pain* The casualty may have already received analgesics or narcotics at the RAP and a careful assessment must be made of his requirements. It is important to remember that shock may have interfered with the absorption of morphine and care should be taken when making the decision to repeat its administration.

c *Evacuation department* The casualty, having received treatment, awaits evacuation to the field hospital in this department. Careful assessment of the casualty's condition must be maintained in order to recognize changes in his condition which may alter his priority for evacuation or require further treatment. Documentation is completed and checked and refreshment is provided for those casualties able to take it.

Air evacuation

Whenever possible, helicopters should be utilized for the evacuation of priority one and two cases to the field hospital, but the constraints listed in Chapter 1 also apply at this level.

MEDICAL TREATMENT AVAILABLE WITHIN FIRST MEDICAL ECHELON IN A CHEMICAL ENVIRONMENT

At the point of wounding

The casualty is dependent upon self administered first aid or that given by his comrade. The scope of treatment available is that contained in the First Aid Training Objectives (All Arms), Objectives 1–10, although the treatment possible under the circumstances of a chemical attack is likely to be severely curtailed. The preservation of an airway and the control of haemorrhage continue to be of utmost importance.

Local decontamination of the wound requires to be undertaken prior to the application of the first aid dressing and whenever possible, a repair to the protective clothing affected. When nerve agent effects are apparent, atropine administration, utilizing the casualty's own supply, should be commenced.

At the squadron, company or combat team aid post

At the squadron, company or combat team aid post, it may be possible to improve on the simple first aid measures already undertaken. Further steps can be taken to ensure the maintenance of the casualty's airway, arrest uncontrolled haemorrhage, adjust dressings and apply simple splintage over protective clothing. It is unlikely that a mechanical means of ventilating the asphyxiated patient will be available at this level and rapid transference of the casualty to the RAP is necessary for this procedure to be undertaken.

At the regimental or battle group aid post

At the RAP, the following procedures are normally undertaken:
a   Maintenance of the airway.
b   Arrest of haemorrhage.
c   Treatment of shock.
d   Splintage of fractures and major soft tissue wounds.
e   Control of infection.
f   Relief of pain.
g   Combat of dehydration.
h   Medical documentation.
j   Assessment of priorities for evacuation.

In a chemical environment and in the absence of a liquid hazard, it should be possible, provided the casualty is able to wear a respirator, to carry out fully almost all the procedures outlined above. However, maintenance of the airway, particularly in the case of the unconscious casualty, is likely to be extremely difficult.

The presence of liquid agent will severely limit the treatment possible, which may be restricted to that which can be undertaken with both medical attendant and casualty clothed in NBC suits. Local decontamination of the wound will be necessary, together with repair of the breached protective clothing and application of splintage over it. The time taken to undertake these procedures will be a further limiting factor.

The fact that chemical casualties may be complicated by a surgical or medical condition causes difficulty in deciding on the treatment priority. In general the following are the priorities of treatment:
a   Treatment of asphyxia, maintenance of the airway and assisted ventilation using a Porton or multi - outlet resuscitator.

b   Arrest of haemorrhage.
c   Use of chemical antidotes (atropine and oximes).
d   Local wound decontamination and repair of breaches in protective clothing.
e   Treatment of those surgical conditions endangering life.

Use of the chemical proof casualty bag

The full or half casualty bag will be available at RAP level for the protection of casualties from both liquid and vapour agents. It may be life saving in the case of those casualties who, because of injury to the head or face, are unable to wear a protective mask. The casualty bag is so constructed as to allow ease of access, sufficiently large to allow the accommodation of a Thomas splint, and permits intravenous therapy to be instituted without loss of its protective properties.

Summary

The use of chemical agents makes the problem of treating casualties within the first medical echelon hazardous and more difficult, but does not alter the aim of that treatment nor the principles involved. The management of asphyxia and the maintenance of the airway are likely to be particularly difficult and further limitations will be imposed by the necessity for both casualty and medical attendant to wear protective clothing.

It is imperative that medical personnel have a complete and full knowledge of chemical agents and their effects and the use of the casualty bag is essential for the treatment of casualties unable to wear a respirator.

CHAPTER 3

Shock and resuscitation

Introduction

Shock is variably classified as hypovolaemic, septic, cardiogenic and vaso-vagal.

Such distinctions distract attention from the fact that there is always a multiple system biological failure with a low cardiac output. This leads to deterioration of the microcirculation and dysfunction of cellular metabolism, particularly noticeable in liver, kidney, lung and skeletal muscle.

The patho-physiology of wounding

Wounding provokes local as well as systemic responses. The local tissue destruction evokes systemic responses through neurogenic and humoral pathways proportional to the extent of the lesion. The main factors are blood and/or fluid loss, tissue devitalization, pain and, ultimately, the effects of infection. The respiratory and cardiovascular systems are primarily affected and involved in the defence mechanisms of the body. Impaired respiratory function with reduced availability of oxygen as well as vasoconstriction with altered distribution of the reduced circulating blood volume to the tissues are factors responsible for deterioration of cellular metabolism. Derangement of function occurs in organs such as the brain, kidney, liver and intestine, giving rise to a variety of symptoms in an unpredictable pattern.

Many effects of injury are obviously harmful while others serve as defence mechanisms. Haemorrhage is harmful but the resulting haemodilution counteracts the oligaemia. At the same time the oxygen carrying capacity of the blood is reduced. The post-traumatic effects are the result of harmless or beneficial physiological mechanisms which become pathological with prolonged or excessive action, and subsequently irreversible. Thus, a serious or even fatal disorder may occur when the duration and/or degree of effects are prolonged.

Definition of shock

Shock is the clinical picture arising from a compensation beyond the limit of circulatory homeostasis and must not be regarded as a static condition. It reflects the dynamic course of the body's adaptation to injury which may result either in improvement or become irreversible; when and how this is established cannot be assessed clinically or by any laboratory method.

The term shock should be used merely to indicate the clinical syndrome resulting from impaired circulation as characterized by tachypnoea, reduced pulse pressure, yielding mean arterial pressure, rising pulse rate, colour changes in the skin (from pallor to cyanosis) with or without sweating, cooling of the periphery, lowering of body temperature, thirst and mental disinterest in the surroundings.

Classification according to pathogenic patterns

In recent years the general trend has been to explain the development of shock on a *hypovolaemic, toxic or cardiogenic basis*.

Hypovolaemia is the problem in severe accident victims and in patients after major elective surgery. There is a demonstratable correlation between the extent of blood loss and the metabolic response. Prolonged shock induces severe changes in carbohydrate and lipid metabolism. Examples of these are altered nitrogen balance, post-traumatic glycosuria and the occurrence of microglobules in peripheral blood. Fat embolism has been thought to reflect altered metabolic pathways in spite of cogent evidence of its origin from the marrow of fractured bones. Recent experience has shown that, in hypovolaemia, blood volume replacement is best carried out by balanced electrolyte solutions with the addition of whole blood as necessary.

Severe infection and septicaemia commonly cause circulatory collapse through the release of endotoxins. This may result from massive killing of bacteria by antibiotics. The pattern of the resulting shock is complex, in which the lipopolysaccharide part of the gram-negative bacterial cell wall plays an important role. The treatment of the condition requires circulatory support as used in hypovolaemic states in addition to antimicrobial chemotherapy.

Cardiogenic shock is typically seen in myocardial infarction. New modalities having dramatic effects on the clinical course are vasodilatory therapy and mechanical support of the failing ventricle. It is of interest in the treatment of shock that there is a release of a myocardial depressant substance from the splanchnic area in particular when exposed to hypoxia, ischaemia or trauma. Myocardial depression may be responsible for prolonged low arterial pressure in spite of apparently adequate volume restitution. Further administration of fluid (blood or plasma expanders) in these circumstances may be unwise as it can weaken myocardial contractility and add to its work load.

Primary or neurogenic shock

This term has survived as vaso-vagal shock, although vaso-vagal hypotension is a more appropriate name.

Strong sensory and emotional stimuli may produce widespread vaso-dilation (and perhaps inhibit vasoconstriction). Following minor trauma or emotional upset pooling reduces the volume of circulating blood. Bradycardia points to vagal activity as a part of the syndrome. Some individuals are more susceptible to it than others. It may occur in association with the manipulation of fractures or other procedures, such as catheterization. It can occur in donors, although the mechanism of fainting may be the result of blood volume reduction.

A variety of signs and symptoms may follow such as yawning, a feeling of heat, sweating, waning of consciousness, fainting and perhaps vomiting; pallor and coolness of the skin, a slow pulse rate, a low systolic pressure and sighing deep respirations. The sign of outstanding clinical significance is the slow pulse. It is important to note that a large dose of atropine given preoperatively may prevent the usual bradycardia. In its transitory form, recovery follows recumbency or lowering of the head. If rapid improvement does not follow in a patient who has been exposed to trauma a more detailed re-examination for haemorrhage is necessary. Should hypotension last for 20 minutes resuscitation with fluid infusion is necessary.

Patients must be watched carefully if vaso-vagal hypotension is complicated by blood loss, as they are liable to collapse suddenly during the induction of anaesthesia.

In head injuries the systolic blood pressure may fall, accompanied by a slow or irregular pulse with irregular, periodic or stertorous respiration. These effects are usually due to disturbance of the medullary centres. In some spinal injuries (as with spinal anaesthesia) paralysis of the vaso-motor fibres in the thoraco-lumbar outflow results in hypotension.

Predisposing and aggravating factors in shock

The degree of circulatory collapse may be hastened or aggravated by fear, fatigue, pain caused by movement of the injured parts, rough handling during evacuation, delay in the application of splints or sudden shifting of the position of the patient. Other factors include dehydration with depletion of electrolytes due to severe vomiting, diarrhoea or sweating.

Gross dehydration is encountered especially in tropical conditions and may lead to a state equivalent to that of hypovolaemic shock. A fighting soldier is invariably short of fluid when wounded. He may lose as much as four litres of sweat in a few hours.

In colder climates the application of external heat in the form of hot water bottles and shock cradles, etc, is particularly dangerous, as they interfere with reactive vasoconstriction.

Over-dosage of morphia, the induction of anaesthesia, prolonged or rough operating, all aggravate shock.

Clinical features

The symptoms are progressive and dependent on the severity of the injury and the amount of fluid loss. Several hours are usually required for the full development of the classical picture, but in some patients the onset may be quick and deterioration rapid. It is important to realize that gross circulatory embarrassment, as shown by a falling blood pressure, may occur late. This is a serious phenomenon, which should be forestalled wherever possible.

Intense peripheral and visceral vasoconstriction is the compensatory mechanism after acute and severe blood volume reduction, enabling the circulation to make the best use of such blood as remains. Thus the patient becomes intensely pale with a cold periphery. At the same time, by relief action, through vagal and sympathetic centres, the pulse becomes rapid, sweating is marked and there may be a tendency to vomit. Consciousness of pain is very variable. The mental state is often deceptively alert and euphoric in the early stages, sometimes tempered with apprehension and an ominous garrulity, but later turns to apathy. Nature's first attempt at repair is to absorb tissue fluid into the circulation in an effort to restore blood volume; this leads to a sensation of thirst. The natural process of repair has a rapid onset, but takes time to be effective and in cases of severe blood loss cannot be accomplished quickly enough to prevent circulatory collapse. In these circumstances, a vicious circle begins. There

Grading of Shock*

Degree of shock	Blood pressure (approx)	Pulse quality	Skin Temperature	Skin Colour	Circulation (response to pressure blanching)	Thirst	Mental state
None	Normal	Normal	Normal	Normal	Normal	Normal	Clear and distressed
Slight	To 20 per cent decrease	Normal	Cool	Pale	Definite slowing	Normal	Clear and distressed
Moderate	Decreased 20 per cent to 40 per cent	Definite decrease in volume	Cool	Pale	Definite slowing	Definite	Clear and some apathy unless stimulated
Severe	Decreased 40 per cent to non recordable	Weak to imperceptible	Cold	Ashen to cyanotic (mottling)	Very sluggish	Severe	Apathetic to comatose; little distress except thirst

*It will be observed that sweating, nausea and vomiting are not mentioned in this table, although these criteria were emphasized in World War I reports. They are not common and not reliable in estimating the extent of shock. They are probably more closely related to psychological factors, the nature of the wound or morphine administration than they are to shock. The pulse rate alone can be influenced by too many other factors to be of much value in estimating degree of shock; pulse quality, however, is important. The factors in the last three columns of the table should be considered when evaluating a patient's condition, and recorded.

is a loss of compensatory powers leading to imperfect cardiac filling and inadequate cardiac output, manifested by a falling blood pressure, peripheral cyanosis and other signs of circulatory failure. Unless treated this will soon become irreversible and finally fatal.

Assessment of shock

The good clinician should recognize the fully established condition as well as the prodromal features which precede it. Neither the presence nor absence of the symptoms emphasized above is an exact indication of the gravity of the condition, because the response to injury varies with the individual. Overall assessment according to the extent and severity of the injuries is more important than individual signs or symptoms.

A serial record of the pulse rate, blood pressure, respiration and temperature should be kept and is most informative. The following factors are important:

a *Blood pressure* A falling blood pressure is always a definite and ominous sign, but individual capacity for compensatory vasoconstriction is a variable feature; it may be intense and maintain the blood pressure for a time, only to collapse suddenly and precipitate a more serious state than if the deterioration had been gradual. Some patients indeed react to blood volume reduction by over-compensation so that, even in the presence of serious injury, the blood pressure may be deceptively high. Nevertheless, the systolic blood pressure can usually be maintained at about 100 mm Hg so long as the blood loss is less than 30 per cent of the blood volume (3½ pints/2 litres).

b *The amount of tissue damage* is another important piece of evidence especially in limb wounds and injuries. The damage done will vary with the wounding agent, its momentum and the region involved, eg the shock following damage to the large muscles of the pelvis, buttock and thigh. Tissue damage can be roughly assessed by using the volume of the human hand as a standard. It is just under a half-litre. For surface wounds the area of the open hand, and for wounds in depth the size of the clenched fist, are used to visualize and estimate the damage.

Based on this concept, wounds may be assessed as:

Size of wound	Hand volume	Equivalent percentage loss of total blood volume*
Small	Less than 1	10
Moderate	1–3	20–40
Large	3–5	40
Very large	over 5	50

*It is notable that the lost blood need not reach the surface. A large vessel leakage may occur into the intramuscular spaces behind a small entrance wound.

c *Other evidence of injury* At the initial examination the quantity of blood or exudate seen on the dressings, clothing and stretcher is a rough guide to the external loss, but may be very deceptive. In closed limb injuries, measurement of the increased circumference of the injured side compared with the normal side will also help to indicate the extent of blood loss and tissue damage. A patient can bleed to death from a closed fracture of the femur or from bleeding in the retroperitoneal space (injury to renal vessels, inferior vena cava or the iliac vessels) without any blood appearing on the skin surface.

d *Variable factors in shock* If a low pressure with a fast pulse is discovered in a patient with only a small wound, an undetected injury or covert haemorrhage must be sought or suspected. Massive infection, such as gas gangrene, must also be excluded. Rapid and adequate transfusion, followed by suitable surgical treatment, is required in both cases. The rate of blood loss is more important than the amount lost and the more rapid the loss the sooner the development of shock.

Prolonged hypotension is more serious than a short-lasting fall in blood pressure because of the anoxia to vital 'cells' in the central nervous system, liver and kidneys. Altered permeability of the capillary wall makes the microcirculation ineffective. After the rapid loss of large quantities of blood the pulse may be impalpable, the blood pressure unrecordable, respiration gasping and spasmodic, consciousness lost and death imminent. Yet, provided this stage is only of short duration, recovery may follow adequate replacement of the blood loss by fast transfusion to restore the blood volume.

Organization of a Resuscitation Ward at the Forward Surgical Centre
Prompt preoperative resuscitation saves many lives. Examination and
sorting of casualties needs considerable clinical experience and acumen
and preliminary instruction of officers for resuscitation duties at a
centralized transfusion and resuscitation centre will frequently prove
rewarding.

The preoperative resuscitation ward should be large and sited close to
the operating theatre. Mobile X-ray apparatus will save unnecessary
moving of patients and good lighting, suction apparatus, oxygen and
masks, airways and tracheostomy instruments are basic requirements. A
generous supply of cuff sphygmomanometers and transfusion stands is
also necessary.

Gentle handling of the patient is important, who must be examined in
the first instance without removal of splints if they have been applied, and
without unnecessary handling before the degree of shock, if present, is
assessed.

Anti-shock treatment

Emergency measures   Only in cases of vascular injury should examination be delayed so that haemorrhage may be arrested or an immediate
infusion given as a matter of urgency.

A clear airway must be established, if necessary by endotracheal
intubation or tracheostomy. Sucking chest wounds must be made airtight
and a tension pneumothorax relieved by inserting a wide bore needle
through the second intercostal space.

Relief of pain (see Chapter 2, page 24)   Pain must be relieved at all stages
of evacuation and treatment. Absorption of morphine and other
substances after subcutaneous or intramuscular injection in shock is so
delayed that it should not be used. Where a rapid effect is required 10 mg
diluted in 10 ml of sterile normal saline should be given in one ml fractions
intravenously until relief is obtained.

If several doses have already been given subcutaneously or intramuscularly morphine poisoning may result, for which amiphenazole (daptazole)
30 mg is the antagonist. This dose may be repeated.

Restlessness   This usually indicates marked and progressive haemorrhage
rather than severe pain. This must be remembered before giving
morphine to allay it.

Transfusion should commence at once or the rate of a transfusion already running increased.

Warmth Wet clothing should be removed and dry covering provided. Though comforting to those suffering from cold and exposure but free of shock, warming will do harm in the treatment of oligaemic shock, as it encourages dilatation of surface vessels, further lowering of the blood pressure and loss of body fluids by perspiration.

Thirst Patients in shock are usually thirsty but should not be given oral fluids for two hours before the induction of anaesthesia.

Oxygen The administration of oxygen by mask or nasal tube is indicated in the management of shock associated with respiratory impairment such as chest injuries, especially due to blast, pulmonary irritants and carbon monoxide poisoning.

Oxygen administration also offers the necessary compensation for a reduced oxygen carrying power where there is a reduction of the circulatory red cell mass (low haematocrit value).

The choice of replacement fluid

The logical approach is to *use the fluid component lost from the circulation;* blood to replace blood loss, as in haemorrhage and wounds; plasma or serum to replace plasma loss, as in crush injuries or superficial burns; blood and plasma in deep burns or in burns associated with other wounds. Experience has taught the lesson, however, that resuscitation with electrolyte solutions enlarges the interstitial fluid compartment and offers the best assistance in the re-establishment of the stability of the circulation.

Evidence exists that the blood volume regulation is a multifactorial system of which only some of the essential aspects are known, such as:
a The Starling mechanism based on pressure differences over the capillary wall;
b The sodium concentration of the extracellular space;
c The red blood cell respiratory forces; and
d The pressure gradients existing over the blood capillary wall and the lymphatic capillaries.

Any therapeutic measure must aim at maintaining as many of these mechanisms as possible intact and so preventing the stage of clinically manifest shock.

Present day treatment principles are based on restoration of blood volume by primary use of some balanced electrolyte solution in order to achieve a speedy reopening of the capillary system in full. If damage to the capillary wall has developed pressure gradients are altered and colloid solutions (dextrans, etc) may be used. However, macromolecular changes seriously alter blood viscosity.

Crystalloid solutions such as saline or glucose remain only temporarily in the circulation. They are indicated in the treatment of dehydration, particularly in warm climates, during long journeys and arduous campaigning. Where oral fluid cannot be retained or is contraindicated, as in abdominal injuries the daily basic metabolic requirement of water (2000 ml daily or more) and sodium chloride must be added to the intravenous colloid fluids. Sufficient quantities should be given to ensure 1200–1500 ml of urine in 24 hours.

In principle resuscitation begins with rapid infusion of electrolyte solution in the amount of 2–3 litres. The effect of this initial measure is assessed by evaluating the patient's clinical response. The achieved result determines the next measure to be taken, ie operation or further observation. For surgical intervention the electrolyte infusion is continued in the preparatory period. If further observation is the choice, infusion is continued until facilities are available for laboratory assessment of the general state of the patient. If haematocrit values go below 30 per cent blood transfusion is required to ensure adequate red cell mass.

Blood The supply of safe, stored blood is limited because of the difficulties of availability, collection, storage, transportation and sterility. The collection of blood from walking wounded or from local donors is only possible under relatively peaceful conditions and on a small scale. For safe usage blood cannot, at present, be stored for more than 21–28 days. During storage, it is liable to haemolysis and the liberation of potassium. Simple recipient grouping with the anti-A only, may permit a choice between stored group O or group A blood. Where even such grouping facilities do not exist, only stored group O blood will be given.

Blood plasma This in dried form will keep well in any climate, and is recommended by some as a substitute for blood in emergency and in the treatment of shock due to burns. When reconstituted it contains the normal content of crystalloids. Five per cent dextrose in water is used as the reconstituting fluid. Plasma increases the blood volume less than does blood, in the ratio of 5 to 8; therefore, the quantity of plasma required to treat shock is greater than blood.

Dextran This is a plasma substitute and a blood volume expander. Dextran is available as dextran 40 (rheomacrodex), which improves flow properties, dextran 70 (macrodex) predominantly a plasma expander and dextran 110. It contains no protein and causes haemodilution and long lasting (days) depression of plasma proteins. Dextran 110 interferes with clotting; therefore a blood sample should be taken from the patient for grouping and cross matching before infusing dextran or other colloids as these cause aggregation of red corpuscles and may interfere with subsequent tests. If a sample is collected after giving dextran, the patient's red cells must be well washed in saline (at least three times) before his blood group is determined; care must be taken to distinguish pseudo - agglutination which may occur in the presence of dextran. The serum of blood samples collected after dextran infusion is not suitable for compatability testing, save by the anti-human globulin technique.

Dextran has been used in starting the resuscitation of severely shocked patients until blood grouping and compatibility tests can be carried out. Not more than 3 litres should be given, unless blood or plasma is not available and the requirement continues, because of the haemodilution and anaemia produced. Blood is needed if the haematocrit goes below 30. Dextran 110 is recommended by some for use in the management of burns.

Dextran is best used in a three per cent solution in 0.9 NaCl, a concentration corresponding to that of plasma-albumin. Reactions are few (about one per cent). If given to subjects with normal blood volume, overloading phenomena occur (precordial pain, tachycardia and headache).

Indications for blood transfusion

The presence of anaemia as a result of resuscitation with electrolyte or colloid solutions is a firm indication to start a transfusion (haematocrit values falling to below 30 per cent). Blood is needed as a part of the supportive treatment during anaesthesia and surgery and in the postoperative period.

If the systolic pressure falls below 100 mm Hg after wounding, infusion should begin as rapidly as possible, and every effort should be made to get the casualty to a resuscitation centre without delay. It is unwise to transport a patient with a systolic pressure below 80 mm Hg.

In less severe cases, if the pressure continues to decline, or remains just above 100 mm Hg for 20 minutes, the restoration of blood volume and pressure should be followed by immediate surgery, during and after which the patient may require to be sustained by further transfusion. There is, however, little point in fully resuscitating a casualty in an area away from surgical facilities unless transfusion can be adequately maintained during the subsequent journey so that he may arrive without deterioration at the place of initial surgery. Smoothness and shortness of ambulance car journeys with an infusion running and the use of helicopter or other air transport should be exploited whenever conditions permit. The use of adequately retained large bore intravenous polythene cannulae inserted well into the major veins, sufficient fluids and well-trained transfusion personnel to use these are essential to salvage critically damaged patients. In practice, it is extremely difficult to maintain a transfusion during evacuation. The speed and amount of intravenous transfusion must be adjusted with caution in those cases where there is embarrassment of the right side of the heart as with blast lung. Ensuring a free airway and stabilizing the chest wall and pleural cavities are important preliminaries (see also Chapter 19, page 203).

Aids to rapid transfusion

In severe shock the selected fluid should be given intravenously as quickly as it can be introduced. This can be helped:

a By exposing a vein without hesitation under local anaesthesia and inserting a cannula or polythene tubing of the largest calibre it will take.

b By inserting cannulae into more than one vein, preferably reaching the superior and/or inferior vena cava.

c By the application of local warmth to overcome any venospasm. Infusion of low temperature fluids in even moderate amounts may lead to hypothermia.

d By the injection of 2 ml of two per cent procaine hydrochloride into the drip or in the use of a local anaesthetic when exposing a vein, to overcome spasm.

e By applying pressure to the plastic bag or positive pressure to the air inlet of the infusion bottle by means of a pump, enema syringe, bellows or sphygmomanometer cuff. When air pressure methods are used the transfusion bag should never be left unattended, and positive pressure should never be applied to a bag containing less than a quarter of its full content. The danger of air embolism must always be kept in mind. This danger is eliminated by using a mechanical rotator pump. Blood is forced along the giving tube by rollers turned by a handle.

Common causes of stoppage of infusion

The main causes of stoppage of infusion are:

a *Displacement of the needle,* due to poor fixation.

b *Perforation of the vein wall* so that the needle point lies outside it.

c *Clotting* either in the needle, cannula or vein due to thrombophlebitis often related to long continued glucose infusions. It occurs more frequently in the leg than in the arm and may cause prolonged disability. For this reason, arm veins are preferred to leg veins. Using the arm allows the patient free movement. A vein in the forearm should be preferred to one at the cubital fossa.

Intra-arterial transfusions

If a quantity of blood is delivered fast enough by the intravenous route, this is more satisfactory and safer than intra-arterially so long as the heart is beating effectively. The intra-arterial route is not free from danger. Air embolism is a greater danger by artery than by veins, and arterial spasm may lead to digital or other distal gangrene.

Noradrenaline and other vasopressors

The use of these drugs is debatable, as a false sense of security may be given since the vasoconstrictors raise the blood pressure even though the circulatory volume has not been adequately restored. These drugs have been successfully used where profound hypotension has failed to yield to orthodox methods. Noradrenaline 8 mg per litre of dextrose solution is given intravenously at 20–30 drops per minute. If the response is poor a 4 mg ampoule of noradrenaline may be added every 10 minutes to the dextrose up to 64 mg per one litre.

Adrenaline, which is inotropic should be given with rogitine, an alpha blocker, to counteract its side effects. Dobutamine is a recently developed alternative, not vasodilator to the kidneys and not a peripheral vasoconstrictor.

Skin ischaemia, necrosis and superficial phlebitis are hazards, and these may be lessened by using pressure locally and adding the noradrenaline after the dextrose solution has been running for several minutes.

Transfusion reactions

Incompatibility The symptoms of a mismatched or incompatible transfusion may appear soon after beginning the transfusion or may be delayed until as much as 500 ml of blood has been given. The severity varies. In a severe reaction, headache, breathlessness, a sensation of heat, flushing and nausea or vomiting occur, often accompanied by pain in the loins. Abdominal and precordial pain may also occur. The pulse, full but slow initially, becomes impalpable. The blood pressure drops and cyanosis develops. A rigor usually occurs. Recovery from this circulatory collapse gradually takes place. Haemoglobinuria is present at first. Subsequently, oliguria and anuria may develop. If the patient has been given morphine, or been anaesthetized the symptoms will be modified or absent. If a haemolytic reaction is suspected, the transfusion must be stopped at once.

Fast transfusion Reactions due to fast transfusion take longer to develop and appear after larger quantities of blood have been given than above. They are not due to incompatible blood. These reactions consist of two phases:

a A phase of vasoconstriction which slows the speed of the drip. The patient becomes agitated and restless with pain in his limbs and back. Severe rigors may follow. Pallor, coldness and tachycardia occur and there is a rise in blood pressure, due to the vasoconstriction. If the drip is reduced in rate rigors abate but this delays the transfusion. They can be controlled with morphine and one ml of two per cent procaine or other adrenalin free local anaesthetic given into the receiving vein. These will relax the veno-spasm and allow the transfusion to proceed, aided, if need be, by positive pressure.

b A phase of vasodilation follows in about one hour with perspiration, flushing and a bounding pulse of over 100 per minute. The blood pressure falls, but if the transfusion has been adequate it should remain over 100 mm Hg. With the onset of this phase restlessness subsides.

Timing of surgery

The aim of resuscitation is to prepare a casualty for surgery. The condition of the patient suffering from, or liable, to shock must never be assumed to be static. He is either improving or deteriorating, and both processes are progressive. There is no advantage in deferring decisions about resuscitation until the condition is stabilized. The rule should be *'when in doubt, infuse'* and the further rule should be *'operate as soon as the patient is prepared for surgery'*.

It is somewhat more difficult to determine both the necessity for additional transfusion and the timing of surgery than these rules would indicate. One may assume that resuscitation has been successful when the blood pressure, pulse rate, colour of the skin and lips and the skin temperature approach normal; when peripheral venous filling is rapid; and when there is no further cyanosis or other evidence of capillary stasis. The pulse rate seldom reaches normal for a number of hours.

Frequent observations are essential. A useful test to determine the fitness of the patient for surgery is simply to raise his head for five minutes by tilting the head of the operating table or stretcher. If the blood pressure, the pulse rate and volume, and the colour of the skin and lips remain unchanged, he will probably be able to stand anaesthesia and surgery with support of further transfusions. If, however, the change of position is followed by pallor, faintness or deterioration in the blood pressure and the pulse rate volume, surgery must be delayed, and additional blood must be administered.

In some cases, because of the nature of the injury, it would be unreasonable to expect that the improvement accomplished by transfusion would be more than temporary, even if fluid and/or blood were given at a rate greater than the rate at which it was being lost. A patient with a gunshot wound of the abdomen, for instance, might respond well to the rapid infusion of 2–3 litres of fluid over a 30 minute period, but then deteriorate even if the rate of infusion were increased. In such cases, it is obviously necessary to open the abdomen at once to control the bleeding and to continue the infusion while the operation is being performed.

During the resuscitation of patients in severe shock a peak of improvement is usually reached, after which deterioration sets in. Increasing the rate of transfusion may result in another period of improvement, but the peak will not be as high as the first. The optimum time for operation is, therefore, just before the first peak is reached. These patients are poor risks, and frequent observation, cool judgement and an acceptance of the calculated risks of surgery at the time are necessary on the part of resuscitation officer, anaesthetist and surgeon if lives are to be saved.

A patient resuscitated from shock is more likely to relapse during or after surgery than a patient who has not been in shock. Since the majority of casualties require surgery, provision must be made not only to treat preoperative shock but to prevent the recurrence of shock during and after operation. If plasma, or a plasma substitute has been used before or during evacuation, whole blood must be used before and during operation.

Early operation is an important factor in survival of patients with large wounds accompanied by toxaemia from infection or from the products of tissue breakdown. Toxaemia may prevent the expected response from resuscitation. When large masses of tissues have been reduced to pulp, as in major fractures of the pelvis and wounds of the buttocks, thigh and calf, profound shock may ensue, and there may be no apparent response to transfusion until all devitalized tissue has been excised. In some cases, especially where there are multiple injuries, staged surgery may be necessary if the patient is to survive. The surgeon must deal with those conditions which imperil life. Later, after restoration of the blood volume, he can deal with less urgent problems, such as the debridement of minor wounds.

Failure to respond to resuscitation may be the result of severe infection. Gas gangrene should be suspected if the response is poor.

Management of shock in mass casualties

The aim will be to save as many patients as possible who have a good chance of survival. Those patients who require large amounts of replacement fluid will be set aside and treatment given to others. Five patients requiring 1 litre of fluid each might be treated first and saved, while the one patient who needs 5 litres of fluid would be treated last, if he survives.

CHAPTER 4

Infection in battle wounds

The purpose of treatment of war wounds is to prevent and control bacterial infection.

Causes and sources of infection

Three main classes of bacteria cause infection:

Clostridia These gram-positive anaerobic bacilli, which are almost universally distributed in soil and dirt of all kinds, are liable to be implanted in the wound at the time of its infliction. In addition, *Cl welchii*, which is almost always carried in the faeces and therefore often found on the skin and clothes of soldiers, is likely to be an autogenous contaminant of wounds and the main cause of gas gangrene.

Gram-positive pyogenic cocci Staphylococci and streptococci may also be present initially or may invade the tissues later. These organisms may come from an extraneous source, as a cross infection in hospital, or may be autogenous.

Gram-negative bacilli These include Proteus, Pseudomonas and Klebsiella, Escherichia, and the anaerobe bacteroides species. The source of these organisms is less well known. The infection may be autogenous, but probably cross infection accounts for their presence in most wounds. Bacteroides often accompany and outnumber *E coli* and other gram-negative bacilli in peritonitis and other abdominal sepsis.

ANTIBIOTICS AND CHEMOTHERAPEUTIC AGENTS

Principles of treatment The aim of treatment is to attain circulating serum and tissue levels of antibiotic three to four times the minimum inhibitory concentration (MIC) of the infecting bacteria, and to maintain adequate levels over the whole 24 hour period.

The Penicillins

These antibiotics are bactericidal, safe and widely available. They are the most valuable group used in war wounds:

a *Benzyl Penicillin*   All principal toxigenic clostridia and haemolytic streptococci are sensitive and resistance does not develop. Staphylococci, although normally sensitive, are now frequently resistant. Its action on coliform bacilli is slight. Bacteroides bacilli are resistant to penicillin.

b *Methicillin (Celbenin)*   has a range of activity similar to benzyl penicillin but is less active against streptococcus faecalis. It is however highly resistant to penicillinase, and therefore, is used in the treatment of penicillin resistant staphylococcal infection.

c *Cloxacillin (Orbenin)*   Its activity is similar to methicillin but as it is acid resistant, cloxacillin may be given orally before meals. It may also be given by intramuscular injection.

d *Ampicillin (Penbritin)*   Like benzyl penicillin it is active against gram-positive cocci and inactivated by penicillinase. However, it has the important advantage of being active against the non-penicillinase forming species of gram-negative bacteria (*E coli* and Proteus). It is well excreted in the bile and is used for biliary tract infections. It may be given orally or by intramuscular injection.

e *Carbenicillin (Pyopen)*   is less active against gram-positive cocci but has valuable activity against Pseudomonas, *E coli* and Proteus. It is one of the few antibiotics that are active against Ps Aeruginosa and should be prescribed preferably only for the latter infection. Large doses are needed for the treatment of Pseudomonas and levels should be increased by giving probenecid. It is administered by intramuscular or intravenous injection.

Complications of Penicillin administration   Penicillin is rarely toxic, but a number of sensitization reactions may occur:

a Anaphylactic shock is the most serious, and although the risk is remote, enquiry should be made as to whether reactions have occurred before. Should sensitivity develop it is likely that the patient will be sensitive to all the penicillins.

b Rare but important side effects of high doses of benzyl penicillin given intravenously are encephalopathy and haemolytic anaemia. Penicillin injections contain sodium or potassium, and the administration of large doses especially to patients with cardiac or renal disease could cause unwarranted effects.

Tetracyclines

Tetracyclines are bacteriostatic to all the bacteria of the three groups except Proteus and Pseudomonas. Most Clostridia are sensitive but resistant strains are appearing. The usefulness of the tetracyclines has recently decreased as a result of bacterial resistance and some hitherto unsuspected side effects.

Complications   Nausea, vomiting and diarrhoea may occur. Enterocolitis is a rare complication. Renal failure may be exacerbated. Liver damage is also a rare side effect.

Chloramphenicol

Cholramphenicol is equal in activity to the tetracyclines against the coliform bacilli, but inferior to these against Clostridia and the pyogenic cocci. It has special indications in other fields.

Complications   Marrow aplasia may follow even small doses, but usually is the result of large repeated courses. The onset of the marrow aplasia may be delayed two months after discontinuing the drug.

Aminoglycosides
a *Streptomycin*   It is active against gram-positive cocci and gram-negative bacilli. Resistance develops rapidly however during the treatment of a patient although it is said to be synergistic with penicillin. The advent of more recent antibiotics enables it to be reserved for cases of tuberculosis.
b *Neomycin*   It is bactericidal against the same organisms as streptomycin. It is too toxic for systemic use but valuable in some bowel infections or for pre-operative sterilization of the bowel. It is also used topically.
c *Gentamycin*   It has the widest activity against gram-negative bacilli as well as being the most active against staphylococcus aureus. Its main use is in Pseudomonas infections, in gram-negative septicaemia and in blind therapy for infections endangering life.
d *Kanamycin*   It is active against *E coli*, Proteus and Klebsiella but not against Pseudomonas. It is active against most strains of staphylococci but streptococci are resistant to it.

Complications   There is a high incidence of toxic side effects including damage to the kidneys and both branches of the 8th nerve.

Polymyxins

The drug in use is polymyxin E (Colistin). They are inactive against gram-positive organisms and Proteus and their main use is in gram-negative infections particularly Pseudomonas. They are frequently used topically. Colistin is less toxic, but less active, and may be given parenterally.

Complications   They are nephrotoxic.

Cephalosporins

Cephalosporins are related chemically to the penicillins. They are powerful bactericidal antibiotics with a spectrum similar to that of ampicillin. They are useful in penicillin-sensitive individuals and in severe infections before antibiotic sensitivities are available. Cephaloridine is the cephalosporin used extensively. Cephalixin is similar to cephaloridine but can be used orally.

Complications   They may cause renal tubular damage in doses in excess of 4 g daily. This effect is enhanced by the diuretic frusemide and these two drugs should not be administered simultaneously. The principal side effect is hypersensitivity.

Marcolides

Erythromycin is the only important member. It has a spectrum of activity similar to that of penicillin but is only bacteriostatic. It is a useful alternative for patients who are allergic to penicillin.

Complications   It may cause temporary jaundice, nausea, vomiting and diarrhoea.

Fusidic acid (Fucidin)

Its main indication is in severe infections caused by penicillin resistant staphylococcus aureus. It is well concentrated in bone.

Complications   Mild gastro-intestinal upset.

Lincomycin and Clindamycin

These have a similar spectrum to penicillin although they are bacteriostatic except in high doses. They may be used for penicillin resistant staphylococci. They are also particularly effective against the bacteroides and other anaerobic infections. Their inability to penetrate tissues should be made use of in osteomyelitis and inaccessible infections due to staphylococci.

Complications   Side effects are chiefly related to the gastro-intestinal tract. Diarrhoea is relatively common with lincomycin. Both preparations can cause a pseudo-membranous colitis which, although rare, can be fatal. Intravenous injection of the lincomycins should be slow, to avoid respiratory depresson.

Nitrofurantoin

Nitrofurantoin is reserved for urinary tract infections caused by a wide range of gram-positive and gram-negative sensitive organisms. Blood levels are low and it should not be used for acute pyelonephritis which can be associated with septicaemia.

Complications   The principal side effect is nausea. Neuropathy can occur if nitrofurantoin is given for prolonged periods in renal failure. A rare but important side effect is pulmonary infiltration with fever, arthralgia, eosinophilia and breathlessness.

Metronidazole

It is bactericidal to most of the clinically important obligatory anaerobes. It is particularly effective against bacteroides fragilis and could be regarded as the drug of choice in abdominal wounds for the prevention and treatment of non-clostridial anaerobic infections.

Complications   No adverse side effects occur with its use.

The sulphonamides

Antibiotics have a more rapid and certain action, and in the circumstances where they can be used should be preferred. Possible uses for the sulphonamides are the prevention and treatment of coliform infection of the urinary tract, and meningitis in head wounds, the suppression of the bowel flora in wounds of the abdomen, and the treatment of penetrating wounds of the eye.

Complications Nausea, vomiting and dizziness may follow large doses. Crystalluria leading to renal tubular blockage is especially liable to occur if the urinary output is low.

Trimethoprim - sulphamethoxazole (Septrin) (Bactrim)

Although both trimethoprim and sulphonamides are bacteriostatic, together they have a synergistic action making them bactericidal. The combination is effective against the gram-positive cocci including the penicillinase forming staphylococci and the gram-negative organisms except Ps aeruginosa. It has a high tissue level and is excreted in the urine. In addition to urinary and chest infection it may be indicated in infections with resistant staphylococci.

Complications In large doses, it may cause malaise, nausea and vomiting.

CHOICE OF ANTIBIOTIC
TREATMENT IN FORWARD AREAS

Soft tissue wounds

Although ordinary cross infection will be a risk, the overriding consideration in forward areas is the prevention of gas gangrene.

Clostridia are sensitive to benzyl penicillin, ampicillin, tetracycline and erythromycin. Of these benzyl penicillin is the first choice as all strains are sensitive, resistance does not develop, and its action is bactericidal. Erythromycin may the best choice if the patient is hypersensitive to penicillin. Tetracycline is unreliable as some strains of Cl welchii are resistant, and others develop resistance rapidly. Benzyl penicillin should be given within three hours of wounding and an effective blood level maintained for five days. Four mega units a day should be administered. At RAP level, the initial dose should be one mega unit followed at the field hospital by one mega unit six hourly. In the severely contaminated wound a combination of ampicillin and cloxacillin should be added.

Chest wounds

Penicillin therapy as used in soft tissue wounds above is recommended.

Head wounds

For the prevention of meningitis following missile injuries, it is necessary to give in addition to benzyl penicillin a drug which appears in the normal CSF at effective concentrations. Sulphadimidine 1 g intramuscularly six hourly is advised.

Abdominal wounds

In addition to the risk of gas gangrene, treatment is needed for the faecal flora. Benzyl penicillin should be supplemented by ampicillin 1 g initially followed by 0.5 g in eight hours intravenously; continue for 48 hours by mouth or intramuscularly, and metronidazole 500 mg given intravenously eight hourly for two days followed by 1 g eight hourly given by suppository or tablet for three days.

Septicaemia

If the condition of the patient or the lack of laboratory facilities necessitates treatment without obtaining the sensitivities of the bacteria a combination of gentamycin, which is effective against staphylococci, coliforms, and pseudomonas but not against streptococci or clostridia, and a broad spectrum penicillin or a cephalosporin provides wide cover.

In infections following intestinal injury, lincomycin or metronidazole should be given to protect against bacteroides infection.

Staphylococcal infections

When the bacteria are sensitive benzyl penicillin is the best antibiotic. For resistant bacteria either cloxacillin or methicillin may be chosen.

If the infection is serious both benzyl penicillin and cloxacillin or methicillin should be given until the sensitivity tests indicate which to choose. For infections with staphylococci resistant to those antibiotics or in patients hypersensitive to penicillin, fucidin with or without erythromycin or cephaloridine may be administered.

TETANUS

Introduction

Tetanus is a disease marked by severe local and general convulsive spasms of voluntary muscle caused by the action of a powerful endotoxin produced by the vegetative forms of the spore bearing and strictly anaerobic Cl tetani. The endotoxin diffuses through the blood stream and spreads cephalad along nervous tissue from the site of infection.

The spores of Cl tetani are found in the soil and in the intestines of animals including man. After an incubation period of 6–12 days, tetanus may follow contamination of even minor wounds with these spores if the tissues are sufficiently devitalized to produce suitable anaerobic conditions for the germination of vegetative forms.

Prevention of tetanus

Tetanus should not occur providing active immunity has been achieved previously and adequate early surgical treatment of all wounds is carried out:

a *Routine active immunization* Active immunity is achieved by a course of three intramuscular injections of 0.5 ml aluminium absorbed tetanus vaccine: the second injection six to eight weeks and the third four to six months after the first. This active immunity should be reinforced with 0.5 ml vaccine five years after the primary course and thereafter at 10–15 year intervals.

b *Tetanus prophylaxis in previously fully immunized wounded:*
(1) Surgery – early, adequate surgical treatment of all wounds is essential in the prevention of tetanus.
(2) Immunization boost – 0.5 ml of aluminium absorbed tetanus vaccine is given intramuscularly with one mega unit benzy penicillin injection at the RAP.

c *Tetanus prophylaxis in non-immunized wounded:*
    (1)   Surgery – as in para b(1) above.
    (2)   Active immunization – 0.5 ml of aluminium absorbed tetanus vaccine and one mega unit penicillin are given intramuscularly as soon as practicable after any wounding and further doses of 0.5 ml tetanus vaccine are given after six to eight weeks and four to six months to complete active immunization.
    (3)   Passive immunization – this should be combined with active immunization in the non-immunized wounded who have major wounds or contaminated minor wounds especially of the leg, thigh, buttocks, axilla and deep puncture wounds. 500 IU (2.0 ml) human tetanus immunoglobulin (Humotet) is given intramuscularly as soon as practicable after wounding (this must be given intramuscularly using a different syringe from that used for the tetanus vaccine and at a different site).

Established tetanus

a *Signs and symptoms*   After an average incubation period of 6–12 days (though this is extremely variable) the warning signs of irritability and insomnia are followed by increased muscle reflexes and sometimes sore throat, dysphagia and difficulty in initiating urination. Muscle tremors and spasm of muscles near the wound occur, and in favourable cases, where immunity is fairly high, the disease may remain thus localized. Trismus and risus sardonicus are signs of established generalized tetanus and are soon followed by painful generalized convulsions, resulting from even minor stimuli, with respiratory distress and hyperpyrexia, then widespread muscle rigidity with opisthotonus and death.

b *Management:*
    (1)   *Human tetanus immunoglobulin (Humotet)*   Humotet is given urgently in a dose of between 30 and 300 IU per kilogram body weight intramuscularly to fix circulating toxin.
    (2)   *Surgery*   To minimize the effect of the release of toxin from the wound during exploration, surgery is delayed until after Humotet has been given. The wounds are then widely excised and decompressed, and all necrotic tissues, foreign bodies, pus and clot removed. Irrigation with hydrogen peroxide may be useful.
    (3)   *Antibiotics* – a full course of penicillin or a tetracycline is commenced.
    (4)   *Sedatives* – in favourable cases where immunity is relatively high

and the condition remains localized, and in early cases where spasms
have not begun, sedation with barbiturates or paraldehyde is combined
with gentle nursing in a quiet, darkened room to minimize stimuli which
may lead to convulsive spasms.

(5)   *Muscle relaxants and intermittent positive pressure ventilation
(IPPV)* – in all established cases muscle relaxants are given, IPPV is set
up via a tracheostomy and blood gases monitored. Full-time heavy
nursing care is required to keep the airway clear, to manage the bladder
by continuous catheter drainage, to prevent pressure sores developing,
mucosal surfaces from drying and to prevent faecal impaction.
Nutrition and fluid balance is maintained via nasogastric tube or
intravenous line. The patient should be kept normothermic; a high
fever allows the condition to deteriorate rapidly. This regimen may be
required for several weeks.

GAS GANGRENE

Introduction

Gas gangrene is due to infection of muscle by anaerobic bacteria of the
Clostridium genus. It is one of the most serious and rapidly progressive
complications of war wounds. Even in heavily infected terrain, if there is a
sufficient number of skilled surgeons to give early and adequate operative
treatment to the wounded, the incidence of infection may be as low as one
per cent, and mortality not much greater than ten per cent. If surgery is
neither early nor adequate, conditions resembling the worst days of World
War I (with an incidence of infection of five per cent and a mortality rate
of 50 per cent) can be expected. Clostridia may be found as simple
contaminants in as many as 50 per cent of all war wounds, the great
majority of which never show any sign of gas gangrene; furthermore, even
when Clostridia are the most important infecting organisms in a septic
wound, the condition may be a localized 'anaerobic cellulitis' and not a
gangrene affecting muscle. Thus the diagnosis must be made on clinical
grounds, and not by the identification of gas forming organisms in the
wound.

Pathology

Gas gangrene is essentially a progressive myositis, going on to destruction of muscle and the appearance of gas in the tissues. Usually several species of clostridia occur together in the wound. The chief species causing toxaemia are Cl welchii, Cl oedematiens and Cl septicum. The toxins of Cl welchii and Cl septicum have a destructive action on tissue, which favours the spread of infection; Cl oedematiens is relatively non-invasive but it liberates a potent toxin. Many other varieties of anaerobic organisms may be present. The Clostridia are found in soil and in the intestinal tract of man and lower animals. The features of the disease are due, first to a local action of the organisms on the sugar of muscle producing acid and gas (the 'saccharolytic group') and on muscle protein causing digestion (the 'proteolytic group'), and second, the production by the organisms of soluble toxins which diffuse into the tissues, causing further tissue destruction. The breakdown products are absorbed and produce a profound and rapidly progressive toxaemia which, untreated, leads to death.

Gas gangrene is most dangerous in the massive muscles of buttock and thigh and in the retroperitoneal muscles associated with injuries of the colon. Usually a group of muscles is involved, but the infection may involve a whole limb or limb segment, especially when there has been interference with the main blood supply. In fact a fundamental factor in the disease is damage to the blood supply. Occasionally, a single muscle, such as the sartorius, is alone affected.

The infection spreads up and down the muscle from the site of the lesion, and has little tendency to spread from muscle to muscle. Even in well established gas gangrene the blood stream is rarely invaded by clostridia until immediately before death. At the advancing edge of the infection the normal purplish-red colour of the muscle changes to brick red, contractility is lost, and the cut surface does not bleed. Gas bubbles may be seen or felt in the muscle, the fibres of which are swollen, more prominent and friable. Behind that the brick-red colour changes to olive green, while at the origin of the infection the muscle becomes purplish - black, glistens and softens to a pultaceous mass. At first the wound is relatively dry, but later a thin exudate containing droplets of fat and gas bubbles can be expressed from beneath the skin edges. The exudate becomes increasingly dark in colour and offensive.

In the early stages there are no marked changes in the appearance of the skin, apart from some bleaching round the wound from pressure. As swelling increases, the skin becomes brownish with marbling of the surface from stasis of the subcutaneous veins. Mottled white patches then make their appearance, and finally greenish-yellow areas in which blebs may form. The skin may appear normal, however, even when lying over massive gangrene. The gas, produced in and between the muscle fibres, is partly responsible for the swelling of the affected part. It eventually escapes into the subcutaneous tissues under pressure, through holes in the fascia, whence it spreads rapidly beyond the confines of the infected area.

These pathological changes are modified when the infection is due to a single species, eg in Cl oedematiens infection, which is relatively common in certain geographical areas, such as the Middle East. Swelling and serous exudate are specially marked features, while gas and smell are minimal.

Of great importance also is the intense necrosis that results in the liver and kidney cells. This accounts for the common terminal symptom of scanty blood-stained urine or even anuria.

An anaerobic cellulitis may occur primarily in subcutaneous or areolar tissue into which blood has been extravasated, eg retroperitoneal haematoma.

Clinical features

There are certain conditions under which gas gangrene is particularly liable to develop:

a Where there has been extensive laceration of muscles, eg in compound fractures of the long bones or penetration by high velocity missiles.

b Where there has been interference with the main blood supply to the affected part, or prolonged application of a tourniquet.

c Where the wound is grossly contaminated with soil and dirt, and where fragments of clothing and contaminated foreign bodies have been carried deeply into the tissues.

d Where operation has been delayed by difficulties of evacuation.

The most striking feature is a rapid change for the worse in a wounded man, until then progressing satisfactorily. In the course of a few hours he becomes anxious, frightened or euphoric: morphine often has little effect. He remains mentally alert till near the end, although sometimes quite unaware of the seriousness of his condition. The face is pale or livid, often with marked circumoral pallor. Pain in the limb was regarded formerly as a constant feature, but in cases occurring in World War II, only some discomfort as a rule was noted, associated with a feeling of increased weight. The temperature may be slightly raised but is often subnormal. A rising pulse in a wounded man who has recovered from shock, and is not suffering from continued haemorrhage, is highly suggestive if it quickly becomes feeble, dicrotic, and running. The blood pressure is low and it may be impossible to record it. Frequently there is practically no response to blood transfusion, even when large amounts of blood are given rapidly. Vomiting may be a feature in severe cases. Unless heroic surgical measures are undertaken without delay, the case goes on to a condition of utter prostration, rapidly fatal. The so-called characteristic smell is not pathognomonic of established gas gangrene; many malodorous wounds contaminated with clostridia do not go on to the profound toxaemic state described. The smell may be absent, expecially when the infection is due to Cl oedematiens. The presence of gas is variable in its significance and may not be apparent clinically until the later stages. Its presence may be due merely to air introduced at the time of wounding and may be palpated subcutaneously in cases of localized anaerobic cellulitis. Gas bubbles may for this reason be seen in an X-ray film of the affected part with or without clostridial infection.

Prophylactic treatment

Every wound of muscle is a potential site of gas gangrene. The primary prophylaxis is early and adequate excision of wounds with removal of debris, excision of dead tissue and fascial release as indicated. Adequate drainage and delayed closure are mandatory.

In addition, all patients with extensive muscle wounds of the buttock, thigh, calf, axilla and retroperitoneal tissues should be given penicillin of the order of one mega unit six hourly commencing as soon as possible after wounding. If penicillin is not available tetracycline is a suitable alternative in the field.

Prophylactic use of antiserum in high risk wounds was shown to be of value in World War II. There should be no need for its use if early and thorough wound excision has been done and penicillin given.

Treatment of the established case

Preliminary transfusion must be rapid and adequate and should be kept running during the operation.

All discoloured muscle, muscle that does not contract when pinched and does not bleed when cut must be excised. This may mean removing the whole muscle from origin to insertion, partial resection of a large muscle or complete removal of a whole group. Amputation may be the only hope of saving life when a limb is disorganized by injury or infection.

Large doses of penicillin are required. Give 10 million units daily, in at least four doses, for a period of five days. Alternatively full doses of tetracycline will be given, ie 0.5 g intravenously or 1.0 g orally every six hours. The results of sensitivity tests may indicate a change in the antibiotic but active treatment should never await these tests. The post-operative period is likely to be stormy. Dehydration, delirium, vomiting, jaundice and anuria may develop.

In severe cases the septic shock will require whatever intensive care facilities are available in the field relative to the work load.

The use of *antitoxin serum* is still regarded by some as controversial in spite of its use in World War II when it was vigorously supported. There should be no need to use it in most wounds but if it is available and it is decided to use it a skin sensitivity test should be done first. Pentavalent antiserum should be used in a dose of two to four vials intravenously, repeatable after four to six hours. The incidence of sensitivity reactions in practice has been low and of relative unimportance.

Hyperbaric oxygen is of proven value as the clostridia are anaerobes and the high oxygen-reduction potential of hyperbaric oxygen inhibits their growth; it also deactivates the toxins. It is supplementary to the main therapeutic measures, ie surgery and antibiotics. In certain circumstances this facility may be available for the treatment of battle casualties.

There is no substitute for early and thorough surgery supplemented by penicillin in the treatment of war wounds.

Differential diagnosis of gas gangrene

Anaerobic cellulitis   In this condition the infection is limited to the subcutaneous tissue. The gas formation being subcutaneous may be greater and more evident than in gas gangrene. The speed of sub-cutaneous gas producing infection may be rapid and extensive; sometimes the condition involves the whole abdominal wall. The brownish purulent discharge has a foul odour. Pain, toxaemia and anaemia are little in evidence and when the affected dirty tissue is removed, the muscle underneath appears healthy, bleeds and contracts normally.

Treatment of this condition is surgical – the relief of tension, the removal of necrotic and grossly infected tissue and adequate drainage.

Penicillin or tetracycline in the usual doses are useful adjuvants to surgery. Anti-clostridial serotherapy is not indicated but hyperbaric oxygen is of value if available.

Anaerobic streptococcal myositis This rather rare complication of wounds develops eight to ten days after wounding and the characteristic toxaemia of gas gangrene is lacking. The blood pressure is little depressed. There is spreading cutaneous erythema and swelling originating in a moist malodorous wound which discharges quantities of this seropurulent fluid. The muscles are boggy and pale at first, then bright red and later purple and friable. Abundant gram-positive cocci and pus cells are found in the exudate.

Treatment – surgery is limited to relaxing incisions through the deep fascia to relieve tension and provide adequate drainage. Penicillin or tetracycline is given as described for gas gangrene.

In true anaerobic streptococcal infection hyperbaric oxygen may be of value.

A limb severely affected by anaerobic cellulitis or streptococcal myositis is in danger of amputation by the inexperienced surgeon who has wrongly diagnosed gas gangrene.

Ischaemic gangrene This is due to loss or impairment of the main artery to a limb. Unless it becomes secondarily infected there is no toxaemia.

Air in tissues Certain wounds may introduce air into the tissues. This may produce surgical emphysema and is not to be confused with gas gangrene.

CHAPTER 5

General complications of the injured

MULTIPLE INJURIES

Introduction

Multiple injuries may consist of multiple closed injuries, missile wounds and/or wounds associated with burns, crush injuries, blast injuries, carbon monoxide poisoning, radiation effects, toxic war gases or frost bite.

Such injuries may occur in various combinations with each other or with ordinary battle wounds.

A disproportionate amount of shock associated with an obvious injury suggests some other cause, eg a head injury does not normally produce a severe degree of shock so that shock might indicate a ruptured liver as a complication.

Management of multiple injuries

First aid surgery is essential at the dressing station, where injuries are dealt with, in the order of the danger threatening life, ie respiratory obstruction, haemorrhage and shock. The problem with many casualties is to ensure they survive long enough to reach the forward surgical centre. The airway must be secured. Haemorrhage is arrested by pad and bandage or ligation of vessel. A haemostat can be applied and left in situ for evacuation. This must be recorded. An intravenous polythene cannula must be inserted and Ringer lactate intravenous infusion started and maintained.

All fractures must be efficiently splinted particularly in the lower limb where the Thomas splint is so effective in preventing further damage and shock.

CRUSH INJURIES

The term 'crush syndrome' is applied to renal failure consequent upon trapping of a limb for an hour or more beneath debris usually the result of falling masonry in air raids.

Ischaemic muscle necrosis liberates myohaemoglobin, and pigment casts and granules block the renal tubules as a result. Haemoconcentration follows the loss of plasma into the crushed tissues and intense arterial spasm is usual. It is also probable that a toxic substance is produced from the injured muscle.

Acute swelling of a limb may follow other closed injuries such as severe fractures of the long bones and prolonged application of a tourniquet. Anuria may also be the sequel of major muscle wounds, gas gangrene, burns and the transfusion of excessive amounts of normal or any amount of incompatible blood. Arterial spasm may well be a factor common to all of these.

Clinical features The crush syndrome should be suspected in a patient with unexplained erythema, wheals or blisters on a limb with gross swelling, loss of sensation or paralysis associated with a diminishing urinary output. The pulse in the limb may be difficult or impossible to feel.

In spite of symptoms of shock due to oligaemia the patient is not necessarily distressed but often mentally alert. The tongue and skin are dry. The urine is dark and scanty, resembling haematuria to the naked eye: if anuria supersedes and is untreated death will occur in six to eight days.

The progressive rise in the blood urea is accompanied by the features of haemoconcentration although these may be masked by haemodilution if overt or internal bleeding has been severe.

Treatment aims at the elimination of pigment and toxin derived from the damaged tissues by promoting diuresis and keeping the urine alkaline. Unless instituted in the first few hours of the 'shock' phase it will be ineffective.

Sodium bicarbonate 1.4 per cent, sodium lactate 2 per cent and sodium citrate 3 per cent have all been used intravenously but care must be taken not to overload the circulation and even produce alkalosis. Oral sodium bicarbonate 2 grams hourly is a useful alternative where possible. Fluids by infusion should not exceed the sensible and insensible loss once oliguria is present and peritoneal or renal dialysis may be life saving.

Attempts to limit the escape and absorption of pigment from the damaged limb by compression bandage or high application of an Esmarch bandage are of doubtful value and there is no place for linear incisions through skin and deep fascia for decompression.

Amputation has a place in cases arriving long after crushing, particularly where the viability of the limb is in jeopardy. Local circumstances such as the availability of an artificial kidney will then be vital in arriving at this decision.

EXPLOSIVE BLAST INJURIES

Explosives are substances which, when detonated, are very rapidly converted to large volumes of gases. When the explosion is confined by a bomb, shell, grenade or rocket casing the high pressure will rupture the casing imparting high velocity to the resulting fragments. These cause injuries in the manner described in Chapter 1. The remainder of the energy then produces a blast shock wave and the displaced air creates a blast wind.

Shock wave

The rapidly expanding gases compress the surrounding air and create a shock wave similar in form to a large amplitude sound wave. There is an extremely rapid rise of pressure of the order of hundreds of thousands of pounds per square inch (psi). The blast wave moves away from the source in the form of a sphere of compressed gas which is expanding very rapidly. The velocity of a shock wave in air is over 3000 metres per second but it soon falls to the speed of sound within a variable distance dependent on the amount and composition of the explosives. Like sound waves, blast pressure waves will flow over and around an obstruction, like a wall, and affect someone sheltering behind it. The pressure level at 90° to the direction of travel of the shock front is called the incident pressure. If the shock front strikes a flat surface in its line of travel the pressure wave will be reflected creating the reflected pressure. The negative pressure, or suction component of the blast wave, is much less than the positive pressure phase and although it follows immediately after the positive wave lasts up to ten times as long.

The blast wave travels much more rapidly through a liquid or solid medium than through air due to the greater density of the media. That is why blast injuries in water are more severe at a greater distance than they are in air and why blast waves transmitted through armour plate, like tanks and the decks of ships, cause severe injuries to casualties in direct contact with the affected surface. Three other physical factors are of significance in understanding the creation of blast injuries.

When any pressure wave progresses through structures of different densities a reflective stress is set up at the interface acting on the more dense. This effect is known as **spalling.** Inertia effects relate to shearing forces which are created between intimately related masses which, because of their different densities, are accelerated at different rates. Finally a pressure pulse will compress and heat small air bubbles as it passes over them. When the wave has passed, the compressed and heated bubbles expand with explosive force creating new shock fronts from their centres and this effect is known as implosion. Therefore, as the blast wave travels through the body it creates specific damage particularly at the interfaces between tissue and air. The most sensitive organ is the ear and eardrums start to rupture at about seven pounds per square inch (psi). The next most sensitive part of the body is the lung. When the pressure reaches about 50 psi damage occurs in the walls of the alveoli of the lung, causing a marked haemorrhagic effect together with oedema of the interstitial tissue and the opening of alveolar-venous fistulae. Similar changes take place, at much higher pressures, when the blast pressure wave travels through the abdomen causing damage in the walls of gas-containing viscera and, if the pressure is high enough, actual disruption of the viscus involved. The mechanism of injury in both chest and lung is probably fairly complicated and certainly as well as spalling it involves differential pressures being transmitted to the lung more quickly through the liquid phase of the vascular system than the gaseous phase of the air in the lungs. Also the lungs are crushed between the diaphragm, which rises violently under the ram effect of the pressure driven abdominal viscera, and the slower reacting rib cage.

Blast wind

The rapidly expanding explosive blast gases displace an equal volume of air. This air rushes out radially at very high speed travelling, at first, immediately behind the shock front. This mass movement of air or windage creates the dynamic pressure. At a distance it may blow the patient over, causing translational injuries of all grades of severity; of particular importance are acceleration or deceleration injuries where internal viscera may be torn from their mesentery or shattered. Closer to the explosion the greater blast wind will cause traumatic amputation. The mass movement of air actually causes parts of the body to be blown off. In the immediate vicinity of the explosion there may be total disintegration of the body.

Explosions in confined spaces cause far worse effects than those occurring in the open. This is particularly true with explosions in tanks, helicopters and fixed-wing aircraft. In confined spaces there is the added effect, apart from explosive blast and primary missiles, of the inhalation of toxic gases and smoke.

Diagnosis and treatment

Hearing   Damage to the ear is usually readily recognizable as the patient is deaf to some degree or has tinnitus.

Lung injuries   Damage to the lung may be apparent immediately but more commonly and characteristically it comes on after a delay of six to twelve hours, the symptoms not being florid but quite often mild without evidence of external injury. A high index of suspicion must, therefore, obtain in those close to explosions. The usual first symptoms are those of mild anoxia with the patient behaving in a rather peculiar fashion; blood gases will show a low arterial pO_2 and a raised pCO_2. Great care needs to be taken in resuscitation of these patients and intravenous crystalloids should be used with the greatest caution as they tend to settle in the damaged portions of the lung causing massive pulmonary oedema. Inhalation anaesthetic agents should also be used with great caution. These patients are better resuscitated with colloid such as dextran 70 or double-strength plasma or blood. The more severe cases will require intubation, intermittent positive pressure ventilation using positive expiratory end pressure (PEEP) and particular care must be taken to watch for an induced pneumothorax. They also require vigorous physiotherapy during the normal period of 36–48 hours of ventilation. Experimental work suggest that high dose steroids of the order of 30 mg per kg of methylprednisolone may have a dramatic effect.

Abdominal injuries   The confident diagnosis of an intra-abdominal lesion following exposure to blast waves may be very difficult because of the varying degree of damage inflicted on casualties close together.

Closed abdominal injuries should be treated according to the symptoms or signs. The most usual injury is haemorrhage into the wall of the bowel but there may also be visceral disruption. If there are signs of a perforated hollow viscus or internal bleeding, exploration should be undertaken.

The following features, especially if present together, indicate the need for operation:

a Severe unremitting abdominal pain, more especially if it increases in intensity.
b Tenderness of the lower abdomen, particularly when there is accompanying melaena.
c Frequent bowel evacuations with melaena, associated with difficulty in micturition or haematuria.
d Loss of liver dullness associated with the presence of sub-diaphragmatic air on a radiograph.
e The presence of guarding or rigidity of the abdominal muscles associated with diffuse tenderness.

Because of possible pulmonary injury from the blast wave, the administration of fluid will require great caution. Colloid solutions should be used and diuretics if necessary.

Those who complain of slight abdominal pain, associated with some tenderness on palpation and slight distension, should be kept under observation for two to four days. The pain may become slightly colicky and be associated with vomiting and a desire to defaecate. Frequent bowel evacuations may even take place without developing signs of peritonitis requiring laparotomy. There may be evidence of large bowel or rectal injury requiring surgical repair. Scrotal contusion and testicular pain are common but in themselves do not call for surgery.

Some apparently mild cases may be diagnosed wrongly as abdominal contusions and treated expectantly, only to develop an intraperitoneal abscess or a faecal fistula later on. Others are less fortunate and after an interval of up to ten days show evidence of an intra-abdominal catastrophe due to an abscess bursting into the peritoneal cavity with diffuse peritonitis. In such cases the perforation may be difficult to locate at laparotomy.

Further difficulty in diagnosis arises because pain and tenderness in the epigastrium may be due to a chest injury stimulating the lower intercostal nerves. The chest lesion may be a single one or additional to an abdominal lesion. The following *diagnostic guides* may be helpful.
a When clinical signs are confined to the upper abdomen, a thoracic cause is highly probable.
b When the clinical signs, at first confined to the upper abdomen, spread downwards to the lower abdomen, an abdominal lesion is certain.
c When the clinical signs are from the first most marked in the lower abdomen, there can be little doubt that there is intraperitoneal damage.

Awareness of blast injuries

The severity of a blast lesion appears to be in direct relationship to the distance from the explosion. Those near the centre of a large explosion will usually be killed instantly while those at a greater distance will survive. The further away an injured person is from an explosion the less likely is the chance of injury. Patients with blast injuries are commonly apprehensive and tremulous and may be wrongly diagnosed as suffering from battle neurosis. They may present no external evidence of injury and unwittingly be returned to their units or treated as walking wounded until shock, dyspnoea or other features call attention to the gravity of their condition. Patients who have sustained other more obvious injuries such as compound fractures may indeed receive general anaesthesia or rapid intravenous transfusion of crystalloid with dire consequences if a condition like blast lung is overlooked. Other inhalation injuries may co-exist and indeed may readily occur under the conditions in which explosive blast damage has been sustained. A person who is clinically shocked, who has been near an explosive device but who has no apparent wounds or contusions may be suffering from blast injury and under these circumstances a high index of suspicion must be maintained.

FAT EMBOLISM

The fat embolus syndrome may be a sequel of high velocity missile injury of long bones but can occur after fractures of small bones such as the patella and os calcis. Rarely it is seen in severe soft tissue injury without coincident fracture.

There is microembolism of capillaries and small arterioles with fat emboli ranging from 15–40 microns (μm) in size.

Etiology The origin of the fat emboli is uncertain, one view presuming them to come from injured fat cells in the marrow passing into damaged veins at the fracture site and the other ascribing them to conglomeration and fusion of tiny chylomicrons in the plasma. This may be the sequel of the release of toxic products, ie thromboplastin and kinins as a result of the missile injury.

The triggering mechanism appears to be an over-compensation in the general metabolic response to trauma associated with haemorrhage, a decreased venous return and increased cardiac output resulting in a metabolic acidosis. The lungs are involved first, with deformable fat globules passing through their capillaries and thence to the systemic circulation. Cerebral fat emboli are responsible for the major signs and may prove fatal.

Presentation A latent period of 48 hours is usual between receipt of injury and the development of the clinical picture. It may however be a few hours only or as long as two weeks.

Pyrexia of 39.4 °C or higher with a tachycardia of 120 or more is seen in the great majority of cases and this may be of sudden onset at about 24 hours. Drowsiness, confusion or coma in a patient previously alert are important presenting features and respiratory symptoms are common, such as dyspnoea, tachypnoea or haemoptysis. Fat globules may be seen in the sputum and moist sounds are heard on ausculation. The chest X-ray typically shows diffuse areas of patchy consolidation.

Cyanosis is uncommon due to concomitant anaemia although the pO_2 is lowered. This can be confirmed by arterial gas analysis.

A petechial rash is seen in about half the cases, developing on the second or third day and only detectable with a hand lens. It may be generalized or involve the root of the neck, deltoid region or anterior axillary fold. The conjunctivae may also be affected and ophthalmoscopic examination may reveal fluffy white exudates and haemorrhages with a macular oedema.

Treatment The most important treatment in the field is early management of shock, respiratory support and immobilization of the fractures. Oxygen by mask will suffice in most cases but mechanical ventilation may be required if this fails to correct the hypoxia. Whole blood transfusion will be necessary to correct anaemia and the metabolic acidosis, if present, must be corrected. Other useful measures include:

a Digoxin to control tachycardia exceeding 120 and in atrial fibrillation and heart failure.
b Calcium gluconate to correct hypocalcaemia.
c Steroids to reduce pulmonary oedema.

DEHYDRATION

Dehydration includes two main components: water deficiency and salt (sodium) deficiency. As encountered clinically there is often a combination of both.

a *Water depletion*   This causes a reduction in the volume of both the extra-cellular fluid and the intra-cellular fluid. When wounded patients are deprived of water they develop oliguria. Provided renal function is adequate, the urine produced is highly concentrated and contains little salt as the body is short of both salt and water. The tongue and mucous membranes are dry. The condition gradually deteriorates and the patient becomes disorientated unless water is provided.

The degree of dehydration can be assessed very roughly as follows: a slight persistent thirst represents a loss of 1 to 2 litres of water, while a marked thirst indicates a loss of 3 to 4 litres.

b *Primary salt depletion*   Loss of salt (sodium) causes a reduction in the volume of the extra-cellular fluid and therefore of the circulating blood volume. Thirst is less marked than with comparable degrees of water dehydration but may result from extra-cellular fluid contraction alone. Marked fatigue, muscular weakness and cramp develop early.

This condition develops in a patient with diarrhoea and vomiting or in a patient with a gastro-intestinal fistula whose fluid intake consists of water only. Profuse sweating, replaced by water only, produces the same picture. Clinically the eyes become sunken and the patient becomes apathetic. The tongue shrinks and becomes smaller. The skin loses its elasticity and tends to become cold and clammy. The urine is scanty with a high specific gravity.

c *Management*   In a temperate climate, an average male requires half a litre of normal isotonic saline to 2 litres of five per cent dextrose daily for his basic fluid needs if he is treated by an intravenous drip.

Abnormal losses should be replaced. Vomit and aspirates from the stomach and intestine should be measured and replaced volume for volume by normal isotonic saline. Fluid lost by excess sweating should be replaced by normal isotonic saline and five per cent dextrose in the proportion of one measure of saline to two of dextrose. This replacement is in addition to the normal basic daily requirements of 2 litres of water (1 litre to replace insensible loss and 1 litre for urine). If oral fluids cannot be administered and absorbed this must be given intravenously as five per cent dextrose solution.

If receiving all fluids by intravenous drip the patient who is suffering from salt deficiency must have one litre of normal isotonic saline every four hours plus half a litre for every half a litre aspirated from his stomach tube until his urinary output is adequate or until fluid status is judged to be correct on clinical grounds or by use of a central venous pressure line. In addition he may require 1.5–2 litres of five per cent dextrose for his water depletion.

Practical indices of adequate hydration are: a urinary output of 1–1.5 litres (2–3 pints) in 24 hours, with a sp gr 1010 or less; moist tongue and mucous membranes; normal appearances and feel of the skin especially over the neck and flexor surfaces on pinching up a fold. The jugular venous pressure should be visible and the blood pressure normal without a marked postural fall.

Oliguria

The most reliable sign of kidney failure in a wounded man is the presence of oliguria when no other cause for decreased urinary output is apparent. Oliguria is here defined as urine volume of less than 20 ml per hour. Other causes of oliguria must be ruled out before acute renal failure (acute tubular necrosis) is diagnosed. These are:

a *Hypotension*   If the systolic blood pressure is below 80 mm Hg in the renal arteries the glomerular filtration rate is reduced. Correction of hypotension requires urgent attention.

b *Metabolic response to injury*   After trauma, including surgical operations, there may be a period of oliguria for 8–36 hours. This temporary reduction of urine flow is apparently physiological (secretion of anti-diuretic hormone). Urine passed will have a high specific gravity and the diagnosis is only justified if the patient's condition is in other respects stable and urinalysis normal. There is a risk of overhydrating in this state.

Anuria

Obstruction of the urinary tract may be the cause, if the patient is anuric. Most patients with renal failure will excrete some urine. Injuries in the pelvic region may damage the ureters or urethra, or cause atony of the bladder or spasm of the internal urethral sphincter.

Careful surgical examination, catheterization of the bladder, cystoscopy or exploration, as indicated, will establish the presence or absence of adequate urinary flow from the kidneys. Obstruction of the urethral catheter by debris or clot may simulate urinary suppression and can be overcome by irrigation, using a measured quantity of saline.

Acute post-traumatic renal failure

When the foregoing conditions can be excluded and the urinary output is less than 20 ml per hour for 12 consecutive hours this diagnosis should be considered. It may complicate prolonged shock, burns, crush injuries, blood transfusion reaction, major muscle wounds especially if heavily infected. An earlier diagnosis can be made by measuring the urinary output than by waiting for the blood urea to rise. If the sp gr of the urine is under 1016 in the absence of glycosuria or albuminuria, or if blood pigment or albumin is present it should be assumed that the patient has acute renal failure.

Early management prior to evacuation

The cause should receive its indicated treatment including antibiotic therapy at once. Remember that the dosage of many antibiotics needs to be modified in the presence of renal failure.

This opportunity should be seized to correct the cause, after which, if circumstances allow, the patient should be evacuated expeditiously to a designated renal insufficiency centre equipped to deal with such cases. (Intraperitoneal lavage and dialysis, the use of the 'artificial kidney' are not feasible except at a special centre having trained personnel.)

If evacuation of the patient with renal failure is impossible or whilst awaiting circumstances favourable to evacuation, the management detailed below is recommended.

Warning There is no evidence that decapsulation of the kidneys or sympathectomy has any influence on the course of anuria-oliguria.

After correction of fluid balance fluid restriction will become necessary unless renal function has been restored. Remember the importance of early replacement of fluid losses: the urgent administration of intravenous saline (if blood and blood products are not available) to wounded men with fluid deficits as soon as possible after injury has been shown to minimize the incidence of acute renal failure.

The patient with acute kidney failure requires special attention to his fluid balance and potassium metabolism. If these two features of his condition are controlled, there will be no symptom or signs attributable to kidney failure for at least three days, and some other disorder must be sought to explain any symptoms or signs such as sepsis, shock and undebrided necrotic tissue.

In this condition in a temperate climate the total fluid intake per 24 hours should be restricted to 500 ml plus the measured output. The basic fluid allowance for replacing insensible fluid loss will be variable depending on climatic conditions. In humid regions of the tropics the basic allowance may be as much as 1000 ml or more. This factor will usually be decided for the local area by consultants. Do not include blood, plasma, or plasma substitutes in the measurement of fluid intake.

The measured output is the total of urine and gastric suction fluid or vomitus; if watery diarrhoea is present, its volume should be estimated and included in the output. Increasing the fluid intake will not increase the urinary output in acute kidney failure, and excessive fluid intake will endanger the patient's life by producing circulatory overloading.

The oral route is best for the administration of fluids provided the patient is not nauseated and there is no lesion of the gastrointestinal tract contraindicating it. However, many patients will require parenteral administration, and it is best to give a continued intravenous infusion at a constant rate.

Infusion by polythene tube or intravenous cannula, introduced by cutting down on the long saphenous vein and passed so that the tip lies in the inferior vena cava proximal to the renal veins, is technically simple and causes little trouble if allowed to remain in situ not longer than five days. Venous catheterization is superior to an intravenous infusion in which a needle or cannula is used and makes movement of the patient easier and better tolerated.

The medical officer should give personal attention to the accuracy of the intake and output. The thirst of the patient should not be allowed to influence the volume of the intake, and close supervision may be required to prevent the patient from over-hydrating himself. The nurse should be instructed regarding measurement and record of intake and output. A warning notice to 'Keep the fluid balance chart' should be displayed on the patient's bed. The maintenance of a daily weight record is also highly desirable, since an increase in weight implies fluid retention and, therefore, over-hydration.

During the conservative management of acute renal failure a daily weight loss of approximately 0.5 kg usually represents correct management of fluid balance after the initial achievement of normal hydration.

Everything possible should be done to reduce the influx of potassium into the plasma and the following points should be remembered:
a *All devitalized tissue must be completely removed.* If there is any doubt about the adequacy of debridement, further debridement is indicated. Wounds should be examined daily for evidence of infection. Bandages and dressings should be thin enough to show early exudate and should not constrict the blood supply. Treatment of superficial or deep infection

should be more aggressive than would be necessary if the patient were passing enough urine to excrete the potassium released by devitalized cells.

b *Avoid hypoxia,* which causes release of intracellular potassium to the plasma. Use local anaesthesia when possible. If general anaesthesia is necessary use a minimum of gases which produce hypoxia.

c *Never administer potassium to an oliguric patient* unless the necessity is proved by electrolyte analysis.

d *Maintain the best possible intake of carbohydrate and fat* by the use of butter-sugar diet. Protein should not be given. Glucose or lactose are the only suitable carbohydrates for the completely oral management of traumatic oliguria. At least 100 g of glucose or lactose should be taken daily. Sucrose is too sweet. This regime soon leads to nutritional problems and the sooner the patient is transferred to a special unit the better.

e *Potassium intoxication cannot be diagnosed clinically* in its earlier phases. This condition is to be suspected whenever a casualty becomes oliguric who has had a major injury to voluntary muscle.

Emergency treatment when evacuation is impossible

a Fifty ml of 50 per cent glucose with 10 units of soluble insulin may be administered into a large vein, preferably the vena cava.

b Calcium is a specific antagonist of potassium. A total of 10 g of calcium gluconate (100 ml 10 per cent solution) can be given intravenously in not less than 24 hours, and this dose may given for two to three days; it should then be reduced to 3–4 g per day. Remember that calcium therapy will not lower the serum potassium level and merely allows some time to achieve this.

c Although sodium also opposes potassium, large amounts should not be used during the first days. In the oliguric period, only that amount of sodium necessary to replace the quantity lost by urinary excretion, gastric suction or vomiting and diarrhoetic stools should be given. This regime is not safe unless it is monitored by frequent measurement of blood chemistry.

In addition to the above, patients who have no intestinal lesions, gastric suction or nausea, may have oral feedings of glucose or lactose (200 g daily) solution. They should not receive food containing protein or potassium, and any fluids they receive by mouth must be measured and their volume subtracted from the intravenous intake. Blood, plasma and plasma substitutes should be given as indicated and should not be counted as part of the fluid intake. 300 ml M/6 sodium lactate or 7½ per cent sodium bicarbonate should be substituted for a like amount of water each day, beginning on the third day of oliguria.

The diuretic phase

Recovery from oliguria usually proceeds as a steplike increase in urine volume, which in the severest cases may be gradual, but in milder cases may be rapid. Then a deficiency of electrolytes is liable to occur. Urine volume may increase to very high levels, 6–9 litres a day, and be entirely independent of fluid intake. This urine should be replaced quantitatively with water. Electrolyte depletion can be prevented by giving 75 mEq of NaCl (½ litre of physiological saline), 40 mEq of KCl (3 grams) and calcium gluconate (2 grams) for each litre of urine passed. Every second day one litre of M/6 sodium lactate (165 mEq) should be substituted for one litre of isotonic saline. It is important not to commence protein feeding until urine volume is at least 1500 ml each day and the blood urea is below 250 mg per cent (25 mmols). Because the concentrating power of the kidney is so poor, and because the catabolic rate may be so high, uraemia may be slow to clear, and too early protein feeding increases the danger of uraemic complications (infection, pericarditis, pulmonary complications, etc).

NUTRITION

All injured patients undergo a catabolic response, the intensity of which is proportional to the severity of injury. This response is particularly severe in major burns, and is made worse by infection.

The catabolic response results in a breakdown of body protein and a negative nitrogen balance. Unless corrected this leads to weight loss, muscle wasting, delayed wound healing and decreased resistance to infection. Anaemia, partly a result of negative balance, further retards wound healing and increases susceptibility to infection.

To counter this nitrogen drain, and the dangers of an increasing catabolism, a high nitrogen, high calorie diet must be provided, together with vitamin and mineral supplements.

Requirements may be calculated thus:

a Nitrogen 0.2–0.3 per kg body weight per 24 hours (1 g N = 625 g protein).

b Calories: 200 kcals per g nitrogen.

A typical requirement would be 120–150 g protein and 2500–3000 cals per 24 hours – best supplied as a light or semi solid diet.

Since anorexia is a frequent accompaniment of severe injury it may be necessary to supplement oral intake with feeding via a naso gastric tube – using one of the many available preparations such as Complan, Clinifeed or Triosorbon. Because of the high sugar contents of these feeds diarrhoea commonly occurs. This is best guarded against by initial dilution of the feeds, and slow administration often by infusion – building up the optimal amounts in three to four days.

Secondary anaemia should be treated initially be transfusion, at the same time ensuring that essential substrates such as iron, folate and Vitamin B12 are provided to promote a normal haemopoietic response.

Requirements In addition to the nitrogen and calorie requirements already calculated, since most preparations contain little potassium, this electrolyte should be added to provide a total of 5 mEq per gram nitrogen supplied. Should any excess loss be occurring this will have to be supplied in addition to the basic requirements.

Vitamins can be supplied by Parentrovite and Konakion; in long term management one unit of blood per week will compensate for most trace elements (Fe, Zn, Co, Cu, Mn).

Formula preparation Since every patient's requirements in terms of their body weight, catabolic state and excess losses will vary, a formula for any patient must be an individual one. The major requirements, fluid, electrolyte, nitrogen and calories, should be calculated: from the preparations available the combination to make good these requirements should be selected. Requirements should be reviewed every 24 hours.

Intravenous nutrition

Indications The parenteral route is more costly, more dangerous and medically more time consuming than oral or nasogastric feeding.

There are, however, three main situations in which it is indicated:

a Poor pre-operative nutritional status.

This is not a common indication in military surgery, but occurs when major surgery is planned for the patient who has been seriously ill for long periods.

b Prolonged gastro-intestinal failure.

This is further subdivided into three groups:

(1) Intake failure – eg coma, head and neck injury or surgery. Parenteral nutrition is preferable here when complications of nasogastric feeding prove difficult to control, eg aspiration, reflux or diarrhoea.

(2) Motility failure – eg prolonged ileus when nasogastric feeding would be ineffective.

(3) Absorption failure – eg high intestinal fistulae.

c Gross hypercatabolic states.

The nitrogen and protein requirements may well be in excess of those which can be practically provided orally.

Route The high osmolality of most of the solutions available for intravenous nutrition produces peripheral thrombophlebitis. If several peripheral veins are available, allowing change of infusion site every 48–72 hours, then these should be utilized. The alternative of central venous catheterization, while allowing administration of hyperosmolar solutions, carries very considerable risks (infection, pneumothorax, septicaemia). A high standard of care and asepsis is required, not only in the introduction, but also in the maintenance of such lines.

CHAPTER 6

Burn wounds

Introduction

Experience in recent wars has shown that burn wounds will form an important part of the work of all Army surgeons. New types of weapons, particularly missiles, will make burn wounds more frequent.

All types of burn are seen in the Army, petrol, flame or flash from explosives, chemical, phosphorus or electric current. Thermo-nuclear devices introduce the possibility of large numbers of burn patients, creating both medical and severe logistical problems.

The extensive petrol burn is generally accidental, often due to negligence, eg handling petrol while smoking a cigarette, or lighting fires with petrol. The classical Army burn, seen both in accidental fires and tank crew survivors, is one involving mainly the hands and face. Army uniform gives excellent protection to flash and to a lesser degree flame, but in summer when soldiers often strip except for trunks and boots the greater exposure of the body means more extensive burns in survivors.

The use of gloves, goggles, protective head gear and flame retardant clothing in high risk personnel at all times must be recommended. Enforcement of safety procedures and existing regulations will minimize accidents.

Patho-physiology

Thermal injury, regardless of cause, results in cell death and damage by coagulative necrosis. Capillary permeability is increased with loss of normal integrity in the vascular system and escape of fluid from the vessels. This oedema forms most rapidly in the immediate post-burn phase and may involve non-burned areas. The loss of serum from the circulating blood reaches a maximum in the second post-burn day, producing hypovolaemic shock. In the first eight hours post-burn this shock can be extremely severe, even fatal if the loss of circulating blood volume is not recognised. Fluid replacement must start as soon as possible after the burn, with the correct fluid and volume spread over 48 hours calculated from the time of burning.

As the integrity of the capillary membrane is restored the fluid is re-absorbed and oedema slowly resolves.

Severity of Injury

This is dependent upon both depth and area of the burn. The area is more important in the early stages, although both factors determine mortality, morbidity and the ultimate functional result.

a   The area: percentage body surface burnt. The burned area is estimated as a percentage of the total body area, excluding simple erythema, employing 'The Rule of Nines' (Fig 5). A percentage estimate of the

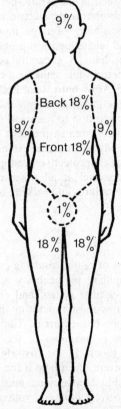

Figure 5   Rule of Nines

body surface burned must always be made and charted. A patient with more than 15 per cent of the body surface area burnt will always require resuscitation and treatment in hospital.

b   *Depth of burns*
  (1)   Superficial burns
      (a)   Epidermal – the epidermis only is injured, leaving the dermis intact. Such burns are always hypersensitive. They vary from simple erythema to mild blistering and heal readily within 7–10 days if not infected.
      (b)   Dermal burns – involve the dermis to a varying degree, although hypoalgesic to pin prick, sensation is not actually lost. Blistering is greater, but pain is less. These burns will heal after three to four weeks, but if any infection occurs full thickness skin loss may rapidly occur.
  (2)   Full thickness burns (deep burns) – in these the whole dermis is destroyed and is leathery hard. Underlying structures such as bone, nerves, joints, etc, may be involved. Sensation to pin prick is absent and underlying vessels may often be seen thrombosed. These burns will always require desloughing and skin grafting for healing. Severe scarring will always result. In thermal injury all degrees are present according to the cause of the burn. Flame burns are commonly deep, while flash burns are more commonly epidermal or dermal. In most cases it is difficult to differentiate between these types. The total percentage of skin surface involved is the primary concern during resuscitation. The depth of burn is unlikely to concern the surgeon in the field, although it will be of importance in the treatment of the patient after two weeks or so.

Early treatment of burn wounds

a   *First aid* – first remove the source of thermal injury from the patient or the patient from the fire. Burning clothing should be extinguished and the burn cooled with cold water to arrest heat uptake. Chemical agents must be washed from the skin surface immediately by drenching with water. In electrical burns great care must be taken whilst removing the patient from the point of contact so that the rescuer will not also be injured. Clothing should not be removed unless it is smouldering or soaked by chemical agents. The patient should be wrapped up in clean sheets or blankets. The Roehampton burns dressing of sheets of sterile polyurethane foam should be applied to cover the burned area. All constricting articles, such as rings, watches, belts and boots should be removed. If the hands are burned the best cover is a polythene bag closed at the wrist by the patient's own shirt sleeve or by a non-constricting bandage. No other local treatment should be attempted and all efforts made to control shock.

b *Airway* – the patency of airway should be assured. Inhalation burns must be suspected in all cases of burns involving the face. Look for singeing of nasal hairs, soot in the nostrils, burns of the tongue and redness in the posterior pharynx. Hoarseness and stridor are early signs.

c *Sedation* – pain is seldom a problem in patients with severe burns, but where the burn is mainly epidermal it can be severe and morphine given intravenously is the drug of choice. In deeper burns anxiety and restlessness are more common and valium given intravenously is of greater value.

d *Warmth* – the patient should be protected from the elements, but not warmed to cause further loss of fluid from sweating.

e *Oral fluids* – fluids should be given frequently by mouth (50 ml/kg/24 hours). The ideal oral fluid is tap water, to which has been added common salt and sodium bicarbonate – five grams salt and four grams sodium bicarbonate per litre (Moyer's solution).

f *Antibiotics* – antibiotic therapy may be commenced at regimental level and continued on the line of evacuation until definitive treatment is reached.

g *Anti-tetanus measures* – conform to accepted military practice and are as essential in the management of a burn as in any other wound.

h *Elevation* – the burned limb should be raised and supported to control oedema. The use of plastic bags enables some self help to be possible, and active use of the hands should be encouraged from the start. In a major burn the patient must be treated as a stretcher case.

Details of anti-shock measures in burn wounds

All burns over 15 per cent will require treatment to prevent the onset of shock. Fluid is lost to the circulation:

    a   from the burn surface,
    b   into the underlying tissues,
    c   by the destruction of blood.

The emergency treatment of burns is initiated with electrolyte solutions intravenously at the first and second echelons. Treatment is continued with intravenous colloid solutions at the third echelon.

A secure intravenous pathway is essential in all cases, and the largest possible venous catheter should be passed into the largest possible vein as soon as possible after the burn. This may involve a cut down through burned tissues. A small needle in a small peripheral vein is of no value in the treatment of severe burns. Intravenous resuscitation must continue for 48 hours, and short term intravenous regimes have no value.

Volume of fluid required   Several formulae exist for the calculation of the fluid needs of the burned patient using body weight and extent of burn. These formulae are merely a guide to the volume of fluid required, which may have to be varied from time to time depending on the patient's response to treatment and the presence of other injuries such as missile wounds.

Firstly estimate the area of body surface burned using the Rule of Nines. Palmar surface of hand is one per cent.

a   *The British Army Burns Unit Formula*

Give 120 ml of colloid per one per cent body surface area burn over the 48 hours from the time of burn divided as follows:

In the first eight hours, **after time of burn** – half the total.
In the next 16 hours – quarter of the total.
In next 24 hours – quarter of the total.
In extensive full thickness burns, blood may be given in lieu of colloid in third phase.

This fluid is given intravenously and is for the correction and prevention of shock alone.

The physiological requirement must be given separately, either by mouth or by intravenous infusion, and is calculated on a volume of 50 ml per kilogram body weight for 24 hours.

b The *Brooke US Army Burns Centre Formula* for estimating resuscitation fluid requirements:

First 24 hours post-burn –

Adult: Lactated Ringer's solution, 2 ml/kg body weight/per cent body
surface burned.*

Child: Lactated Ringer's solution, 3 ml/kg body weight/per cent body
surface burned.*

NB: Rate of infusion adjusted according to patient response.†

Second 24 hours post-burn –

Colloid-containing fluid to replace residual plasma volume deficit.
Electrolyte-free water to maintain urinary output.

* One half of estimated volume is infused in the first eight hours after burn.
† More than estimated volume is often required in patients with delayed resuscitation and for those with high-voltage electric injury.

Nature of replacement fluid The fluid lost from the circulation is protein-containing and therefore a colloid is the logical choice in replacement. This should start at the second echelon:

a *Colloids*

(1) Dextran (preferably 110, some use 70) is the usual plasma substitute in the treatment and prevention of burns shock. It may be used in concentrations of three to six per cent diluted with saline solution. Dextran 110 influences cross-match of blood and so, if immediate transfusion is indicated because of other injuries, blood should be taken for cross-matching before starting.

(2) Reconstituted plasma – still used but becoming more difficult to obtain and may occasionally transmit the causative agent of Virus B hepatitis. Freeze dried and deep frozen plasma are to be made available.

(3) Human plasma protein solution (HPPS) is replacing dried plasma and is stored in liquid state in glass bottles. Because of the expense of stockpiling it is of less value in the field. It is deficient in certain essential factors, and this must be remembered if other injuries are present as bleeding may occur.

b *Blood:* 50 ml for each one per cent whole skin loss during early phase of treatment.

c *Electrolyte solutions* – Ringer lactate, saline or Hartmann's solution is used at the first and second echelon and to replace transudation and physiological requirement later. The volume of electrolyte solution alone required in the treatment of shock is four to six times that required if colloid solutions are used. The patient becomes very oedematous, but the method may be of value if colloids are not available, provided the fluid is given in the huge volume required to maintain circulation, eg over 20 litres per 24 hours in some patients with extensive burns. Not advised for general use – only in emergency.

Assessment of treatment

A formula provides the surgeon with an order of the volume of fluid requirement and is not a set of instructions to be followed blindly. Frequent, regular assessment of the patient's general condition and response to treatment must be made and the volume and rate of infusion varied accordingly:

a *Pulse rate* A steady fall in the pulse rate is a good index of adequate treatment.

b *Assessment of peripheral tissue perfusion* Skin colour, temperature and capillary filling.

c Together with the *patient's general demeanour,* restlessness, nausea or vomiting, etc.

d *Urinary output* is the most effective means of assessing the satisfactory response to treatment. The severely burned patient must be catheterized. Hourly urinary output should be measured and an output of between 35–60 ml per hour is ideal. Less than 30 ml per hour is evidence that the fluid replacement is inadequate.

e *Hb and Haematocrit* Frequent monitoring of these two values is of value in assessing treatment; a rising haemoglobin concentration warrants increasing the rate of infusion.

f *Central venous pressure* Where other injuries co-exist, may be of some help to the surgeon in the third echelon hospitals.

Measures for the general condition of the burn patient

In burns, as in all forms of wounding, the casualty as a whole must receive consideration as well as his wounds. All wounded pass into a state of negative nitrogen balance for longer or shorter periods and in burn injuries this is of particular importance as the catabolic state is particularly severe and prolonged. It is therefore important to make good the protein deficiency by adequate diet and by supplementary feeding of proteins, vitamins and iron.

Burn injuries are commonly associated with a failure of bone marrow resulting in anaemia, which may persist for some weeks after the burn. The haemoglobin level must be monitored regularly and, where required, blood transfusions given to correct a falling haemoglobin level.

In the late stages of burn injuries infection is the commonest cause of death and septicaemia in major burns is a common complication. All measures in treating the burn wound must be carried out with the fullest aseptic technique and great care taken in ensuring that intravenous treatment does not introduce organisms. Bacteriological monitoring of the burn wound is essential to detect the onset of pathogenic contamination.

Surgical treatment

a *Escharotomy* Circumferential coagulation of the skin of a limb may result in impaired circulation to the distal unburned parts. Similarly the chest wall movements may be restricted by a dense deep eschar. To prevent secondary ischaemic necrosis or to ease respiration, an escharotomy may be necessary to relieve constriction caused by oedema beneath the inelastic unyielding eschar. The procedure can be carried out without an anaesthetic since it is performed through insensitive full thickness burn. The incision is made with a sharp knife and is carried throughout the whole length of the full thickness burn to ensure adequate release of the vascular compression. Blood loss is not excessive, provided care is taken to incise burned tissue only.

b *Tracheostomy*   Tracheostomy in severe burns may be life saving and the indications for this operation are those which exist in any other surgical patient, namely – acute laryngeal or upper airway obstruction, inability to cough out secretions and associated chest wall injuries. Severe smoke inhalation with respiratory insufficiency is an indication for tracheostomy as the patient may require ventilation. These patients are best evacuated at the first possible moment and tracheostomy should be performed before movement to avoid the risk of an acute airway obstruction in transit. The operation may have to be done through severely burned tissues, but the method is as described on page 262.

c *Wound care*   Care of the burn itself should follow treatment of shock:

(1) *Initial cleansing*   The initial cleansing of the burn is important and should be carried out aseptically with the usual operating theatre techniques. A general anaesthetic is rarely required as intravenous analgesia is usually sufficient. Intramuscular Ketamine will be of value in the field. The burn wound is washed with savlon solution followed by saline and all blisters are removed. Scrubbing must be avoided, otherwise valuable epithelial elements will be destroyed. The choice of treatment thereafter depends on the availability of nursing personnel, expertise and the battle situation. Exposure of the burn is the ideal form of treatment, but where early evacuation has to take place closed dressings are to be preferred.

(2) *Exposure*   The exposure method is applicable to burns of the head and neck, the front of trunk, the arms to the wrist, the legs and perineum. In these situations the burn, after thorough cleansing, is left exposed to the air and the patient is nursed on sterile sheets or on special absorptive sheets of foam. After 48 hours the burn is usually dry and in the next few days a dry, firm eschar develops, giving good bacteriological protection. This may be speeded up where rapid cover is required, particularly in the tropics, by the use of a spray, eg Nobecutane or Opsite. In epidermal burns this separates in 7–10 days,

but where the eschar is still present after 14 days it is advisable for a definitive operation to remove the eschar and graft, where necessary, the areas of skin loss.

(3) *Indications for absorptive dressings* All cases for evacuation. Circumferential burns of limbs and the trunk, burns over other injuries, eg fractures or missile wounds, and patients requiring tangential excision (see below) should be treated by absorptive dressings. After thorough cleansing of the wound a single layer of vaseline gauze or furacin gauze is applied to the wound. This is covered by layers of dry gauze, cotton wool and a firm bandage to retain the dressing in position. This dressing is left for 3–5 days before it requires changing.

(4) *Hands* Hands should always be treated in plastic bags to allow movement of the fingers and self help. After thorough cleansing a cuff of gauze is loosely applied to the wrist. Silver sulphadiazine should be applied to the hand. A clean polythene bag is then applied over the hand and lightly occluded at the wrist. A rapid accumulation of serous exudate will be found, but the bag should not be changed unless absolutely necessary. A second bag applied over the first may give additional mechanical protection. The hands should be mobilized and the patient encouraged to feed himself. In a mass casualty situation patients with only hands and face burns may, by the use of these hand bags, be employed as helpers for other more seriously injured patients.

(5) *Standard surgery of the burn wound* The majority of burns, other than hands and eyelids, will be treated by conventional means where the time and expertise required for tangential excision is not available. Whatever method of treatment has been employed in the early stages the necrotic area of skin will have demarcated and all epidermal burns will have healed on the fourteenth day post-burn. At this time it is possible to deslough the wound and cover the skin defect by auto-graft skin. The sloughs or dry eschars are removed by sharp dissection, using scissors, scalpel or skin graft knife, until viable tissue is reached. This usually involves excision down to the fascia in deep burns. Bleeding can be severe and blood in adequate volume should be available for transfusion. Following a full deslough auto-graft skin should be used to give cover as postage stamp grafts or by meshing the split skin graft (Chapter 9). Where sufficient auto-graft skin is not available homograft or porcine skin is used as a biological dressing, but failing this a topical agent such as Furacin, Silver Sulphadiazine or Betadine ointment, liberally applied will be of value in preventing infection until such time as suitable donor skin is available.

(6) *Tangential excision and split skin grafting* With early evacuation to a burns unit it is advisable to treat deep and deep dermal burns of hands and special areas by this method. Three to five days post-burn the deep dermal burn is shaved to the level of punctate bleeding, using a normal skin graft knife and covered by a split skin graft. Firm dressings are used to keep the grafts in place. Early healing of the wound is of particular value in burned hands, where the classical form of treatment at the 14th day often leaves much stiffness in the fingers and functional impairment.

Evacuation

It is inadvisable to move the patient while failure of the circulation is pending, but advisable as soon as the shock phase has been treated.

The burn patient tolerates movement by either ground or air well in the early post-burn period before the development of septic complications makes movement hazardous. The patency of the airway must be ensured at all times throughout the evacuation procedure and a secure intravenous cannula, through which the appropriate fluid can be administered, is essential. Absorptive dressings are required for the burn wound.

Adequate documentation of the patient's condition before evacuation and in transit is maintained and should accompany the patient at all times. Particularly important is an adequate record of fluids administered, urinary output, medications administered and other serial assessments, such as the haemoglobin and haematocrit.

The seriously ill, extensive burned patient travels best by rail or air and should be accompanied by personnel trained in treatment of burn injuries.

Mass casualties

Large numbers of burn patients can occur, either from thermo-nuclear explosion or from missile wounds.

The treatment of the typical Army burns of head and hands has been detailed. With mass casualties the same treatment, with polythene bags on the hands and with exposure of the face, allows the soldier to help himself.

It is probable that burns up to 20 per cent will have to be treated by oral fluids only and in this situation Moyer's solution – five grams sodium chloride plus four grams sodium bicarbonate per litre tap water, should be used. This is one teaspoon of salt and one teaspoon of sodium bicarbonate per litre of water.

Patients with burns of greater extent than 40 per cent are unlikely to survive since intravenous fluids are unlikely to be available in sufficient volume. In extreme situations a difficult decision will have to be made to treat those extensive burns by adequate relief of pain and oral fluids only.

Nursing care in this situation will be extremely difficult and patients with minor injuries will have to help with those more seriously injured. The simplest possible treatment is essential, concentrating on the prevention of early infection in treatable burns by the topical application of Betadine or Silver Sulphadiazine ointment and closed dressings left for as long as possible.

Phosphorus burns

Many anti-personnel weapons employed in modern warfare contain white phosphorus. Fragments of this element, which ignites on contact with the air, may be driven into the soft tissues. Most of the injury resulting from phosphorus burns is due to the ignition of clothing, and is treated as a conventional thermal injury. The first aid treatment of patients with embedded phosphorus particles consists of drenching the area with water and the removal of identifiable particles. This is then followed by covering the area with a saline or water soaked dressing, which is kept moist until the patient reaches a definitive treatment area. Patients with phosphorus burns require immediate wound care in contrast to those with conventional burns. The wounds containing embedded phosphorus particles may then be rinsed with a diluted (one per cent) freshly mixed solution of copper sulphate. This solution combines with the phosphorus on the surface of the particles to form a black phosphide covering, which impedes further oxidation and facilitates the identification of retained particles.

Under no circumstances should copper sulphate solution be applied as a wet dressing and retained on the body.

Following treatment the wound must be washed thoroughly with saline to ensure that all of the copper solution has been removed. Thereafter treatment is as for conventional means, but a closed dressing is advisable.

A SYNOPSIS OF TREATMENT FOR THERMAL BURN INJURY

1 Assessment of the patient   Extent of burn – Rule of Nines (palm of hand = 1 per cent). Depth of burn. Haematocrit at regular intervals. Other injuries.

2 Start records   Diagram per cent body surface surface burn: time of burn: weight of patient (kg).

3 Treatment   Immediate. Remove burning clothing. Cool burn to arrest heat uptake. Sedation.

4 Fluid balance   Aim urine output 50 ml/hour. Control by Foley Catheter.
a *Oral* 50 ml/kg/24 hours: Moyer's solution. (5 g NaCl + 4 g $NaHCO_3$ + one litre H_2O is isotonic) (+ 'Jungle Juice' crystals to taste.)
b *Intravenous* for burns of over 15 per cent body surface burnt. Route: Polythene Cannula (large bore).
   (1) Regimental Aid Post: Echelon one – Hartmann's solution, one litre.
   (2) In transit: Echelon two – Hartmann's solution, one litre.
   (3) Hospital: Echelon three

British Army Formula:
(a) Colloid: Dextran or Plasma: Rate 120 ml per one per cent burn in 48 hours. Divide total: Half in first eight hours from time of burning: quarter in next 16 hours; quarter in next 24 hours.
(b) Blood: 50 ml for each one per cent whole skin loss during early phase of treatment.
(c) Electrolyte to cover physiological requirement deficit from oral or intravenous electrolytes.

US Army Formula: The Brooke US Army Burns Centre Formula:
First 24 hours post-burn –
Adult: Lactated Ringer's solution, 2 ml/kg body weight/per cent body
surface burned*.
Child: Lactated Ringer's solution, 3 ml/kg body weight/per cent body
surface burned*.
NB: Rate of infusion adjusted according to patient response.†

Second 24 hours post-burn:
Colloid-containing fluid to replace residual plasma volume deficit.
Electrolyte-free water to maintain urinary output.
*One half of estimated volume is infused in the first eight hours after
burn.
†More than estimated volume is often required in patients with delayed
resuscitation and for those with high-voltage electric injury.

5 Airway: Consider intubation: or tracheostomy if absolutely necessary.
Escharotomy of chest burns.

6 Local care: Aim – maximum efficiency with minimal work and
minimal materials. Consider Neuroleptic; IV analgesia; General
Anaesthetic.

7 Definitive local care: Methods of preference
a. Absorptive – Clean surface.
Pressure dressing – Tulle gras if superficial – two layers gamgee tissue.
Change 7–10 days (review earlier if wet).
b Occlusive method – HANDS and FEET. Clean surface.
Apply Silver Sulphadiazine or other ointment.
Cover with plastic glove/bag/envelope.
Change daily.
c Exposure treatment – Limited application except for
head/neck/perineum. Requires intensive nursing care.
May be used for fractures, associated with thermal injury, on skeletal
traction.
d Excision/grafting – Within 72 hours of injury if possible.
Autograft.
Heterograft: Lyophilised freeze dried porcine skin.
e Antibiotics – Only for: established infection, respiratory burns.
f Circumferential limb burns should have escharotomy before
evacuation.

CHAPTER 7

Anaesthesia and analgesia in forward areas

Personnel

It is an accepted principle that medical anaesthetists of mature judgement must be made available to cover forward surgery. With mass or multiple casualties they may be responsible for several patients under anaesthesia at the same time and careful planning will be necessary to ensure maximum safety, particularly as the assistants available may be only partially or hastily trained.

Equipment

The field apparatus for general anaesthesia is based on the air drawover principle, being independent of a supply of logistically undesirable cylinders of medical gases but with provision for oxygen supplementation. Flammable agents are not normally included in the scale but ether must be considered in many countries as the most readily available local agent.

Special conditions

Climate and topography may affect the choice of anaesthetic and consideration must also be given to situations in which the anaesthetist finds himself separated from his equipment and obliged to improvise.

Preparation of the patient

The airway Obstruction of the airway is one of the most frequent and rapid causes of death in casualties, who survive initial trauma. In unconscious patients, and many of those with maxillo-facial injuries, clearance of the airway, extension of the head and neck, support of the jaw and the use of the prone or semi-prone position will often suffice to maintain the airway until the patient arrives at the reception area of the surgical centre; but immediate action to preserve the airway may be required in the resuscitation department in the form of endotracheal intubation, or, more rarely, opening the air passages below the obstruction. General anaesthesia is contra-indicated at this stage in an obstructed patient and infiltration or topical local analgesia are rarely necessary because the patient is often actually or virtually unconscious because of hypoxia. Cricothyrotomy is usually effective, simpler and safer than tracheostomy in such circumstances. Every field anaesthetist should be familiar with the surface markings of the cricothyroid membrane. Two or more wide-bore needles (size 16 g or larger) inserted through the membrane, with oxygen administered through one of them if necessary, may save life. The use of modern disposable needle and cannula systems such as the Medicut is a further refinement which will enable blunt plastic cannulae to be left in place. Cricothyrotomy itself can be carried out by inserting the first 2 cm of the tip of a solid-bladed knife, which is then twisted vertically. This manoeuvre opens up the wound prior to the insertion of a tracheostomy, endotracheal, or some other suitable tube or catheter. Special trocar and cannula systems have been designed for cricothyrotomy but the use of the knife is probably safer and equally effective. In recent wars cricothyrotomy has been successfully undertaken by para-medical personnel at the site of wounding as an advanced first aid procedure.

Tension pneumothorax   The insertion of a chest drainage tube under local analgesia for the relief of respiratory distress due to tension pneumothorax is another life-saving measure which may be required. The anaesthetist must be familiar with the techniques involved in inserting a chest drain and the use of a simple underwater seal or a Heimlich valve. In emergency situations the insertion of a 16 gauge disposable intravenous cannula in the 3rd interspace in the mid-clavicular line will be life saving until formal underwater seal drainage can be instituted.

Blood volume   Hypovolaemic shock due to loss of blood volume is the main pre-anaesthetic problem encountered.

General anaesthesia must necessarily be the technique of choice for the surgery of major casualties under battle conditions. It is, however, in these cases that blood loss is greatest and hypovolaemic shock likely to be most severe. All general anaesthetics cause vasodilation and some (thiopentone, and halothane for example) can also depress myocardial action if administered too freely. The combined results of these effects in the grossly hypovolaemic patient may rapidly precipitate the fatal sequence of profound hypotension – coronary insufficiency – cardiac arrest and death.

Estimates of the degree of hypovolaemia based on the measurement of arterial blood pressure can be grossy misleading. An initially fit soldier can lose up to 30 per cent of his blood volume (1 to 2 litres) and still remain normotensive or even be slightly hypertensive due to excessive compensatory vasoconstriction. Care should be taken to observe the other signs of hypovolaemia including vasoconstrictive pallor and tachycardia and to estimate, and at least partially replace, volume loss before general anaesthesia is induced (see Chapter 3). Oxygen should be administered if available to make the best use of the depleted haemoglobin.

Dehydration due to vomiting, sweating, evaporation from wounds and exposed viscera, and fluid sequestered as wound oedema, can greatly add to the degree of hypovolaemia.

The decision whether a patient has been sufficiently resuscitated for general anaesthesia must be taken jointly by the anaesthetist and the resuscitation officer. If the military situation is static and secure, there are very few traumatic conditions, other than the rupture of a major artery, which call for immediate operative intervention. It is nearly always safer to wait for the patient to be resuscitated with adequate quantities of the appropriate intravenous fluids. Under active war conditions, however, less than complete volume replacement must often be accepted. The greatest care must be taken in choosing and administering general anaesthesia to patients still suffering from hypovolaemic shock (see page 109). Experience has shown that a rising systolic blood pressure of 80 mm Hg or above, a steadily decreasing pulse rate and improvement in the peripheral circulation, as evidenced by the warm, pink, dry skin on the forehead and the tip of the nose, provide sufficient indication that the cautious induction of general anaesthesia may be undertaken.

Catheterization and estimation of urinary excretion is another useful means of monitoring fluid replacement. A volume in excess of 30 ml/hr is satisfactory.

Routine preparation   Techniques of anaesthesia which guard against the danger of vomiting and regurgitation must be used routinely. These consist of:

a   The use of head up tilt whenever possible.
b   Pressure on the crichothyroid cartilage during induction of anaesthesia.
c   The intubation of all patients who may be liable to vomiting or regurgitation.

The mouth should be checked and any broken fragments of teeth and dentures removed.

Urine should be voided but the routine testing of urine in a basically fit military population under emergency conditions is a procedure of doubtful value.

Analgesia and premedication   The patient may well have received morphine or one of its derivatives or substitutes intra-muscularly before arrival in the resuscitation area. There is a well documented danger of an excessive extra dose of morphine narcotic being given intramuscularly because the first dose appears to be ineffective. This is because the first dose has been retained around the site of the injection as a result of the intense vasoconstriction. Subsequent vasodilatation during resuscitation causes both doses to be released into the circulation at the same time and severe respiratory depression may ensue. This danger must not, however, be exaggerated. The importance of ensuring that patients receive adequate analgesia in the resuscitation area must never be under-estimated. Morphine narcotics should be given intravenously in incremental doses titrated to alleviate the patient's pain (see page 106). Removal of clothes and many other preparatory manipulations can be carried out under general analgesia provided by intravenous morphine alone. The respiratory depression due to morphine narcotics usually affects respiratory rate rather than depth and if very severe (a respiratory rate of less than 12 per minute) may be reversed by an intravenous injection of naloxone 0.1 mg doses given incrementally at two minute intervals. This may be repeated as necessary. Premedication before surgery in the field will usually be by morphine narcotics, already given for the relief of pain, with the addition of atropine (0.6 mg), but given intravenously immediately before induction. Trichloroethylene and halothane are less irritant than ether and the necessity to dry up bronchial secretions correspondingly less important. In dry, dehydrated, pyrexial patients the use of atropine is contraindicated and the requirements may be diminished in the presence of tachycardia unless suxamethonium or ketamine is to be used.

General anaesthesia

The need for as complete a restoration of blood volume as possible before the induction of general anaesthesia has been fully discussed above.

General anaesthesia is the only practical technique for the surgery of multiple trauma and usually the only one psychologically acceptable to the severely wounded man. The possible use of local analgesic blocks to supplement it for abdominal relaxation and to provide relief of post-operative pain is considered on page 108.

Induction and intubation   Tracheal intubation is both the key to safety and a mandatory part of anaesthetic techniques involving controlled ventilation. Intubation is also the surest way of achieving the gas-tight continuity between the apparatus and respiratory tree of the patient, so essential for the successful use of the drawover systems provided for use in Surgical Centres.

An intravenous infusion should always be started before induction of general anaesthesia in order to guarantee an open vein. A three-way tap should be inserted between the cannula and the intravenous infusion tubing. In the field, the infusion will normally be set up in the resuscitation area.

The inspired air should be enriched with oxygen for a few breaths before induction of possible, so that the patient will have a high arterial oxygen tension to carry him through any unavoidable period of apnoea or respiratory obstruction which may occur.

Two alternative techniques of intubation designed to prevent the inhalation of gastric material are recommended; intravenous induction and muscle relaxant technique of intubation. This is the so-called 'crash' induction so popular with British anaesthetists.

Passage of an endotracheal tube   The patient is positioned in a slight head up tilt with his head on a pillow to extend the head on the neck as for mouth to mouth resuscitation – the neck is not extended.

A cuffed endotracheal tube and catheter mount is tested and lubricated and an assistant stands beside the patient with his fingers lightly on the cricoid cartilage. While the patient is breathing oxygen enriched air anaesthesia is induced using an intravenous agent followed immediately by a short acting muscle relaxant – Suxamethonium Bromide. As soon as the patient is unconscious the assistant applies firm pressure to the cricoid cartilage while the anaesthetist, standing at the head of the patient, aids the patient's ventilation by gently squeezing the reservoir bag until he is fully relaxed.

Holding the lighted laryngoscope in his left hand the anaesthetist checks the extension of the patient's head and opens his mouth with the thumb and index finger of his right hand and gently introduces the laryngoscope blade slightly to the right of the mid line towards the right tonsil. Checking that the lips have not been caught between the blade and the teeth, the laryngoscope is advanced until the right tonsil or tonsillar bed is seen. The tip of the blade is then moved towards the mid line keeping the tongue behind the shoulder of the laryngoscope blade.

When the epiglottis comes into view the tip of the blade is inserted between the base of the tongue and the epiglottis – in the vallecula. Keeping the left wrist rigid, the larynx is exposed by a firm pull in line with the laryngoscope handle. On no account must the tip of the blade be rotated upwards by levering on the upper teeth. As the larynx is seen the lubricated endotracheal tube, in which a well lubricated malleable introducer may be placed, is introduced from the right side of the mouth and advanced between the vocal cords into the trachea. The laryngoscope and introducer, if used, are then removed and the catheter mount is connected to the anaesthetic supply. Whilst listening to the chest the anaesthetist gently inflates the lungs by squeezing the reservoir bag to ensure that both lungs are being aerated and that the stomach is not being inflated. The cuff of the endotracheal tube is then inflated with air just sufficiently to prevent the escape of gases between the trachea and endotracheal tube.

If cuffed endotracheal tubes are not available, a regurgitation-proof and air-tight seal may be obtained by packing the throat with a gauze pack soaked in water using Magill forceps under direct vision with the aid of laryngoscope.

Intubation of the unanaesthetized patient 'Awake intubation' should be practised more often. Experience in the United States of America has demonstrated that this is a safe and acceptable method which need not cause undue distress to the sedated patient.

The best sedation for awake intubation is the intramuscular or intravenous injection of a morphine narcotic (see page 106) which the patient will probably have already received. Morphine narcotics leave the patient co-operative, which is essential for the success of the technique, and also, to some extent, obtund the pharyngolaryngeal reflexes.

Five millilitres of 4 per cent lignocaine are drawn up into a syringe with a needle attached. The patient is asked to open his mouth and 1–1·5 ml of 4 per cent lignocaine are sprayed from the syringe on to and over the dorsum of the tongue. The patient is asked to close his eyes and breathe deeply.

He is then quietly reassured by the anaesthetist as the well lubricated laryngoscope blade is gently introduced over the tongue until the tip of the epiglottis comes into view; a further 1–1.5 ml of 4 per cent lignocaine are sprayed on the epiglottis. The vocal cords are exposed. The remaining 2–3 ml of the 4 per cent lignocaine is now sprayed into the upper larynx and between the cords. When the vocal cords are widely abducted the endotracheal tube may be passed gently into the trachea and the cuff inflated. The patient coughs a little but soon tolerates the tube and, now that the airway is isolated, general anaesthesia can be rapidly induced with the intravenous agent of choice.

In the case of a moribund patient, intubation prior to inhalation anaesthesia may be effected without drugs as in emergency resuscitation.

The draw-over apparatus   A draw-over apparatus consists of one or more calibrated vaporizers for different volatile agents, through which ambient air is drawn, via an unidirectional valve system, either by spontaneous respiration, or by controlled ventilation by the manual operation of a self-inflating resuscitator bag or a mechanical ventilator. Provision is also made for a T-piece reservoir to allow enrichment of the entrained air with oxygen. This is particularly desirable with spontaneous ventilation and at the beginning and end of a controlled ventilation technique.

The particular apparatus provided for the use of surgical teams has two separate Oxford Miniature Vaporizers (OMVs) designed to vaporize calibrated percentages of the non-flammable agents trichloroethylene and halothane. It has replaced the Epstein Mackintosh Oxford (EMO) apparatus.

Controlled ventilation technique for the maintenance of general anaesthesia.

After intubation as described above ventilation is controlled using comparatively low concentrations of any volatile agent in air (eg trichloroethylene 1–1.5 per cent, halothane 1–2 per cent, ether 6–10 per cent). The air is preferably supplemented with oxygen through the T-piece reservoir system. The short acting relaxant suxamethonium bromide will begin to wear off after a few minutes and spontaneous respiratory movements be observed.

The patient is then paralysed with one or other of the longer acting muscle relaxants (see page 104). Controlled ventilation continues with the chosen volatile agent. The concentration is gradually reduced as time passes. Both trichloroethylene and ether should be discontinued well before the end of the operation as they are cumulative. The oxygen may be turned off during maintenance.

At the end of the operation atropine 0.6–1.2 mg is injected intravenously to control side effects such as bradycardia, before the residual action of the muscle relaxant is reversed by the intravenous injection of prostigmine (2.5–5 mg). Ventilation is assisted until spontaneous respiration is adequate. It is useful to turn on the supplementary oxygen (1 or 4 litres per minute) at this stage. This enables relatively long pauses to be made in ventilation in order to build up the blood carbon dioxide level to normal again after the almost inevitable hyperventilation of controlled ventilation. A length of about 30 cm of corrugated anaesthetic tubing, inserted between the catheter mount and the one-way expiratory valve, will add dead-space and assist in the process of building up carbon dioxide to normal levels.

If the patient does not breathe immediately patience is required. On no account must more than a total of 7.5 mg of prostigmine be given. This is the maximum effective dose; further dosage will serve no useful purpose and may promote, rather than reverse, apnoea. Consideration should be given to the possibility of residual respiratory depression from morphine narcotics administered in the pre-operative period, which will be shown by the presence of constricted pupils; naloxone in 0.1 mg incremental doses should then be injected intravenously.

An intravenous dose of doxapram hydrochloride (40–100 mg) may be effective in starting spontaneous respiration, if it is evident from the tone of the jaw that the muscle relaxant is reversed, but apnoea persists because of a temporary loss of the power of automatic discharge of the respiratory centre. Relative respiratory insufficiency does not usually continue once spontaneous respiration has started in basically fit young subjects.

Apnoea persisting for 10–15 minutes after the administration of suxamethonium is not uncommon but rarely causes concern as its duration is shorter than the surgical operation. If apnoea due to suxamethonium persists after the end of the operation the best policy is to continue controlled ventilation until spontaneous respiration starts again. There is usually a change in the type of neuro-muscular block, from depolarizing to non-depolarizing, after about one hour. Atropine and prostigmine may then be tried in cautious increments. If they are administered before one hour has elapsed prostigmine may aggravate the depolarizing block and prolong apnoea.

A controlled ventilation technique is essential for intrathoracic operations, safe and reliable for abdominal surgery and neurosurgery and satisfactory for body-surface surgery. It is the easiest and safest technique to use with draw-over apparatus, especially in the absence of oxygen supplementation.

Recovery after this type of anaesthesia is normally rapid because of the low concentrations of volatile agents used. This is a considerable advantage in a busy surgical centre in which the number of personnel who can be spared to look after unconscious post-operative patients is minimal (see page 106).

Spontaneous respiration technique for the maintenance of general anaesthesia

The patient is induced and intubated as described on page 98. The effect of the suxamethonium bromide is allowed to wear off and, as it does so, the concentration of volatile anaesthetic vapour is gradually increased. The patient may strain a little but laryngeal spasm is not possible because the patient is already intubated. It is often useful to give a dose of naloxone 0.1 mg incrementally to increase the tidal volume if substantial doses of morphine narcotics have been given in the pre-operative phase.

The combination of trichloroethylene (1–1½ per cent) and halothane (1–3.5 per cent) from separate vaporizers is a satisfactory mixture for spontaneous respiration. These agents may be delivered in ambient air (enriched if possible with oxygen 1–4 litres per minute) from the two separate OMVs of the field drawover apparatus. Neither of these two agents is very satisfactory as a sole agent. Spontaneously respired halothane alone is a good anaesthetic but it causes respiratory depression and hypotension as well as being a poor suppressor of reflex reaction to surgery. Trichloroethylene alone is a better general analgesic than anaesthetic but it has a tendency to cause tachypnoea, which may be controlled by 10–15 mg of pethidine given intravenously. In combination, the two agents are complimentary.

Ether (8–20 per cent) delivered from a vaporizer is a mild respiratory stimulant if not pressed to deep anaesthesia. Apart from its flammability it is the most satisfactory agent for a spontaneous draw-over technique. Ether is suitable for use without oxygen supplementation but too great a volume and concentration are required for it to be satisfactorily used in an OMV vaporizer. Trichloroethylene may be used in an ether EMO vaporizer (the 6 per cent ether setting is equivalent to approximately 1 per cent Trichloroethylene). Halothane should not be used as it will corrode an ether EMO.

The draw-over technique with spontaneous respiration can be used for body-surface operations but it requires more minute to minute adjustment of the vaporizer settings than the muscle relaxant, controlled ventilation, draw over technique (see page 100). A greater concentration of volatile agent is also required and recovery consequently tends to be slower.

The combination of light spontaneously respired volatile agents with intercostal block or caudal block for lower abdominal and perineal surgical procedures also deserves consideration for use with general anaesthetic and local analgesic agents (see page 108).

Selection of intravenous induction agents and muscle relaxants

This paragraph is concerned only with the drugs provided in the current scale for surgical teams:

a *Induction agents:*

(1) *Thiopentone* – (100–500 mg) has long been popular as an induction agent. Its margin of safety is narrower than is the case with some other agents including ketamine but it is a drug with comparatively few side effects. It acts long enough to permit an early transition to intravenous maintenance. A relative overdose of thiopentone can cause temporary apnoea but this is not important if the patient is to be paralysed with suxamethonium bromide, intubated and ventilated (see page 100).

Thiopentone must be administered slowly and cautiously to all seriously ill patients. It causes vasodilatation and some cardiac depression leading to hypotension which may be unwise if the patient has not been fully resuscitated after hypovolaemia. It can however, be used safely in hypovolaemic shock provided it is administered cautiously in small doses allowing for the reduced blood volume and slowed circulation in such cases.

(2) *Ketamine* – (100–300 mg) is a drug which has a unique value as a sole agent under emergency conditions (see page 104) but it is also a useful induction agent prior to more conventional anaesthesia. It has a wide margin of safety. Its special value in emergency situations lies in its sympatheticomimetic action which makes it useful for induction of cases in which hypovolaemic shock has not been completely treated.

The subsequent administration of a volatile anaesthetic agent virtually eliminates the psychogenic emergency problems sometimes associated with the use of ketamine. Ketamine may also be given intramuscularly in doses of 200–500 mg (see page 105).

b *Muscle relaxants:*

(1)   Suxamethonium Bromide (100 mg) is the short acting depolarizing agent ideal for intubation. Under field conditions the powdered product of the bromide is supplied as it is more stable than the more familiar liquid solution of suxamethonium chloride. It should not be administered in the presence of anoxia owing to the danger of cardiac arrest and it should always be preceded by atropine 0.6 mg unless an antisialogogue has been given with the pre-medication.

Suxamethonium should not be used in burns cases over 10 days old due to the risk of cardiac arrest following potassium release from damaged muscles and that produced by suxamethonium itself.

(2)   Tubocurarine (15–30 mg) is a non-depolarizing agent. It has an indefinite storage life. It will paralyse the patient for 30–45 minutes. It is liable to cause hypotension and should be used with caution in the presence of hypovolaemic shock and halothane.

(3)   Pancuronium (4–8 mg) is a most useful non-depolarizing muscle relaxant for field units. It has a limited shelf life of about six months at temperate room temperatures and will therefore only be added to the field unit scale on mobilization.

It is rapid in onset, with about the same duration as tubocurarine and slightly elevates blood pressure and increases cardiac output. Its excretion is little affected by impaired renal function and it is particularly appropriate for use in cases with incompletely corrected hypovolaemic shock. It should not be used in conjunction with ketamine in normovolaemic, normotensive patients, as a potentially dangerous degree of hypertension may develop; but this combination is of value in the hypotensive patient.

Ketamine as a sole anaesthetic agent

Ketamine is a unique drug with a wide margin of safety. It has special indications in emergency anaesthesia but its limitations should be clearly understood.

Ketamine produces the unusual highly analgesic, trance-like state known as 'dissociative anaesthesia.' The laryngopharyngeal protective reflexes are preserved under ketamine alone better than under any other agent or combination of agents, but they are always partially suppressed. The suppression will be increased if any form of sedative or analgesic premedication has been used. The airway therefore always requires careful supervision. Ketamine stimulates the secretion of saliva and a preliminary or concomitant injection of atropine is desirable.

Ketamine (100–300 mg) is effective intravenously within 45 seconds. It is also unique as the only consistently effective intramuscular anaesthetic agent (200–500 mg). If administered intramuscularly it reliably induces anaesthesia within three minutes. This time is only slightly prolonged by the vasoconstriction of hypovolaemic shock.

Intravenous ketamine suppresses reflex response to surgery for 5–15 minutes, but amnesia persists for up to one hour. The duration of its action when administered intramuscularly is variable, but it can allow about one hour of operating time and its effects may last for well over two hours.

A satisfactory technique for longer procedures is to inject a full dose of ketamine intravenously and follow it immediately with a dose of 200–500 mg intramuscularly. Further reflex suppression is obtained by intravenous increments of approximately 100 mg. Alternatively the first injection can be intramuscular if no veins can be found. Ketamine does not produce respiratory depression even in relatively high doses but may do so very temporarily if a large dose is given intravenously too rapidly. A rate of injection of 100 mg in 30 seconds should not be exceeded.

Ketamine raises blood pressure and probably increases cardiac output. It is thus the induction agent of choice if general anaesthesia must be administered in the presence of incompletely corrected hypovolaemic shock. In these circumstances the full calculated mg/kg body weight dose can be given intramuscularly or slowly intravenously.

Ketamine is often regarded as unsatisfactory as a sole agent for abdominal operations but this really depends on the degree of muscular relaxation which is acceptable. It may be supplemented by local analgesic intercostal block.

Both objectively observed delirium and subjective hallucinations occur in some patients in the recovery phase from Ketamine. They can be controlled by the intravenous injection of diazepam (5–10) at the end of the operation but this greatly prolongs recovery. Ketamine, used with discretion, is a very useful anaesthetic as a sole agent in emergency and also in the later management of trauma and burn casualties to cover such procedures as multiple dressings.

Recovery from general anaesthesia

Under field conditions it is often desirable to leave the endotracheal tube in place longer than would be the case after elective operations. The temporary discomfort to the patient regaining consciousness is more than counterbalanced by the element of increased safety. Extubation should, whenever practicable, be carried out with the patient on his side and he should be kept in that position pending recovery unless the nature of the operation makes it impossible.

It is vitally important that adequate post-operative analgesia is provided. The intravenous injection of increments of morphine analgesics, titrated to the need of each patient, is one of the most satisfactory methods of pain control (see below).

The control of post-operative vomiting can be effected by the intravenous or intramuscular injection of metoclopramide (10 mg) or perphenazine (5 mg).

General and local analgesia

Wide use of general and local analgesia saves time and reduces the number of personnel required to supervise unconscious patients:

a *General analgesia*

(1) *Intravenous analgesia* Intravenous injections of morphine narcotics are particularly useful for the manipulation of closed fractures and dislocations and as background analgesia for the intubation of the conscious patient (see page 99). In emergency situations intravenous morphine has been used to cover amputations without subsequent recall by the casualty (see page 117).

Morphine should be diluted to 2 mg/ml, papaveretum to 4 mg/ml and administered in 4 mg (papaveretum 8 mg) increments until the desired effect is obtained. 15 mg morphine or 20 mg papaveretum should be regarded as the maximum intravenous dose ordinarily permissible. Careful observation should be kept on respiration and naloxone (0.2–0.4 mg) used as required.

Pethidine diluted to 10 mg/ml and given in 10 mg increments to a maximum of 100 mg may also be used in this way but it is less satisfactory than morphine or papaveretum as it has little tranquillizing action on the cerebral cortex.

Pethidine (or morphine or papaveretum) administered with the tranquillizer diazepam (5–15 mg intravenously) is an effective combination. Smaller doses of morphine analgesics and substitutes are required if diazepam is used than if the analgesics are used alone. Respiratory depression is less but recovery time is longer than with intravenous analgesia alone.

(2)   *The inhalation of Trichloroethylene*   This is a powerful analgesic and the inhalation of 0.5–0.7 per cent of the vapour in air produces a useful analgesic state short of full general anaesthesia. A system consisting of one Oxford Miniature Vaporizer or an improvised vaporizer (see page 117), a piece of wide bore tubing, a one-way anaesthetic valve and a mask can be used. The patient should always be asked to hold the mask himself as a safety precaution against loss of consciousness. Trichloroethylene can also be inhaled from a Schimmelbush open mask or improvised gauze sponge. It is eminently suitable for burn and wound dressings and to augment local analgesia.

b   *Local analgesia*

(1)   *Indications*   The main uses of local analgesia in the Surgical Centre are: topical 4 per cent lignocaine (for the eye and for oral, nasal and urethral catheterisation or endoscopy), infiltration with lignocaine (for clean minor lacerations in any part of the body), nerve blocks and regional intravenous analgesia with lignocaine or bupivacaine for the limbs and intercostal block for muscular relaxation under general anaesthesia.

(2)   *Lignocaine* is a most suitable agent for cutting surgery. It is rapid in onset and reliable in its action. It is used in 1 or 2 per cent solution and the maximum safe dose is about 20 ml of 1 per cent solution without adrenaline or 40 ml of 1 per cent solution with 1 : 250 000 adrenaline in an adult. The duration of action is about one hour without adrenaline and two hours with it.

(3)   *Bupivacaine* is slower in onset than Lignocaine. It is an effective long-acting agent of 5–16 hours duration. The maximum safe dose is about 30 ml of 0.5 per cent solution in an adult with or without adrenaline. Bupivacaine is normally used in 0.5 per cent solution but can be diluted to 0.375 per cent if required. Its long action has opened up the possibility of using it as a nerve block under general anaesthesia to provide analgesia into the post-operative period.

(4)   *Toxicity*   Toxic effects are rarely seen provided the dosages of local analgesic agents are kept within the maximum safe dose recommended. True allergic reactions to a small dose of local analgesics are rare.

(5)   *Topical analgesia*   Four per cent lignocaine produces excellent

analgesia of the larynx and pharynx. Four per cent cocaine is often preferred for the eyes and nose because of its vasoconstrictive effect.

(6)   Infiltration analgesia is simple and a knowledge of the anatomy of the subcutaneous nerves useful, as it will reduce the volume of solution required, especially when dealing with the head, neck and scalp. 0.5–1 per cent lignocaine with adrenaline 1 : 200 000 to 1 : 400 000 is normally used.

(7)   *Nerve blocks for the extremities*   The safest and most reliable are axillary brachial plexus block and digital blocks in the upper limb and those around the ankle in the lower limb. 1.5 per cent lignocaine is a convenient solution.

Adrenaline should not be used for digital blocks for fear of producing gangrene due to vasoconstriction at the tip of the finger.

(8)   *Intravenous regional analgesia*   This is a very satisfactory technique for the arm but is not recommended for the leg for which a large volume of solution is required.

A blood pressure cuff or, preferably, an orthopaedic tourniquet is placed in position high up on the arm. An indwelling needle is inserted into a vein on the back of the hand. The arm is exsanguinated by an Esmarch bandage, by elevation for three minutes or by the use of a pneumatic fracture splint. The tourniquet is inflated to well above arterial pressure (ie 200–300 mm Hg) and 40–60 ml 0.2 per cent bupivacaine (4 ml 0.5 per cent solution in each 10 ml) or 0.5 per cent lignocaine without adrenaline is then injected into the indwelling needle. Full and complete analgesia is obtained within five minutes.

A second cuff may be placed below the first, which is then deflated if the patient complains of pain at the site of the tourniquet.

The cuff should not be deflated before 20 minutes have elapsed. This avoids releasing a large bolus of local analgesic solution into the circulation, thus causing a toxic reaction. Sensation returns very soon after the removal of the tourniquet, whichever agent has been used.

(9)   *Intercostal block*   This is not a satisfactory technique in the conscious patient in a Surgical Centre but it is excellent for producing analgesia and muscular relaxation of the lower abdomen (T9 to 12) under light general anaesthesia and for prolonging analgesia of the whole abdomen (T6 to 12) and thorax (T5 to 12) into the post-operative period if 0.5 per cent Bupivacaine is used.

Blocks should be carried out under the lower border of the ribs in the mid-axillary line, injecting 3–4 ml at each site.

The technique can be criticized because of the possibility of producing a pneumothorax but this can be avoided if the needle is always kept on the syringe, the tip of the needle never advanced more than 0.5 cm obliquely under the lower border of the rib and if an aspiration test for air or blood is repeatedly carried out. Aspiration should indeed be practised in any local analgesic technique to avoid intravascular injection.

Spinal, caudal and lumbar epidural analgesia are contraindicated in the field.

CHOICES OF TECHNIQUE FOR PARTICULAR CONDITIONS AND INJURIES

A 'standard' general anaesthetic technique for forward surgery

The sequence described on page 97 can be described as 'standard' anaesthetic regime for forward surgery (viz the institution of intravenous infusion – preliminary inhalation of oxygen – intravenous induction – suxamethonium bromide – intubation – long-acting non-depolarizing muscle relaxant – controlled ventilation with a volatile agent in air – reversal of muscle relaxant with prostigmine covered by atropine – extubation and supervised recovery).

General anaesthesia for patients in hypovolaemic and toxaemic shock

The aim should always be to avoid the administration of general anaesthesia to casualties in whom hypovolaemia has not been adequately corrected (see page 95) but this may not always be possible in field surgical centres under battle conditions. If anaesthesia must be induced in a patient suffering from hypovolaemic shock, the patient should be positioned with the legs elevated (to allow maximum venous return) but with the trunk horizontal to permit maximum excursion of the diaphragm. The agent of choice for induction is ketamine (see page 103). Pancuronium is the most satisfactory muscle relaxant for use with the standard technique in these cases (see above). Special resuscitative measures including the use of intravenous antibiotics and hydrocortisone (see Chapter 4) may be required. Intravenous agents must be injected slowly to avoid overdosage in the presence of a slow circulation or congestive heart failure due to anoxia and overtransfusion.

Abdominal injuries

General anaesthesia is usually mandatory for abdominal operations (see page 97). The 'standard' anaesthetic technique (see page 100) is almost invariably the method of choice.

The insertion of a nasogastric tube (at least size 7 mm) is often unnecessary before induction but highly desirable before the end of the operation to permit aspiration of stomach contents and avoid post-operative abdominal distention.

Thoracic procedures

The 'standard' general anaesthetic should be used for thoracic procedures but aspiration of a haemothorax should normally be carried out under local analgesia before induction.

Open wounds of the chest should have been sealed by a dressing as a first aid measure. If a wound is too large for such a seal to be effective 'paradoxical' respiration will be taking place into the lung of the opposite side causing hypoxia and hypercarbia. Early intubation, general anaesthesia, a long-acting muscle relaxant and controlled ventilation are indicated, pending surgical closure of the wound.

Controlled ventilation is essential in the 'standard' technique and at the end of operation a chest drainage tube with one-way underwater seal must be inserted by the surgeon. Controlled ventilation will expel air and blood from the residual pneumothorax by air bubbling through the underwater seal after the chest is closed. The effectiveness of the system can thereafter be observed by the rise and fall of the water level in the glass tube of the underwater seal. Bottles for underwater seals are easily improvised. A Higginson's syringe applied to the short glass tube of the system will ensure a negative pressure. This may be desirable in the case of an air leak due to lung damage. The wound itself must be airtight before spontaneous respiration is re-established. This means that all deep layers should have been sutured and the skin stitches started before atropine is given and prostigmine administered to reverse the long-acting muscle relaxant.

Head injuries

The requirement is to prevent a rise, or a further rise, in the intracranial pressure. This may be caused by coughing or straining, or the use of local infiltration analgesia but the difficulties of maintaining an airway in the position required for surgery, and the positive advantages of controlled ventilation in reducing intracranial pressure, usually indicate that light general anaesthesia and the 'standard' technique (see page 100) is preferable.

Recent work suggests that the power of autoregulation of the intracranial pressure is lost at systolic blood pressures above 140 mm Hg and that cerebral perfusion is impaired below 60 mm Hg. Every effort should be made to keep the systolic blood pressure between these two limits. Thiopentone is preferred to ketamine as an induction agent as the latter tends to cause hypertension and thus raise intracranial pressure. The dose of suxamethonium should be increased and the vocal cords and trachea sprayed with 4 per cent lignocaine to avoid coughing and straining during intubation as this would markedly increase intracranial pressure. Tubocurarine, which tends to cause hypotension, is generally preferred to pancuronium which elevates blood pressure. Controlled ventilation reduces blood pressure and intracranial pressure.

Blood replacement with colloid or other solutions should not exceed blood loss and should preferably be allowed to fall slightly behind it. This will avoid an increase in venous pressure which would cause a further rise in intracranial pressure and encourage bleeding. Mannitol 20 per cent (250–500 ml) may be given to dehydrate and reduce the size of the brain. An indwelling catheter should be inserted to prevent restlessness due to a distended bladder in the post-operative period. Dexamethasone 20 mg (or hydrocortisone 200 mg) should be administered intravenously followed by 5 mg (or hydrocortisone 50 mg) intramuscularly every six hours. If the prone position is adopted for surgery, care should be taken to ensure that the chest and abdomen can move freely during spontaneous respiration or controlled ventilation. This may be achieved by placing rolled blankets or sandbags under the upper chest and the front of the pelvis. A nasogastric tube should be introduced before the patient is turned into the supine position.

Maxillo-facial injuries

The primary objective is to secure the airway. Sometimes intubation may have to be achieved in the face of severe intra-oral bleeding (see pages 94 and 98). Anaesthetists trained to intubate orally in the lateral position are at a considerable advantage. In most cases, an oral tube can be passed with the aid of suction under the chosen induction agent and Suxamethonium Bromide. Ketamine is possibly a better induction agent in these circumstances than thiopentone. 'Awake intubation' (see page 99) will be required in some cases. The greatest care must be exercised in manipulating gags and laryngoscopes, as a simple fracture of the jaw can easily be converted into a compound fracture by rough handling. In a few cases, tracheostomy under local analgesia will be necessary to enable the anaesthetic to be administered through the tracheostomy tube. The latter is, however, a difficult and dangerous procedure when the patient is obstructed because the airway has not been secured by intubation.

The surgeon may well request nasal intubation, particularly for operations on the mandible. In the presence of bleeding, it may be safer to secure the airway with an oral tracheal tube first and then to pass the nasotracheal tube through the nose at leisure. The oral tube should be removed under direct vision when the tip of the nasal tube can be seen in the back of the pharynx ready to enter the larynx. The assistance of a Magill intubating forceps may be required for the final insertion. Anaesthetists who are experienced in passing blind nasal endotracheal tubes may find it easier to use this method provided the intra-oral bleeding is not too severe.

A nasogastric tube (7 mm) should be introduced through the other nostril after endotracheal intubation (see page 100). A gauze throat pack should be inserted around the endotracheal tube in the back of the pharynx whether or not a cuffed tube has been used. This should be soaked and squeezed out in water as saline packs tend to increase the tendency to post-operative sore throat. The pack should not be too tight. It may be introduced either under direct vision with a laryngoscope and the Magill forceps or by pulling the jaw forward and pushing the gauze over the back of the tongue with the forefinger. If the latter method is used, care should be taken not to scratch the back of the palate with the finger nail. It is good practice to write the word 'pack' with a ball-point or other marker on the adhesive strapping used to secure the tube.

The depth of anaesthesia should be as light as possible to facilitate recovery. The 'standard' technique with controlled ventilation (see page 100) is accepted for this reason.

At the conclusion of the operation the anaesthetist must confirm with the surgeon that all the packs inserted or used by him have been removed.

The gauze throat pack is the special responsibility of the anaesthetist.

The nasogastric tube should be left on open drainage into a plastic bag.

The jaws may be wired together at the end of some operations and maintenance of the airway after these and similar procedures is best ensured:

a   By leaving the endotracheal tube in position until the patient has regained consciousness.

b   By shortening the tube and nursing the patient in the semi-prone 'tonsil position' with the under arm drawn behind the back and the upper arm thrown over a pillow. An indwelling endotracheal tube should always have a safety pin inserted through it just outside the nostrils.

Eye injuries

Superficial eye operations are frequently undertaken under local analgesia but more serious operations on the globe are better done under general anaesthesia.

The most usual procedures under field conditions will be closure of a penetrating wound of the eyeball and excision of the globe. If there is an open wound of the eyeball ketamine and suxamethonium, both of which increase ocular pressure, should be avoided as they are liable to cause extrusion of intraocular contents. Smooth intubation under thiopentone, a long-acting non-depolarizing muscle relaxant (pancuronium or tubocurarine) and topical lignocaine, and controlled ventilation by the 'standard' technique (see page 100) is the best method. Supplementary topical analgesia and specialized local analgesic blocks to the eye by the surgeon are to be encouraged. These are added precautions against spasm of the extraocular muscles or elevation of intraocular pressure due to coughing or straining on the tube or at extubation.

Burns

The initial toilet of burnt areas can often be accomplished under general analgesia (intravenous morphine narcotics or Trichloroethylene by inhalation) as described on page 106. Adequate and continued correction of hypovolaemia with colloids and electrolyte solutions is essential before dressing burns (see Chapter 6).

Endotracheal intubation or tracheostomy may be indicated for patients with serious facial burns. Oxygen by nasal catheter may be required for those who have suffered from burns of the respiratory tract, for whom the prognosis is very grave. If general anaesthesia is required for patients with burns, the 'standard' technique (see page 100) will be satisfactory. Suxamethonium bromide is not contraindicated at this early stage (but see below). The removal of sloughs and the provision of skin cover is usually undertaken after evacuation to a Base Hospital. Suxamethonium Bromide is contraindicated in the period two to seven weeks after burning because of the effect on the heart of the release of potassium from damaged muscles. This may cause cardiac arrest. Ketamine is useful for repeated procedures and especially for those on the head and neck without intubation. General intravenous and inhalation analgesia (see page 107) is useful to relieve the pain and discomfort of extensive burn dressings.

SPECIAL CONDITIONS AFFECTING ANAESTHESIA IN FORWARD AREAS

Extreme cold

Locations, in which anaesthesia is administered, are usually warmed by some means in cold climates. Heating devices are often oil-fired and primitive and the atmosphere is frequently dry. There is a consequent likelihood of the development of static electrical charges and a constant danger of fire. Both for this reason and because cold atmospheres are frequently associated with high altitudes volatile flammable ether is contraindicated; and the non-flammable agents provided in the present scale for Field Surgical Units are the agents of choice. Complications due to cold usually result from the exposure of apparatus and drugs or the patient to cold during transport to the operating theatre rather than in the theatre itself:

a *Exposure of apparatus and drugs to cold*   The OMV vaporizer is insulated against temperature changes by a large water reservoir but it does not have an elaborate temperature controlling mechanism. It is, however, remarkably accurate over normal room temperature (15 °C to 25 °C). If cooled below 15 °C by transport in, for example, the baggage compartment of an aircraft, it should be stood in water at 25 °C before use until it has warmed up to at least 20 °C. The ether EMO is temperature compensated by a thermostat. If the indicator provided shows that it is below accurate operating temperature (about 13 °C) water at 25 °C may be substituted for that already in its water-jacket.

Contents of glass ampoules sometimes freeze during transport and the ampoule cracks on rewarming. They should be placed in well insulated containers as should intravenous fluids.

b *Exposure of the patient to cold*   Vasoconstriction due to cold prevents the absorption of intramuscular injections, causes veins to be less easy to enter and makes the action of local analgesics less reliable. If the body temperature of the patient is below 35 °C (the lowest temperature usually measurable by a clinical thermometer) he must be treated with great caution. His temperature would undoubtedly fall further during surgery and there is a danger of ventricular fibrillation below 30 °C. Most of the patients encountered under field conditions will be fit and have had a relatively short exposure to cold. Fairly rapid rewarming is therefore permissible. Core warming is better than surface warming as there is liable to be a less uneven distribution of blood volume as vasodilation occurs. Such measures as passing all intravenous fluids through a coil immersed in water at 42 °C and warming inspired gas mixtures are important. A simple warmer/humidifier can be made by passing gases through a bottle or vacuum flask containing warm water with two wide but short tubes above the surface of the water. Humidification will also mitigate the effects of irritation of the respiratory tract by the dry atmosphere which often accompanies extremely cold conditions.

Extreme heat

In most static situations in hot countries operating theatres are cooled. Problems have arisen from hypothermia. The best that can be expected in the field, however, is an electric fan playing on a block of ice. Field surgical units must expect to have to function in hot, confined conditions even in temperate climates:

a *Exposure of apparatus and drugs to heat*   Vaporizers warmed above their specified operating temperature will read high. This is less of a problem with the higher BP volatile agents used in the OMV than it is with ether in the EMO. Even at 30 °C the delivery of trichloroethylene or halothane vapour from the OMV is only 25 per cent higher than that expected from the setting of the control lever. The ether EMO is thermocompensated up to approximately 35 °C but, should the indicator show that it is above its maximum operating temperature (probably due to exposure during transport) it may be cooled. This can be accomplished either by putting cold water at 20 °C in the water-jacket or by drawing air over the ether with the bellow, thus cooling the vaporizer by evaporation. Rubber and some plastics perish rapidly when exposed to bright sunlight. Bags, tubes and other equipment made from these substances should be kept cool and in the dark when not in use. Certain drugs decompose or lose potency when warmed and/or exposed to sunlight. Suxamethonium chloride solutions are particularly affected and the powdered bromide has therefore been substituted in field surgical scales. Pancuronium bromide also deteriorates. Medical gas cylinders, including oxygen, should be stored in a cool place under cover.

b *Exposure of casualties in hot climates*   In hot countries casualties exposed after wounding rapidly become dry and dehydrated. This greatly aggravates the hypovolaemic state caused by blood loss and causes further problems due to lack of sodium. Attendant personnel should not be discouraged from administering small amounts of water by mouth to conscious patients even after abdominal wounds. Fluids should be given intravenously immediately on arrival in the resuscitation area; later 20 per cent mannitol (250–500 ml) may be given to improve kidney function. The patient should be kept naked and sponged with tepid water and, if possible, cooled by an electric fan. Convulsions have been described under practically all known agents but they are most frequent under ether. The pyrexial, hot, flush, dehydrated septic patient is the most likely subject. Atropine should be avoided in such cases, as in all dehydrated patients. Convulsions usually start with muscular fasciculation round the eyes. Treatment consists of withdrawal of the volatile agent, the administration of thiopentone and oxygen and the institution of controlled ventilation with muscle relaxants if this technique is not already being used. Cooling may be assisted by placing the corrugated tubing joining the apparatus to the patient in bowls of cold or iced water to lower the temperature of the inspired gas mixture.

Patients under general anaesthesia are thermolabile. Dangerous degrees of hypothermia have occurred after patients have been removed from cooled operating theatres to wards at ambient temperatures. Patients must be kept cool under such circumstances.

Dry and dusty conditions

Dust can cause problems under both cold and hot conditions. It irritates the respiratory tree. Humidification of inspired mixtures is desirable. An inexpensive metal gauze condenser (a 'Swedish nose') both filters and humidifies. Dust can be drawn into vaporizers in drawover systems and may jam or damage the control mechanisms. A simple dust filter can be placed on the air intake (eg a dust filter to British Standard 1969/2091, a condenser humidifier, a car air intake filter or a gas mask filter).

In the current surgical team scale the explosion hazard is eliminated by supplying only those agents which are not flammable.

The biological pollution hazard is theoretical rather than actual in a surgical centre, but it may be unpleasant for the team to work in a confined and ill-ventilated atmosphere laden with a volatile agent. Fortunately it is often easy to direct exhaled vapour to the exterior through tubing attached to the expiratory part of the one-way valve of the drawover system. The carbon absorber from a service gas masks will remove volatile agents if attached to the expiratory port, or purpose-built filters can be obtained.

Mass casualties

Anaesthetic equipment is inevitably limited in amount as is the number of personnel, who can undertake surgery and anaesthesia. The accent must be on careful patient selection and a rapid turnover of casualties rather than on the number of simultaneous procedures undertaken with anaesthetists and untrained assistants under their supervision. No general directions can be given about the choice of anaesthetic agents in these circumstances.

Improvised techniques

The ability of anaesthetists to improvise when they find themselves separated from sophisticated equipment is almost legendary. Some examples are:

a Intravenous morphine.

b Ketamine, of inestimable value in emergency.

c Controlled ventilation with inhalation agents. Several successful techniques have been developed using intravenous agents and muscle relaxants, intubation and controlled ventilation with air alone delivered from a resuscitator bag. These methods include:

(1) Thiopentone, pethidine and tubocararine.

(2) Morphine premedication, thiopentone, tubocurarine and hyper-ventilation.

(3) Ketamine and tubocurarine.

d *Improvised vaporizers* Vaporizers for use with controlled ventilation using a resuscitation bag or for spontaneous ventilation with a one-way valve can easily be improvised from screw-capped jars or beer cans approximately the size of a Boyle's bottle (diameter 7.5 cm, height 13 cm). This will conveniently deliver 1 per cent trichloroethylene or 8 per cent ether.

e *Ether:*

(1)   *Open ether*   Gauze or padding with a central hole for the nose and mouth should be placed over the face. Ether is at first dropped and then poured intermittently onto a domed mask, covered by gauze, closely applied to the pad on the face.

(2)   *Flagg's can*   This was originally made from a metal ether can but can also be improvised from beer cans and other food and drink containers. A central hole for the tubing and several peripheral holes are made. The patient breathes air 'to and fro' over the surface of the ether in the can. The device is best used for the maintenance of anaesthesia after the patient has been intubated following induction with intravenous drugs or open ether. This is the only volatile agent, which should be used in Flagg's can. Condensed expired water vapour sinks to the bottom of the can beneath the ether but, with other agents, the water vapour forms a layer floating on top and very soon prevents vaporization. An alternative is to stretch cotton gauze over a funnel attached to the intubated patient by a wide-bore tube. Ether is then dropped on the gauze.

f Intermittent thiopentone and thiopentone infusions.

g *Hypnosis and distraction*   These are hardly techniques that can be practised easily in forward areas but anaesthetists must always remember the value of suggestion and a confident and cheerful manner.

In the unfortunate but less harried atmosphere of a prison camp hypnosis, local analgesia and even pressure on nerves with close osseous relations may all be useful.

CHAPTER 8

Treatment in the Fourth Echelon, the General Hospital Area

Introduction

The surgical tasks in a General Hospital Area, normally a group of general hospitals, are two-fold:

a Initial surgery on local conventional casualties and wounded who have by-passed forward surgical centres.

b Delayed primary suture (dps) and later procedures on patients who have had initial operations at forward centres, ie most first priority cases.

This is a greater commitment than in the past and organization and disposition of surgical facilities to meet it will require planning by the medical administrative staff. The number and grouping of hospitals to handle the anticipated number of casualties, their dispersal to avoid crippling surgical loss in the event of attacks on the area; the allocation of tasks among hospitals; the grouping of special facilities for neuro-surgical, thoracic, orthopaedic and burns management; the nomination of mobile surgical teams and alternative hospital arrangements for disaster conditions pose problems, the solution of which is vital to the success of the surgical plan for the force. The early phase of a future battle will see a greater need for initial surgery only to be carried out in general hospitals in the field. Second stage delayed primary suture will then be performed, after further evacuation, at the base hospitals. Wherever second stage surgery is done the same surgical principles apply.

Femoral and complicated fractures, neurosurgical, maxillo-facial, thoracic, vascular and peripheral nerve injuries are best segregated in special centres. These should be situated sufficiently far back to draw cases from several routes and in hospitals large enough to hold them for some considerable time. Sometimes it may be of value to site the light sections of neurosurgical and maxillo-facial units in the Rear Forward Combat Zone (FCZ) temporarily attached to a major unit, to provide the best early treatment for the severely wounded and to screen off the relatively trivial cases – provided these can be held for a few days until sutures can be removed.

Initial surgery on non-priority cases

After stabilization, casualties who did not require urgent surgery forward have been evacuated to this area for operation. Whenever possible these groups will have included head wounds, spinal injuries, maxillo-facial, ophthalmic and such casualties whose evacuation to special centres is preferred to operation forward. Wound toilet and excision will follow the usual technique with the same restrictions against primary wound closure. Some who have regressed during transit require resuscitation and others may have evidence of early wound infection, but unless evacuation has been unduly delayed these should be minimal. Management is similar to that described at forward centres. The management of special cases is given under the appropriate chapters.

Subsequent surgery and treatment

Wounds which have already received surgical debridement in the forward area will arrive in one of three conditions depending on when and how efficiently the primary operation was performed and on the measures taken to ensure immobilization and bacteriostasis en route. When campaigns are progressing smoothly casualties should arrive at the general hospital within two to four days if coming by road, and earlier if flown. Wounds may be either clean and suitable for delayed primary suture, mildly infected or grossly infected. Their subsequent management differs accordingly.

The clean wound – delayed primary suture

When the wound debridement has been well performed and bacteriostasis has been effective the wound should be ready for closure on the third to fifth day.

Unless on admission there is an indication for immediate surgery, there should be no interference for 24 hours. There must be no inspection of the wound except in the operating theatre. During this period of 24 hours the patient rests, his blood is investigated (erythrocyte count, haemoglobin, haematocrit, electrolytes, plasma proteins). And he is transfused and X-rayed if necessary.

Next day in the operating theatre the patient is anaesthetized and the dressings are removed. A swab is placed over the wound, the surrounding parts are shaved if necessary and widely and scrupulously cleaned with soap and water and painted with spirit or other alternative. The wound is disturbed as little as possible, the edges are separated, any blood clot is removed or the wound may be gently irrigated with saline. Any tag which has been missed is excised. Since haematoma formation will ruin the prospects of success, any bleeding point must be dealt with, avoiding ligatures if possible.

In deep wounds the track should be explored in case anything has been missed at the primary operation. After excision of any necrotic tissue it is usually wise to delay suturing for a further two days. Drainage is avoided, but it may be considered wise to drain the angle of an amputation stump to prevent haematoma formation or obviate the collection of serum.

The skin edges are undermined if necessary. No freshening of the skin edge is permitted. Undermining of skin and subcutaneous fat to a depth of 1 cm, by which cover is provided without tension on the sutured edges, is safe in most areas up to 6 cm. Care must be taken over haemostasis. Dead space should be obliterated and the suture line should be lax and not under tension.

Any tension militates against successful closure. If dead space cannot be obliterated and the suture line kept lax, an alternative method should be used (flap or free graft). The edges are brought together by interrupted sutures of nylon or serum proof silk, inserted so as to give accurate apposition with eversion of the edges.

Few defects of more than 6–8 cm can be closed by approximation, however extensive the undermining. Much smaller wounds on the forearm and hand, and of the leg below the calf, may need grafting for stable cover.

A pressure dressing of gauze-wool is applied and the limb is again put at rest in a padded split plaster of Paris splint and not disturbed for 10–12 days (deep wounds should be inspected in the theatre after five days). Patients treated in this way must be held until the stitches are removed. They are better nursed in separate wards away from open wounds.

The stitches are removed in the theatre 10–12 days (12 if there has been any tension). Exercises are commenced next day and in the ordinary uncomplicated case the patient should be fit for transfer to the rehabilitation unit 7–12 days later

Locally infected wound

a *Secondary toilet* – The presence of infection and its degree must be assessed from the clinical appearance and odour of the wound. Although all degrees of wound infection may occur, for practical purposes an important distinction should be made between those in which the infection is localized to the wound itself (locally infected wounds) and those in which infection has extended into surrounding tissues (gross wound infection). Their management is different.

Local wound infection results when initial toilet was incomplete and devitalized tissue or extraneous material was left for organisms to multiply in, although prevented by penicillin from actively invading adjacent tissue. It also results when, because of delay in evacuation, the wound was already infected at the primary toilet.

Delayed primary excision On many occasions, particularly when missile injuries have been treated in civilian hospitals, wounds will be seen that have, incorrectly, had primary suture after no or inefficient primary excision. In all these cases the sutures must be removed and the wound inspected as soon as possible.

Mildly infected superficial wounds and more heavily locally infected wounds will require secondary wound toilet in order to remove dead tissue which was missed at primary toilet and to relieve tension by splitting the fascia. Although it is now too late for thorough excision and the attempt would do more harm than good, the removal of dead tissue and the provision of drainage will reduce toxaemia and appreciably reduce the time before bacteriostasis in the wound permits its closure. Many of these wounds can still be closed some days later by delayed primary suture. Wound cultures should be taken and if penicillin resistant organisms are found a change of antibiotic is indicated. This should not be done, however, until the surgeon is sure that no dead bone or other necrotic tissue remains in the wound, otherwise resistance to the new antibiotic will follow. Estimation should be made of the haemoglobin and serum protein values, as a fall in either is a common cause of delayed wound healing and must be corrected by blood transfusion and a high protein, high calorie diet. Immobilization of the wound, often with elevation of the limb, is important.

b *Secondary suture* – When wound closure has been delayed beyond about 10 days, healing by granulation develops to an extent which makes subsequent closure 'secondary suture' rather than 'delayed primary suture,' although there is no sharp dividing line between the two. By this time, complete closure by approximation of skin edges is often impossible and skin cover by grafting is necessary.

Secondary suture should be performed when possible using a pneumatic tourniquet to reduce bleeding. The tissues by now will have become indurated and no longer pliable, with a growing epithelial edge of which the blood supply is inadequate. This new epithelium must be excised, the skin edges undercut, the granulation tissue gently scraped off the wound surface and, after releasing the tourniquet and securing haemostasis, the edges approximated and sutured. If scar tissue has had time to develop (after three weeks or so) this must be excised from skin and subcutaneous layers until healthy fascial planes are exposed. If there is any undue skin tension the attempt at closure will fail unless relieving incisions are made. The resulting raw areas should be covered with split skin grafts.

Major wound infection

With the methods of early wound management already described and the use of antibiotics, major wound infection is uncommon. It occurs after unavoidable delays in evacuation, when a combination of extensive skin loss and subjacent bone involvement has prevented early closure. It will also occur in a high proportion of cases if wounds are closed at the time by primary suture and the patient then evacuated.

When wound infection involves soft tissue only it can usually be brought under control by appropriate measures but when bone is involved management is more difficult and there is danger of chronic wound infection developing.

Localization of infection – bacteriological control is essential for organisms aerobic and anaerobic must be identified and their sensitivity determined. In the early stages localization may be obtained merely by increasing the dosage of penicillin and adding the appropriate antibiotic. It is essential to take all surgical measures necessary to prevent the development of chronic wound sepsis during the limited period available before antibiotic resistance develops.

Surgical toilet – is indicated as soon as antibiotic cover has been started. Free drainage is essential and any pockets of pus must be opened up. The underlying cause must, if possible, be identified and removed whether it be a retained foreign body, dead tissue or bone, infected blood clot or dead space resulting from an unreduced fracture. Having performed adequate secondary toilet, corrected any bone displacement and eliminated dead space, and having provided free dependent drainage the part must be effectively immobilized by the use of plaster in elevation. Where applicable strict immobilization and free drainage are essential during the days that follow if the infection is to remain controlled and healing is to result.

Early skin cover – is important for reducing the protein drain and improving the patient's general condition. Split skin grafts are suitable at this stage and should be applied early to those parts of the wound ready to receive them. Glycerine makes a good dressing for such wounds and by its local hygroscopic and bacteriostatic action will often quickly convert an offensive wound into one ready for grafting.

General and post-operative management of wound casualties

a   *Nutritional requirements* – All patients with wounds go through a phase of negative nitrogen balance which is proportional to the degree of injury. This active breakdown of body proteins is a response to trauma apparently to provide certain essentials for tissue repair. It is, however, a wasteful process and unless active measures are taken to restrict the nitrogen drain by ensuring a high protein intake, it will retard wound healing and prolong convalescence. The red cells of the blood are involved in the general protein catabolism and a progressive secondary anaemia results which must be corrected.

Apart from the anaemia and fall in blood proteins, the catabolic phase, if severe and prolonged, shows itself clinically in delayed healing of wounds, in a tendency for wounds to break down and gape after suture, and in a lowered resistance to wound infection. It also increases the difficulty in securing skin cover by reducing the percentage take following split skin grafting.

Measures necessary to counter the post-traumatic nitrogen drain are three:

(1)   A high calorie, high protein, vitamin rich diet.
(2)   Iron administration.
(3)   Blood transfusion, repeated if necessary, when the anaemia reaches a degree which is retarding healing.

The daily food requirements are at least 3500–4000 calories, including at least 150 grams of protein. The food should be rich in vitamins. A suitable initial diet is the 'light diet, fluid' of the Military Hospital Dietary, but this should be supplemented by supplementary feeds of egg flip, malted milk, etc, reinforced by one of the milk protein preparations, eg

Complan. Tube feeding may be required. Later, 'light diet, solid' similarly reinforced can be substituted. While iron administration may be sufficient to correct minor degrees of anaemia following lesser wounds, patients with severe post-traumatic anaemia need repeated small blood transfusions preferably using fresh blood. The haemoglobin should not be allowed to fall below 13 grams/100 ml.

b   *Faecal impaction* – is not uncommon amongst the seriously wounded, particularly if they have had frequent moves between medical units. This adds considerably to their distress. Enemata may have to be supplemented by digital removal of hard faeces or drugs such as Dorbanex.

c   *Active rehabilitation* – must start from the time of admission. Each patient should be given a programme of graduated exercises for both wounded and unwounded parts of his body. They should be done at frequent intervals, not only under the supervision of the physiotherapists but by the patient himself. The importance of this in reducing the time for recovery cannot be over emphasized. Whenever possible, early ambulation should be encouraged. Mental rehabilitation is equally important, with occupational and diversional therapy carried out under bright and cheerful surroundings.

Mass casualties

It is important that a heavy weapon attack on the General Hospital Area should be anticipated. The layout and organization of general hospital surgical centres should offer wide dispersal to minimize the effects.

CHAPTER 9

Plastic surgery methods of wound closure

Introduction

Many wounds can only be closed satisfactorily by plastic surgical methods and work of this nature would normally be the responsibility of plastic surgeons, recognizing that early skin closure of wounds is one of the most important aspects of war surgery, second only to the initial wound excision, in determining the successful outcome of treatment. On it may depend the whole future of a wounded man.

In war plastic surgeons may not be available and evacuation of patients not always possible; general surgeons therefore must understand the basic principles involved in certain simple plastic procedures.

Most missile wounds are closed by delayed primary suture. The methods described here are used when the tissue loss is too great for closure of the skin by approximation of the edges. They are of special value too as primary methods in certain sites, such as the hand and face, when the wound has exposed tendon or nerve which should be given a primary cover of viable skin and fat to prevent drying out and when simple approximation has been tried and failed. Experience and judgement will determine choice of method in individual cases, but great care should be taken to see that the skin closure over a fracture site is not under tension, and that dead space or tenting is obliterated in the use of flaps by a layered closure when necessary.

The procedures described in this chapter should be reserved for the situation where the patient can remain for at least 10–14 days, and for units which have the necessary equipment and experience to perform them.

Certain basic surgical techniques are essential for all these procedures, they include the careful cutting of skin flaps with a sharp knife, avoiding bevelling of the skin, the gentle handling of flaps using skin hooks and fine instruments, and the use of fine needles and suture materials. Sutures should always be interrupted and never tied under tension.

Methods available

A wound may be closed by:

a *Direct approximation* – delayed primary suture as described elsewhere.

b *Free grafts:*

(1) Continuous – a sheet of split skin covering the whole defect.

(2) Discontinuous – patch grafts of split skin spread over a defect, or meshed grafts applied to cover the whole defect.

c *Flaps:*

(1) Local flaps – with free graft if necessary to cover the secondary defect.

(2) Distant flaps – these methods, or a combination of them, may be used primarily, or when primary excision has been done two to five days earlier.

When in doubt general surgeons should *always* use free skin grafts.

Free grafts

General principles Split skin grafts will take satisfactorily on almost all tissues, except for exposed bone and tendon. When it is decided that a wound is to be closed by free skin grafting, the aim must be to cover the entire wound with split skin in order to obtain the earliest possible complete healing of the wound. Even if this skin does not take on bone or tendon, it acts as a very satisfactory biological dressing until such time as some other method can be contrived.

All forms of graft can be lost by infection, haematoma or inadequate fixation. A continuous sheet of skin may easily be floated off its bed and therefore it is probably better always to use discontinuous grafts, which allow for discharge of pus or blood between the patches. In this respect, meshed grafts are ideal and should always be used, if available, when infection is to be feared. When the area is a clean fresh wound, typically three or four days after primary excision, larger sheets may be employed with success and should be used, whenever possible, over flexion creases of the limbs.

There should be no doubt, however, as to the value of a flap cover if major vessels, nerves or joints are exposed, and in these situations, split skin grafts will not give such good results.

In older wounds, when free grafts are to be applied to granulating surfaces, if there are firm and healthy granulations, the grafts may be applied directly on them, but if there are pale and avascular granulations, they should first be either excised or curetted together with their fibrous base, before applying the free skin grafts. In these circumstances, it is often better to wait for a culture of organisms from the wound before applying split skin, as the presence of a haemolytic streptococcus in the wound will always destroy free skin grafts, and organisms such as pseudomonas will certainly destroy much of the graft. Where there is a profuse purulent discharge, this should be treated by suitable local applications, such as eusol, to obtain clean, healthy granulations before applying split skin.

The surgeon should always take more graft than he requires, and store the balance unused for application in the future. If it is then not used, it will still be useful as a homograft dressing for other wounds.

Graft cutting and application   Modern hand held skin graft knives are most commonly used, and patterns such as the Cobbett, Braithwaite or Campbell knives are ideal. These knives have disposable blades which are always sharper than the Blair knife; this sharpness is essential in the cutting of large skin grafts. The thickness of the graft is adjustable, but in general use the thinnest possible skin graft should be cut for use in military surgery, as thin grafts take better than thick grafts under difficult circumstances.

Donor sites for hand cut skin are usually limited to the lower and upper limbs, but with practice, skin can be cut from the back, chest and abdomen, although the sheets so obtained are not so satisfactory. The ideal donor site is the posterior and lateral surface of each thigh, where large sheets of skin may be easily obtained. The commonly used antero-medial surface of the thigh should not be used unless absolutely necessary, since the skin in this region is thinner and much more mobile, the grafts more difficult to cut and the quality of the grafts obtained not as good as in the other areas. Another suitable donor site in the leg is the calf, taking sheets from each side and posteriorly, but the front of the skin should never be used. The arm and forearm may also be used as donor sites, but bony prominences and flexion creases must be avoided.

A general consideration in selecting the donor site should be to avoid the injured limb, or to avoid using donor sites proximal to wounds, as the constrictive dressing around the donor site may impede the proper healing of the wound.

When cutting skin by hand the donor site should be lubricated with liquid paraffin or glycerine, and with an assistant holding the limb up so that the operator can cut upwards. Allowing the graft to fall back over the knife, the operator concentrates on a regular to and fro movement, avoiding rotation around the limb, and limiting the movements of the knife to the guard end-beads, thus avoiding a saw toothed edge to the skin graft. Firm pressure on the knife is maintained at all times, and the tension on the skin is increased by the use of a grafting board held in the opposite hand, pressing firmly on the skin one centimetre in front of the cutting edge.

Using this method large sheets of thin split skin can be obtained; these are then carefully spread on vaseline gauze, raw surface upwards, and the excess vaseline gauze trimmed off. The spread skin may then be either applied directly or cut into strips 2–3 cm wide, for application to the affected area.

Total cover of the area should be attempted with slight overlaps at the edges. If there is insufficient skin on the donor site to perform this using continuous or patch grafting, the skin grafts should be meshed by passing them through the mesh cutting machine, which will expand the area covered by the graft by as much as three times. The raw areas, diamond shaped between the strips of meshed skin, heal very rapidly, usually within one week, and this method is very useful for extensive wounds of the trunk, or where donor sites are very limited, because of injuries.

Mechanical methods of cutting skin are also in use, and these are:

a *The electronic dermatone,* by which means strips of skin three inches wide are quickly and easily obtained by the experienced operator from almost any of the recognized donor sites.

b *The Padgett dermatone,* which requires much more experience in use, and employs a glue on a cylindrical drum, by which means the skin is lifted before cutting. This instrument is most useful for cutting skin from the trunk, particularly the abdomen and flanks, where hand and electric dermatones are not so useful. It requires much more expertise for general use and is probably only found in specialized units.

Once the skin has been spread and applied to the affected area, the only dressing required is one layer of vaseline gauze to give total cover of the wound, followed by a layer of dry gauze, a layer of wool and a firm bandage, at all times ensuring that adequate cover and overall even pressure is obtained. It may be necessary to immobilize some limbs by plaster slabs, to ensure the immobility required until the grafts have healed.

Donor sites should be treated in a similar manner by thick pressure dressings. A newer method of treatment for donor sites employs a water vapour permeable plastic film, with a suitable adhesive, which is stuck over the donor site and on the surrounding skin, on top of which a firm dry dressing is applied. This speeds up the healing and removes much of the discomfort commonly found in donor sites. It is not suitable for large area donor sites.

Storage of skin   Unused skin may be stored for future use and under suitable conditions may be kept for two to three weeks after cutting and still used with very satisfactory results. The skin is spread on vaseline gauze, as before, and trimmed to size. The skin is then folded on itself, so that the raw surfaces are together, rolled into a cylindrical compact bundle, and enclosed with a saline moistened swab, in a dry sterile jar, which is then sealed, labelled with the patient's name and date of operation, and stored in an ordinary household refrigerator at 4 °C.

This autograft skin may subsequently be required to cover raw areas on the patient, but if not required for the patient for whom it was intended, may still be of great value as homograft skin on other patients with more extensive wounds, where there is insufficient skin available for full biological cover of the wound. These fresh homografts are of particular value in burns cases, where they may be used in conjunction with freeze dried homografts from store, or with heterografts which are becoming increasingly used, particularly porcine skin.

First dressing after skin grafts   Once applied, skin grafts should be left for at least five or six days to consolidate, before being exposed for dressings. Care must be taken in removing the dressings not to pull off any attached skin graft and the nurse must have some experience in performing such dressings. In the first dressing, only the top layer of vaseline gauze need be removed and the original layer of vaseline gauze used to spread the split skin need not be removed immediately. This can be done at the second dressing, when the graft is more firmly adherent. At this first dressing, any blisters should be removed, and any dry, loose pieces of graft overlapping the healed edge should be cut away. A wound swab should be taken for culture in the laboratory and, with the minimum of interference thereafter, a suitable dressing is applied. This should either be one layer of vaseline gauze, or furacin (nitrofurazole) gauze, which is then covered with dry gauze in several layers, wool and a firm bandage. This dressing should be adequate for three or four days before a further change is required; but if profuse purulent discharge occurs, or if the dressing smells badly, it may be necessary to redress the wound, as this indicates infection which must be treated. Following this, dressings are required every two to three days, but should not be performed daily until such time as the wounds are fully healed and the skin grafts stable.

Flaps

Indication   Flap cover of wounds in the early stages of treatment is only indicated to obtain skin cover over tendon, bone, exposed joint, major blood vessel or nerve.

Limitation of flaps   With certain exceptions which will be detailed later, great care must be taken to ensure the vascularity of flaps, which is usually an entirely random supply of blood vessels. To ensure the safety of a flap the length/breadth ratio should never exceed 1:1 (except as detailed below). This ensures that there is adequate arterial supply and venous drainage of the flap.

The greatest killer of flaps is venous obstruction from whatever cause, and great care must be taken to ensure that flaps are not kinked, rotated, stressed or pressed upon at any time. Haematoma under the flap is another cause for the loss of skin flaps, and suitable precautions must be taken. Flaps in the early stages should never be covered by dressings so that the surgeon may inspect them at all times and, if necessary, the vascularity of the flap tested. Careful nursing techniques are essential in the care of flaps to ensure that they are rolled adequately to empty them of static venous blood within the flap, and to evacuate haematoma from under the flap.

Local flaps

a *Simple undercutting and approximation*   This method is very limited in obtaining wound cover, but the advancement of the skin edge may be augmented by creating a double pedicle (or strap) flap, by a relief incision parallel to and some distance from the edge of the wound. This creates a long flap which in size is limited to twice the length of each base, and so does not exceed the normal length/breadth ratio. It retains its attachment at both ends. The flap of skin and fat is carefully dissected free, displaced as required, and a free skin graft applied to the secondary defect.

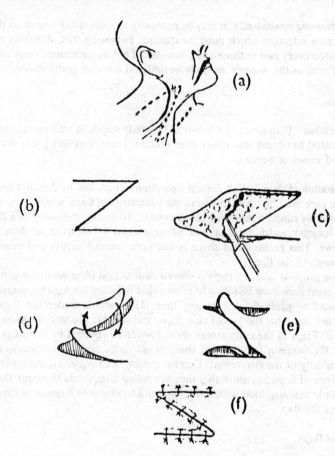

Figure 6 Z Plasty

a Linear contraction of the neck. Dotted line indicates site of incision.
b Shape of incision producing two triangular flaps.
c Flaps undermined and raised.
d Apices of flaps interposed in opposite directions.
e Flaps inset in the triangles created.
f Suture line complete.

b   *V–Y advancement*   This is used for small defects. The defect or scar, which should be V shaped to start with, is under-cut and the edges advanced so that the incision is closed in Y form. Care must be taken to ensure there is no tension in the closure. The *Z-Plasty* is based on a similar principle used in correcting small linear contractions.

c   *Rotation flaps*   In many sites, the tissues are better suited to closure by swinging a flap into a defect rather than by advancement in one plane. This method is used to repair larger defects, especially triangular defects, if there is sufficient laxity of skin in the neighbourhood, and if a large enough flap can be raised. The scalp, buttocks, thighs and trunk are suitable areas. Where skin is scarce and tight, for example below the knee and in the hand, it is inadvisable to use a rotation flap. The defect is cleanly excised in triangular form, and a curved incision made as a continuation of the short side of the resultant area and about four to five times its length. The flap so outlined and widely undermined and raised is

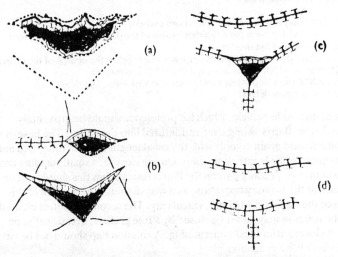

Figure 7   V–Y Advancement

a   Dotted line indicates site of V-shaped incision, open end towards wound.
b   Triangular flap undercut to include fat. Original wound has been excised and suture started.
c   Suture of original wound complete. Incision being closed in 'Y' form.
d   Closure completed.

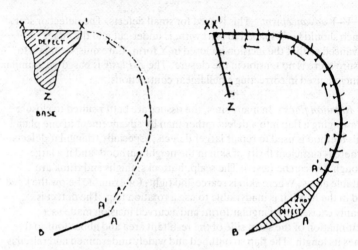

Figure 8   Rotation flaps

XX'Z is a triangular defect which has been excised.
X'A' is a curved incision from the shorter side of the defect approximately four times the length of the shorter side.
AB a straight incision ending at B perpendicularly below the open Z of the defect.
BZ Pedicle on which the undermined flap BAX'Z is rotated.
B, A', XX'Z show flap rotated and sutured leaving secondary defect.
BAA' – secondary defect.

hinged on a wide pedicle, which for preference should be proximally placed. This flap is swung over and sutured into the defect. The base of its pedicle should again comply with the usual length/breadth ratio, and must be as great as the length of the flap. During closure, a small standing cone of skin may be produced when the flap is rotated, but this should not be excised at the primary operation, as it may diminish the breadth of the base of the flap, and so impair vascularity. The secondary defect created by the rotation may either be closed by a free graft or, occasionally, by direct closure after local undermining. A rotation flap should not be cut from over bone or tendon.

Distant flaps   These long term procedures are best undertaken in hospitals where special plastic surgical services exist. Cross limb, belly-arm or tube pedicles are commonly used methods, but these flaps are worthy of special attention. These are axial pattern flaps, that is the flap contains one or two arteries supplying the flap and concomitant veins, draining the flap adequately to one particular point. The flaps are:

a *Delto-pectoral flap* This flap is based on the second, third and fourth intercostal spaces on the front of the chest, and runs along the line of the blood vessels below the clavicle, as far as the point of the shoulder. The length/breadth ratio of this flap is safely three or four to one, and it is of great value in that it can be rotated up to the face, as far as the orbit to give safe skin cover for massive defects in this region. The resultant defect at the shoulder is closed by free graft.

b *The groin flap* This single pedicled axial flap is raised along the line of the inguinal ligament, and is based on the superficial circumflex iliac artery and vein. It is of immense value in resurfacing the hand and the forearm in emergency, but it can also be used in place of a standard tubed pedicle. Used on the hand and forearm, the breadth of the flap within reasonable limits should be that required to cover the defect, and its length has been that required by the technical needs of the transfer itself. The flap, in effect, may reach as far as the lateral border of the erector spinae muscle.

c *Forehead axial flaps* This flap is based on the superficial temporal artery and vein, and may have a length/breadth ratio of 6:1. It is of value in covering defects of the scalp, where brain is exposed. The secondary defect is covered by a free graft, but the cosmetic effects in this type of flap are not very satisfactory, and it should be used only with great care.

In using these flaps from a distance, it must be stressed that previous experience in their use is necessary for both surgeon and nursing personnel, but in emergency for severe hand injuries, the groin flap is extremely safe to use.

Avulsion flaps

In vehicle accidents, it is not uncommon to find that the skin and fat have been flayed from the underlying fascia and bone. This is commonly called a de-gloving injury. When large areas of skin are detached in this way, the whole of the de-gloved skin will die if it is sutured back in position, since it has been de-vascularized. The only answer is to excise the whole of the de-gloved area of skin and fat, leaving a huge, raw area underlying, which is treated with a closed, dry dressing. The de-gloved skin is then cut as a split skin graft by any of the methods detailed above, and the free skin graft is stored for application to close the defect by delayed primary closure, on the third to fifth day after injury.

Any de-gloving injury, which raises flaps of skin which exceed the normal length/breadth ratio for flaps, should be treated in this manner and attempts to sew back larger areas must **never** be undertaken.

Smaller, distally placed flaps in the lower limb, may also require treatment in this manner.

CHAPTER 10

Hand and foot wounds

Introduction

The management of hand and foot wounds are considered together, because both structures anatomically are similar. Each has an intrinsic musculature attached to a bony skeleton associated with fascial compartments that do not take kindly to tissue tension. In cases of multiple injury, the hands and feet are often involved, but frequently are the last areas to receive attention.

First aid

Attention should be directed to the prevention of oedema as soon as possible after injury. After the application of a generous gauze and wool dressing to the injured part, the limb is elevated. The injured hand should be placed high in a sling. Walking should be discouraged on an injured foot. The injured part is splinted, in the hand using roller bandages and a palmar slab, and in the foot a padded Cramer wire splint bent to accommodate the contour of the extremity. Occasionally haemorrhage may be severe and its control requires pressure dressings in addition to elevation.

Initial surgery by FST

Examination of the extremity without an anaesthetic may confirm a neurological deficit or vascular injury which might influence the decision to amputate or save a damaged digit. An X-ray is valuable.

Injured hands and feet require wound debridement under a general anaesthetic. Initial cleansing is important using a detergent solution such as Savlon. The object of wound debridement in hand and foot injuries is to clean and remove indriven debris and to prevent tissue tension which would kill the intrinsic musculature. A good light and a fine set of instruments are essential.

A detailed knowledge of anatomy is mandatory in this type of surgery. Viable skin should not be sacrificed as it is the extremities most valuable asset. Only a minimal amount of skin edge is trimmed at debridement. Generous skin incisions should be used. In the hand these should, if possible, follow the palmar creases. In the foot, longitudinal incisions should be placed between the metatarsal heads. It is wrong to approach injuries of the palm of the hand or sole of the foot from their dorsal aspect. Access will be difficult and exposure inadequate without increasing destruction of bone.

The use of the tourniquet is recommended to facilitate identification of nerves, blood vessels and tendons. Once identified, debridement can be carried out. Release of tissue tension by incising the palmar fascia, transverse carpal ligament and intrinsic muscle fascia becomes mandatory in the swollen hand to prevent intrinsic muscle necrosis. Just occasionally removal of the inter-metacarpal fascia through dorsal incisions will be necessary to decompress the dorsal interossei. A tourniquet, if used, must be released to confirm viability of musculature.

Nerves Damaged nerves are noted. No attempt at repair is undertaken, but their ends approximated to prevent retraction.

Tendons Injured tendons are identified and, after debridement of their tatty ends, left unsutured. Exposed tendons on the dorsal aspect should be cleaned and covered with one layer of tulle gras. Any attempt at providing skin cover at initial operation will usually fail due to post-operative oedema. There is no place for swinging flaps of skin to cover a defect at the time of wound debridement.

Bones Fractured bone ends are cleaned with a curette and aligned. A rigid skeletal scaffolding is sometimes required to preserve blood supply or allow future reconstruction. It is permissible in some cases of multiple fractures to use internal fixation. Kirschner wires are most suitable for this purpose.

Digits Only digits which are irretrievably damaged are amputated. Amputation of the thumb is a last resort. Grossly damaged fingers should still be saved if possible, for the skin from such a finger may be used later to provide skin cover for the injured hand. Digital nerves may be repaired primarily if time allows.

Delayed primary closure In most cases it is best to delay closure of the wound for several days after initial surgery. Post-operative oedema always occurs in hand injuries and primary closure will only result in loss of skin from tissue tension. In addition at the time of delayed closure one can be sure the wound is free of sepsis and necrotic tissue. Skeletal fixation may also be undertaken.

Dressings

Dressing consists of well fluffed gauze applied evenly and snugly over a single layer of tulle gras. In the hand the metacarpo-phalangeal joints are held in aproximately 30 to 40° of flexion and the inter-phalangeal joints in 15 to 20° of flexion. Unaffected digits should be left free to move wherever possible. Their tips should be left exposed so that they can be inspected regularly to determine the adequacy of blood supply. It is essential that the limb is elevated post-operatively in order to reduce oedema.

The keynote to success in hand injuries is the preservation of skin and all viable tissue, the prevention of oedema and early mobilization.

CHAPTER 11

Vascular injuries

Missile wounds of major arteries are usually accompanied by soft tissue injury of sufficient magnitude to compromise the collateral circulation. Ligation of a main limb artery is, therefore, likely to lead to amputation and provided adequate surgical facilities are available every effort should be made to repair vascular damage. Early diagnosis and treatment are of paramount importance for irreversible ischaemic changes may develop within four to six hours of wounding.

Diagnosis

In any limb injury it is wise to maintain a high 'index of suspicion' concerning artery injury. The position of the missile track or the presence of a subfascial haematoma may indicate possible arterial injury. Of all the clinical physical signs of acute ischaemia the palpation of distal pulses is the most important. If after resuscitation the distal pulses remain impalpable in the injured limb urgent surgical exposure of the possible site of arterial injury is essential. In this situation 'look and see' is wiser than 'wait and see.'

Types of arterial surgery

a *Complete transection*   In missile injuries transection is usually accompanied by loss of a variable length of entire artery.

b *Arterial laceration*   In this injury the vessel remains in continuity but a portion of its wall is avulsed or torn open. Profuse bleeding accompanies this injury and if the artery is deeply placed a 'pulsating haemotoma' or false aneurysm results.

c *Arterial contusion*   This lesion can occur at some distance from the track of a high velocity missile or follow a blunt crushing type injury with no external wound. The artery remains macroscopically intact but intimal rupture and local thrombosis occur. The external surface of the contused segment may look bruised but because of the soft nature of the contained thrombus may continue to pulsate. Arteriotomy is often required to establish the true nature of the injury.

d *Arterial spasm*   This occurs when major arteries are stretched abruptly by a 'near miss' injury. It is a rare occurrence and should never be diagnosed without direct inspection of the vessel. Even then it may not be possible to differentiate between spasm and contusion without open arteriotomy.

e *Arterio-venous fistula*   A missile track may involve adjacent artery and vein. An arterio-venous communication is established immediately. This type of injury causes little external bleeding and peripheral pulses may remain palpable, though reduced in volume. It is recognised by a palpable thrill in the region of the fistula and a loud continuous murmur on auscultation. Acute ischaemia of the distal limb does not occur and there is usually no immediate urgency for definitive treatment.

Management of arterial injury

After standard resuscitative treatment to restore blood volume every effort should be made to repair the arterial damage. Ligation of major arteries should not be done unless the poor general state of the patient or local circumstances preclude the more lengthy procedure of arterial repair. The incidence of limb gangrene after major arterial ligation for trauma is of the following order:

High axillary and brachial artery	— 45–60 per cent
Common femoral	— 80 per cent
Superficial femoral	— 45 per cent
Popliteal	— 85 per cent

Ligation of the profunda femoris or single arteries in the forearm or leg is usually safe from ischaemic sequelae. Injuries of the extracranial portion of the carotid system are sometimes accompanied by neurological evidence of cerebral ischaemia. In carotid lesions with established hemiplegia ligation of the vessel is the best course, because re-establishment of blood flow may cause death from haemorrhage into the fresh cerebral infarct.

Surgical repair

Arterial injuries should be treated definitively as early as circumstances allow, and preferably within six hours of injury. After this time tissues of high metabolic activity such as muscle may have suffered irreversible damage. Debridement of the wound is done by standard technique and bleeding from the damaged vessel controlled with bulldogs or vascular clamps. Adequate exposure is essential and additional anatomical exposure of the proximal and distal vessel is usually required. Undamaged branches of major arteries should be preserved and temporarily controlled by double encirculation with fine ligature material.

With most arterial injuries, and particularly those associated with high velocity missiles, it is essential to have an adequate length of artery exposed, because damage may be more extensive than immediately apparent. Before repair is completed it is essential to check that free forward bleeding is obtained from the proximal segment and adequate back bleeding from the distal segment. If there is doubt about distal patency a Fogarty balloon catheter should be carefully passed. The region of the anastomosis should be washed frequently with heparinized saline and this solution should be injected into the distal arterial tree.

Arterial spasm is easily provoked in young subjects and may occur despite a careful and gentle technique. It is best overcome by the passage of graduated dilators through the arteriotomy incision.

Techniques of repair

a *Arterial laceration*　　Direct repair by suture is only applicable in small clean cut lacerations of large arteries. Large ragged defects or injuries inflicted by high velocity missiles are unsuitable for direct suture. In appropriate cases the distal and proximal arteries are controlled by arterial clamps and the laceration sutured by a continuous suture of 00000 or 000000 synthetic vascular suture. The stitches should be inserted 1 mm apart and about 1 mm from the wound edge. Care should be taken to avoid entangling strands of adventitia in the suture line. As with any arterial anastomosis bleeding through the suture line after release of the clamps should be controlled by packing for at least five minutes, and additional sutures only used if bleeding continues after such treatment. Lacerations of small or medium sized arteries should not be sutured directly but the defect repaired with a patch graft of autogenous vein (Fig 9). In this way stenosis at the site of repair will be avoided.

b *Complete transection*　　With defects of up to 2 cm the proximal and distal vessels can usually be mobilized to allow direct anastomosis without tension (Fig 10). More extensive damage requires replacement by autogenous vein graft (Fig 11). With small arteries the damaged ends should be resected obliquely to enlarge the suture line area. The prepared ends are approximated by two sutures placed at opposite poles and then carried as a running suture around each side. It is helpful to place stay

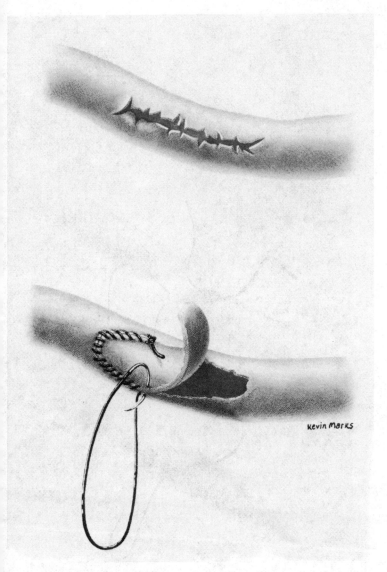

Figure 9 Repair of linear arterial laceration. Ragged edges are excised and the defect filled with a vein patch.

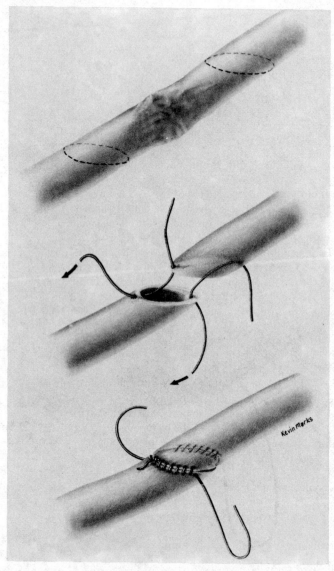

Figure 10 Excision of traumatised segment with direct end-to-end anastomosis. Note – oblique line of transection.

sutures at each lateral mid point.

c *Arterial contusion*   The intimal damage is usually too extensive to allow resection and anastomosis, and replacement by vein graft is the method of choice. Once the decision to use a vein graft has been made the length of vessel resected is unimportant and it is better to err on the side of over rather than under resection in order to reach undamaged artery (Fig 11).

The long saphenous vein is the best vein for use as an arterial substitute but the cephalic vein can also be utilized. If there is extensive concomitant venous injury in a leg the saphenous vein should be obtained from the opposite limb.

The appropriate length of vein should be dissected cleanly and all branches tied off carefully. The excised segment will invariably be in spasm and should be restored to normal diameter by inflation with saline or preferably blood. Loose adventitia should be removed from each end of the vein and the anastomosis made in the oblique manner described above (Fig 11). The vein segment should be reversed to obviate obstruction to flow from the venous valves. The proximal anastomosis should be done first and with the proximal arterial clamp released and a bulldog on the distal vein the correct length of vein for the distal junction can be accurately judged.

d *Arterial spasm*   This is a dangerous diagnosis and should not be made without direct inspection of the artery concerned. Even then it may not be possible to distinguish between spasm and contusion with intraluminial thrombus. If doubt exists open arteriotomy should be done and the intimal surface inspected. True spasm can sometimes be relieved by soaking the segment with papaverine hydrochloride but mechanical dilation through a proximal arteriotomy is immediately effective.

With any arterial repair it is important to cover the suture line with viable tissue, preferably a muscle belly, mobilised if necessary, to lie comfortably over the region of the anastomosis. If a vein graft is used the entire venous segment is covered in this way.

Concomitant venous injury

Major accompanying veins should be repaired whenever possible. Lateral suture of defects is more often possible in venous injury because of the larger diameter of main venous trunks.

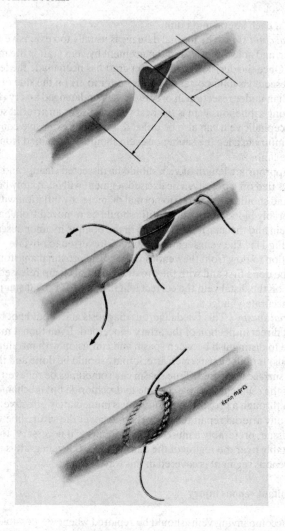

Figure 11 End-to-end vein graft anastomosis after resection of length of damaged artery.

The arterial segment is cut obliquely and the vein graft incised longitudinally for a similar distance. The corners at the end of the vein graft are trimmed obliquely.

Artery and vein are then approximated by two equidistant mattress sutures and the anastomosis completely by continuous suture.

Fasciotomy

Increased tension in the compartments of the lower leg often follows vascular injury and fasciotomy is indicated:

a In wounds directly involving the calf.

b Where there is concomitant major venous injury.

c Where calf or anterior compartment tension becomes evident in the immediate post-operative period.

d Where the ischaemic state has existed for longer than four to six hours before arterial repair.

CHAPTER 12

Missile wounds involving bone

First aid

Treatment of the fractured limb should begin as early as possible. Temporary splintage not only reduces pain but also prevents further damage to the soft tissues caused by the broken bone. Missile wounds should be covered by sterile dressing before the application of splints. In the upper limb, either a sling or bandaging the arm to the side may be sufficient. In the lower limb, the other limb or some sort of emergency splint is used.

On arrival at the dressing station splintage should be checked to make sure that it is not too tight and in the case of a lower limb, consideration should be give to application of a Thomas splint for femoral fractures or air splint for injuries below the knee.

MANAGEMENT BY THE FIELD SURGICAL TEAM

General principles

Management of these wounds differs in no way from a soft tissue missile injury. Careful assessment of the patient in respect of blood loss, both internal and external, must be made and measures to prevent haemorrhagic shock taken. A vascular and neurological assessment must be made of the extremity distal to the injury. The presence of a distal pulse does not exclude damage to a proximal major vessel.

Along with tetanus toxoid, antibiotics should be given to combat potential infection especially as bone is involved.

Operative management

The principles of wound debridement must be adhered to and in this respect wide decompression is necessary in all these injuries. At operation there is often an enormous haematoma associated with much devitalized tissue. In the upper limb surgical debridement can be facilitated by the temporary use of a tourniquet to identify the neuro-vascular structures before proceeding with excision of devitalized tissue. If used it must be released to confirm viability of damaged muscle.

Bone will frequently be shattered into many pieces, but these invariably have some soft tissue attachment. No bone should be sacrificed. Contaminated bone should be cleaned in situ with a curette, irrigated with diluted hibitane and left in place. Soft tissue should be cleared from the bone ends and an attempt made to reduce the fracture.

Internal fixation of bone is not permissible in these injuries unless it is required to protect an accompanying arterial anastomosis or in some injuries of the hand and foot. Accurate reduction of bone fragments is never essential at this stage and a reasonable alignment of the fracture should be accepted.

The joint must be thoroughly inspected through an incision and copiously irrigated to remove foreign matter. Metallic fragments, especially lead, should be removed. Articular cartilage should, if possible, be covered at the end of operation by one layer of tissue, preferably synovium.

At the end of wound debridement, haemostasis having been secured, all these wounds are left open for subsequent closure 4 to 10 days later. Lightly fluffed gauze should be placed in the wounds as a dressing in order to allow adequate drainage. Plugs of vaseline gauze must be avoided.

Splinting after initial surgery for evacuation

Splinting of the limb is employed not only to hold the bone fragments in a satisfactory position, but also to rest the soft tissue. It is best carried out using a padded plaster or a Thomas splint with skeletal traction. Whatever type of splintage is employed, it must be remembered that these wounds frequently swell after operation and, therefore, plaster should be well padded and split prior to evacuation. Gangrene of a limb as a result of ignoring these rules is a preventable surgical catastrophe.

Evacuation facilities must be taken into account when considering the type of splint to employ. Different types of transport require different splints and it should be remembered that there may only be a minimal amount of attention to the patient during his journey.

Immobilization methods – lower limb

a *Fractured femur including knee joint* At the forward dressing station a Thomas splint should be used. Fixed traction via the boot can be by either metal clip or clove hitch. The boot lace should be loosened and a small pad of wool placed under the tongue of the boot prevents sloughing of the skin on its dorsal aspect. Over distraction is harmful.

Once at the field ambulance traction via the boot should be stopped and skin traction applied.

After initial surgery, skeletal traction will be employed using either fixed traction via a windlass or a tensator spring. Provided sufficent support is given to the posterior aspect of the shaft of the femur using padded Cramer wire and plaster slings (Fig 12), it is seldom necessary to wrap up the splint in plaster.

High fractures of the femur, those that involve the neck and trochanteric regions, are not suitable for the application of a Thomas splint and require a padded hip spica, though evacuation can be difficult.

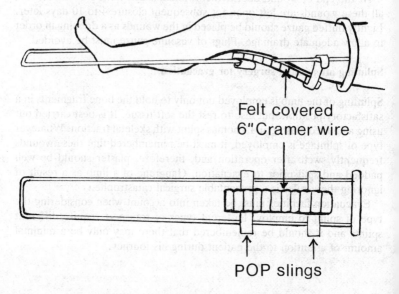

Figure 12 Immobilization methods – fractured femur including knee joint.

b *Fractured tibia and fibula* The best splintage for wounds involving the tibia and fibula is an air splint. This should only be used during initial management from the time of wounding until operation. Care must be taken not to over inflate, as this reduces capillary blood flow. It is applied directly over the boot and clothing of the patient. There are many other forms of temporary fixation for a fractured tibia, including temporary padded Cramer wire splints.

After initial surgery these fractures are invariably treated in a well padded plaster, which extends from groin to toes. The knee should be flexed at 10 to 15° and the foot placed at a right angle. There should be no bandages beneath the plaster which is split throughout its entire length before evacuation.

Immobilization methods – upper limb

a *Fractures about the shoulder and arm* After initial operation a pad of wool is placed beneath the axilla between the arm on the injured side and the chest wall. The arm is well padded with cotton wool and is then fixed to the chest using crepe bandage following an over-lay of elastoplast strapping. In the rare instance it may be desirable to use plaster fixation in which case no bandaging or strapping should be used under the plaster. Check the radial pulse after immobilization.

b *Fractures about the elbow and forearm* Following operation the wounds are left open and a well padded POP is applied from the middle of the upper arm to the proximal transverse palmar crease. The elbow should be at a right angle and the plaster split throughout its length before evacuation.

c *The hand* Following wound debridement, the hand should be elevated. Adequate splintage is provided using a generous padding of cotton wool and crepe bandage.

Post operative evacuation

In this type of injury there is no restriction to early evacuation. However, in view of the inevitable oedema that accompanies such injuries, especially missile wounds involving the femur, it is advantageous to delay evacuation for 48 hours after operation.

MANAGEMENT IN THE GENERAL HOSPITAL AREA

General management

If possible all patients sustaining missile wounds of bone should be evacuated to orthopaedic units.

The object of treatment is to provide suitable skin cover for the wound and align the bone fragment in the best possible position. Satisfactory skin cover will, in part, prevent the onset of sepsis and of late chronic osteomyelitis, which is such a common feature of wounds containing shattered bone.

All wounds should be inspected five to seven days after the time of the initial operation, with a view either to wound excision if devitalized tissue is still present or to provide skin cover. At this time post-operative oedema is usually settling and delayed primary closure of the wound can be carried out. At operation there may be an opportunity to correct bone alignment. The dead space should be obliterated by suturing the muscle sheath. The skin is closed.

Skin closure may not be possible due to either skin loss or persistent limb swelling. It is desirable to provide skin cover of some sort. An attempt should be made to close the skin using a partial thickness skin graft.

In all these wounds prime consideration must be given to healing of the soft tissues before tackling the bone problem.

Treatment of major individual fractures

Principles Splintage should be simple and provide immobilization for the fracture, allowing in some cases movement of the joint above and below to prevent stiffness as union takes place. Distraction of the bone fragments with subsequent delayed union may occur from over traction.

Lower limb fractures

a *Upper femur* Fractures of the femoral neck and trochanteric region should be treated by the application of skeletal traction from the tibia, with the limb balanced in two well padded slings, one placed beneath the thigh and one beneath the thigh and one beneath the calf. A Thomas splint is not usually suitable for this injury as the fracture is just where the ring of the splint comes in addition perhaps to a posterior wound. The use of a Povey splint can be recommended. The amount of skeletal traction required to produce and maintain reduction varies and a check made on limb length as well as X-ray control should be used to avoid over distraction.

Frequently the upper fragment with the powerful pull of the abductors and hip flexors lies upwards and outwards and in order to maintain correct bone alignment the lower fragment has to be placed in a suitable position of abduction.

b *Shaft and lower femur*   Fractures of the mid and lower third of the femur can be adequately treated in a Thomas splint or Povey splint. Such fractures have a tendency to sag posteriorly. The usual flannelette bandages employed to support the back of the thigh are frequently unsatisfactory and cut into the skin. It is much better to provide a more rigid support using orthopaedic felt covered Cramer wire slung under the limb with two strips of plaster of Paris. (See Fig 12.) When employing this method, the Cramer wire should be bent slightly convex shape, the proximal end aligning with the posterior rim of the Thomas splint and the lower end stopping just short of the knee joint.

c *Tibia and fibula*   Satisfactory fixation can be obtained using a long leg plaster from upper thigh to metatarsal neck. On occasion, however, it may be desirable to inspect or dress the wounds. If a window cut into the tibia is not suitable, the limb may be left exposed using skeletal traction with a Steinmann pin either through the lower tibia or os calcis, the limb resting on a soft pillow.

More rigid fixation can be provided using external skeletal fixation. Two Steinmann pins are placed above, and two below the fracture. The pin ends are attached to longitudinal bottle screws or other external fixator. Bone cement can be used to fix the ends of the pins to the longitudinal struts in the absence of more sophisticated apparatus. This method is especially useful in wounds of the tibia accompanied by skin loss due to burns. (See Fig 13.)

Upper limb fractures

a *Humerus*   Injuries involving the lower half of the humerus are best treated using a U plaster, dependency of the limb acting as counter traction. The U plaster should not be extended over the tip of the shoulder joint as this defeats the object of the weight of the limb maintaining bone alignment. Fractures of the upper third of the humerus

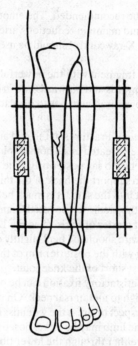

Figure 13   External fixation – fracture tibia and fibula.

are probably best treated using a shoulder spica of wool, crepe and elastoplast as in operations for recurrent dislocation of the shoulder, or in a shoulder plaster spica. The latter are, however, uncomfortable in bed and when travelling.

b *Radius and ulna*   Padded forearm plasters adequately serve to maintain fixation of these fractures.

c *Hand injuries*   The management of these injuries is discussed in Chapter 10.

Complications

Constant vigilance is required at all stages of treatment to detect the onset of vascular complications or infection.

Tissue tension with subsequent necrosis of muscle may occur even in the presence of a distal pulse. *In addition to external factors, such as the constricting effect of hard, dried blood on dressings, inadequate decompression at initial operation results in tension.* Common sites for closed compartment compression are the forearm muscle groups and the anterior tibial compartment. Increasing pain beneath the plaster in association with pain on passive extension of the fingers or passive plantar-flexion of the toes is an indication of tension and incipient muscle necrosis. Do not be fooled by normal looking toes, the presence of a peripheral pulse or even the absence of any sensory loss. Beware of the innocent looking gun shot wound of the fibula, for this bone is connected to all four fascial compartments of the lower leg and tension may develop in any one of them due to bleeding from the bone ends, or a torn peroneal artery.

Increasing pain beneath a plaster may also herald the onset of infection. The presence of pain and a rising pulse rate demand immediate inspection of the limb free of its dressings to exclude the possibility of early gas gangrene.

Bone infection

Bone infection occurs either by haematogenous spread or direct entry of organisms through an open wound. In the context of military surgery almost all bone infections are due to the latter cause.

Significant infection in military surgical wounds is uncommon despite the degree of contamination caused by high velocity missiles.

The incidence will be increased by:

a Unavoidable delay in surgical wound excision beyond six hours.

b Gross fracture comminution with impaired fragment blood supply.

c Contamination from associated bowel injury, especially the large bowel in pelvic and hip wounds.

d Association with vascular injuries of limbs.

Prevention depends upon thorough wound excision with meticulous cleansing and lavage of bone fragments, repositioning only those with retained periosteal attachment and discarding all free fragments unless an unacceptable defect would be created by so doing. Synovial fluid has some anti-bacterial properties provided it is not overwhelmed and this emphasises the importance of thorough joint toilet.

Established bone infection will delay healing of both the fracture and the overlying soft tissues and may impair the long-term functional recovery. It will prevent the delayed repair of associated tendon and nerve injuries. Eradication of such established bone infection is difficult, prolonged and costly.

Treatment   Acute episodes with systemic toxaemia will require urgent administration of an appropriate antibiotic.

Chronic infection is unlikely to be cured by antibiotic administration alone although some, such as fusidic acid, are claimed to produce high effective levels in dead bone. Prolonged administration is required. Topical antibiotics and irrigation systems may also be useful occasionally.

Surgery is necessary to remove sequestra and to permit adequate drainage of large infected cavities. All dead bone should be removed – the instability created being treated by external cast splintage, by traction or, preferably, by intero-external fixation with transfixion pin insertion well away from the wound site. (See Fig 13.)

Only when the osseous infection is quiet and skin cover obtained can the non-union or bone defect be treated by autogenous cancellous bone grafting.

Chronic infection should usually be overcome by aggressive surgical and therapeutic management, so avoiding amputation and complications such as amyloid disease and neoplastic change in chronic sinuses.

CHAPTER 13

Missile wounds of joints

General

Missile wounds of joints endanger life and limb from sepsis. Synovial fluid has natural antibacterial properties but the haemarthrosis resulting from a penetrating war wound provides an ideal sequel from which toxins are freely absorbed. Infection can be avoided by early appropriate surgery. Treatment of a septic joint is repeated aspiration of the joint cavity with instillation of antibiotics supplemented by large doses of broad spectrum antibiotics systemically. Constitutional effects may be severe with hyperpyrexia, marked toxaemia, hypoproteinaemia and anaemia. The articular surfaces, capsule and ligamentous structures will be disorganized and fibrous or bony ankylosis may be expected.

Principles of treatment

The object is to prevent infection by the use of the following prophylactic measures:

a *Excision of the wound* The joint is cleansed and, if possible, the synovium and capsule closed.

b *Immobilization of the joint* The joint is placed in the physiological position to ensure the best chance of functional recovery.

c *Aspiration of the joint,* repeated at intervals.

d *Installation of antibiotics* into the joint. This is in addition to the systemic antibiotic cover.

When infection is established the following steps must be taken:

a *Drainage of the joint* to reduce the destructive effects of pus under tension and to minimize systemic effects.

b *Immobilization of the joint* in the position of function anticipating ankylosis.

Treatment in forward area

As for wounds of bone (see Chapter 12).

If evacuation is delayed a swollen joint should be aspirated and 100 000 units of penicillin instilled.

Priority of evacuation – most wounds involving joints are Priority 2. The aim is to ensure surgical treatment within 12 hours of injury, or earlier if possible.

Wounds associated with extensive muscle damage such as may occur around the hip and shoulder and those with multiple injuries and associated vascular complications would place the casualty in Priority 1.

Through and through missile wounds of low velocity without evidence of gross damage to the joint may be assessed as Priority 3.

Treatment at the field hospital

a *Treatment of shock*   Assessment of management.

b *X-ray* in two planes should be carried out whenever possible to locate opaque foreign materials and to show the extent of bone damage.

c *The operation:*

(1) *A formal arthrotomy is required*   Thorough exploration is facilitated by the use of a tourniquet when possible and diathermy should be available. After debridement of the wounds, the joint is opened either by extension of the original wound or by standard arthrotomy, whichever will give the better exposure as all recesses must be explored. All clot, loose pieces of bone or articular cartilage and foreign material are removed. Metallic fragments which are deeply embedded in bone and inaccessible are left. The joint is irrigated with saline. The tourniquet should be released at this stage and haemostasis secured by fine ligature or by diathermy.

(2) *Closure*   If possible, the synovium and capsule should be closed with interrupted absorbable sutures. The soft tissues and skin are left open. Extensive tissue mobilization to obtain closure is contraindicated and small advancement or rotation flaps considered only in favourable circumstances. Should closure be impossible the wound is covered by a single layer of vaseline gauze followed by light fluffed gauze. Exposed articular cartilage may necrose. Joints left open should be given a higher priority for early evacuation. Penicillin (100 000 units in 3–5 ml of sterile water) is instilled into the joint if closure was possible.

(3) *Dressing*   The wounds are dressed as for a wound of bone. No encircling gauze or bandage should be used under the plaster.

(4) *Immobilization*   The position and type of splint is indicated in the table below.

Plasters other than the Tobruk and Thoraco-Brachial must be split from end to end, including the padding and gauze, on the side opposite to the wound. If a window is cut over the joint to permit access for aspiration and further antibiotic instillation, the window is replaced and held with a bandage. A plastergram, which includes instructions about aspiration, should be drawn on the cast.

d *Post operative care* The limb is elevated. The joint should be inspected every 48 hours with aspiration and antibiotic instillation, or sooner if indicated by pain or by the presence of fever and toxaemia. Systemic antibiotics are given as for any other wound.

e *Associated injuries* Penetrating wounds of the lower abdomen and pelvis may involve the hip joint. Any evidence of such injury strongly indicates the need for a posterior arthrotomy to establish drainage.

Optimum positions for joint immobilization

The physiological position is that in which ligamentous structures are put on stretch to prevent contractures so that, in the absence of intra- articular stiffness, the best functional recovery can be expected.

The functional position is preferred if ankylosis is likely to occur.

Joint	Position	Splint
Shoulder	Abduct 45° Flex 30° Medially rotate 70° from neutral	Thoraco-Brachial plaster
Elbow	Flexed 90° neutral rotation. If both elbows – extend dominant to 80° and flex other to 100°.	Above elbow plaster as Thoraco-Brachial for severe injuries.
Wrist	Dorsiflex 30°	Above elbow plaster.
Fingers	Physiological: Metacarpo/phalangeal joints well flexed. Interphalangeal joints, minimally flexed. Thumb: well abducted in line of radius. Functional: all joints flexed 30°. Thumb abducted.	Splint affected digits only. Malleable finger splints with or without below elbow cast. Boxing glove dressing may suffice.

Hip	Flex 20° Abduct 5° Neutral rotation	'One and a half' spica plaster or Thomas splint (with posterior half of ring cut away) and incorporated in plaster of Paris (POP) round trunk as a spica.
Knee	Physiological – Flex 15° Functional – Flex 5–10°	Tobruk splint
Ankle	Physiological: right angle. Functional: 5° plantar flexion. Avoid any varus deformity.	Below knee plaster

Treatment at the general hospital

The general condition of the patient may require attention. Urgent surgery will be required in those cases of failed joint closure or when there is evidence of gross sepsis.

a. If *not infected* – the wound is closed. If tissue tension is too great rotation flaps or preferably split skin grafts may be necessary. Immobilization is necessary until the wound is healed. Early successful closure will permit a more rapid return of function.

b. If the joint has *been infected but now under control* immobilization should be maintained for four to six weeks. During this time static contraction of muscle groups such as the quadriceps should be practised.

c. If *frankly infected,* the joint must be freely drained – the choice of incision influenced by the optimal gravitational drainage. The joint is immobilized in the functional position for expected ankylosis. So great is the constitutional disturbance in established suppurative arthritis of a major joint that drastic measures may be necessary to ensure adequate drainage such as the extensive removal of bone. Amputation may be considered if life is threatened. Traction may be necessary in major weight bearing joints such as the hip both for comfort and to prevent dislocation.

CHAPTER 14

Amputations in war

Introduction

Amputations are of two kinds: emergency and final. An emergency amputation may be only a stage in treatment and foreshadow a subsequent amputation. A final amputation, as the name implies, is intended to be the last operative treatment which the injury demands. It is devised to give the best possible function after fitting of a prosthesis.

The ideal final amputation has a myoplastic stump which provides maximum muscular control, proprioceptive sensation and pumping action for venous return. It may be through a joint or through bone with an osteoperiosteal flap to cover the medullary cavity. Such an amputation cannot be performed in forward areas in war because in it the muscles are brought together with some tension and this is unacceptable in a potentially infected limb.

Amputations in a war zone are therefore emergency amputations and in performing them the surgeon must consider the possible sequelae:
a His emergency amputation may in fact be the final one although not ideal. This is the most likely outcome in war wounds.
b A myoplastic amputation may in fact be performed later.

He must therefore plan his site of amputation and his flaps with both these possibilities in mind and he should be familiar with the details of the myoplastic stump as outlined on pages 166 and 167.

The final definitive amputation should be performed whenever possible at special centres by orthopaedic surgeons who also understand prosthetic fitting. At such centres it may be decided that the emergency amputation as it stands will suffice. This would apply particularly in a mass casualty situation in total war when large numbers of amputations would have to be performed to save life.

Emergency amputations – indications

Remember that amputation is irrevocable. The decision to amputate both for primary and complicated injuries is often difficult, and a source of anxiety. Wherever possible a second opinion should be obtained. While any doubt remains and while the patient can be retained under observation amputation should not be performed.

In recent injuries of major blood vessels the possibility of vascular repair must always be considered.

The **indications for amputation** are:

a *The severity of the damage*
In the case of recent injuries (first 24 hours) amputation of the upper extremity should only be considered when part of the limb is mangled and devitalized and it is judged that the damage to the soft parts is such that there is no chance of the recovery of function of any part of the hand, fingers or thumb.

In the case of the lower extremity after recent injury, amputation may be considered justifiable when the limb is mangled and grossly contaminated, particularly if the blood supply is impaired, or when damage to a main nerve and artery is accompanied by such muscle and skin damage as to prohibit attempts to restore vascular or nerve continuity. Loss of bone without concomitant nerve and vascular injury does not justify it.

b *Overwhelming infection,* eg clostridial gangrenous myositis of segmental type.

c *Established gangrene* due to vascular injury.

d *Continued infection* associated with severe nerve or bone injury.

e *Secondary haemorrhage,* if all other measures fail.

f *Multiple injuries,* especially in a gravely shocked and ill patient, may affect the decision. In such cases amputation as the simplest and fastest means of removing excessive amounts of damaged muscle may be life saving.

Levels for amputation

The emergency amputation should be at the lowest level at which the tissues are viable. When there is a fracture just above this level the amputation should be performed through the fracture.

An exception to this rule is in uncontrollable secondary haemorrhage in a gunshot wound involving bone when amputation may have to be done through the fracture. In such circumstances it is important to remove all blood clot surrounding the vessels and to define and tie securely each artery and vein separately with non absorbable ligatures.

In infected cases it may be necessary to amputate above the infected area because amputation provides good drainage.

The temptation to perform high definitive amputation in the battle zone must be resisted. However useless the stump may appear it may yet be functional and the more distal the wound the safer and better another definitive and final amputation will be.

Operative technique in emergency amputations

a Patients requiring amputation are often profoundly shocked and in dire need of vigorous resuscitation, but in the presence of continued haemorrhage operation must not be delayed. Surgeons must be prepared to operate rapidly. A tourniquet may be necessary, but is best avoided as it makes it more difficult to judge which structures are viable and distorts the flaps.

b Skin incision – in general *all viable skin should be preserved* and is used at the time of delayed primary suture to obtain skin cover. The incision is often dictated by the wound. Otherwise if formal rounded flaps are necessary they should be made as long as possible and in general anterior and posterior with a combined length of at least one and a half times the diameter of the limb at the level of bone section. If, however, it would appear that a future myoplastic stump may be possible flaps could well be fashioned as indicated on pages 166 and 167, ie above knee and through knee, lateral flaps; below knee, anterio-medial and postero-lateral but when there is doubt about the viability of the skin a long posterior flap may be used. The deep fascia is incised at the same level as the skin and reflected up with it as a single layer. The muscles should be preserved if viable and division made through the tendons. If this is not possible they should be divided at least half an inch distal to the proposed level of bone section. The main vessels should be identified and tied individually when possible with non-absorbable ligatures. A main artery should have two proximal ligatures. The nerves are cut through cleanly just above the level of bone section. They are not ligated, injected nor pulled down forcibly before division. The bone is sawn through using an amputation retractor. No periosteal cuff should be reflected.

c If a *tourniquet* has been used it should now be released and all bleeding points secured. The flaps are allowed to fall into place and not sutured. Care should be taken that drainage of the stump is free. Dry dressings and wool padding are applied and the stump is immobilized. Delayed primary suture follows as for any other wound.

d In *wounds of the foot and hand* no attempt should be made at formal amputation at this stage, but a simple removal of non viable tissue is performed. Splinting should be applied to prevent contractures of the ankle and wrist.

e When amputation is indicated in the *region of the knee,* section through the joint itself is preferable to a bone section. The operation is performed as on pages 166 and 167 for a myoplastic stump, but no attempt is made to suture the muscles at this stage.

f In order to *prevent flap retraction* where the amputation flaps are scanty, it is advisable to apply traction to the skin above the amputation level by means of a sterile adhesive such as mastisol and a stockinette cuff fixed to a Cramer wire cage incorporated in a plaster.

Evacuation

Before evacuation the patient's condition must be stabilized, shock and blood loss overcome and invasion infective controlled. If the evacuation journey is to be long, the stump should be immobilized in a well padded plaster cast. This plaster should include the joint above and be made easily removable. A good way to do this is to incorporate a greased rubber tube which when withdrawn allows easy splitting. Important instructions for after care should be written on the cast as well as in the notes. Ensure that thorough drainage from the stump is not impeded. Redressing en route should not be necessary. When possible the patient should be retained for 48 hours after amputation lest a reactionary haemorrhage occur.

Delayed primary closure

The first dressing of the stump will ordinarily be done in the operating theatre three to seven days after the emergency operation. The procedure adopted will follow the well established principles of wound closure, but there are certain differences in the case of amputation stumps.

a Where it has been possible to leave enough skin and muscle at the primary operation to allow a myoplastic stump at a later stage the surgeon should close the wound by skin suture without suturing the muscles over the bone ends leaving as much muscle and skin flaps as possible.

b When enough muscle and skin has not been left for a myoplastic stump the tissues should be fashioned into an acceptable stump as low down as possible. In doing this it must be borne in mind that, although a myoplastic amputation may be performed later at a higher level, this emergency amputation may be the final one.

c Split skin grafts at or near the end of a stump are not acceptable in fitting a prosthesis and they should not be used in delayed primary closure in this situation because this may be the final amputation. This rule does not apply to the hand where all viable tissues should be preserved to allow for subsequent reconstruction in a specialized unit. Useful split skin may be obtained and stored from the amputated limb before discarding.

The **method of skin closure** is therefore:

a *The hand* – defects are covered with split skin grafts. These may be regarded as the best form of dressing. They may be replaced by full thickness cover at a later stage.

b *All other situations* – by full thickness skin flap and not by skin graft. If necessary, re-amputation should be made a little higher in order to obtain closure without tension.

Whichever of the above procedures be adopted, it is important to ensure haemostasis before closure and to drain the wound at its most dependent point. The drain is removed after 24–48 hours and any collection of serum aspirated before re-dressing the stump. Dressings should be copious and bandaging firm to reduce oedema.

After treatment   Apart from removing the drain the dressings should be left for 10 days if there is no evidence of infection. Firm bandaging must be continued after the wound has healed to prevent oedema.

Active movements of all proximal joints must be encouraged and flexion contractures of hip and knee must be prevented.

The psychological trauma which the loss of a limb produces must be counteracted throughout the after care by encouragement to use the limb and resume a normal life quickly. A pylon should be fitted within the first two weeks and the patient encouraged to walk on it pending the provision of a prosthesis.

Final amputation

An amputation performed in the war zone as described above may allow for the fitting of a satisfactory prosthesis without further surgery.

Any further definitive surgery should be postponed until the wound is soundly healed and the patient in the home base having been assessed for prosthetic fitting. The ensuing details of final amputation are therefore inserted only as a guide to the forward surgeon on the future management of the patient in that this may influence his technique in performing an emergency operation.

The upper limb There is no site of election, the amputation being made as low as possible. In the hand as much tissue as possible, particularly of the thumb, is preserved. Surplus skin of useless digits may be used in the reconstruction of a functional hand. Above the wrist; bone ends are covered with osteoplastic flaps as described below and opposing muscles of their tendons are sutured together over the bone ends to create a myoplastic stump. Equal skin flaps are designed so that the suture line is at right angles to the suture line of the muscles.

The lower limb Amputations are made at as low a level as possible consistent with the fitting of a prosthesis. They may have end-bearing stumps through the foot, ankle or knee or total-bearing stumps below or above the knee. In the latter the weight bearing is conveyed to the prosthesis spread throughout the whole surface of the limb from the stump end to the bony prominences above, eg in the below-knee stump up to the tibial condyles and the under surface of the patella. Bone section is made at the level at which the muscles may best be sutured over it and which allows the several inches needed to fit an artificial joint.

The foot Amputations through the digits as far back as the base of the metatarsals are satisfactory, but section through the tarsus gives a stump which tilts owing to muscle imbalance and should be avoided.

The ankle The classical Syme amputation (not the Elmslie modification) is recommended. The heel pad is filleted and covers the bone ends sawn across through the bases of the malleoli.

Disarticulation at the knee The patient is prone. If anterior and posterior flaps are used the anterior flap is made a hand's breadth below the tibial plateau. The posterior flap is two fingers breadth below the plateau, so that the suture line will be just behind the weight bearing area of the condyles. The anterior flap is filletted down to bone and includes the patellar tendon. An alternative method with less risk of sloughing of the flaps is to make equal lateral flaps which begin just above the insertion of the patellar tendon. Ligaments are cut at tibial plateau level and muscles at their insertions. The hamstring tendons are sutured to the medial and lateral quadriceps expansions, the patellar tendon and the posterior capsule to the cruciate ligaments in the inter-condylar notch. This operation produces an excellent end-bearing stump but it is essential that if an anterior skin flap be made it should have an adequate blood supply

Below knee   The patient is prone. The best site for bone section is at the level of the musculo-tendinous junction of the gastrocnemius. The skin flaps are antero-medial and postero-lateral to give a diagonal terminal scar. A preliminary bone section 3 cm below the final section is made to allow the cutting with a sharp chisel of osteoperiosteal flaps on each of the three surfaces of the tibia and on the fibula. These are fashioned into an osteoperiosteal bridge between the ends of the two bones. The fibula is cut 0.5 cm above the tibial section and the anterior edge of the tibia is bevelled enough to obviate a bony protrusion under the skin. Any sharp edges are filed smooth. The calf muscles are split longitudinally, the medial part being sewn over the bridge to the anterior tibial muscles and the lateral part, thinned if necessary to avoid a bulbous stump end, completes the muscle sling.

Above knee   The patient is supine. Lateral flaps are made at the suprapatellar level. The quadriceps aponeurosis is divided above the patella and the hamstring tendons near their insertion. The bone section is 12 to 15 cm above the joint line with a periosteal flap turned up from 3 cms below this. The muscles are sutured with overlapping musculo-tendinous junctions over the bone end under slight tension, medio-lateral flaps first and then the anterior overlapping the posterior flap.

CHAPTER 15

Plaster of Paris splinting

Plaster room

Plasterwork should be carried out as far as possible in a plaster room, preferably adjoining the operating theatre. Following surgery the patient can be moved from the operating room to the plaster room for application of a cast. This will prevent plaster debris on and around the operating table and will limit the requirement for cleaning and enable the theatre to be prepared for the next operation.

In larger hospitals it is preferable to have a second plaster room for the use of up-patients and walking wounded.

In improvised buildings a plaster trap must be constructed from flyproofing wire mesh below the sink to prevent the obstruction of waste pipes.

Materials and instruments

Plaster of Paris will be available:
a in individual rolls of 4 in and 6 in widths,
b in pre-prepared emergency splint packs with two pre-cut folded slabs and the conforming crepe paper bandage contained within a polythene bag. This bag, if carefully opened, can be used as a water container to wet the slabs and
c dispensers of slabs of 4 in and 8 in widths which can quickly be cut to selected lengths.

Padding of rolls of synthetic plaster wadding will be required along with adhesive and plain felt. Where increased absorbency is necessary, or where excessive swelling is expected, standard rolls of cotton wool may be preferred.

Cramer wire splinting is useful for reinforcing plasters and malleable padded aluminium digital splinting should also be available.

Essential instruments are plaster shears, blunt pointed bandage scissors, plaster knives and a scalpel; wire cutters, one gallon bucket and a broad felt tipped indelible pen. Slabs can easily be soaked in a bucket and no special trough or flat tray is necessary. A plaster cutter of the oscillating type is ideal especially where plasters are to be split soon after application if swelling is expected.

Plaster application and technique

Depending on the circumstances of the fracture or underlying injury a complete cast or slabs will be used, the latter for preference. Slabs can be applied over clothing if necessary, provided that all wrinkles are avoided and buttons are padded or removed. The technique of applying such a cast is:

a A back slab is applied first with the joint in question maintained at the desired angle followed by

b a lateral U-slab completed with

c an encircling bandage of cotton or crepe paper. This has the advantage of being easily removed and less likely to produce circulatory problems should swelling occur within the cast.

It should be appreciated that slabs applied with a cotton bandage can become tight due to shrinkage of the bandage in drying and it is advisable for the encircling bandage to be cut along the whole length of the cast after the slabs have set. Circulatory embarrassment can be due to constriction from the original wound dressing gauze or the encircling cast wadding, especially if this has been blood soaked and subsequently dried. *In such cases it is essential to split all encircling materials to expose skin from end to end of the cast.*

There is no place for the use of unpadded encircling casts in forward areas. All plasters should therefore be padded with particular reference to points of bony prominence and where peripheral nerves are at risk of pressure from the edges of a cast, the lateral popliteal nerve at the fibula neck being the best example. Plaster bandages should be applied rapidly and there should be no adjustment of joint position after application as this tends to produce wrinkles and folds within the cast which may subsequently produce skin irritation and damage. Provided the cast is well padded moulding can be applied to maintain reduction of the fracture.

Cast windows

The cutting of windows in the cast to permit inspection and redressing of the underlying wound is not advised in the early stages as swelling may tend to occur through the area of the window. The site of the fracture or wound should be marked on the overlying plaster surface and the area of the window to be cut at a later stage delineated. If windows are cut for removal of sutures they can be replaced after the dressing is completed either by an encircling crepe bandage or, preferably, a few turns of the plaster bandage.

Immediate splitting of casts

When the casts are dry it is essential that they are split from end to end before evacuation. It will not be possible to retain patients with casts for any significant time prior to evacuation and this will facilitate the opening of the cast during transportation of required, particularly if plaster shears are not available. The siting of the linear cut will normally be along the front of the leg and the flexor aspect of the arm, but will be influenced by the presence and location of any underlying wound. The limb should be elevated after application of the plaster and early movement of fingers or toes encouraged. Definitive plasters should immobilize only those joints required and in the optimum position leaving joints which are no involved entirely free.

Special points in application

The extent of the cast applied will be governed by the underlying injury In the upper limb the cast may be limited to the forearm alone or may require the incorporation of the elbow or even the shoulder. Joints so immobilized should conform to the rules suggested in Chapter 13 on missile wounds of joints so far as optimum position is concerned. Long leg casts should extend from the upper two thirds of thigh to the base of the toes and short leg casts from below the knee also to the base of the toes The foot should be plantigrade, in other words at right angles to the tibia and in neutral position for valgus and varus. Limb casts should permit free and full movement of the digits.

Special plasters

Patients with spinal injuries, including those of the cervical spine, should travel on a turning frame employing traction if necessary. The application of the Minerva type of jacket for cervical spine fixation is time consuming difficult and not advised. There is no place for the use of plaster beds for evacuation purposes.

Hip spica casts are also seldom required, being time consuming, difficult and wasteful of materials. The Tobruk plaster is the logical alternative.

Tobruk splint   This method of splintage is ideal for the transportation of patients with femoral fractures, missile wounds of knee or other extensive bone and soft tissue injuries of the lower limb.

The steps of application of a Tobruk cast are shown in Figs 14a to 14g. After wound surgery and local dressing a suitably padded Thomas splint is applied, following which an extension strapping is applied to the limb reaching as far as can be permitted by the size of the bandage or the wound. This is maintained by an encircling elastic bandage and fixed traction established to the splint with the foot supported by a padded adjustable foot support which provides also stabilization on the stretcher poles and elevation of the lower end of the splint. The whole limb is then padded using cotton wool or gamgee and an encircling cast applied reaching as high as the ring of the Thomas splint at the top and to the toes distally. This is moulded at the edges to provide greater stability and comfort and finally a diagram drawn on the surface of the cast showing details of the injury and its location.

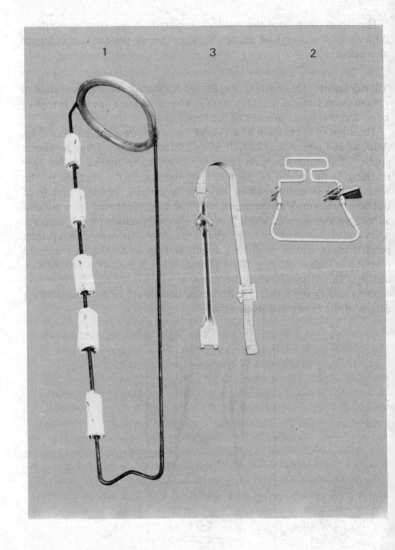

Figure 14a   The Tobruk splint
1 Thomas splint
2 Footpiece and support
3 Stretcher bar and adjustable strap, buckle and locking device.

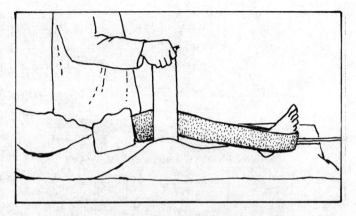

Figure 14b Extension plaster applied and suspension bandage to flex knee 10 degrees.

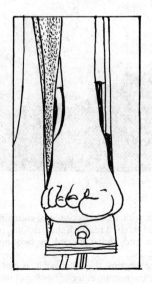

Figure 14c Arrangement of spreader and cord

Figure 14d

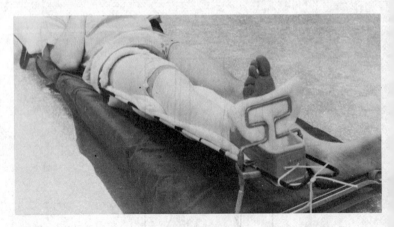

Figure 14e

Thomas splint in position with fixed traction and countertraction. A spreader is shown but equally effective traction results if the strapping is taken around the sides of the splint, tied to the end and tightened by twisting with a stick 'Spanish windlass' fashion (see Fig 14e)

A pad keeps the ring snugly against the tuber ischii. A pad of wool is placed under the fracture site to restore the normal anterior bowing of the thigh. Ample wool has been placed under the limb. The foot is held at right angles to the leg on a footpiece adequately padded under the sole and heel.

Figure 14f Wool envelops the limb, filling the gaps between it and the side bars of the splint, completing in front the padding which has already been done behind.

Figure 14g The limb and splint are encased in plaster as described in the text. It is moulded to grip the side bars. If the foot is included in the plaster, the traction strapping must be kept free to allow effective traction and tightening of the windlass.

Fractures involving the trochanters or neck of the femur are not well immobilized in a Tobruk plaster and may be put up in a very carefully applied plaster spica. Leg. Severe fractures are best immobilized in the Tobruk plaster. Less serious fractures may be put up in a padded plaster cast from groin to metatarsal necks with the knee flexed 10 degrees and the foot placed at right angles. The splint is split throughout its entire length before evacuation. The limb and plaster may be slung.

Thoraco-brachial cast The thoraco-brachial cast is a useful method of providing comfortable support for the upper arm and shoulder injury. The steps involved in its application are shown in Figs 15a to 15f. Wool padding is placed in the axilla and the elbow maintained at right angles, ideally with a collar and cuff support. Protective padding is required over the shoulder and around the elbow on the injured side and also on the thoracic wall and the axilla on the uninjured side. Plaster should include the original collar and cuff support, leaving the hand and wrist free unless there is an associated nerve injury or forearm injury which would require more extensive support. While the plaster is setting moulding is applied both anteriorly and posteriorly to the surface between the chest wall and the injured upper arm. It is preferable that the patient should be conscious when the plaster is applied.

a Collar and cuff support

b Placing of four pads

c Circular bandage keeping pads
   in position

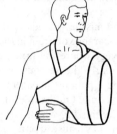

d Round shoulder and elbow of
   the injured side

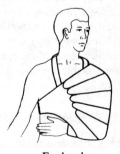

e Fan bandage

f Final circular bandage

Figure 15   Thoraco-brachial plaster

CHAPTER 16

Head injuries

Introduction

Missile wounds of the head are divided into penetrating wounds, in which the dura is pierced and non-penetrating wounds in which the breach of tissue is limited to the scalp alone or to the scalp and skull. The severity of a wound is to be judged more by its effects on the patient's state of consciousness and on the focal signs, such as hemiplegia, which may be found on clinical examination, than on the actual extent of the wound itself.

Extensive missile wounds of the head with wide fracturing of the skull and the appearance of brain in the superficial tissues are compatible with a good recovery where the injury is confined to certain parts of the brain and particularly the regions of the frontal and occipital poles. Indeed many of these patients may remain conscious, or lose consciousness for a few minutes only. On the other hand a small missile wound, particularly a high velocity missile, which has penetrated deeply to the brain tissue or brain stem may cause death, either immediately or in the succeeding hours or days during which the patient remains in deep coma.

The physio-pathology of brain injury is such that there is a marked difference between wounds caused by high velocity missiles and those due to low velocity missiles. The high velocity missile causes a devastating brain injury with highly unstable intracranial pressure dynamics and raised intracranial pressure. Such patients do not travel well and in any event have a poor prognosis. Low velocity missile wounds of the brain are different, however, and many such cases are suitable for transfer to a neurosurgical unit for definitive brain surgery.

Factors in the management of head wounds and closed injuries

a *Arrest of surface haemorrhage* is a first priority. Bleeding can be severe from scalp arteries, particularly where the wound is around the 'hat band' area. Fortunately for the majority of scalp wounds a shell dressing firmly applied will arrest bleeding. Where this is not effective and a scalp artery is seen spurting, it can be stopped by underrunning a stitch through the scalp or applying a Spencer Wells forceps to the galea aponeurotica and the blood vessel for a few minutes. Occasionally severe venous bleeding may occur where wounds over the midline, or across the back of the head, have torn the sagittal or transverse venous sinuses. This type of bleeding can be recognized by the situation of the wound, and the character of the blood, which is dark and comes out in a continuous stream. The best way to arrest this is to prop the patient into a semi-reclining position for a few minutes and apply a firm dressing. Make sure there is no obstruction to the venous return from the head by clothing about the neck.

b *Intracranial haematoma* is a major complication and its early detection is important. Untreated the haematoma will give rise to cerebral compression and death unless it can be evacuated by surgical operation as soon as possible. The haematoma may be extradural, subdural or intracerebral and may follow non-penetrating as well as penetrating head wounds and closed head injuries. The accumulation of blood within the cranium is accompanied by a progressive lowering of the patient's conscious state, or the development of fresh focal signs on neurological examination or both. For these reasons, therefore, regular observation of the patient's clinical condition is essential. When the compression becomes severe the pupil may dilate and become inactive on the same side as the clot. The most constant sign of cerebral compression, however, is progressive deterioration of the patient's responsiveness. This is most obvious where at one stage after the injury the patient has regained full consciousness and then relapsed – the so-called 'lucid interval' – but it should be remembered that the classical 'lucid interval' is not common. The progressive deterioration may also be recognized where the patient has been less than fully conscious from the time of injury, provided regular observations of how the patient reacts at each examination have been recorded. Intracranial haematoma is not a common complication, but is more likely to give rise to symptons and signs in circumstances where natural decompression has not already been afforded by the injury. Thus a massive penetrating missile wound is less likely to be complicated by an intracranial haemotoma with cerebral compression than is a machine-gun bullet wound with only a small entry wound. In the latter case if a clot develops, its immediate removal at a forward surgical centre is necessary if the patient's life is to be saved. Some clots, however, develop slowly and thus permit the patient to be transferred to a neurosurgical centre.

c *Infection* is the third factor. Virtually all head wounds are contaminated with a mixed bacterial flora. The infection which may develop is usually due to staphylococcus aureus, less commonly to streptococcus pyogenes, and rarely to gram negative organisms. Clostridial infection may occur and at times frank gas gangrene, especially in temporal and occipital wounds where scalp musculature is present. Infection of head wounds is serious because, in addition to the complications that may accompany all infected wounds, there are the particular complications of brain abscess, ventriculitis or meningitis, all of which carry a high mortality rate. Although these complications are most likely to arise in penetrating missile wounds they can also arise from time to time where the dura is intact and have even been seen to follow simple scalp wounds. Careful treatment of all scalp wounds is therefore paramount. In addition to the careful cleansing of the wound to be described below and the use of antibiotics, efficient scalp closure as soon as possible is important in preventing infection. In closed head injuries if there is a discharge of cerebro-spinal fluid from the ears or nose, meningitis is a likely complication so long as the discharge persists. Prophylactically both sulphadiazine and pencillin should be given. Sulphadiazine may be given by mouth – 2 g followed by 1 g four-hourly – or by intravenous injection if the patient is unable to swallow. The leak of cerebro-spinal fluid may persist until the dura is repaired by intracranial operation. If the leak comes from the nose and the patient is conscious he should be warned not to blow his nose.

d *Treatment of the unconscious state* is the fourth factor to be borne in mind. If the patient is unconscious following a missile wound of the head or a closed head injury from a road accident, he may develop chest complications unless the airway can be kept clear, or metabolic disorders unless his state of nutrition is maintained. As a general rule these patients should be nursed on their sides and turned two-hourly. The patient may be apnoeic immediately following head injury and may require assisted ventilation until respiration returns. If the breathing is not free a simple airway should be provided and secretions accumulating in the mouth mopped or sucked away. The use of endotracheal tubes is preferable in the early stages of treatment: tracheostomy may be needed in selected cases if simple measures do not suffice. If the patient remains unconscious for more than 24 hours after the injury and is then unable to swallow safely, a feeding tube should be passed through the nose into the stomach. Fluids, such as milk and water in equal parts, should be given up to 4 or 5 pints (2–2½ litres) every 24 hours. Intravenous fluids may be preferred in the early days following head injury and this enables electrolyte balance to be more readily maintained. Paralysed or weak limbs should be protected from injury.

Following a closed head injury of any severity most patients are unconscious at the outset and some may remain unconscious for many days or even weeks. This does not mean that recovery is not possible, although it should be recognized that penetrating high velocity missile wounds of the head do carry a very high mortality and such patients have a low treatment priority. By contrast scalp wounds, depressed skull fractures, intracranial clots and low velocity missile wounds are all capable of excellent recovery given correct surgical treatment and nursing management.

First treatment

The hair is cut away for about one inch (2.5 cm) all round any wound and one of the local topical antibiotics such as penicillin-sulphamezathine powder or polybactrin is applied. A shell dressing is then applied and secured firmly by bandaging or strapping, attention being given to the comments on bleeding (see above).

Treatment against tetanus will be the same as for other wounds. Morphine should be avoided if possible. It may be necessary to give it for the relief of pain in other wounds in a conscious patient. The following entry should be made on the field medical card (F Med 26):

a Date and time of wounding.

b Date and time of examination.

c Site of wound.

d State of consciousness (the level of responsiveness should be briefly described so that deterioration at a later stage may be more easily recognized). Useful descriptions are:

   (1) 'Alert, orientated in time and space'

   (2) 'Alert but confused'

   (3) 'Drowsy but responds to name or command'

   (4) 'Comatose but reacting to pain in the limbs'

   (5) 'Comatose and unresponsive to all painful stimuli'

e The presence or absence of weakness or paralysis of the limbs.

f The size and reaction of the pupils.

g Respiration and pulse rates.

h Presence or absence of injuries to other regions.

En route to definitive treatment or surgical units/centres, entries should be made wherever possible on the clinical state, with the time of the observation stated.

Management at the dressing station

a *Examination of the patient* The patient's conscious level and the findings on examination of the central nervous system are repeated and compared with the findings on the field medical card. Particular care is taken to exclude the presence of other injuries. Where the full extent of the head wound is not apparent close clipping of the hair may be needed to ensure that other scalp lacerations have not been overlooked.

b *Diagnosis* of a penetrating wound is usually easy, either on the appearance of the wound, or where there are focal neurological signs corresponding to the site of injury. This is not invariably true. In other cases the extent of the injury and the brain wound may only be defined at operation. If, therefore, operation is undertaken at the advanced surgical centre it should be so conducted, that if the wound is found to be more extensive than was at first supposed, the operation can be terminated and completed later at a neurosurgical centre if necessary. It is however preferable that operation when undertaken should be the definitive one; hence the need for good clinical evaluation since the intracranial dynamics can be seriously disturbed by the need for undue manipulation of brain tissue and additional anaesthesic agents should be avoided if possible since they raise the intracranial pressure, sometimes by a remarkable amount.

c *Resuscitation* Shock is not common in uncomplicated head injuries unless there has been serious haemorrhage from surface vessels, in which case blood transfusion may be needed. Otherwise the presence of shock should re-direct attention to the possibility of some other injury which may have been overlooked, or the possible development of gas gangrene. Sedatives should be used cautiously for restlessness. Adjustment of the patient's position or the relief of a distended bladder are often more effective than drugs. If they are required chlorpromazine 25–50 mg or diazepam 10 mg given intramuscularly or intravenously would be appropriate. *Where morphine has to be used it should invariably be in small doses and not more than 10 mg exceeded.* In larger doses morphine depresses respiration and so raises intracranial venous pressure.

d *Early care* See page 178.

Evacuation

In general, if a patient can be evacuated to a neuro-surgical unit within 72 hours from the time of wounding this is the correct disposal. Brain wounds cannot be treated satisfactorily without the aid of preliminary X-ray examination. It is often necessary to have more sophisticated radiological apparatus to assess the patient before embarking on wound toilet. Whilst it is generally true to say that head casualties travel well, this is not true of the high velocity brain wound (see below).

Where there has to be priority of evacuation, pride of place should be given to those patients who are well and conscious with penetrating brain wounds such as compound depressed fractures of the skull or low velocity missile injuries. Next priority includes patients unconscious following closed head injuries but with equal and reacting pupils and responding to stimulation by normal and purposeful movements. With full nursing care, which can be provided at the general hospital area, their chances of recovery should be good. In cases for immediate evacuation, penicillin or broad spectrum antibiotics should be given intramuscularly and also 3 gm of sulphadiazine by mouth. This dose should be repeated twice daily on the line of evacuation. Clinical observation should be continued and recorded.

On the other hand, those patients who have been in coma from the outset of their injury and particularly those in whom the pupils are fixed and dilated, showing no reaction to light, or who only react to pain by abnormal movements, should have a low category for evacuation.

Where the military situation prohibits transportation within 72 hours from wounding or when complications develop which make immediate operation essential, operation must be conducted at the advanced surgical centre. In battle conditions it may not always be possible to evacuate all head injuries to base and patients with scalp lacerations or compound fractures which have not penetrated the dura would then be treated forward.

SURGICAL PROCEDURES

Pre-operative preparation

If the patient is comatose the operation may be conducted under regional block anaesthesia with one per cent lignocaine. In other cases a general anaesthetic is given through an endotracheal tube. It is important to see that the airway is at all times clear since the slightest obstruction may cause embarrassing swelling of the brain. Deep anaesthesia is not needed for head wounds. Pre-medication should normally be by atropine (0.2 mg) only. Under anaesthesia the whole scalp is shaved and thoroughly cleaned with one per cent cetavlon or soap and water.

Methods of haemostasis in brain surgery

Haemostasis must be much more carefully secured in operations on the head than elsewhere. The scalp, dura and brain cortex are extremely vascular, and patients with head injury tolerate blood loss badly. An accumulation of clot within the skull after operation can be rapidly fatal. The wisdom of wide surgical exposure in arresting bleeding applies as much in neurosurgery as in other disciplines:

a *Scalp*   The line of incision should first be marked by scalpel and then assistants should compress the scalp digitally on each side of this line until artery forceps are applied to the galea aponeurotica. It is impracticable to catch individual scalp vessels; complete haemostasis can be obtained by applying light artery forceps to the galea aponeuritica at intervals of about one cm. When these are removed at the end of the operation no ligatures need be applied, for the closing suture should effectively stop all bleeding, especially if the scalp is closed with fine silk in two layers. In penetrating wounds or unclean wounds it is not advisable, however, to leave deep silk sutures and a single layer closure is to be followed.

b *Bone*   Bleeding from the cut edge of the bone may sometimes be considerable and is always persistent. It is effectively stopped by bone wax.

c *Dura mater*   Bleeding from the middle meningeal artery may be stopped by diathermy, small silver clips or by ligature, or by a combination of these techniques. In certain cases it may prove impossible to visualize the bleeding source and packing with hot cotton wool packs may be necessary, continuing for 10–20 minutes. Bleeding from the surface of the dura near the bone edge can be stopped by stitching the dura to the pericranium or by muscle 'stamps.' Take a small piece of temporal muscle, or muscle from the anterior compartment of the leg, hammer it out flat and lay it gently on the bleeding point, covering it for the time being with a piece of old rubber glove, through which it can be firmly pressed into place. It adheres in a few minutes and the sheet of rubber can then be removed without dislodging it.

d *Venous sinuses*   Bleeding from the superior longitudinal or other sinuses may be fierce and difficult to control. If the wound is small a curved clamp will usually control it, and a muscle graft can then be prepared and applied. With gross injuries of the sinus the bleeding can be temporarily controlled by pledglets of cotton wool wrung out in Ringer's solution or normal saline. If the operating table allows, and the patient is not exsanguinated, he should be gradually sat up. This lowers the pressure in the sinus, sometimes to such an extent that there may be a risk of air being sucked into it. The gaping edges of the sinus can then be approximated by silver clips or by silk suture. Gauze packing should hardly ever be necessary, but if used should be removed in 24 hours.

e *Brain*   The large cerebral vessels are on the surface of the brain: thus bleeding from the white matter is usually slight, and can be stopped by temporary application of wool pledgets. Surface vessels are best stopped by diathermy, or, in the case of the larger arteries, by Cushing's silver clips. Small muscle grafts are sometimes useful. It should never be necessary to leave a gauze pack against the brain, and ribbon gauze should never be used for drainage.

As an alternative to using small muscle grafts to secure haemostasis on the dura and in the brain a haemostatic substance, such as oxycel or gelatin sponge, may be used.

Exploratory operative measures in closed head injury

A burrhole or trephine hole placed one inch (2.5 cm) above and in front of the ear will disclose many of these clots. If an extradural haemotoma is found the bony opening can be enlarged and the clot evacuated. If a subdural haematoma is present, as manifested by a bluish appearance of the dura, the dura may be opened and the blood allowed to escape. In cases of subdural haematoma bilateral exploration is required since localizing signs may be misleading and clots are not infrequently bilateral. Exploration should always be made to the local sites of injury such as fractures, scalp bruising or laceration, if the temporal exploration has proved negative and the clinical evidence for cerebral compression is strong.

Operative measures in head wounds

Before operating on head wounds the surgeon should consider the following points:

a *General considerations:*
(1)   The main aim is to convert an open wound into a clean, closed wound.
(2)   Apparently trivial scalp wounds may turn out to be serious penetrating wounds of the brain. In all cases and particularly where there is doubt as between a penetrating and non-penetrating wound, the operation should be conducted in stages layer by layer as described below.

(3)   Incision and excision of the scalp may be attended by severe blood loss unless performed by standard technique (see below). Inspection of the deeper layers of the wound cannot be carried out without adequate haemostasis.

(4)   Dislodgement of indriven bone fragments in the region of the sagittal or transverse sinuses may be attended by disastrous bleeding and these are best left alone unless full facilities are available.

(5)   The brain must at all times be handled gently and blind exploration for foreign bodies whether with instruments or with the finger may produce irreparable functional damage, resulting in such disabilities as hemiplegia.

(6)   Wide removal of undamaged bone is unnecessary in the majority of brain wounds and it is not necessary to provide a decompression except where the operation is mainly undertaken for the symptoms and signs of cerebral compression.

(7)   Head wounds should not be packed or plugged with gauze and drainage is rarely necessary.

b *Scalp*   The wound is opened and if necessary prolonged, or two separate wounds are joined to facilitate exposure of the deeper parts. Blood loss is prevented by finger pressure on the wound edges until the galea aponeurotica can be picked up with light artery forceps placed at intervals of one cm, or a pair of self retaining retractors can be introduced which also effectively controls the bleeding. The subgaleal plane should be thoroughly explored for dirt, hair, bone chips and missiles which sometimes lodge at a considerable distance from the wound edge due to the mobility of the scalp over the bone. The edges of the wound are excised.

c *Skull*   Fissured fractures are best left alone. If there is visible dirt in the crack it may be scraped gently till clean. Contaminated periosteum should be removed and a more generous excision made if the wound has involved the temporal or occipital muscles. In depressed fractures all contaminated, depressed and loose bone fragments should be removed. As a general rule this should begin with a trephine or burrhole through healthy bone adjacent to the depression to determine the plane of the normal dura. The bone to be removed is then gradually nibbled away from this. If the dura has been torn, bone should be removed so as to expose a healthy margin of dura about ¼ inch wide all round. An intact dura should be left unopened except in the rare instances where it is obviously blue and tense from an intradural clot or the operation is being conducted for clinical signs of compression where an incision in the dura to evacuate the underlying clot may be needed.

d *Dura* If an unsuspected penetrating wound with tearing of the dura is disclosed and full neurosurgical facilities are not available, it may be possible for the surgeon to terminate the operation at this juncture by closure of the scalp as described below and arrange evacuation to a neurosurgical centre. Where the full operation is being conducted or an emergency operation is undertaken to relieve cerebral compression, the dural rent is carefully opened although rarely if ever does it require enlargement.

e *Brain* The rent in the dura is usually plugged with blood clot and necrotic brain tissue and on opening it up pulped brain and clot can be removed by gentle suction and irrigation. Where an intracranial clot has formed and has caused cerebral compression this simple procedure may be effective in allowing it to discharge itself and thus relieve the immediate situation. Under emergency conditions it may be possible to terminate the operation at that stage having relieved the immediate compression and defer the formal examination of the deeper parts of the brain wound until arrival at the neurosurgical centre. Otherwise the necrotic brain and clot are gently irrigated away and usually bone chips are brought to the surface by this manoeuvre. Others which are readily visible are also removed, but it is harmful to search blindly for indriven fragments. Irrigation with warm normal saline or Ringer's solution will usually produce haemostasis and at the end of this part of the operation the brain should be slack, and pulsating. As a general rule it is safe to leave the dura open, although dural closure is now practised in neurosurgical units where a definitive procedure has been effected. Otherwise the dura is left unclosed since there may well be a dural deficit as well; and the aim must be to secure sound scalp closure.

f *Closure of the scalp* The superficial layers of the wound are now dusted with penicillin sulphamezathine powder or polybactrin and then the scalp closure begun. Accurate closure without tension is a most important step in the operation. No attempt must be made to pull the skin edges together under tension when closure is difficult. Flaps can be undercut or the wound turned into a small flap by a rotating incision, or the wound extended in a triangular fashion. Once the skin edges come together readily they are sutured together in two layers with fine silk. The deep layer through the galea holds the edges together and controls the bleeding and the skin stitches then need not be tied tightly and can be removed in four days time. Closure in one layer is also acceptable provided the stitch goes through all layers and the tension is evenly distributed throughout the wound. In this event they must be left in longer (six days). At the end of the operation any pent up blood beneath the scalp is removed through a blunt brain cannula inserted beneath the scalp, and this manoeuvre may be repeated on the following day when the dressing is done. Alternatively a portex drain may be inserted beneath the scalp, well clear of the incision.

g *Wound dressing*   The wound is covered with one layer of tulle gras or vaseline gauze followed by gauze. Large gauze dressings which can be wrapped round the whole head stay in place better than smaller ones. A firmly and evenly applied bandage to cover the whole head then completes the operation.

Where the patient is likely to be restless or confused, or if the wound is low in the temporal region this should be anchored to the skin by strapping, or better still a full head dressing with chin straps is used. The position and size of the wound, the presence of a drain and the date of the operation are then marked on the dressing in blue pencil.

Post operative treatment and disposal

The importance of the nursing care if the patient is unconscious, attention to the airway and the fluid intake have already been mentioned. Administration of penicillin and sulphadiazine should be continued for at least five days after the operation, depending on the patient's condition. When sulphadiazine is used the usual precautions against tubular precipitation should be taken. If there is any suspicion of intracranial infection a lumbar puncture should be performed and the CSF examined.

As soon as the patient has recovered from the immediate effects of the operation, he should be evacuated to the nearest neurosurgical centre. Where an incomplete operation has been performed this should be completed as soon as the general condition allows.

CHAPTER 17

The early treatment of injuries of the spinal cord and cauda equina

Aetiology and prognosis

The spinal cord may be injured by missile wounds, or by fractures and dislocations. In missile wounds the missile may score a direct hit on the theca, or may pass nearby with little damage to the spinal column. In the latter case spontaneous recovery from paraplegia may occur; if it is sufficient to be useful, some recovery of function will usually be evident within the first week, and this statement also applies to injuries of the spinal cord resulting from fractures and dislocations. High velocity missile wounds may cause severe disruption of spinal cord function even though the missile has not itself traversed the cord. The symptoms of missile wounds of the lumbar and sacral vertebrae are for the most part due to injury of the spinal roots of the cauda equina, and in these cases a large amount of recovery, especially motor recovery, is to be expected, but it may not begin for several weeks after the injury.

Complications

In injuries of the spinal cord death is most commonly due to urinary infection, bedsores or chest infection. In complete lesions spontaneous recovery of spinal cord functions may be seriously interfered with by these complications. Adequate treatment in the first few days will prevent them.

Early management

Emphasis must be placed on the following points:
a Diligent and continuous nursing care.
b Definitive management of the paralysed bladder.
c Attention to a high fluid intake and to protein and calorific requirements.
d Care of the chest.
   Frequently a missile penetrating the chest or peritoneal cavity also damages the spine. Clearly, in such cases operation on the spinal wound is

usually secondary to the management of the chest or abdominal injury. In other cases, if the condition of the patient permits, the wound should be excised in the usual way to diminish liability to infection. The spinal cord should not be interfered with, and usually no search should be made for missiles or bone fragments, nor should the spinal cord be decompressed, for the damage to the spinal cord is almost invariably due to the violence of impact, rather than to continued pressure of a missile or displaced bone fragments. If there is a leak of cerebro-spinal fluid the skin around the wound should be cleaned with special care using one per cent cetavlon or soap and water and a large firm dressing applied. Sulphadiazine should be given by mouth as a prophylactic against meningitis.

When the military situation prevents rapid transfer to a neuro-surgical unit it may be necessary to carry the treatment of the wound a stage further in the forward area. Here, as for wounds in other situations, delayed primary suture is the treatment of choice. Laminectomy should be considered at this stage only if there is a persistent cerebro-spinal fluid fistula requiring closure by fascial graft or in the rare event of advancing spinal compression from haemorrhage.

At a later stage laminectomy may be performed for:

a Gross deformity.

b Foreign body within the theca in cases where there is an incomplete lesion, as assessed by incomplete disturbance of function.

c Arrest in progress of recovery in cases of an incomplete lesion when the effects of spinal shock have passed off, especially when there is evidence of a spinal block to the flow of cerebro-spinal fluid.

d Severe and persistent nerve root pain.

Paraplegic patients should be evacuated as soon as the military situation permits to a neuro-surgical unit.

Transportation of the paraplegic

Ideally, these patients should be transported on a turning frame such as the Stryker or Emesay. If such a turning frame is not available the same principles of management can be achieved using two identical Service stretchers. The two Service stretchers should be prepared, one to act as a bottom and the other as a top. On the bottom stretcher several pillows or sorbo rubber pads are arranged transversely so that nothing hard will press on the patient's skin. A hole is cut from the canvas of the bottom stretcher to allow for bowel attention and the cleansing of the peri-anal area. Similarly, on the top stretcher holes are cut in the canvas for the face and for catheter drainage from the bladder. The patient is then placed on the prepared bottom stretcher, great care being taken to move him with the spine in a neutral position. Turning should be carried out every two hours. When being turned, more pillows should be arranged over the front of the patient's body and the top stretcher applied. The two stretchers, with the patient enclosed, like a sandwich, are strapped together and the turning carried out. The patient is nursed flat, and in fractures and dislocations of the spine a mild hyperextended position at the site of the fracture may be maintained by an extra pillow.

Reduction of cervical dislocations and flexion fractures

In dislocations of the cervical spine and flexion fractures, paralysis of delayed onset may be caused by haematoma formation or by gradual forward displacement of the proximal segment of the spinal column. In either instance, the prognosis is better than in paralysis of immediate onset, and reduction is indicated.

The patient is either anaesthetized in the supine position or is kept under sedation during manipulations.

There are two methods of traction:

a Traction can be applied to the head by a halter or chin strap. In an emergency, the battle helmet can be used, with the strap in position. The deformity is then reduced by strong traction.

b If this method fails, skeletal traction is applied by means of a caliper inserted in the parietal bones of the skull. Under local analgesia, symmetrically placed small circular incisions are made in the shaven scalp one inch (2.5 cm) above and slightly behind the apex of each ear. When the diploe has been entered on each side by a small trephine, the points of the caliper are introduced and are securely fixed by a double screw-locking device. A small dressing is applied around each incision.

Traction is begun by using 15 lb (7 kg) over a pulley fixed to the head of the stretcher or bed. Reduction is frequently obtained at once or within a few hours. If it is not, the weight may be increased to 30 lb (14 kg) until reduction has been secured. Then the weight is reduced to 15 lb, and later to 10 lb (4.5 kg).

Whatever method of traction is used, the head of the bed is placed on blocks for purposes of countertraction.

Casualties with fractures of the cervical spine are evacuated with skeletal traction in situ, the neck being immobilized by small, firm pillows on either side. The use of traction is not a contra-indication to regular turning of the patient in transit.

In order to reduce spinal cord oedema and to improve spinal cord function, the patient should be given dexamethasone 4 mg six hourly, either intramuscularly or intravenously.

Prevention of pressure sores

These tend to develop rapidly in anaesthetic and paralysed parts, for example, over the sacrum, the great trochanters, the head of each fibula, on the heels or, when the legs are tied together or in close contact with one another, over the internal malleoli. These sores always become infected and may produce a fatal septicaemia. To prevent sores it is necessary to avoid undue or prolonged pressure on any part of the insensitive skin. Clearly, therefore, it is of the utmost importance to ensure that the paraplegic patient is turned regularly, at least every two hours. This rule should apply, not only in hospital, but particularly when the patient is being evacuated. Such patients should be prominently and clearly labelled in block capitals, 'UNABLE TO MOVE. PLEASE ALTER POSITION TWO-HOURLY DURING TRANSIT'. Special care should be taken during transportation to avoid creases in bed linen and hard objects causing pressure necrosis on anaesthetic skin. The skin should be washed twice daily with soap and water and care should always be taken, after washing, to dry the parts thoroughly. If the skin is soft it may be rubbed regularly with alcohol. Special care should be taken to avoid wetting of the skin with urine. It is important to protect the head of each fibula from pressure against the edge of the stretcher during transport, thereby preventing palsy of the lateral popliteal nerve, the onset of which in incomplete lesions of the spinal cord and cauda equina may ruin the chances of a good functional recovery of the legs. A pad and bandage may be placed with advantage over the head of each fibula.

Care of the bladder

All complete and most incomplete injuries of the spinal cord or cauda equina cause paralysis of the bladder and retention of urine. In these cases infection of the bladder which spreads to the kidneys is the commonest cause of death. The management of the paralysed bladder due to injury of the spinal cord demands rigorous care from the time of injury, in order to prevent infection and to ensure good bladder function in the future. The paralysed bladder should not be allowed to over-distend. At the onset of paraplegia the bladder does not require emptying as routine until it fills;

this can usually be determined by palpation. It should then be emptied by means of intermittent catheterization under a strictly aseptic technique and using a small size soft catheter. This can be done twice daily in the early stages until some form of continuous drainage can be instituted in a neurosurgical unit. There, or if the military position prohibits evacuation, at the advanced surgical centre, continuous bladder drainage should be instituted using an indwelling Foley catheter size 16–18. As an alternative, a length of 2 mm diameter polythene tubing previously blunted at the end by flaming and suitably sterilized, may be introduced under aseptic technique through the urethra so that a sufficient length lies curled up inside the bladder to retain itself. Where the forward situation precludes catheterization under proper conditions, the distended bladder may be relieved by suprapubic aspiration with a long needle and a syringe. This may be repeated once, but not oftener owing to the risk of extravasation of urine. During a long evacuation, a Foley catheter draining into a bottle and left undisturbed, is the safest method of bladder drainage, provided the patient's high fluid intake is maintained. Suprapubic cystostomy should be avoided.

Catheters and the bladder should be washed out daily with a bland antiseptic solution to prevent infection and encrustation. With an indwelling catheter particular care should be taken to avoid traction or kinking of the urethra. This is liable to occur during turning of nursing treatment with a drag on the catheter or penis, and may occasionally lead to pressure necrosis and urethral fistula. A penile dressing consisting of gauze dipped in flavine or suitable antiseptic should also be applied to the tip of the penis and the catheter exit point.

Prevention of Urinary Infection

A high fluid intake must be maintained and about six pints (3.5 litres) per day should be given. In order to prevent and treat infections of the urinary tract sulphonamides may be given with alkalies, but these should be alternated with acidifying agents such as mandelamine to reduce phosphatic deposits. Antibiotics should not be used routinely for urinary infection but should be reserved for established infection in which the organism and its sensitivity are known.

Care of the bowel

The bowel is at first atonic. In the first few days after injury it may not require special attention but on arrival at base the rectum should be emptied. Hard faeces may cause considerable discomfort, and enemata may have to be supplemented by digital removal of accumulated faeces. Later on, retraining of the bowel is important so that the patient can be mobilized in comfort and can be done with the help of drugs such as Dorbanex, Dulcolax and a regular bran supplement in the diet.

Physiotherapy

All joints of the extremities should be gently put through a whole range of movements twice daily. Flexion deformities of the knees, clawing of the toes and plantar fixation at the ankle joints must be anticipated and should be prevented by suitable treatment. From the outset the patient should be encouraged to use fully those muscles which escaped paralysis. On their strength and development his future rehabilitation depends.

Nutrition

A profound anaemia and plasma deficiency may develop quite rapidly in paraplegic patients and particularly where there is sepsis. The diet should be rich in protein and vitamins. A blood transfusion is often the best way of counteracting anaemia in these patients and quickly improving their general well being. Iron may also be prescribed but its constipating effect should be borne in mind.

CHAPTER 18

Injuries of the peripheral nerves

Introduction

In high velocity missile injuries affecting limbs, peripheral nerves may be injured alone or more commonly there may be an associated vascular injury or long bone fracture. In such a complicated wound, where bone, vessels and nerves are involved, the nerve injury is the last in sequence of repair. It should only be carried out when the joints and soft tissue are in the best condition for surgery.

When an axon is divided, whether motor or sensory, the part distal to the cut is physically separated from its nucleus and dies. No matter how immediate the suture of the nerve, death of the axon cannot be avoided. The object of nerve suture must be to oppose the axons of the proximal face of the cut nerve to the tunnels or tubes of the Schwann cells in the distal face. Perfect recovery of axonal function can only occur if this is done.

Initial wound toilet and management

When a missile wound reaches the FST surgeon it is explored and a wound excision is carried out removing all dead and devitalized tissue and foreign material. There may be evidence of nerve injury and the two ends of the divided nerve may be clearly visible in the wound, with a gap between the two ends. No prolonged search should be carried out to find the proximal or distal stumps of the divided nerve. Even if the two divided ends of the nerve are in reasonable apposition, a primary nerve suture is not justified at this stage, since large neuromata are a complication of high velocity missile injuries involving peripheral nerves.

A detailed account is recorded on the F Med 26 as to whether the peripheral nerve is totally or partially divided. If the division is complete, the location of the nerve ends should be clearly noted, with a measurement of the gap between the nerve ends.

After wound excision, nerve tissue is preferably covered with muscle or fat so that when gauze is laid over the wound, viable nerve tissue will not be injured when drying out. Elevation of the affected limb is essential to lessen oedema, and immobilization in a padded plaster is the recommended way of splinting a limb.

Protection from further injury to anaesthetic skin is essential, ie in median nerve injury, cigarette smokers should be warned about burns to the fingers.

Splinting for evacuation

Splinting to afford relaxation of affected muscles, and padding to avoid pressure necrosis of the insensitive skin are necessary for transportation in peripheral nerve injuries. The padding must be smooth and there must be frequent changes in the position of the pressure bearing areas.

The hand is put in the position of function. A cock-up splint is applied for radial nerve injuries with wrist drop. Splints should not extend beyond the distal palmar crease and the thumb must be prevented from falling into the palm for if it stays in this position too long, the power of abduction will be lost. From the beginning active and passive movements of the joints should be carried out to prevent stiffness and maintain mobility.

In sciatic nerve injuries, a padded posterior plaster splint is applied with the foot at 90° in the neutral position, ie neither inverted nor everted.

Delayed primary suture

Repair of a divided nerve is not carried out at this stage for various reasons including the following:

a There is always a risk of sepsis in missile wounds.

b The microscopic extent of the damage to a nerve is more than is macroscopically apparent.

c Elaborate dissection to mobilize a nerve for suture without tension is harmful.

d The nerve sheath is friable and becomes less friable later.

e The scar involving all injured tissue will be continuous so that the line of nerve suture would be liable to be dragged on.

The aim at this stage is to obtain uncomplicated healing of the wound with a minimum of scarring.

Complications

The object of treatment before and after definitive nerve suture is carried out, is to maintain nutrition and mobility in the joints in the paralysed muscles. The two chief causes of stiffness are oedema and muscle shortening. The best way of controlling oedema is to elevate the limb, and muscle shortening should be prevented by suitable splinting. Fixed deformity is caused by the pull of the non-paralysed opponents of the paralysed muscle groups, the action of gravity, or the contraction of the scar.

Splints

Splints should be simple and easily reproducible. In radial nerve palsy a cock-up splint is advisable. In an ulnar nerve lesion, small improvised finger splints of metal should prevent clawing of the fingers, ie hyper-extension of the metacarpo-phalangeal joints of the little and ring fingers. For median nerve paralysis, a piece of adhesive to hold the thumb in opposition for part of the day and night is all that is required. In sciatic nerve injury with a foot drop the foot should be held at right angles to prevent contracture and a right angle splint applied when the patient is in bed.

Joint movements

Whether the paralysis is widespread or not, every joint should be put through the fullest possible movement several times a day, actively or passively. If pain is present, analgesic drugs may be required for these movements to be carried out. The patient himself must be instructed how to help himself, take an interest in his condition, and in finger and hand injuries to keep the joints mobile passively if active movements are not possible. Once any stiffness has developed, it may take months for intensive physical treatment to correct this.

Definitive surgical treatment

The importance of adequate preliminary investigation must be emphasised. The findings at the initial examination, ie wound excision, are most important, in particular whether the nerve is completely divided or not. If the nerve was divided, how big was the defect? With a partial division of the peripheral nerve, EMG studies will indicate the extent of the denervation and clinical examination using Tinel's sign will indicate axonal regeneration.

If a high velocity missile has passed in the vicinity of a peripheral nerve causing paralysis and the anatomical state of the nerve is unknown, there is much to be said for early exploration of the nerve. It is a necessary step in the diagnosis and the higher in the limb the lesion is, the earlier should be the exploration.

Arguments in favour of a secondary nerve suture are valid. The skin, joints and soft tissues should be in the best condition for surgery. The extent of the damage to a nerve can accurately be assessed. The nerve sheath is sufficiently thickened when a secondary suture is carried out to make handling and suture technically easier for the surgeon. There is strong evidence that the earlier the suture of the divided nerve is carried out, the better are the chances of recovery, and the best time for repair is in the third week provided there is no sepsis. Should a repair be carried out after six months results are progressively worse.

The technique of suturing individual nerves is different at different sites and is usually concerned in gaining sufficient length to suture the nerve without tension. In an ulnar nerve lesion anterior transposition at the elbow may be carried out to lessen the tension on the nerve. If the length is gained by joint flexion, subsequent stretching must be done slowly enough to avoid disruption of the nerve or a late traction lesion. It is best to leave the joints flexed until the nerve suture is sound, and then stretch by serial plasters. An elbow flexed at right angles can take six weeks to extend sufficiently to discard the plaster. It is better to gain length in forearm nerves by elbow flexion than wrist flexion because finger function is inhibited by wrist flexion.

Extension mobilization is not justified as the blood supply to the nerve may be affected. Defects are bridged by cable grafting to avoid tension.

CHAPTER 19

Wounds of the chest

General considerations

Any combination of parietal and visceral injuries may occur. In crush or blast injuries, there may be extensive visceral damage without visible injury, but in most other cases there is a parietal wound. All chest wounds, except those which are obviously superficial, should be regarded as potentially serious however small the wound and however good the patient's condition at the first examination. Cardiopulmonary functional disturbances may take several hours to develop. The following are the most important results of injury: haemothorax, pneumothorax, tension pneumothorax, open pneumothorax, stove-in-chest, bronchial obstruction, cardiac tamponade. The nature of these is primarily mechanical and they are often easily recognized and remedied.

Haemothorax

After a chest wound, blood may accumulate in the pleural space from both the lung and the chest wall. Bleeding usually occurs slowly and ceases spontaneously. The volume of the haemothorax is further increased by effusion from the pleura so that the haemothorax, although it has the appearance of pure blood, may have a low haemoglobin content. The clinical signs are those of a pleural effusion combined with those of loss of blood. The position of the mediastinum, ascertained by palpation of the trachea and the apical impulse of the heart, is an important indication of the size of the haemothorax. Displacement of the apex beat to the left is easier to appreciate than displacement to the right.

A haemothorax large enough to cause mediastinal displacement and dyspnoea at the first examination is infrequent, and indicates bleeding from a large pulmonary or systemic vessel. The bulk of a haemothorax usually remains liquid, but a variable degree of clotting occurs. Fibrin is deposited on the pleural surface and, if the haemothorax persists, may become organized, loculated and prevent re-expansion of the lung.

Pneumothorax

Some air escapes into the pleural space from most wounds of the lung. The diminution in volume of the lung and in the vital capacity is proportional to the size of the pneumothorax. A small pneumothorax is usually absorbed over a few days and alone has little importance. A pneumothorax of significant size can usually be diagnosed by hyper-resonance and reduced breath sounds on the affected side.

Tension pneumothorax

In some cases, the pulmonary wound from which air escapes is valvular, so that the pneumothorax compresses the wounded lung and, by displacing the mediastinum to the opposite side, also the sound lung. It can be recognized by the signs of pneumothorax with displacement of the trachea and apex beat to the opposite side and by the accompanying dyspnoea, pallor and cyanosis.

Surgical emphysema

Air may escape from a pneumothorax into the soft tissues about the parietal wound, where crepitus can be readily palpated. When the pneumothorax is of the tension variety, much air may be forced into the parietal tissues. The appearance which follows, inflation of the face, neck, trunk and, to a lesser extent, the limbs, is impressive, but surgical emphysema is not of itself dangerous, and does not require treatment. The air is rapidly absorbed when leakage from the lung stops or is treated.

When surgical emphysema begins at the suprasternal notch or is largely confined to the neck, it suggests a wound of the trachea, a major bronchus or the oesophagus, the air passing up the mediastinum to the neck.

Open pneumothorax

A wound of the chest wall which permits air to enter and leave the pleural space during respiration causes a sucking sound. The lung on the affected side falls away from the chest wall and its function is grossly disturbed. As dyspnoea increases, mediastinal movement becomes more violent and impedes the venous return to the heart, so that the cardiac output is diminished. The mechanical disturbance can be abolished by closure of the parietal wound.

Stove-in-chest

Similar effects to those of open pneumothorax are produced when an area of the chest wall loses its rigidity as a consequence of multiple fractures of the ribs, particularly double fractures of one or more ribs. The mobilized part of the chest wall moves paradoxically, being drawn inwards during inspiration and outwards during expiration. Paradoxical movement and its consequence can be reduced by a firm dressing.

Bronchial obstruction

Haemoptysis is frequent with wounds of the lung. It is rarely profuse. Suppression of cough because of a painful wound of the chest wall, or ineffective cough related to severe disturbances of respiration, may result in retention of bronchial secretions. Bronchial obstruction causing pulmonary collapse is therefore likely to occur.

Cardiac tamponade

A wound of the heart, if the pericardium remains intact, may be followed by bleeding which fills and distends the pericardium. This obstructs the venous return to the heart and prevents normal atrial filling. Cardiac tamponade can usually be recognized by tachycardia, the small pulse and pulse pressure and distension of the neck veins. If it is allowed to persist, death from circulatory failure may follow, but it can be relieved by the release of blood from the pericardium.

Blast injuries

Death may be instantaneous, but many less severe cases survive. The ribs are often not fractured and there may be no chest bruising. Shock, restlessness, severe dyspnoea and chest pain are accompanied by cyanosis and tachycardia. The clinical picture may lead to a faulty diagnosis of 'acute battle neurosis' since the patients are extremely apprehensive and tremulous. Injury to intercostal nerves may cause abdominal rigidity leading to a suspicion of intraperitoneal injury. Haematomata of the lungs along the lines of the ribs are present and this causes slight haemoptysis but more strikingly, the ineffective expectoration of frothy mucus. The X-ray appearance of lung mottling occurs early.

Thoraco-abdominal wounds

Both cavities may be damaged by a missile entering from the abdomen or from the thorax. Thoraco-abdominal wounds are more frequent than abdomino-thoracic ones and have a better prognosis, as have wounds on the right side than those of the left. A through and through wound on the right may traverse the pleura, diaphragm and liver and yet cause surprisingly little upset; on the left side the hazards of such wounds include rupture of the spleen and perforation of the colon, small intestine and stomach. A large tangential wound of the diaphragm may cause a severe hernia later.

Diagnosis

Abdomen This may be difficult because missile wounds of the lower thorax without peritoneal damage may cause abdominal pain and rigidity and can lead to unnecessary laparotomy. It is essential in all cases to consider carefully the probable course of the missile since this may indicate with certainty that the abdomen has been penetrated. X-ray studies are of great value. Persisting abdominal rigidity, adsence of peristaltic sounds and rising pulse rate indicate peritoneal involvement. Shoulder tip pain may indicate irritation of the under surface of the diaphragm (phrenic referred pain).

The chest When radiological facilities are not available, the diagnosis must be made on clinical examination. Damage to the chest wall is for the most part readily recognized.

A missile may enter the chest after passing through the arm, neck, abdomen or spine. The presence of, say, a compound fracture of the upper end of the humerus when there is no visible wound of the chest wall may distract attention from pulmonary damage. A sucking wound round the scapula may allow the passage of air only intermittently according to the position of the scapula. In the assessment of respiratory dysfunction, it is of particular importance to detect deviation of the trachea and displacement of the apex beat.

It may not be possible to differentiate a pneumothorax from prolapse of the bowel through a diaphragmatic wound, but the possibility of this occurrence must be kept in mind and calculated from the position and type of the injury. Similarly, prolapse of the liver on the right side may stimulate a haemothorax. The anatomical features of a wound, unlike its physiological consequences, cannot usually be exactly appreciated without radiological help or direct inspection at thoracotomy.

The **treatment of chest wounds** follows the principles of wounds in general and **four special principles** derived from knowledge of the respiratory and circulatory disorders:

a *Normal Intra-thoracic Pressures*   Normal pleural and pericardial pressures must be maintained. The pleural space should be kept empty. This entails stabilization of a stove-in-chest, closure of an open pneumothorax, aspiration of a large pneumothorax and aspiration of the pericardium for cardiac tamponade.

b *Clearance of bronchi*   The bronchial tree must be kept clear from obstruction. Clearance of the bronchi can be aided in a number of ways of which the adjustment of the pleural pressure, as described above by making coughing more effective, is the first and most important. The relief of pain of a parietal wound may allow deliberate coughing, on instruction. A productive cough is very effective in clearing the bronchi. When haemoptysis contributes to obstruction, the posture of the patient, lying on the wounded side with the head slightly lowered, favours clearance of the bronchi, at least of the undamaged lung. Blind tracheal aspiration and bronchoscopic aspiration are most valuable when they are available. Tracheostomy may be necessary to facilitate frequent aspiration of secretions or to improve ventilation by reducing ventilatory dead space and resistance. Finally, standard physiotherapeutic methods may be used.

c The *arrest of haemorrhage and replacement of blood*   Bleeding from a large vessel in the chest is likely to cause death before medical aid is available. Bleeding in a patient who has reached the regimental aid post may be from intercostal, internal mammary, or pulmonary vessels and in most cases does not require immediate operation for its control. It should be appreciated, however, that several pints of blood may be gradually lost into the pleural space and it should be replaced as for any other wound. Facilities for continuous measurement of central venous pressure are of great value.

d *Wound toilet*   Excision or debridement of a penetrating wound of the chest wall is liable to result in an open pneumothorax; therefore if excision is judged necessary precautions for dealing with an open pneumothorax must be taken. The patient should be under general anaesthesia with controlled ventilation. Similarly, if laparotomy is performed in a patient who has a wound traversing the diaphragm, an open pneumothorax may be produced and cause serious difficulty unless the same facilities are available.

Treatment applicable at various stages of evacuation will be considered in the light of these principles.

Management at the RAP and Dressing Station

a An *open sucking wound* is closed immediately. This is best done by covering with a shell dressing, preferably slightly moist. The dressing must be secure. It may be satisfactorily kept in position with strapping, but, especially where it tends to be dislodged by movement of the scapula, skin sutures may be necessary.

b *Stove-in-chest* A dressing firmly strapped over the mobile segment of the chest wall will usually relieve the respiratory embarrassment of a stove-in-chest. The strapping must be adjusted by trial so that the best extent and tightness are used and the function of the normal side is not limited.

c *Resuscitation* If there has been severe bleeding, including intrapleural bleeding, the patient should be evacuated without loss of time and with an intravenous drip using plasma or plasma expander if blood is not available. If there is haemoptysis, the patient should lie on the wounded side with the head lowered. Oxygen should be given if there is cyanosis.

d *Sedation* The control of pain in thoracic injuries is of importance and morphine is contraindicated whenever respiratory embarrassment is present. Narcotics which do not depress the repiratory system are preferred. Any narcotic should be used sparingly.

e *Antibiotics* Antibiotics should be started early.

f *Priority of treatment* Closure of an open pneumothorax, stabilization of stove-in-chest and relief of tension pneumothorax take precedence over the replacement of blood.

g *Evacuation* After first aid treatment, all thoracic casualties are evacuated down the line. Maximum priority is given to cases of continued intrapleural bleeding, cardiac tamponade, tension pneumothorax and thoraco-abdominal injury.

Management at forward surgical centre

If need be, the bronchi are cleared and the pleural pressures are adjusted anew.

a *Large haemothorax or pneumothorax* If there is clinical evidence of a considerable pleural collection of blood or air and especially if this is associated with mediastinal shift to the opposite side, the pleural space is emptied by aspirations as completely as possible, care being taken to avoid the entry of air.

Method of aspiration   The patient is propped up comfortably so that the axillary and posterior areas of the chest are clearly exposed: the site of the area to be punctured is best estimated by studying the PA and lateral chest films. The commonest error is to aspirate too low, for the diaphragm has often risen in these patients. After the skin and intercostal plane have been anaesthetized by local anaesthetic injection, a really large bore needle attached to a two-way syringe is introduced. Too fine a needle is readily blocked. The aspiration should be thorough.

If air escapes through the needle under pressure it signifies the presence of a tension pneumothorax. A large calibre needle should be introduced into the pleural space through the second interspace anteriorly and left there. A rubber finger cot with a small slit in its end is tied over the needle to act as an escape valve. An intercostal tube drain with a water seal is more efficient for this purpose in suitable circumstances, but should be used only in hospitals because the tube without attention is likely to become blocked and is easily contaminated. During evacuation the water seal is apt to be raised too high, allowing the liquid it contains to enter the chest. The *Heimlich flutter valve* should be used for choice.

The possible development of tension pneumothorax after a sucking wound has been packed is to be kept in mind.

b *Cardiac tamponade*   If there is evidence of cardiac tamponade, the pericardium is aspirated. The needle is inserted in the angle between the xyphisternum and the costal margin and passed upwards and backwards at an angle of 45°, to enter the pericardium. It is unnecessary to empty the pericardium completely. Repeated aspiration may be required but if unsuccessful thoracotomy may be necessary. Evacuation to the nearest thoracic unit is arranged immediately.

c *Thoracotomy*   Thoracotomy may be required for the following conditions:

    (1)   Continued intrapleural bleeding or escape of air.
    (2)   Thoraco-abdominal injury with suspected intraperitoneal damage.
    (3)   Wounds of the trachea, major bronchus or oesophagus.
    (4)   Cardiac tamponade.
    (5)   Sucking wounds.

If possible, a pre-operative radiograph of the chest is taken. This will increase the accuracy of diagnosis and help in planning the exact operative procedure required. It will also show the position of metallic foreign bodies.

General anaesthesia with controlled respiration by endotracheal intubation is required for all cases.

A standard lateral thoracotomy through the sixth interspace or the bed of the sixth rib gives good access to all the intrathoracic organs on the same side.

Pleural foreign bodies and foreign bodies which are readily accessible are removed. Search for others which have been shown radiologically is to be avoided.

At the end of the operation and, if the patient can be retained, intercostal drainage with a water seal is used for 24 – 72 hours. The drain is removed before further evacuation. Oxygen is given by face mask during the 24 hours after operation.

If there is a large defect in the chest wall, making the usual closure of all layers difficult or impossible, sliding grafts of skin and muscle may be made to close the defect. Some stability must be given to soft tissues covering a large defect and this may be done by applying a dressing as for stove-in-chest.

In cases of continued intrapleural bleeding, all blood and clot, of which there may be a large amount, is first removed from the pleural space and the bleeding vessel, usually an intercostal or internal mammary artery, is secured. Pulmonary resection is rarely necessary. A severely contused lung may recover remarkably. Any one great vessel of the pulmonary hilum may be ligated without causing necrosis of the lung. Bronchial leaks are closed by ligation unless the bronchus is a main one, when repair of the defect by suture may be possible. A leak from a segmental or lobar bronchus may require resection of the lung supplied by the bronchus.

If cardiac tamponade recurs soon after aspiration, a thoracotomy should be performed. The pericardium is opened from apex to base. The wound in the heart is necessarily a small one but on release of pericardial pressure may allow the escape of a forceful stream of blood. This is controlled by digital pressure and sutures are passed across the wound while the finger is in position and tied as the finger is withdrawn. The pericardium is only loosely closed so that pericardial effusion may escape freely into the pleural space, whence it can be aspirated. An oesophageal perforation can be closed by suture. Liquid feeding may be given 24 hours later.

d *Thoraco-abdominal wounds*   If there is a sucking chest wound this must be dealt with as described above. The difficulty here may be greatest with the clean through and through wound. If this is on the right side, and the only organ apparently wounded is the liver a conservative approach may be the correct one. A careful watch must be kept on the abdomen and chest.

Frequently these cases have a haemothorax which will require aspiration. Occasionally the aspirating needle will remove bile from the thorax. These cases notoriously go on to empyema formation. Large shell fragments seen on the radiographs in right-sided wounds should be removed, preferably through the thorax, for they often cause subphrenic abscess.

If the wound is a left thoraco-abdominal one with a track involving the dangerous left subphrenic area of the abdomen or if radiographs demonstrate a fragment of metal retained in this region, the thorax should be dealt with first and access to the upper abdomen obtained through the diaphragm.

If the chest injury is thought to be insignificant but there are signs of serious intraperitoneal damage a full laparotomy should be performed and the lesions dealt with appropriately. If, after the abdominal lesions have been dealt with, a small opening is seen easily accessible in the diaphragm it should be closed by suture; but no time should be wasted if the approach to this indicates a difficult operation.

e *The Thoraco-abdominal approach*   This is easily performed by those with some experience of thoracic surgery; the commonest error is to attempt to deal with serious lesions through a quite inadequate length of incision. Under general endotracheal anaesthesia the chest wound is excised; if this wound lies over the 7th, 8th, 9th or 10th rib the incision is enlarged from just in front of the transverse process to the costal cartilage, and the appropriate rib is excised subperiosteally.

If the original wound does not permit an adequate thoracotomy the chest is opened along the line of the excised 8th rib; the chest is held widely open by the use of a rib-spreader.

The haemothorax is sucked out and any bleeding from the lung is checked; the lung is then covered with a moist saline pad. The diaphragm is inspected and the hole is enlarged. This enlargement must be free and adequate and later can be sutured with ease; the abdomen is explored through this opening; splenectomy and suture of gastric or small intestinal wounds can be readily performed through the incision. If the colon is damaged, in most instances it is wise to exteriorize it through a stab incision in the abdominal wall.

After the abdominal portion of the operation has been completed the diaphragm is repaired. The chest is then closed in layers, the skin being left open for later delayed primary suture.

f *Blast injury.* Treatment is by oxygen, warmth, control of shock and maintenance of a clear airway. Absolute rest is mandatory. These patients stand general anaesthesia badly. If at the close of operation the chest is 'bubbly' the retained secretions should be aspirated by a trans-nasal catheter or through the bronchoscope. Great care in transfusion is indicated since oedema may be precipited. Tracheostomy is extremely valuable in these injuries.

Post-operative care and evacuation

In the post-operative treatment the rules that govern the care of the abdominal wound and the management of the haemothorax must be followed meticulously.

In the early post-operative period bronchoscopic aspiration may be necessary for the relief of bronchial obstruction. Within three or four days of thoracotomy most of these casualties are fit for transfer to rear hospitals. Others not requiring surgery are evacuated as soon as possible.

CHAPTER 20

Wounds of the abdomen

Introduction

Abdominal wounds require urgent treatment as the patient who has been wounded in the abdomen is almost certain to die unless he is treated by operation. The time factor is of cardinal importance for the outlook is grave unless he is operated on early and mortality increases with increasing time from injury to operation. He requires not only expert surgery but also skilled resuscitation and nursing. All operative and pre-operative attention may be wasted unless he is retained after operation in the same unit until fully fit to travel further. Ideally, bowel function should be re-established and naso-gastric suction no longer required before evacuation.

Sorting officers must be alert to discover intra-abdominal injuries especially as the entry wound may be remote from the abdomen. Men wounded in the chest, trunk, thighs or buttocks should be questioned for any abdominal symptoms. Patients whose condition is worse than their wounds seem to warrant or who are vomiting and have a rising pulse rate, or those who fail to respond to resuscitation should be closely and repeatedly examined for signs of abdominal injury.

Wounding agents

The severity and the prognosis of abdominal wounds varies with the causal agents.

a *Bullets from hand guns* in general are of low velocity These have a tendency to cause small entrance wounds and to be retained in the body. They usually cause simple damage to viscera without extensive disruption.

b *Rifle and machine gun bullets* have a high velocity and may pass right through the body, causing a perforating wound. If the rifle bullet is unstable or fragments readily, it tends to be retained in the tissues and will therefore give up more of its energy than the stable bullet. Thus very severe disruptive wounds can occur with widespead damage at a distance from the missile track.

c *Bomb, mortar, mine, shell and rocket fragments* may be large or small. They have a high initial velocity which rapidly falls off due to the irregular unstreamlined shapes. The entry wounds are usually ragged and the damage to the tissues depends on their velocity. High velocity fragments cause damage similar to high velocity bullets. Low velocity fragments may cause damage similar to low velocity bullets, but the effect may be more serious because of unstable ragged fragments. Very small fragments from explosive devices travelling at high velocity may produce minute superficial wounds which may be associated with surprisingly severe internal damage. An intra-abdominal catastrophe can easily be overlooked unless examination is most careful and observation maintained in all suspected cases.

d *Blast* may damage viscera by direct or indirect trauma. Underwater explosions likewise cause severe damage at considerably greater distances. In addition to petechial haemorrhages throughout the tissues, there are often multiple ruptures of hollow viscera. The caecum, large intestine, small intestine, bladder and stomach may be injured in that order of frequency.

e *Crush injuries* and falls from a height may also cause intra-abdominal injury, especially to the fixed organs such as liver, spleen, pancreas and the bowel at its points of fixation.

Management at the RAP and dressing station

The treatment of penetrating abdominal injuries is surgical and, there-fore, the main concern of all who handle these casualties in the forward areas must be to get the patients to a surgical centre without delay. Shock in these patients is compounded of many elements, the most serious of which are:

a bleeding from mesenteric vessels and solid organs and
b leakage from torn viscera into the peritonal cavity.

These cannot be combated by ordinary measures of resuscitation and early operation is required.

Initial action in advance of the surgical centre follows the normal rules of skilled first aid, dressing of wounds, intravenous fluid, antibiotic therapy and rapid evacuation. Once the need for operation has been determined, morphine may be given if the pain is severe, for it may render an ambulance journey over rough country tolerable, and lessens fear and excitement. It must be recorded clearly on the F Med 26 and marked on the patient's forehead with indelible marking ink. (If a morphine syrette has been used the empty syrette should be attached to the patient's collar.)

On reaching the dressing station, the patient is assessed according to the urgency with which he requires resuscitation and surgery and is allotted a priority. If possible, he is sent at once to the surgical centre. Three questions may arise at this stage:

a Should the patient be tranfused before he reaches the surgical centre? In abdominal wounds the commonest cause of death is from haemorrhage. Shocked abdominal patients resuscitated by electrolyte solutions, plasma or blood tend to relapse within three to four hours. That is just at the time when operation may be contemplated. A second transfusion does not resuscitate them as well as the first, and indeed may fail to render them fit for anything but a hurried operation. If evacuation from the dressing station to the surgical centre is not long – say, less than two hours – it is better as a rule to refrain from transfusion until reaching the centre. If, on the other hand, it is felt that the patient will collapse en route it is justifiable to start an infusion of Ringer lactate (Hartmann's) solution and to continue it during the ambulance journey. Blood should be taken beforehand for grouping and later cross-matching. Time must not be wasted.

b Should the patient be sent to the nearest FST in a field hospital or to another surgical centre further down the line in a general hospital? Major haemorrhage demands treatment at the earliest possible moment; the closure of intestinal leaks is a less urgent matter and survival in most cases where infection is the chief problem depends more on the care and thoroughness with which the operation is done and the continuity of the after treatment, than on early surgery. A patient who is badly shocked two hours after being wounded in the abdomen and whose shock is increasing, is suffering above all from loss of blood and should be dealt with by the nearest available operating unit.

c Should the patient be sent by air? Here, there are two considerations. On the one hand, abdominal casualties travel badly by air, on the other hand they stand the rough journey by road badly and tend to deteriorate rapidly if it takes much longer than two hours. Where the choice is between half an hour in a plane and a longer journey over unmade tracks then the first would be preferred.

Management at the surgical centre

a *Diagnosis* When the patient marked as a case of suspect abdominal injury has reached a surgical centre the surgeon must decide:

(1) Does the injury actually involve the peritoneal cavity?

(2) If so, what structures may be injured?

If operation is necessary, should it be done immediately? Very often this question involves deciding the priority between several patients awaiting operation. A study of the history of the case and an examination of the wounds and abdomen will nearly always answer the first question. Apart from evidence of visceral damage, the welling up of blood, intestinal contents or urine, or protrusion of omentum from a wound is sufficient proof that the peritonal cavity has been penetrated. The need to remember the latent case and to question every patient who looks unaccountably ill cannot be over-emphasized. In the heat of battle a man may not realise the severity of his wound but, usually, when a hollow viscus has been injured, there is pain similar to that of a perforated duodenal ulcer. Vomiting is common.

b *Differential diagnosis* is difficult in the following types of wound:

(1) *Chest wounds* The rigidity present in some thoracic wounds can usually be differentiated by the fact that it is variable, and relaxes somewhat when respiratory movement changes from expiration to inspiration.

(2) *Superficial wounds* Tangential wounds and lacerations or contusion of the abdominal wall cause shock, localized tenderness and guarding. If there is no intra-abdominal injury the shock tends to diminish and the tenderness and the guarding to subside, or at most remain stationary. Bowel sounds are usually present and the abdomen does not become distended.

(3) *Intra-abdominal wounds* Increasing shock, a rising pulse, tenderness at some fresh site such as the rectovesical pouch, and guarding that has spread to a fresh and uninjured area of the abdominal wall, are signs of intra-abdominal damage. Auscultation should always be practised. Peristaltic sounds are occasionally heard even when the intestine has been perforated, but silence is virtually always an indication for laparotomy.

A plain radiograph, if available, may show free gas under the diaphragm.

(4) *Perforating wounds* In through and through wounds the direction of the track will give an indication of viscera likely to have been injured, but too much importance must not be attached to purely anatomical deduction. The relation of the abdominal parieties to the underlying

viscera at the time of wounding was probably very different from that with the man lying on a stretcher.

(5) *Penetrating wounds*   In single penetrating wounds an estimate of the direction of the track is difficult without knowledge of the location of the foreign body. Radiographic screening or antero-posterior and lateral films may give the needed information to determine the track of the missile but is rarely advisable if only because it delays operation.

(6) *Buttock wounds*   The importance of wounds in the buttocks cannot be overstressed, for they are often accompanied by injury to the rectum, bladder or pelvic vessels. They are therefore dangerous and carry a high mortality.

General management

When penetration of the abdominal cavity is proved or inferred, operation is imperative and should be done as soon as possible. The best time for operation on an abdominal injury is the earliest at which the patient can stand it. Very often the decision to be made is not so much the best time for any particular patient, but the priority in which a number of wounded patients shall be operated on. Cases where haemorrhage is the chief problem should take precedence over those in which intestinal perforations dominate the clinical picture. A badly shocked man should be resuscitated while a less shocked one goes to the theatre. The operating list should be considered as a whole, and if the unit is over-burdened, or if the number of patients with abdominal injuries is greater than can be dealt with within a reasonable time and additional surgical aid is not available it may well be correct to send on those who are in the best state to stand the journey to another unit further down the line of evacuation. Patients with traumatic perforations of the small, or even the large bowel, have recovered spontaneously on supportive treatment. Such cases are rare, but the knowledge that recovery is possible without surgery offers hope under conditions where active surgery is impossible. The principles of treatment are rest, morphine, intravenous transfusion, nothing by mouth, naso-gastric suction and antibiotics.

Men with abdominal injuries are sometimes brought in several days after wounding, having laid out on the field or having been cut off in some raid. Those who have survived so long without medical aid have usually succeeded in localizing their injuries, and should be treated expectantly, surgery being reserved for some definite indication such as the draining of an abscess or the closure of a fistula.

Pre-operative care

a *Classification of casualties for operation*   The cases of abdominal injury in the pre-operative ward of a Surgical Centre fall into four groups:
(1)   Those in whom there is no evidence of visceral damage. These are kept under careful and continuous observation.
(2)   Cases with evidence of intra-abdominal injury who are fit for immediate operation.
(3)   Cases with evidence of intra-abdominal injury, but not yet fit for operation because of shock.
(4)   Moribund cases: included in this group may be some of those with multiple injuries (eg head, abdomen, femur), and those who have arrived late with advanced peritonitis and a failing peripheral circulation. They may be mentally alert but restless and often in pain. They should be made comfortable and screened off from other patients.

b *Aetiological factors in shock*   Shocked patients must be resuscitated but the period of resuscitation must be actively supervised. The shock of an abdominal casualty is due to a number of factors – loss of blood, exhaustion, dehydration from sweating and shortage of water during the fighting, loss of plasma from wounds and into the peritoneum and toxaemia from early infection. Some of these can be overcome, but others, particularly the bleeding from mesenteric vessels and leakage from torn viscera, will continue while shock is being treated. Experience has shown that an absolute limit of two hours must be set upon resuscitation.

c *General management*   After wounds have been examined, the probable nature of the injury determined, and the scope and risk of the operation assessed, the patient should be made as comfortable as possible. He should be given morphine if in pain, preferably intravenously in small quantities in order to obtain rapid relief and keep accurate control. Fluids by mouth or by the rectum must be avoided, even if perforation of the alimentary tract can be excluded, but intravenous fluids should be given to every serious case, and the drip should be kept running when the patient is taken to the theatre.

d *Transfusion*   A severely shocked patient with an abdominal wound is nearly always suffering from loss of blood that cannot be controlled until the abdomen is opened, and he must be given fluid and blood as quickly as possible. More than one intravenous drip may have to be set up. Ringer lactate (Hartmann's) solution should be administered at a rapid rate, followed by blood if available, and the aim should be to get the patient into the theatre in a condition that will allow the surgeon to find and control the bleeding.

After one litre of fluid has been given it is usually possible to decide whether the shock is being overcome, or whether the loss is being barely balanced by the inflow. In the first case the transfusion should be continued at a slightly reduced but still rapid rate till a systolic pressure of 100 mm or over has been reached, when the operation can be started. In the second case the patient, unless moribund, should be taken to the theatre with the drip running fast and, where possible, more blood should be kept in reserve. The surgeon must make a rapid attempt to find and deal with the source of the bleeding. Once this has been achieved then resuscitation may continue. The patient's condition will improve and the operation may then be completed. Estimation of blood loss in combat casualties is likely to be grossly inaccurate; therefore the amount and speed of the replacement fluid and blood should not be determined by estimated losses but by the response to fluid administration in terms of the clinical condition. This involves monitoring the systemic blood pressure, pulse, skin colouring and temperature and the urinary output.

Surgical procedures

a *Management of other wounds*   Multiple wounds are common in warfare where bombs, mortars, grenades, rockets and mines are the main weapons, and the treatment of wounds other than the main abdominal one calls for fine judgement. All wounds should be excised, but in the case of wounds of moderate severity this excision becomes of secondary importance to the treatment of the main abdominal wound. If the injured viscera are not repaired the patient will certainly die; if the wounds are not excised they will go septic, but with delayed surgery and antibiotics the sepsis may be brought under control.

When other wounds coexist with the abdominal one, for instance if there is a major fracture or penetration of a large joint, or if an amputation is necessary, a second surgeon should preferably operate simultaneously. When it is necessary to perform two operations, one on the front and one on the back, it is important to do the latter first, for experience has shown that turning a patient onto his face after a laparotomy may cause profound shock.

b *The incision*   The wounds in the abdominal wall, like all other wounds, should be excised but time must not be wasted on this step when the clinical picture suggests that major intra-abdominal bleeding has occurred. Such wound excision can be carried out on completion of the intra-peritoneal operation.

If the wound is unsuitable for enlargement, or if widespread intra-abdominal damage is suspected, a full laparotomy incision should be made. For severe injuries a generous full length mid line incision is best. The right or the left paramedian or rectus splitting incisions are all good. The oblique or transverse incisions in the lateral aspects of abdomen are acceptable but transverse incisions across the rectus muscle are bad in war wounds and are often followed by ventral herniae.

c *General plan of operation*

(1) First pass a catheter and note whether there is any blood in the urine.

(2) *Toilet of abdominal cavity* The abdominal cavity usually contains free fluid, blood or intestinal contents, which must be rapidly evacuated before the damage can be traced.

(3) *Haemorrhage* Haemorrhage is the chief cause of death and must be dealt with first. Peritonitis is a secondary and less urgent danger. When the abdomen is full of blood, the most likely sources of the bleeding are the mesentery of the small intestine, the liver, spleen, kidney and pancreas, and the large veins on the posterior abdominal wall. The bleeding points must be found and ligatured with fine thread, which is preferable to catgut, to avoid slipping of ligatures and spreading mesenteric haematomas.

Injuries of the large blood vessels are usually lethal. Severe bleeding from the liver can be controlled temporarily by compressing the hepatic artery and portal vein in the free edge of the lesser omentum, but haemorrhage from tears in the liver has as a rule ceased by the time the abdomen is opened or can be arrested temporarily by light packing.

This manoeuvre is shocking and expert anaesthesia is required for it does facilitate the control of bleeding and the exploration of the abdominal cavity.

(4) *Alimentary tract* When he has dealt with the haemorrhage the surgeon must find and repair all perforations in the alimentary tract. The perforations may be in unexpected places, very small, and when recent not recognizable by touch. All must be found as a successful operation will fail if one is missed. The structures in the line of the missile track should be examined first, but all the organs that may have been injured must be inspected. It is usually wise to postpone any repair until all the injuries have been discovered and assessed as a total, since resection may be more sensible than multiple individual repairs.

(5) *Small bowel* The small intestine is the part most frequently

injured and will usually be examined first and repaired before dealing with the colon. Loops many feet apart in continuity may lie adjacent in the abdomen, so that the whole length should be inspected methodically from caecum to duodeno-jejunal junction, each perforation or tear as it is encountered being repaired or held by an assistant with swab or forceps applied to its edges. When the mesentery has been torn from the bowel the length involved should be noted to consider later resection. Much time is saved if the bowel is handled only once.

(6) *Colon* After the small intestine, the stomach, colon and solid viscera should be examined in turn. A retro-peritoneal haemorrhage or emphysema in the region of the ascending or descending colon, or signs of the wound track being in their vicinity, should lead to a most careful search for any perforation of the bare areas. It may be necessary to mobilize the colon by incising the parietal peritoneum lateral to the ascending and descending colon and stripping it medially in order to expose the posterior surface.

(7) *Stomach* When examining the stomach the posterior wall must be exposed by opening the gastro-colic omentum. The duodenum will be inspected after the stomach, and this, like the colon, has a bare area that may have been injured. The duodenum must be mobilized by Kocher's manoeuvre and must be examined closely.

(8) *Rectum and bladder* Finally, the pelvis should be examined for injuries to the rectum or bladder, and where the lesion in the latter is large enough to admit the finger its cavity should be explored for any foreign body, since fragments and bullets have been discovered therein on a number of occasions. At the same time damage to the base of the bladder can be assessed and dealt with.

(9) *Wound closure* When all the lesions have been found and considered together, they must be repaired individually by methods that will be considered in greater detail in the section on regional injuries. At the end of the operation, the abdominal cavity should be cleaned by suction and swabbing. The abdominal incision should be closed in layers and this should be reinforced by tension sutures of stainless steel or synthetic materials inserted as the first step in closure and tied as the last, over a gauze roll or short lengths of rubber tubing. If there is a grossly contaminated wound the skin incision should be left open with a sterile dressing in place and closed later by delayed primary suture.

Large abdominal war wounds should be thoroughly excised. If the resultant defect cannot be closed without tension by local soft tissues, marlex or similar synthetic mesh may be used even in the presence of contamination. Alternatively, a practical method for field use is to cover the defects with moist packs to prevent evisceration. Adhesions and granulations will form on the presenting abdominal contents later.

c *Drainage*

(1) *Intra-peritoneal* An operation for the repair of a penetrating abdominal injury is never a clean one. Many of the haemostatic measures are not completely secure and some of the sutures may be under tension. Therefore drainage is always a wise precaution. A reactionary haemorrhage is recognized at once if there is a drain, and a failed anastomosis leaks to the surface instead of bursting into the peritoneum.

A drain is less liable to result in adhesions than is a slowly resolving or fibrosing collection of blood and exudate. Except in completely clean cases, drainage is mandatory and the drain should be led down to areas of soiling, damage or extensive repair. The drains may be in tube or corrugated form. They should be brought out through a separate, generous incision rather than through the original wound or the laparotomy wound and should be placed so that gravity drainage is thereby facilitated. Good pelvic drainage may be achieved by placing a drain to the recto-vesical pouch. They should be gradually shortened and usually withdrawn about the third or fourth day after operation.

(2) *Retro-peritoneal* The retro-peritoneal tissues are very vulnerable, for cellulitis and clostridial invasion from contaminated colon contents are likely. Gross infection in these regions is a lethal complication. Whenever the ascending or descending colon has been injured the retro-peritoneal space should be generously drained, any blood clot and debris being thoroughly cleaned out first. Drainage is best achieved through separate incisions in the flanks and drainage tubes can be passed upwards and towards the kidney regions and separate tubes may be placed running medially. If there is any question of peri-vesical soiling the retropubic space should also be drained. Presacral drains are essential for the drainage of low rectal injuries.

REGIONAL INJURIES

Alimentary tract

The **stomach** is wounded in about 10–15 per cent of all abdominal cases. Wounds may be small or large perforations, linear tears or complete trans-sections. It is important to remember that a posterior perforation may be the only injury.

Wounds of the stomach carry a high mortality because they are usually associated with injury to neighbouring organs such as the transverse colon, jejunum, liver, spleen, pancreas and left kidney. Isolated wounds are relatively benign, for the stomach walls are resistant to injury and have a good blood supply. Tears of the fundus and the body should be closed by a double layer of sutures; those wounds near the pylorus which leave a narrowed lumen after repair may require the addition of a gastro-jejunostomy.

Duodenum Wounds of the duodenum are rarely encountered by surgeons because of the high associated mortality from coincident injuries of the pancreas, liver, stomach, kidney and great vessels. Patients with wounds of the duodenum often have severe haemorrhage. Minor wounds of the duodenum should be treated by excision and closed transversely after mobilization of the duodenum and examination of the posterior wall. More severe disruptive wounds may be treated by partial resection and gastro-jejunostomy. The duodenum must be kept decompressed and particular attention must be paid to drainage of the site of the anastomosis and the retro-duodenal area.

The small intestine is wounded in at least 30 per cent of abdominal cases and almost always the wounds are multiple. The perforations may be small and often cannot be felt, so that they may be missed unless the whole length of the gut is rapidly, but carefully, inspected. A single hole should be mistrusted for there should be another. The perforations are often sealed by pouting mucuous membrane, so that they may not actually leak. Blood in the peritoneum is therefore far more characteristic of small intestine injury than the presence of intestinal contents.

Perforations of the small intestine should be closed by local sutures if at all possible. The edges need minimal trimming and a single layer of interrupted, invaginating sutures is usually enough. Resection of gut is indicated:

a When simple suture is mechanically unsatisfactory, as when a group of perforations are so close that their repair would overlap; when so many

injuries are found in a given segment that resection of the segment will save valuable time; or often when the injury is on the mesenteric border.
b When the viability of a loop of gut is destroyed, by crushing, by thrombosis of the vessels or by detachment of its mesentery.

End to end anastomosis is best done by the method with which the surgeon is familiar. A single layer of invaginating sutures is adequate, rapid and safe.

Colon Wounds of the colon occur almost as frequently as those of the small intestine. They are less often multiple than those of the small intestine but they are more serious because:
a They are often retro-peritoneal injuries and therefore easily overlooked. These retro-peritoneal injuries may be caused not only by primary missiles but by secondary missiles such as bone.
b The walls of the colon are thinner and the blood supply is less good. Simple perforation is uncommon and extensive damage, bruising and rupture of the outer coats of the colon is the rule.
c The contents usually escape earlier and in greater quantities than from a perforation of the small intestine and are grossly infected.
d Retro-peritoneal cellulitis, which is often an anaerobic infection, is a common and often fatal complication.

Perforations in the colon should be looked for carefully as those that are in the fixed portions and on the mesenteric aspects of the transverse colon are difficult to demonstrate and easily missed. A search for hidden wounds will require incision of the lateral peritoneal reflexions to mobilize the colon and permit direct inspection of the retro-peritoneal areas. The absence of soiling does not preclude perforations.

The parts of the wall of the colon which are contused or discoloured should be repaired, resected or exteriorized. A haematoma in the mesocolon or in the right or left paracolic gutter calls for a minute examination of the adjacent bowel wall. A faeculent smell may draw attention to a hole that can scarcely be seen.

The treatment of colon injuries is based on the known insecurity of suture and the danger of leakage. Simple closure of a wound of the colon, however small, should never be attempted in the field. *The rule that injured segments of colon should either be exteriorized, or functionally excluded by a proximal colostomy, is one that every surgeon should follow at an advanced field surgical centre.*

The whole colon above the recto-sigmoid junction is either mobile or can be readily mobilized. Injuries of these portions may therefore be brought onto the surface of the abdomen. A small perforation may be converted into a loop colostomy, the perforation being temporarily controlled by the blades of a spring clamp introduced through a lateral incision and used to ease the gut through it. A larger perforation will usually require resection of the damaged portion. Mobilization must be sufficient to allow the colon above and below the injury to be approximated without tension, as in all colonic surgery. The injured segment should be resected and the cut ends above and below it closed with crushing clamps and brought to the surface of the abdomen as a double-barrelled colostomy. Wounds of the lower pelvic colon must be repaired as well as possible and the faecal stream diverted by a proximal defunctioning colostomy. It is essential that drains should be placed into the retro-peritoneal space or led down to the sites of repair in colon injuries. Under field conditions a proximal colostomy must be established or a damaged loop of bowel exteriorized for these are life-saving measures. Common mistakes are inadequate mobilization of the colon because of inadequate lateral peritoneal incision and improper positioning of the incision on the abdominal wall causing the colon to be brought out under tension. This results in retraction and defeats the purpose of the colostomy. The separate colostomy incision should be made in a muscular part of the abdominal wall. The transverse colon is easily exteriorized. The left colon may be exteriorized through an incision in the left hypochondrium or the left iliac fossa.

Right colon   Wounds of the right colon are not satisfactorily managed by exteriorization. Modern methods of stoma therapy have, however, solved the problems of digestion of the abdominal wall and maintaining a fluid balance if an ileostomy is required. The treatment of these wounds depends upon the extent of the injury to the colon and associated visceral damage.

The alternatives available are:
a Resection of the damaged colon with the formation of an ileostomy and exteriorization of the proximal end of the colon as a mucous fistula.
b Right hemicolectomy with end-to-side ileocolostomy and exteriorization of, or a catheter, in the cut end of the colon proximal to the anastomosis. (See Fig 16.)
c Right hemicolectomy without anastomosis but double-barrelled exteriorization of both ileum and colon.
d Simple suture with caecostomy. This should only be considered for the smallest perforations known to have resulted from low velocity missiles.

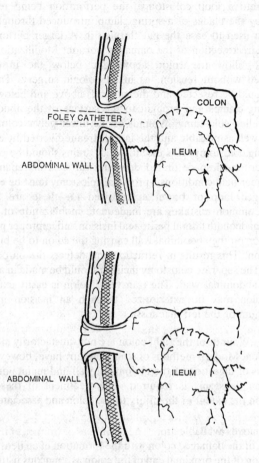

Figure 16   End to side anastomosis of colon and ileum
Acknowledgement: Operative surgery. Rob and Rodney Smith)

Gross contamination is usual in severe wounds of the colon and adequate post-operative drainage of the utmost importance. Particular attention should be paid to the paracolic gutter and sub-hepatic spaces and posterior dependent drainage is frequently required.

Left colon Left colon injuries, like those of the transverse colon, can usually be exteriorized but adequate mobilization of the colon is imperative so that there is no tension in the exteriorized bowel. When there is severe disruptive injury or a devitalized segment, resection may be performed with end colostomy and the establishment of a distal mucous fistula. When there are small wounds of the lower sigmoid colon which cannot be exteriorized, they may be closed in two layers with the addition of a proximal defunctioning colostomy. When severe injury occurs to the lower sigmoid colon, it may be necessary to resect the injured colon to form a proximal colostomy and to close the distal colon in two layers in the fashion of a Hartmann's operation as a blind pouch. It is important with all left colon injuries to drain the left para-colic gutter and the pelvis thoroughly.

The damaged colon or the colostomies should be brought out through a separate incision so placed that further contamination of the traumatic wound or the surgical incision does not take place, and that an appliance can be readily applied to the proximal stoma.

Rectum Wounds of the rectum have a high morbidity and mortality for they are often complicated by fractures of the pelvis, perforations of the small bowel, perforations of the bladder and damage to the urethra, major nerve injuries and haemorrhage from iliac blood vessels. It is very important that penetration of the rectum should be proved or excluded at the first examination. Whenever such an injury is at all possible, or when blood had been passed, the rectum should be examined digitally and with a proctoscope and sigmoidoscope. The treatment of wounds of the rectum is by repair, thorough drainage and the formation of a defunctioning colostomy for it is imperative that the faecal stream is diverted. The distal rectal segment should be irrigated at the time of initial surgery. Drainage must never be omitted. When the wound is on the peritoneal surface of the rectum in its upper third, a broad strip of corrugated rubber may be introduced beside the injury to the bottom of the recto-vesical pouch and led out through a stab incision in the left iliac fossa. When the wound involves the side or back of the upper third of the rectum or any part of it in its extra-peritoneal course then the retro-rectal space must be drained by drains introduced through the wound if this is in the buttock or the sacrum but otherwise through an incision placed in the median raphe between coccyx and anus. The space between the sacrum and the rectum can then be opened up to allow excellent dependent drainage. Coccygectomy is occasionally required to facilitate drainage. In large wounds of the perineum or buttock encroaching on the anal region but not injuring the sphincters, a colostomy is often advisable in order to prevent faecal soiling of the wound and to facilitate early suture or skin grafting.

Liver

The liver is damaged in about 20 per cent of abdominal wounds. It is most vulnerable in right sided thoraco-abdominal injuries. Liver wounds may be broadly divided into three grades of severity. Low velocity bullets and fragments may pass through the liver or be retained within it, leaving only an oozing cored out track which may well heal spontaneously. If there is not active bleeding from the liver wound when it is exposed at operation it should not be disturbed but external drainage must be performed and such drainage must be thorough.

More severe wounds are due to missile fragments which cause shattering of the liver parenchyma and the resultant haemorrhage is moderate or severe. If there is evidence of haemorrhage, the liver wound should be cleaned of clot and fragments and pressure firmly applied to the damaged area using a swab wrung out of hot saline; excision of the damaged tissue followed by further haemostasis by suture will be required. External drainage is imperative but biliary tract decompression by T tube may or may not be indicated.

High velocity bullets and missiles cause extensive shattering of the liver substance. Liver is particularly vulnerable to the cavitation effect of high velocity missiles, so much so that almost the whole liver substance may be pulped. This is always associated with severe haemorrhage which comes not only from the liver substance but from the hepatic veins or the intra-hepatic vena cava. There should be no hesitation in extending the incision into the right side of the chest for control of haemorrhage and the prevention of air emboli. This procedure allows the liver to be mobilized and rotated forward so that the hepatic veins and vena cava above the liver can be controlled. Any means of controlling haemorrhage which seems feasible should be used, from digital compression of the hepatic artery and portal vein in the free edge of the gastro-hepatic omentum to the use of partial occluding clamps or tape occlusion of the vena cava, hepatic veins, portal vein and abdominal aorta. The mortality of such operations is very high.

T tube drainage of the common duct should not be used routinely for the less than severe injuries, but it is acceptable in the disruptive injury which has resulted in excision of so much damaged tissue that a partial hepatectomy has resulted. Thorough external drainage is mandatory and this is best accomplished through the posterior aspect of the right flank.

The right paramedian or mid-line incision gives adequate exposure and these may be readily extended into the right side of the chest if necessary. The line of liver resection, during wound excision, should be at the edge of the devitalized tissue; packing to control liver haemorrhage is not recommended whereas the use of deep sutures through intact liver substance well away from the wound and hot packs are very useful in controlling the haemorrhage and exposing the field of operation.

Major complications of liver wounds include secondary haemorrhage, infection which may be subphrenic, sub-hepatic or intra-hepatic, and biliary fistulae. These complications have usually occurred because of failure to excise necrotic or devitalized liver tissue, the strangulation of viable hepatic tissue by the injudicious use of sutures, by inadequate drainage and by gross contamination of the liver tissue from the commonly associated injuries of colon, small bowel and stomach.

Spleen

The spleen is less often damaged than the liver due mainly to its smaller size, but its friability and greater vascularity make it more susceptible to blows, crush injuries and blast injury. The treatment of injuries of the spleen is splenectomy. The mid-line or left paramedian incision may be used and gives adequate access. The left subphrenic space must be drained because subphrenic infection is the commonest complication of splenectomy and is usually related to injuries of other viscera.

Pancreas

Wounds of this organ are not often met by the surgeon in the field because they are complicated by proximity of major vessels and often lethal. The pancreas must be examined, at laparotomy, whenever there is a wound in the upper abdomen. Minor injuries of the pancreas in which there is minimal contusion or laceration should be treated by thorough dependent drainage through the posterior aspect of the flank. When there are more severe injuries which involve the pancreas, particularly when there is disruption of pancreatic tissue and ducts, they should be treated by resection of the distal pancreatic remnant and ligation of the proximal end of the divided pancreatic duct. The pancreatic capsule should be closed if possible and thorough posterior dependent drainage is imperative. Preservative operations on missile injuries of the pancreas should not usually be attempted because it is safer to resect the injured portion and establish good drainage.

Kidney

The kidney may be wounded alone or with other organs in an abdominal injury.

Closed injuries should be dealt with along lines similar to those employed in civil practice. Coincident fracture of the transverse processes of the upper lumbar vertebrae or the lowest three ribs should be excluded by X-ray and intravenous pyelography is essential in assessing the renal damage. Cystoscopy may be useful in identifying the side of the haematuria and nephrectomy will be required in only a small proportion of cases, particularly those with damage to the pedicle.

The possibility of delayed rupture, initially contained within the capsule, should always be borne in mind.

Intraperitoneal haemorrhage from injury of the kidney occurs in war wounds and penetrating wounds either from the loin or anteriorly. Renal injury is also seen in some thoraco-abdominal wounds. Surgical exploration may reveal damage to the cortex communicating with the pelvicaly-ceal system but partial nephrectomy or suture with perinephric drainage and perhaps nephrostomy will usually be possible rather than nephrectomy. Injuries of the ureter are very rare and may only become apparent by the development of a urinary fistula many days later. Early repair is important, usually over a ureteric catheter with proximal nephrostomy but this is a problem to be dealt with at a genito-urinary centre.

Bladder and urethra

Wounds of the bladder and urethra require treatment at the first unit with surgical facilities. The distended bladder is more vulnerable than the empty one, protected by the bony pelvis, and it must be remembered that the bowel, vagina and uterus may be injured at the same time.

Urinary diversion by suprapubic cystostomy, sited as high above the symphysis as possible, is usually all that is required as primary treatment.

Intraperitoneal rupture of the bladder demands suture of the bladder tear as well and this may be possible in extra-peritoneal injury. If not, suprapubic cystostomy and prevesical drainage will suffice.

Rupture of the urethra, commonly associated with fractures of the pelvis is treated in the first instance by urinary diversion. Evacuation of the patient to a genito-urinary centre for definitive treatment of the urethral injury should be arranged as soon as possible.

Major blood vessels

Wounds of the aorta and of the vena cava are usually fatal although cases have been recorded of tears in the latter being controlled by suture, muscle graft or packing. Wounds of major vessels such as the iliac can be treated by lateral suture, resection and end to end anastomosis or replacement with autogenous vein graft. The use of prosthetic materials has not been successful due to the problem of sepsis; the presence of a large foreign body leads to catastrophe in most cases.

Fractures of the pelvis

Injury to the bones of the pelvis is usually of secondary importance when dealing with abdominal wounds. Displacement of bony fragments rarely demands special measures other than the immobilization implicit after laparotomy, except that it will have to be prolonged for a period varying from eight to fourteen weeks.

Crush injuries usually produce fractures involving one side of the pelvis with coincident rupture of the bladder or urethra in approximately a quarter of the cases.

Separation of the symphysis or fractures of the ischio-pubic rami occur anteriorly and posteriorly; there may be separation of the sacro-iliac joint or fracture of the adjacent ilium or sacrum.

Treatment   A strong canvas sling suspended from an overhead beam with the cords crossed so as to compress the pelvis is usually all that is required. In rare instances traction on the leg is necessary to overcome proximal displacement but this should only arise at general hospital level, as should exploration for internal fixation of fragments, which has a very limited place in management.

Postoperative management

Evacuation   Evacuation in the immediate postoperative period is particularly harmful and may well lead to the patient's death. Patients must be held in the surgical centre for at least seven days, preferably ten. Spontaneous bowel action should have occurred, abdominal distension should have subsided and the laparotomy incision should be healed or free from acute infection before they are moved.

Position   Patients with abdominal wounds cannot be nursed efficiently on stretchers. Beds are a necessity in any surgical centre prepared to deal with abdominal casualties. The Fowler position should be avoided, at any rate as a nursing routine or for more than short periods. Patients should, as a rule, be allowed to take up the position in which they are most comfortable, but they should be encouraged to abandon the position from time to time, to change from side to side and from lying flat to sitting up. The following points are emphasized.

Gastric suction   Ileus must be anticipated rather than treated when it appears. An endogastric tube should be passed through a nostril before operation. In the ward gastric suction is maintained until the return of peristalsis is heard and flatus has been passed. For gastric suction, simple syphonage using an inverted bottle should be preferred to more elaborate apparatus. It must be remembered that one medical asssistant may have to keep twenty suctions going. Any elaboration involving changing of bottles or repeated suction should be avoided. Plastic naso-gastric tubes should be used as they cause less irritation to the naso-pharynx than rubber. It must be remembered that if a naso-gastric tube is kept in for too long oesophageal stricture may follow.

Intra-venous fluids
a Blood should be given whenever the haemoglobin estimation shows that it is needed.
b Patients on post operative gastric suction require continuous intra-venous administration of fluids to supply the basic needs of water and electrolytes, in addition to the replacement of fluid lost through gastric suction. The clinical state and the response to therapy must be assessed frequently. An intake and output chart must be accurately kept. If kidneys are undamaged and the blood pressure is normal, the human body is able to compensate very efficiently for moderate electrolyte imbalance.

Homeostasis following severe injury and multiple transfusions must be monitored closely by measuring the arterial blood pressure, the central venous pressure, the character of the pulse, skin capillary perfusion and hourly urinary output. Accurate intake and output recordings are essential to guide rational fluid therapy. Measured urine output should exceed 50 ml in the hour. Insensible loss of 2 litres in a normal sized man may be expected in a temperate climate provided there is no abnormal loss. The intake should be 2–3 litres in a 24 hour period and this can be either Ringer Lactate (Hartmann's) solution or normal saline and 5 per cent dextrose solution in a ratio of ½ litre of normal saline to 2 litres of 5 per cent dextrose. In addition to this, isotonic (normal) saline should be given to replace what has been withdrawn from the gastric tube, measure for measure.

After two or three days of intravenous therapy potassium supplements may become necessary. Approximately 60–80 mEq should be given each day. This can be as 2 g of potassium chloride in each litre of the intravenous fluid or, if it is possible, be taken by mouth. It may be given in solution or in fruit juice.

Antibiotics   The antibiotics of first choice in abdominal penetrating injuries are:

a   *Aqueous Penicillin* intravenously 1 000 000 units initially and 1 000 000 units every eight hours, together with

b   *Ampicillin* 1 g initially followed by 0.5 g every eight hours intravenously.

c   In patients who are sensitive to penicillins *tetracycline* may be given 1 g initially intravenously followed by 0.5 g every eight hours.

d   *Metronidazole*   500 mg (0.5 g) given intravenously every eight hours for two days, followed by 1 g given by suppository or tablet eight hourly for three days.

When circulatory collapse has been controlled, antibiotics may be given by the intramuscular route. Once oral feeding is permissible, administration of antibiotics may be by this route. After three to five days, the patient's condition and the effects of the antibiotic therapy should be evaluated and any change that is necessary may be made.

Postoperative peritonitis   Peritonitis following penetrating wounds of the abdomen is the most frequent serious complication and leads to significant morbidity and delayed mortality. It is one of the major problems to be met with in missile wound surgery. Associated complications which contribute to the gravity of the situation are wound infection, wound dehiscence, persistent ileus, intestinal obstruction, atelectasis and pneumonia, intra-abdominal abcesses and stress ulceration.

The signs and symptoms of peritonitis after operation may be florid and readily diagnosed or they may be so slight and insidious that they may be regarded as part of the normal process of recovery. Careful examinations, repeated frequently, are necessary to detect post operative peritonitis. After operation for intra-abdominal injuries, the normal course of events is that the abdomen becomes soft, peristalsis is restored and the temperature, pulse and respiration return to normal within three to four days. When peritonitis develops, the abdomen usually becomes distended, the peristaltic sounds may not return or are infrequent, tenderness and rigidity are demonstrable and the patient tends to lie still in bed because movement causes pain. The pulse and temperature do not return to normal and rectal examination may reveal tenderness.

Peritonitis after operation almost invariably results in intra-abdominal abscess formation. In addition to pelvic and subphrenic abscesses, abscesses may occur in the paracolic gutters and between loops of bowel. When localized abscesses are detected, appropriate posterior or lateral dependent drainage should be accomplished and maintained. Abdominal abscesses which result from war wounds are frequently multiple and in general the abdomen should always be formally explored for these. At operation for drainage, the cause of the sepsis may well be detected, for instance a leak at an anastomosis, a missed visceral injury or necrotic tissue that has not been excised. These conditions can be corrected at the time of operation and before thorough drainage is established.

It is most important to remember that patients wounded in the abdomen tolerate repeated operations poorly, and therefore, every effort must be made at the time of the original operation to elimate all sources of infection by thorough excision of damaged tissues and by adequate dependent drainage. If intra-abdominal sepsis is not controlled early, there is an increasing danger of septicaemia and pyaemia with spread of infection to the lungs, brain, kidney and liver; once this has occurred there is little chance of survival.

Intra-abdominal sepsis is one of the major cause of morbidity and mortality in missile wound surgery. Only the most scrupulous attention to details of the treatment of colon wounds in particular will reduce the complications and mortality to a minimum acceptable figure.

Re-operations for complications of abdominal injury   These commonly occur in the first three weeks, emphasizing the teaching that the casualty should not be evacuated following abdominal operation for seven days. It is important that during this time the surgeon who did the original operation should be available for frequent evaluation of the case. If there is a heavy patient work load and evacuation becomes necessary the least seriously injured patients should be selected rather than those who have had extensive intra-abdominal injuries.

This will allow earlier diagnosis and treatment of the complications that might occur in this high risk group.

a *Dehiscence*   Wound infection is the prime cause of dehiscence but in addition the failure to place tension sutures and the evacuation of patients with post-operative ileus by air contribute to the condition.

b *Missed intra-abdominal injury*   It is inevitable that some significant intra-abdominal injury may be missed when dealing with these severe, and frequently multiple injuries. To reduce these failures to a minimum, it is necessary to pay particular attention to several points. The laparotomy incision must be adequate in size and well placed. If in doubt the generous mid-line incision is best for exposure and because of the ease with which it can be made and closed. An adequate incision allows a thorough and systematic exploration. The injuries that are most commonly overlooked at laparotomy are those involving the retro-peritoneal structures, the fixed portions of the colon and the viscera bordering the lesser sac. These areas must be thoroughly explored by mobilization of the viscera if necessary to ensure that the missile entering another part of the body has not penetrated the abdominal cavity. To this end an adequate history of the position of the patient when wounded, the type of missile that has caused the wound and the use of abdominal radiographs may be of help by identifying an intra-abdominal metallic fragment.

c *Intestinal obstruction*   This is a complication which usually occurs within the first two weeks after injury. Early operation may correct the obstruction more successfully than conservative methods. The usual cause of the obstruction is adhesions and abscesses that are present between loops of bowel. This condition should not be confused with the prolonged ileus that may occur in the immediate period after injury.

d *Intra-abdominal haemorrhage*   Haemorrhage occurring within the abdomen, following operation, is usually secondary haemorrhage. It is usually the result of infection within the abdomen which allows erosion of a blood vessel of significant size. Such haemorrhage is usually profuse and only urgent operation may save the patient. Most vessels within the abdomen can be ligated securely and the problem usually arises with those vessels in the retro-peritoneal tissues particularly when a haematoma, resulting from a blood vessel wound is not explored. The haematoma gets infected and eventually an abscess or cellulitis causes a significant haemorrhage.

e *Intra-abdominal abscesses*   These are one of the commonest complications of the surgery of missile wounds of the abdomen. They are often associated with other complications such as obstruction, fistula or stress haemorrhage. Most of these abscesses present in the first weeks after operation but some may be chronic and present at a much later date. The treatment consists of drainage of the abscess, and the appropriate antibiotic. Once again great importance is placed on adequate and skilfully placed drainage, the use of sump drains, suction and in some cases irrigation with saline or antibiotic solutions to prevent recurrence.

f *Abdominal wall defects*   Extensive damage to the abdominal wall may result in the loss of a considerable portion, either directly or because of the necessary excision of contaminated tissues. If primary closure is attempted undue tension will lead to failure to heal and respiratory embarrassment. It is not practicable to leave small bowel to become the base of the granulating wound by covering with saline dressings, in other than an emergency situation, because of the risks of intestinal obstruction and fistula formation. It is possible, even in infected cases and provided adequate wound excision has taken place, to insert a synthetic mesh prosthesis to replace the defect of the abdominal wall. It is securely sutured to the under surface of the surrounding tissues. In the course of time this becomes covered with healthy granulation tissues and may be covered by skin grafting.

g *Fistulae*   These are usually rather late complications and should be treated by conventional methods. Suction, protection of the surrounding skin and tissues, investigation to confirm that no distal obstruction is present and finally operation to close the fistula by a variety of methods should be done. They are commonly complicated operations and would normally be done at base hospitals.

h *Colostomy problems*   Retraction or necrosis of a colostomy or ileostomy may occur in the immediate period after the operation. This is particularly true if a segment of bowel has been exteriorized under tension. Tension is usually the result of inadequate mobilization of the lateral peritoneal reflections of the colon, in particular the division of the suspensory ligaments of the hepatic and splenic flexures. It is also important to secure the mesentery of the involved bowel to the parietal peritoneum, taking particular care that the blood supply is not damaged in this manoeuvre. At a second operation it may be possible to mobilize the involved bowel further to produce an easy delivery of the involved segment onto the abdominal wall or it may be necessary to mobilize bowel and form a colostomy or ileostomy proximal to the old site.

It is most important to establish the stoma in a fashion that will allow it to function without any problems until such time as it is closed.

j *Haemorrhage from stress ulcers*   Stress ulceration occurs from the stomach and duodenum following major injury. It is most common after severe burns and intra-abdominal wounds, particularly those that have resulted in sepsis. The bleeding is commonly severe, it usually occurs after about ten days, and may well have to be controlled by surgical rather than medical means.

CHAPTER 21

Ophthalmic injuries

Incidence

Up to 10 per cent of all battle casualties sustain an ophthalmic injury, of which 15 per cent are bilateral.

Type of injury

Fifty per cent of eye injuries are penetrating wounds of the globe and 15 per cent have hyphaema. Corneal abrasions, corneal foreign bodies or conjunctival lacerations are extremely common.

The surrounding structures are frequently injured: 25 per cent have lid and facial wounds and 20 per cent orbital floor fractures. In 15 per cent there are associated wounds of the cranial vault and brain. For optimum efficiency the ophthalmic team needs to be working closely with neurosurgical, plastic and ENT surgeons.

Source of injury

In addition to the effects of blast and high velocity fragments from many modern weapons, low velocity injuries from road crashes, knives and sticks are seen.

Management at RAP – Dressing Station – Forward Surgical Centre

History   A careful history is essential and must be recorded.

Examination should be in the following order:
Measure visual acuity.
Inspect lids and lashes.
Inspect cornea, conjunctiva and sclera with the help of focussing torch, the lids being pulled back by the fingers resting on the upper and lower rims of the orbit without putting pressure on the globe.
Assess depth of anterior chamber.
Critically assess pupil shape and reactions.

Test ocular movements – both eyes together and each eye separately.
Ask about diplopia in the nine cardinal positions of gaze.
Inspect fundi.
Assess infra-orbital anaesthesia.
Assess jaw opening and closure.

Treatment

a *Lids and facial wounds*   Protect eye and stop bleeding. If necessary tack sutures to hold wound edges approximately together. Pad and bandage is applied and patient evacuated.

b *Conjunctival foreign bodies and lacerations.*   Wash out conjunctival sac with saline and pick out any loose foreign matter. Non penetrating conjunctival lacerations will heal (if black uveal pigment is visible penetrating scleral wound co-exists and evacuation is essential). Local antibiotic drugs (chloramphenicol) four times daily. No pad – the conjunctival sac when closed is an ideal incubator of organisms.

c *Corneal foreign body and/or corneal abrasion*   Instil a couple of drops of local anaesthetic (amethocaine or benoxinate). If foreign body (non penetrating) is present remove it with a large sterile needle tip, the shaft of the needle approaching the cornea tangentially. Scrape out any rust from the ulcer crater thus left. This leaves the patient with a corneal abrasion.

Corneal abrasions may be visualized more easily by the instillation of a couple of drops of fluorescein. Treat the abrasion whether traumatic or post foreign body removal with a few drops of mydriatic (hyoscine, homatropine or cyclopentolate) – remember the effects of atropine last up to two weeks – and a few drops of antibiotic (chloramphenicol or neomycin). This will reduce the pain from ciliary spasm, prevent infection and minimize secondary iritis.

Pad the eye.   Inspect the stain with fluorescein every 24 hours until no further staining of the abrasion occurs. Then discontinue the pad. Continue antibiotic drops three times daily for a week.

d *Hyphaema*   Blood in the anterior chamber is present in 15 per cent of ocular injuries. Hyphaema occurs with non penetrating injuries more commonly than with penetrating injuries. The danger of hyphaema is that eyes tend to have a secondary bleed on the third, fourth or fifth day after injury and the secondary bleed is often worse than the primary bleed leading to total hyphaema, secondary glaucoma and corneal staining with blood. This secondary hyphaema is almost impossible to manage easily and must be prevented. It is best prevented by total ocular rest, ie:

Complete bed rest.

Mydriatic drops (homatropine, hyoscine not atropine) to prevent the pupil moving.

Antibiotic drops.

Pad on both eyes.

Evacuate.

e *Penetrating injury*   If no other injuries are present the injured eye requires antibiotic drops and a pad. The patient requires systemic antibiotics and tetanus toxoid and must be evacuated on a stretcher. If the penetrating injury coexists with other injuries which require emergency surgery, the eye should be treated in exactly the same way with antibiotic drops four times daily, an eye pad and systemic antibiotics and tetanus toxoid. The pad should be changed at each instillation of drops and the lashes bathed with saline and kept clean.

It is essential that the cornea be covered while waiting for evacuation and during transit.

If the lids are torn or split a single key suture should catch the skin near the margins of both lids so that the lids are approximated.

An eye should never be removed by a general surgeon unless it is totally disrupted, has no perception of light and there is likely to be delay of 10 days before evacuation to an ophthalmic unit. Sympathetic ophthalmia does not develop before 10 days after penetrating injury and only very rarely before three weeks. There is usually, therefore, abundance of time for the patient to reach a specialist ophthalmic surgeon and for the latter to give a reasoned opinion on the case before drastic action need be taken.

In recent conflicts where early and definitive ophthalmic surgery was carried out by ophthalmic surgeons the incidence of sympathetic ophthalmia was virtually zero.

f *Orbital injuries*   Twenty per cent of ocular war injuries have fractured orbital floors. Some have zygomatic fractures. Carefully palpate the orbital margin. No emergency treatment is required.

Antibiotics and tetanus toxoid should be given.

Evacuation to an ophthalmic unit for treatment is required if there is:

(1)   Diplopia.

(2)   Enophthalmos.

(3)   Inability to open jaw.

(4)   Flat cheek and infra orbital nerve anaesthesia.

If eyes and useful vision are to be retained ophthalmic injuries must be accurately assessed and evacuated for ophthalmic assessment and treatment.

Do not ignore an eye injury.

Do not squeeze eyes or lids.

Do not use ointment.

Do not use scoline.

Do not patch up.

Management at forward ophthalmic unit

Function of unit It prevents patients with minor injuries, diseases or broken spectacles being referred back to base, and enables them to return rapidly to their units. With major injuries operative interference should be reduced to a minimum and confined to that necessary for conservation of vision.

*No surgical treatment which requires long
post-operative immobility should be attempted*

Assessment of injury An eye is potentially useful so long as it retains perception of light. A gross diminution of vision may be due to temporary causes which may clear up and an eye which may appear useless soon after the injury may eventually recover sufficiently to allow some vision — a matter of extreme importance in cases where the injury involves both eyes.

An eye wound is dangerous as it is liable to cause sympathetic ophthalmia if there is a rupture or penetrating wound of the globe, particularly in the ciliary region and especially when complicated by a prolapse of the uvea or lens capsule. A retained foreign body associated with a small self-sealing wound, although it may lead to complete disorganization of the eye, does not usually give rise to sympathetic ophthalmia unless accompanied by prolapse of the uvea or lens capsule. A suppurating eye rarely gives rise to sympathetic ophthalmia; it is the angry red eye or the quiet iridocyclitis that is the greatest danger. An eye which has not been perforated does not develop to sympathetic ophthalmia; but remember that a minute perforation may require extreme accuracy in examination for detection and is easily missed.

Sympathetic ophthalmia is now extremely rare and the remote

possibility of its occurrence should not unduly influence the management of an injured eye.

Surgical procedures The operations which should be done at this early stage are as follows:

a *Excision of the eye* Usually this need only be done in extensive irreparable ruptures of one eye. In such cases, if the eye is blind, it should be removed within the first ten days after injury. When both eyes are ruptured, excision should not be undertaken immediately; the operation serves no useful purpose, it inflicts unnecessary shock and is bad psychologically. Such cases are best dealt with at the base where there is ample time to verify the hopelessness of the condition. If excision of an eye is indicated at an early stage complete evisceration should be performed. Complete excision of the globe in the ordinary way, by cutting the optic nerve, has led to fatal meningitis in the past.

b *Prolapse of the uveal tissue or lens capsule* should be excised.

c *Corneal wounds* should be sutured and the anterior chamber reformed.

d *Gaping scleral wounds* should be sutured and protected by a conjunctival flap.

e *Gaping corneal wounds* which cannot be closed by direct corneal suture, should be covered by a conjunctival flap. The best technique in all cases is the total purse-string flap. It is important that the cornea be circumcised close to the limbus and that undercutting be extensive so that the flap may be drawn over the cornea without any tension. If this flap is formed under tension, the patient will reach the base with a partially retracted flap and an exposed cornea traumatised by sutures.

Foreign bodies

a *Intra-ocular foreign bodies* Too enthusiastic attempts at the removal of a foreign body should not be made in a forward ophthalmic unit. A large proportion of those foreign bodies are non-magnetic or are only magnetizable to a slight extent, frequently necessitating accurate localization, close approximation of the magnet and repeated attempts at extraction. Since posterior extraction is often necessary involving the use of diathermy or cryotherapy followed by prolonged convalescence, such cases are not usually suitable for forward surgery.

If the foreign body is either: in the anterior chamber or adhering to the magnet when it is presented at an already existent scleral wound of entry, its removal by the magnet at this stage is permissible.

b *Foreign bodies peppering the cornea,* either of metal, powder or dirt, are troublesome to remove. If they are numerous and not causing irritation they should be left alone. If they are superficial and causing irritation, they should be picked out with a sterile needle. As a rule, deep foreign bodies are best left for some days; if they cause a reaction this will facilitate their removal; if they are well tolerated, they may be left permanently.

c *Foreign bodies in the orbit* are best left alone. The tendency is for haemorrhage or cellulitis with proptosis to subside with general antibiotic treatment. If cellulitis is severe it should be treated by incision and drainage, but blind attempts at removal usually cause more harm than good.

Control of infection   In all penetrating wounds of the eye and wounds of the orbit, general treatment by the administration of antibiotics and tetanus toxoid should be instituted at the earliest possible moment.

a For slight injuries instillation of antibiotic drops is sufficient.

b When infection is suspected or obvious and the intraocular tension is normal, the most efficient treatment is a sub-conjunctival injection of gentamycin or cephaloridine with systemic antibiotic therapy.

c If the eye is penetrated antibiotics will pass the blood-aqueous barrier. The best initial systemic antibiotics by injection are Ampicillin 1 g six hourly or cephaloridine 1 g six hourly. Ideally, these should be given pre-operatively and may be continued post-operatively along with broad-spectrum antibiotic eye ointment.

Intra-ocular infections are best prevented by minimal surgical intervention in field units and by the use of systemic and local antibiotics.

Steroids   Steroids are useful agents in the control of post-traumatic uveitis. Because they retard the initial healing of ocular tissues they are not advised as an immediate application but after the second or third day are safe. If administered at an early stage in presence of a large corneal or scleral wound good coaptation by the liberal use of sutures is desirable. After the fifth day or so on the appearance of post-traumatic iridocyclitis they may be used liberally, either topically, by sub-conjunctival injection or systemically. All casualties with intraocular foreign bodies should be evacuated to the base marked and annotated.

Evacuation   During evacuation to the base, if there is any danger of corneal exposure the lids should be approximated by a skin suture as described above, or if this is difficult, a complete conjunctival flap should be made. During evacuation, arrangements should be made for the eye or socket to be gently irrigated with saline and dressed at least once every 48 hours.

All cases of intra-ocular perforation are to be evacuated on stretchers.

Management at base

General considerations Treatment at the base involves general ophthalmological principles and it is here that final operations such as the treatment of traumatic cataract, the reposition of a detached retina and the removal of difficult foreign bodies should be undertaken. It is here, that the really difficult problems regarding excision must be faced.

Foreign bodies The following general principles are important:

a Many non-magnetic foreign bodies are well tolerated. No foreign body should be considered magnetically inactive unless it has failed to give a response on several occasions.

b If the foreign body is either in the anterior chamber, or in the lens, it should be extracted by an electric magnet through an ab externo incision at the limbus.

c Because of the poor magnetic quality of missile fragments all magnetic extractions of foreign bodies in the posterior segment should be done by the posterior route. The foreign bodies' magnetizability can be estimated:

(1) If seen with the opthalmoscope, by observation of movement when it comes within the field of force of the magnet.

(2) If not visible, by a change of position on X-ray or by its response to the foreign body locator. If the foreign body is magnetizable, lies in the vitreous or the periphery of the fundus, the site of election for the incision is through the pars plana of the ciliary body, 7.5 to 8 mm behind the limbus: the operation is easily carried out in the outer and lower quadrant of the globe. If the foreign body is embedded in the posterior part of the fundus, or feebly magnetizable, it must be located precisely by X-ray and, if possible, opthalmoscope. The incision should be as near as possible to the site of the foreign body.

A conjunctival flap is retracted and surface diathermy or cryo is applied as a prophylactic measure against subsequent retinal detachment. The sclera is steadied by appropriate scleral sutures and incised, the head and eye being turned so that the wound itself lies uppermost to minimize the risk of vitreous loss. The terminal of the magnet is introduced into the lips of the wound (but not into the vitreous) and the current turned on. After removal the scleral sutures are tied and the conjunctival flap reposed. If there is a scleral entry wound it may be used for extraction; this is rarely advisable since it is usually too small and seldom in the right place. It should be emphasized that one trial with the magnet is not sufficient to determine whether a foreign body is magnetizable. Several attempts must be made with the large magnet on several occasions; if the slightest response is elicited its removal should be attempted in the above manner. Occasionally with a similar scleral incision it may be possible to pick up a foreign body with fine iris forceps, or even extract it with a snare of wire passed through a large sized syringe needle, a tricky and difficult operation.

Traumatic cataract   Unless the eye is obviously and violently irritated, or the tension is markedly raised and will not come down, removal of a traumatized lens of the extraction of a cataract is best left until the eye has settled down and is white.

Burns

a *Emergency treatment*   Burns in the region of the eye should never be tanned, nor should dye preparations be used; this almost invariably results in extensive ectropion from cicatrical contraction leading to exposure keratitis, frequently followed by permanent loss of vision or rapid loss of the eye. Emergency treatment: the burnt area of the lids should be thoroughly cleansed with saline, any blisters opened, and an antibiotic cream applied over the denuded area. This should be covered by a tulle gras dressing and a large pad of dry cotton wool under a firm bandage. The cotton wool should always be changed before it becomes soaked with exudate, lest bacterial contamination occur.

   With exposure treatment of burns of the face chloramphenicol eye ointment is applied to the eye four hourly and one per cent atropine drops twice daily following cleansing with saline.

b *Skin grafting*   Whole-thickness skin burns of eyelids should be excised and grafted at the earliest possible moment; this offers the speediest hope of healing and reduces subsequent scarring to a minimum. If this is not done at an early stage skin grafts should be applied to the raw surfaces of the lids as soon as granulations appear to reduce scarring. If these fail to take they must be repeated.

c *Protection of cornea*   During the whole time of healing the cornea must be kept covered, if necessary by tarsorrhapy. If these measures are not successful a protective soft contact lens is a valuable temporary measure. Where this is not available, a pedicle flap from the forehead or temple stitched to the orbital margin right over the exposed eye is a temporary emergency expedient of great value. Provided the cornea is protected the subsequent complete reconstruction of the lids by grafting at leisure need give rise to no anxiety as far as the ultimate function and appearance is concerned. Protection of the cornea is the only immediate necessity.

Plastic surgery   Plastic surgery of an extensive or ambitious nature is to be deprecated in theatres abroad. When an eye is still present and the lid is partially destroyed, every effort should be made to make an eyelid for protection and, if necessary, using the procedures noted above. If there is no eye, particularly if there is lid destruction as well as a contracted socket, the patient should be transferred to the home base. The minor operation of closing the socket may be used when the evacuation is likely to be delayed.

Partial reconstruction and mucous membrane grafts in sockets have not given good long term results. Numerous ill-devised operations are not in the military interest and generally make subsequent and permanent reconstruction a much more difficult, or even an impossible, procedure.

Reconstruction is best carried out in co-operation with a plastic surgeon.

CHAPTER 22

Maxillo-facial injuries

Introduction

The following notes are to help those obliged to undertake the primary treatment of injuries where disposal to special units is delayed or for any reason impossible. In the treatment of jaw injuries there must be the closest co-operation between the dental surgeon, the field surgeon and the anaesthetist.

At each echelon the condition of the patient requires critical assessment as to what surgical measures are essential to make him fit to travel to a more favourable centre for treatment.

Initial surgical treatment should be minimal, consistent with the patient's safety. The facilities available, including anaesthetic skill, the time and distance in transport and quality of skilled attendance on the way to a special maxillo-facial centre must be evaluated.

It cannot be too strongly emphasized that surgical treatment of face and jaw wounds is best conducted by special units having a dental and plastic surgeon working in close proximity and with the co-operation of specialists in anaesthesia, oto-rhino-laryngology, neurosurgery and ophthalmic surgery. Technical assistance and workshop facilities are also needed for the preparation of intra-and extra-oral dental appliances. At least 25 per cent of maxillo-facial injuries have associated injuries of the head or eyes. Experience has shown that it is better for the patient to arrive at a special unit up to 48 hours after being wounded than that he should have had an earlier but incomplete or mismanaged primary operation.

Evacuation

Patients with maxillo-facial injuries normally travel well by air if at an altitude not requiring the use of an oxygen mask. Certain types of mandibular fracture are painful and limit the ease with which the patient can swallow. These patients should be immobilized by means of elastic traction or placed face down on a stretcher in a semi-prone position. A tracheostomy should be performed prior to travel on patients in whom respiratory difficulty is anticipated. The idea that a suture through the tongue is adequate control is short sighted and since tracheostomy is a life saving procedure creating little or no psychological trauma this is the preferred treatment.

It may be necessary to release the intermaxillary fixation and so fixation by elastic bands is the method of choice. By accepting this as a standard procedure one can eliminate difficulty during the patient's subsequent travel. Attendants travelling with maxillo-facial cases should be specially instructed in the dangers of respiratory obstruction and the methods of dealing with emergencies as they arise. They should see that the patient has a device for feeding, such as a feeding cup with rubber tubing or a teaspoon, for long journeys.

Clinical examination

A routine method of visual inspection and careful digital palpation should be carried out by regions. Both sides should be examined simultaneously for comparison. Areas of contusion, swelling and emphysema, points of tenderness, alteration or distortion of bony landmarks, eyeball levels and nose are noted.

Testing should always be done for diplopia and analgesia indicating nerve injury. The examiner should look especially for subconjunctival haemorrhage, cerebrospinal otorrhoea and rhinorrhoea. He should discover whether the temporo-mandibular joint is functioning normally or has restricted movement. The palate and buccal sulci and the alignment of the upper and lower teeth and alveoli require detailed attention. Haematoma, bruising and tears of the mucous membrane of the cheeks, gums and floor of the mouth will suggest damage to the body of the mandible. Examine dental occlusion – if it is abnormal, try to determine the cause. A 'gagging' or open bite is commonly due to fractures of the ramus or fracture/dislocation of the condyle of the mandible but may be caused by a horizontal fracture of the tooth bearing area of the maxilla (Guerin fracture), a loose or displaced tooth, or haematoma over a posterior fragment.

INITIAL SURGICAL CARE

Respiratory obstruction

For the emergency relief of respiratory obstruction see Chapter 2 page 28.

Indications for tracheostomy (Tracheostomy page 262)

a Where there is any doubt about the continuing patency of the airway with inadequate supervision post-operatively and especially during evacuation.

b Wounds of the jaw associated with laryngeal and some pharyngeal injuries.

c Intermaxillary fixation (IMF) of the jaws, accompanied by nasal airway obstruction due to fractures or other causes (any indication of respiratory obstruction requires release of IMF).

General measures

a *Arrest of haemorrhage* In bleeding from deep wounds, eg bullet in maxillary antrum, packing is necessary. Otherwise locate the site of bleeding with suitable retraction, good light and suction. Digital or gauze pressure will, given adequate time, usually arrest oozing. A light haemostat may be then precisely applied to any remaining bleeding point and the vessel ligated. Proximal ligation of the external carotid artery is rarely necessary.

b The *treatment of shock* will follow accepted usage. Severe pain is not a usual feature of maxillo-facial injuries. However, if the patient is suspected of having cranio-cerebral injury and is complaining of pain, paraldehyde or chloral hydrate may be given. Morphine is contraindicted where there is respiratory obstruction and in all cases with associated cranio-cerebral injury. The evacuation of stomach contents and the avoidance of fluids by mouth for some four hours previous to general anaesthesia must be kept in mind, having regard to the technical hazards connected with injuries of this region.

c *Prevention of infection* (See Chapter 4.) Except in ascending ramus and condylar lesions almost all facial fractures are compound. Careful toilet of the teeth and frequent and adequate irrigation of the mouth with a mild antiseptic solution until healing is complete are important.

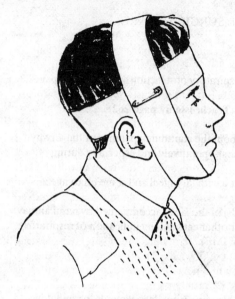

Figure 17 Vertical bandage

Figure 18 Elastic sling

Wound toilet and primary closure

Repeated lavage with soap and water or a suitable detergent washing all layers of the wound is a necessary preliminary to surgery. Ingrained dirt may lead to infection and scar pigmentation and must be removed by gentle scrubbing with a soft brush (eg toothbrush) aided by fine forceps and needle or scalpel point. It is wise to cut the hair short but the hairline should be marked or left to serve as a guide for the accurate placement of skin flaps. The eyebrows should not be shaved. Tissues should be handled gently, preferably using skin hooks and fine forceps. Only 1–2 mm of skin edge should be trimmed to provide non-contaminated non-bevelled edges which can be accurately approximated. Ophthalmic scissors and a sharp No 15 blade are used. Soiled tags of deeper tissues and mucosa are removed by scissors. The closure is carried out after any dental or fracture fixation. The initial closure is done intra-orally on the mucosa following which the wound is cleaned of saliva by gentle scrubbing and saline lavage. Facial closure may be by approximation after undermining of the skin edge for 2–5 cm. This approximation should never be allowed to produce tension anywhere. The blood supply of facial tissues is so adequate and the resistance to infection so high that primary closure is preferred to delayed two-stage closure.

Distortion of the lips and eyelids   When a closure is impossible without such distortion a free graft or flap may be considered (by an experienced surgeon) or if the wound involves all layers of the cheek a muco-cutaneous suture should be employed. Where there is bone destruction in addition, the mucous membrane of the buccal surface should be sutured to the margins of the skin in such a fashion that the fractured surfaces of bone are covered. Defects of bone will be replaced by grafts after healing.

Where a defect is large, or on account of its position, difficult to close, the surgeon should concentrate on a thorough toilet and careful removal of grossly soiled and dead tissue. All flaps of skin unless obviously gangrenous must be conserved. After fixation of bone fragments the flaps are replaced in their normal position and retained by means of a few sutures tied without tension.

Surgical care of bone fragments

The rule is to conserve all viable bone fragments except those that are grossly soiled by indriven foreign bodies which will later sequestrate.

Detached fragments can be sterilized in boiling water and replaced to act as chip grafts. If the mouth has not been excluded by a watertight closure of the mucous membrane, the fracture site should be drained to the exterior. The drain is removed in two to five days. Bone should not be left bare but should always be covered by soft tissue. A mandibular stump should be covered by suturing mucous membrane to the skin edge.

The problem of teeth in fractured jaws

At the time of the primary operation only teeth that are completely loose should be removed. Firmly embedded teeth near fracture lines are best left alone. Even damaged and injured teeth will be useful for the immobilization of fractures during the early weeks. Molar teeth in otherwise edentulous fragments are especially valuable for fixation. Dead, carious and loose teeth may cause infection and act as sequestra and their extraction may be indicated later after the primary operation in order to control infection of fracture sites. The risk of dislodging a major bone fragment by dental extraction must be assessed.

Haematomas should be avoided by draining large facial wounds but care must be taken in the closure of face wounds after conservation excision in order to encourage primary healing and the minimizing of scar formation. Tension must be avoided. For the skin, the finest nylon or serum proofed silk is used, preferably mounted on fine eyeless needles. Stitches should be introduced close to the skin edges and close together (3 mm apart). When possible the application of a pressure bandage is indicated for the prevention of haematoma and oedema. Sutures should be removed after four days and skin relaxing steristrip applied, and permitted to remain for four to five days. The oral mucous membrane is closed with fine chromic catgut. A watertight closure over a fracture is desirable. When the wound is through and through or involves a muscle layer it should be closed in layers.

Methods of immobilization of fractured jaws

Immobilization is necessary for the early union of fractures; fixation of bone fragments is done at the primary operation. It generally follows the toilet and debridement and precedes the closure. Since dental splints take time to construct it is advisable that a uniform type of wire splint be used on most cases involving associated facial lacerations and that fixation be with elastic traction. This will assure rapid treatment of a primary nature and facilitiate early evacuation of the patient. The jaw can be immobilized by the following methods:

a Elastic bands;

b Intermaxillary wires;

c The patient's dentures may be placed in position and inter-denture fixation done by means of wire; it is advisable to remove one or two anterior teeth for feeding purposes;

d A lower denture may be fixed to the mandible by circumferential wiring but it is also advisable to immobilize the mandible to the maxilla;

e An upper denture may be fixed to the maxilla by suspension from the zygomatic arches by means of circumferential wiring and by trans-alveolar wiring.

NB: If intermaxillary fixation is done and oedema or haematoma of the floor of the mouth is present, a review of the patient's respiration is necessary to ensure that it is unobstructed. In bandaging the jaw it is essential to secure vertical support for the mandible. A backward pull, such as that of a four-tailed bandage, leads to retraction of the mandible, the malposition of fracture surfaces and respiratory embarrassment.

Some cases with multiple fractures and edentulous jaws or irregular dentition cannot be fixed by wiring. For these, extra-oral pins or cast metal cap splints may be used. If possible, this provision should be made before operation. When these fractures do not communicate with the mouth direct wiring of fragments is satisfactory.

Feeding and nursing

As with patients suffering from other injuries, a balanced, high calorie, high protein diet is important and should commence as early as possible.

Patients without intermaxillary fixation can be given minced meat, eggs, pounded fish, soft cheese, soft fruits and mashed vegetables, and all ordinary fluids.

Patients with intermaxillary fixation will require their diet thin enough to suck through a tube. Milk reinforced with cream, milk powder and lactose or glucose, thin custards and thick soups at two-hour intervals and at least four ounces in quantity are usually given to make up 2000 – 3000 calories daily.

Certain cases will require feeding through an intra-nasal or intra-oral gastric tube. A drinking cup with an 8 inch spout (20 cm) of rubber tubing attached is useful to introduce a fluid diet well back over the tongue or a clean bottle with a length of tubing and filled with fluid food, inverted and suspended at the bed head or on a stand, can be used.

Owing to the dribbling of saliva, dressings of wounds become rapidly soaked unless protected by waterproof covering. A large waterproof infant's bib should be worn to protect clothing.

The lips may need protection from the wires used for IMF and pieces of gutta percha may be used. Lubrication of the lips and nostrils helps to prevent fissures and sores. After each feeding the teeth are cleansed with a soft brush and the mouth should be washed out with two per cent bicarbonate of soda or saline solution, followed by a mild antiseptic.

It is important to instruct and make these patients perform their own mouth and teeth toilets. This will benefit their morale and lessen the strain on the nursing staff.

INDIVIDUAL INJURIES AND FRACTURES

Multiple fractures of the mandible

a *Location*   A blow on the point of the chin may cause bilateral fractures of the condyles or may fracture the centre of the body near the symphysis menti. A strong force striking the lateral aspect of the mandible will fracture it at the site of impact and may also fracture the bone near the canine tooth or the condylar neck of the opposite side. Fractures of the angle, ascending (vertical) ramus, condyle and coronoid processes also occur. Always suspect multiple fractures in this bone.

b *Clinical features*   The normal movement of the jaw is usually restricted. A tender spot or abnormal mobility may be felt. Tearing of the gums and compound injury into the mouth is common. There may be irregularity of the teeth and abnormal occlusion with the teeth of the maxilla or deviation to one side. Swelling and bruises of the fauces, lateral wall of the pharynx and soft palate may be seen in severe fractures of the ascending (vertical) ramus.

c *Methods of fixation*

(1)   Vertical bandage; adhesive bandage; elastic sling attached to a canvas headcap (see Figs 17 and 18).

(2)   Where teeth are present in both fragments of mandible and maxilla; interdental and intermaxillary wiring using non-corrosive steel ligature or cap splinting (See Fig 19).

(3)   Teeth in both fragments of mandible with loss of bone substance: interdental wires until cap splints are made and fitted.

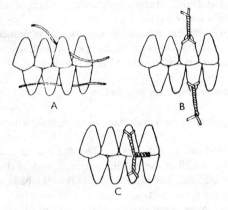

"Direct method"

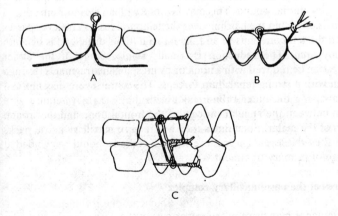

"Eyelet technique"

Figure 19 Interdental wiring

(4)   Edentulous mandible and maxilla; interlocking upper and lower plastic splints resembling dentures, or circumferential wires.
(5)   Fracture of ascending (vertical) ramus: cap splints or interdental wiring. Immobilize for 14 days.
(6)   Fracture of condyle or fracture/dislocation: try to reduce at once as for simple dislocation. Do not perform open reduction at this stage. Immobilize in correct occlusion using elastic traction.

Fractures of the malar-maxillary complex

Fractures of the zygomatic arch and of the malar-maxilla are due to direct violence. The malar prominence, or zygoma, is flattened but the deformity may at first be concealed by swelling. Where the lower fracture line is low, the lateral wall of the maxillary antrum will be damaged and the cavity filled with blood. The infra-orbital nerve may be injured. If the roof of the antrum is fractured there will be subconjunctival haemorrhage and the level of the lower outer margin of the orbit is depressed causing diplopia. Depression of the zygoma impinging on the coronoid process may interfere with the opening and closing the mouth and there may be dental malocclusion.

Treatment   Depressed fractures should be reduced at once provided there is no external wound. This may be done with an elevator introduced by an incision within the hairline over the temporal fossa. The lever passes between the temporal muscle and the fascia until its distal end is beneath the bony arch. The reduction is usually stable. Some of the easier fractures can be reduced with a hook or by grasping the fragments through the skin with a strong tenaculum forceps. The more severe decompressions, involving the outer orbital floor with diplopia, may require wire fixation between the angular process of the frontal bone and the frontal process of the malar. Sometimes they will require maxillary antral packs to raise the orbit level. These more serious methods should be avoided at the stage of primary treatment.

Fractures of the naso-maxillary complex

Direct violence may drive in the upper part of the nose near the glabella. The bridge of the nose is depressed and the tip tilted upwards. The upper part of the septum and ethmoid as well as the nasals and the nasal processes of the maxilla are fractured. If the impact on the nose is lower down, separation of the nasal bones in the midline occurs with their lateral margins overlapping the nasal processes of the maxilla resulting in marked broadening. The septum may be fractured or dislocated. Lateral violence will splay the nose to one side. The nasal bone on the side of the impact will be driven beneath the opposite nasal bone, raising it.

Treatment Haemorrhage may be so profuse as to require intra-nasal packing with ribbon gauze moistened with sterile saline, but this should be removed as early as possible to effect early reduction. Packing is contraindicated in the presence of cerebro-spinal rhinorrhoea. Early correction of the deformity and restoration of the nasal airways is obligatory. Nasal forceps are used to reduce septal deformity and manipulate the nasal bones into the normal position. Every effort should be made to restore the height of the nasal bridge. In the absence of nasal forceps, blunt-pointed scissors or a sponge-holding forceps can be used. Lateral displacements can usually be corrected by finger manipulation. Nasal forceps with one blade on each side of the septum are used to correct septal dislocations. To disimpact nasal bones one blade should be inside and one outside the nose. The blades of the forceps or scissors used should be protected by rubber tubing. When the reduction is complete the position is often stable without splinting but finger cots packed with wool may be inserted in each nasal cavity for 24 hours. Lubricated soft rubber tubing passed through each nostril back as far as the level of the soft palate is useful and re-dressings should be performed under direct vision. External splinting is sometimes required to maintain the corrected position and small plaster slabs, rubber pads, stent, or soft lead or layers of adhesive tape may be used. To retain very unstable fractures of the nasal bridge, through and through wire sutures tied over such outside support may be necessary. Open wounds of the nose are treated by toilet and excision and careful primary closure without tension as for wounds elsewhere on the face. The adjoining skin may require undermining to effect apposition without tension. In major skin loss muco-cutaneous suture will be necessary to obtain soft tissue cover of exposed bone and fractures. Avoid distortion of the lips and nostrils in such closure.

Bilateral naso-maxillar fractures

In these major fractures the maxillae are displaced backwards 'en bloc' between the malar bones. At first there is marked swelling of the whole central area of the face which conceals intitially the depressed 'dish face' deformity. There may be associated eye, ear and brain damage. Many show cerebro-spinal fluid leaks (rhinorrhoea or otorrhoea.) They should be transferred as early as possible to a special centre where neurosurgical and other specialists are available. Penicillin and sulphadimidine will be given. Diplopia may be present because the upper part of the fracture displaces the floors of the orbits. There will be malocclusion and the upper teeth lie behind the lower. The lower border of the maxilla may be rotated upwards so that only back (molar) teeth can meet. This is one of the causes of 'open bite.' The maxillae may be 'floating' ie grossly displaced and freely movable with a blocked airway.

As with all injuries of the facial skeleton early reduction of the deformity is important and because of the associated injuries in the region of the ethmoid and floor of the anterior fossa of the skull reduction of the displacement will diminish the risk of infection of the meningeal spaces and of other areas. Impacted fractures can readily reduced within the first few days but firm union takes place rapidly and restoration after 10 days is difficult and not without danger.

Treatment   The nasal airway is first restored as described under nasal injuries. The maxillary alveolus is gripped with strong sharp-toothed forceps and rocked if necessary to disimpact the displacement. The maxillary fragment must then be immobilized in correct occlusion with the mandible. The mandible is then connected externally to a plaster skull cap by means of outside rods and universal joints. In some cases, in order to maintain the forward position of the main bone fragment, wires are inserted through both maxillae and brought outside through the skin of the cheeks and attached to a plaster head-band.

Open wounds of the maxilla

The fixation of displaced and mobile fragments in open maxillary wounds is as for closed fractures. Conservation of alveolar bone fragments and those of the floor of the orbit is essential.

Fractures of the palate

a *Palatal alveolar fractures*   Here a section of the alveolus with its teeth is displaced. It may involve the maxillary antrum and the nasal floor. Replacement and fixation is secured by cap splints, or by interdental splinting.

b *Horizontal fracture* – separation of the palate (Guerin.) This follows a blow in the region of the nasal spine which separates and drives the palate backwards. There is malocclusion with the upper incisor teeth behind the lower. The main fragment may be rotated causing an 'open bite.'

Reduction is effected in the same manner as described for major bilateral naso-maxillary fractures.

c *Vertical separation fracture of the palate*   This causes separations of the upper incisors with splitting of the palate in the midline.

Reduction is by manual pressure approximating the two sides and is retained by elastic inter-dental bands or cap splinting and approximation by means of a horizontal adjustable palatal rod.

CHAPTER 23

Injuries of the ear, nose and throat

External ear

Lacerations Wounds of the pinna and external auditory meatus require careful cleansing with early replacement of the damaged parts. Should a portion of the auricle be lost, the defect should be defined by suture of the anterior and posterior skin layers over the exposed cartilaginous edge. The remaining fragments of the auricle should not be sutured to each other out of the normal position.

Should the external auditory meatus be torn through completely, careful suture should be made using catgut, the lumen of the meatus being packed with narrow ribbon gauze soaked in paraffin and acriflavine. Should injuries of the meatus be neglected, stenosis will occur. This is to be avoided at all costs.

A haematoma of the pinna should be treated by aspiration or evacuated under strict aseptic precautions, and the ear protected with a firm sterile dressing.

Middle ear

Rupture of the tympanic membrane Injury to the tympanic membrane is common and is often associated with other and frequently more serious injuries. It is thus prone to be overlooked immediately. Damage may be caused by: direct penetration; fracture of the base of the skull involving the tympanic ring; sudden compression of air in the auditory meatus. The last may cause diverse effects varying with the degree of trauma. In its simplest form small haemorrhages may occur into the substance of the membrane, or there may be rupture of the outer fibres of the drum, a linear tear or complete disintegration. The great subsequent danger is infection.

Symptoms of injury to the middle ear may be obscured or absent. When damage to the drum is suspected, the ear should be examined with care, observing strict aseptic precautions.

Should rupture have occurred, all interference should be avoided and the outer ear protected with a sterile dressing or loose sterile cotton wool.

The latter is less desirable as it may become forgotten and remain for a long period in situ with consequent liability to infection. No drops or local medication should be allowed in the ear and on no account will syringing be done if there is any suspicion of a rupture of the drum.

Wax, when present, should be left undisturbed for a period of approximately one month from the date of injury unless there are local indications for its removal, eg pain or deafness. In this case treatment by an aural surgeon is required.

Rupture of the tympanic membrane associated with damage to the pinna sufficient to require treatment, necessitates packing the meatus with sterile wool whilst preliminary cleansing of the outer ear is being undertaken.

Avoidance of acute naso-pharyngeal infection is of great importance until the tympanic membrane is healed. During this period blowing the nose is contra-indicated and should further exposure to blast be inevitable, ear protection should be provided.

Chemotherapeutic and antibiotic agents The administration of chemotherapy or antibiotic agents as a routine measure is not required but is necessary in the presence of concomitant otitis externa or tympanic rupture complicating a basal fracture.

Spread to the meninges may be rapid in a case of basal fracture with a concomitant tympanic rupture. Sulpha, penicillin or other powders will not be insufflated into the meatus. It leads to caking and removal may later cause difficulty.

Aero-otitis; otitic barotrauma Sudden alteration of pressure on either side of the tympanic membrane, such as may occur in aviation or in diving, cause ear changes. The initial precipitation factor is blockage of the Eustachian tube, followed by extreme retraction of the tympanic membrane, oedema of the mucosa lining the middle ear cleft and, in more extreme cases, the formation of a serous exudate which is sometimes blood-stained and often mixed with bubbles. Deafness is pronounced whilst pain may be severe.

If early inflation of the Eustachian tube fails, puncture of the tympanic membrane by a fine gauge sharp needle after cleaning the meatus by spirit is indicated. The procedure is painless, and anaesthesia is not required.

Equalization of pressures immediately relieves symptoms.

Internal ear

Injuries Damage to the inner ear may be caused by continuous loud noise, blast, otitic barotrauma.

There may or may not be evidence of middle ear injury.

The presenting symptoms are: deafness, high-pitched tinnitus; vertigo in some severe cases.

It is essential that such patients avoid exposure to further acoustic trauma for at least a month to obviate permanent damage. If vertigo and tinnitus are severe they may be relieved by administration of betahistine hydrochloride 8 mg three times daily. Vertiginous symptoms may also be relieved by use of Avomine 25 mg twice daily.

Nose and para-nasal air sinuses

Haematoma of the nasal septum After thorough cleansing of the anterior nares a free incision is made, under aseptic conditions, into the anterior and dependent portion of the haematoma, which is evacuated of blood. A small roll of sterile gauze is then affixed over the nostrils, being held in place by tapes tied across the back of the head.

Neglect of a septal haematoma leads to infection, abscess formation, cartilaginous necrosis, and nasal deformity.

Fractures of the nose (see page 252)

a *Simple* If treated early, ideally within 48 hours, reduction and the maintenance of the fragments in position will seldom present any difficulty. For accurate replacement of fragments complete disimpaction is essential. External splintage will be required; this is conveniently made either of dental compounds such as stent, plaster of Paris or from thin lead sheet.

Badly comminuted fractures showing considerable collapse of the nasal bridge will require full support after reduction. This is best achieved by through and through sutures of nylon or silkworm gut or alternatively of fine wire, tied over small lateral lead plates.

b *Compound* Thorough cleansing and early reduction are essential. Should the wound be clean, immediate closure with bony fixation as stated above is recommended. Free drainage should be provided and chemotherapeutic or antibiotic cover given.

Maxillary antrum

a Simple *effusions of blood* into the antrum are usually quickly absorbed and best left alone. If infection be suspected proof puncture and lavage should be employed.

b *Foreign bodies*   When the maxillary antrum contains foreign bodies or bony fragments, it should be opened by the sub-labial route, cleaned out and counter drainage established into the inferior meatus of the nose.

c *Depressed fractures*   In the cases of fracture with depression of the orbital floor and/or anterior wall, it will be necessary to elevate the fragments and retain the position by means of an antral pack impregnated with penicillin or pigment iodoform compound BPC.

Malar depressions or similar fractures of the zygomatic arch should be elevated as soon as possible by means of a lever introduced between the temporal muscle and temporal fascia through a small incision within the hair line, over the temporal fossa.

Other fractures may sometimes be reduced by grasping the fragment through the skin with tenaculum forceps and manipulation by means of a finger introduced into the mouth high up in the buccolabial sulcus.

In difficult and, in particular, difficult late cases, a combined operation employing the Caldwell-Luc approach with that of the temporal route is recommended. After reduction, suspension to wires attached to a bracket embedded in a plaster head-cap is required.

With severe deformity and much bony loss, replacement by bone graft taken from the iliac crest is necessary.

Frontal sinus   Injuries to the forehead involving the frontal sinus require both functional restoration and cosmetic repair. The external approach is necessary. In severe injuries a scalp incision following the hair line may well give the best exposure. All loose fragments of bone and blood clot should be removed from the sinus which is drained into the nose by a plastic or rubber tube surrounded by a Thiersch graft.

When the posterior wall of the frontal sinus is fractured and the dura torn, a repair by fascia lata graft is necessary. The case is more properly one for the neuro-surgeon. Fascia lata is also required for fractures of the ethmoidal region complicated by cerebro-spinal rhinorrhoea.

Ethmoidal labyrinth   After injury, operation on this area should, if possible, be avoided for at least fourteen days. Approach by the external route is the only feasible method. Early penicillin cover is essential.

Should obstruction of the fronto-nasal duct seem likely insertion of a skin graft will be required.

Aero-sinusitis Sudden alteration in barometric pressure produces definite changes in the mucosa of the paranasal sinuses. The symptoms are those of acute pain referred to the general area of the affected sinus.

Within a sinus, small petechial haemorrhages may be seen in the lining mucosa, a submucosal haematoma may form or there may be actual haemorrhage into the sinus cavity. In very severe cases the lining mucosa may be torn and detached from the bony walls.

Treatment is conservative, consisting of rest, sedation, simple inhalations of menthol together with instillation of 0.5 per cent solution of ephedrine in normal saline into the nose. If interference is avoided it is unlikely that infections will supervene. Should acute suppuration develop, simple intra-nasal drainage is recommended.

Pharynx

Injuries Wounds of the naso- and oro-pharynx are commonly associated with extensive neck wounds, fractures of the maxilla or the ascending ramus. If the patient survives a perforating wound or through and through injury, the danger is from haemorrhage or from infection of the para-pharyngeal space. The internal wound should be treated by suction toilet, digital exploration and removal of dead pieces of tissue.

Wounds involving the laryngo-pharynx are serious, as saliva and secretions can contaminate the tissue planes of the neck. A wide and well planned exposure is essential so that haemostasis and cleansing of the wound may be affected. Where primary repair of the pharynx by approximation is possible this should be done. Where this is impossible due to tissue loss and removal of devitalized tissue, a pharyngostomy should be planned, suturing the skin to the exposed pharyngeal mucosa. The defect may be filled by means of a shell dressing of a vaseline gauze tampon.

Antibiotics will be given as early as possible to restrict the spread of infection. This is of paramount importance.

Larynx

Indirect effects of injury Blows on the neck and wounds in the region of the larynx may cause a laryngeal haematoma and/or damage to one or both vagus nerves. Treatment is complete rest with the patient in the sitting position, ready for an immediate tracheostomy should this prove necessary. It is better to perform a tracheostomy too early than to temporize and leave it too late.

Simple direct injuries   Blows on the structure of the larynx may cause a dislocation or a fracture of the cartilages of the laryngeal cage, or may injure its intrinsic soft tissue. These injuries are not serious per se, but there is an immediate danger of laryngeal obstruction from oedema or from submucosal haemorrhage. Complete rest, sitting up in bed, is essential. Although tracheostomy is to be avoided if possible, all must be held in readiness should any deterioration be observed. The most careful observation is required and evacuation over any distance postponed until danger of acute laryngeal obstruction has passed.

Compound injuries   Compound injuries are of the utmost seriousness, on account of haemorrhage into the trachea, surgical emphysema, infection of the tissue planes and perichondritis of the laryngeal cartilages.

The immediate treatment is to maintain a clear airway and prevent ingress of blood into the lungs. Suction may be life-saving.

Tracheostomy through the second and third rings of the trachea should be performed as early as possible.

A local anaesthetic is the method of choice.

Coughing should be encouraged and the patient is nursed in the sitting position to avoid pulmonary complications. For this reason too, morphine is contra-indicated.

The cartilages of the larynx and of the trachea are vulnerable. Improvised airways and tracheostomy tubes, if left in contact for more than a few hours, will cause perichondritis and subsequent stenosis.

Effects of war gases and smoke   Inhalation of irritant gases produces intense congestion, quickly followed by a massive oedema of the laryngeal mucosa. This quickly breaks down with ulceration, secondary infection occurs and perichodritis quickly follows. Tracheostomy should be performed as soon as signs of laryngeal deterioration are observed.

Plastic repairs for late sequelae   All operative procedures to relieve the effects of wounds in and around the laryngeal area are long-term measures and are delayed until healing is completed. The late sequelae of injuries of the larynx include fixation of the vocal cords and laryngeal stenosis from perichondritis or organization of granulations into scar tissue. Fixation of the crico-arytenoid joints, paralysis of the recurrent laryngeal nerves and tracheo-oesophagael fistulae also occur. Recovery of function after a vagus nerve injury may occur up to two years.

Trachea

Emergency tracheostomy

a *Indications in field surgery*   Clinical discrimination must be used. It is better to perform a tracheostomy early and possibly unnecessarily than too late.

(1) Mechanical obstruction   Inflammation of trachea and larynx; burns of the face, mouth or air passages; maxillo-facial injuries. Injuries of the neck, foreign bodies in the larynx or air passages.

(2) Interference with pulmonary ventilation, due to secretions. Head injury; chest injury; burns of the respiratory tract, the effects of war gases; blast injuries; fat and air embolism; tetanus; barbiturate poisoning; post-operatively – usually head, maxillo-facial, neck and chest operations if there is doubt in the operator's mind about the continuing adequacy of the airway especially as to facilities for proper supervision during the post-operative and evacuation stages.

b *Technique*   A low tracheostomy is preferable. Only under rare circumstances or urgency and in the hand of an inexperienced operator should the incision involve the first tracheal ring or the cricoid cartilage. If it is difficult to get the patient in the proper position it may be necessary to do a high tracheostomy as a life-saving procedure. This should, however, be followed by a revision, making it into a low tracheostomy. With the high tracheostomy there is danger of laryngeal stenosis.

The position of the patient is very important. He should be placed supine on a table (or bed), and the shoulders raised on a sandbag or folded linen so as to extend the neck. Analgesia, if indicated and permitted, is produced by the usual method of infiltration with one per cent novocaine or xylocaine. The injection should be subcutaneous, beginning above the suprasternal notch and carried upwards in the midline to the level of the thyroid cartilage.

The incision may be longitudinal or transverse. The transverse incision is preferable and will ensure a better cosmetic result, but the longitudinal incision will ensure an almost bloodless and faster exposure of the trachea.

Making a longitudinal incision from the cricoid cartilage down to the suprasternal notch, the incision is carried in the midline through skin and platysma. Bleeding is usually minimal because there are no large vessels in the midline. The strap muscles are then split in the midline by blunt dissection and retracted, thereby exposing the trachea. The isthmus of the thyroid is often encountered and this is cut between clamps and tied. If small, the isthmus may be retracted downward.

If available, a few drops of four per cent solution of cocaine are now injected into the tracheal lumen to reduce the cough reflex. The pretracheal fascia over the cricoid is divided transversely and stripped downward. There is only one ideal level at which to cut the trachea, and that is at the level of the second and third tracheal rings. By holding the trachea firmly with a tenaculum a small circular area of tracheal cartilage is removed, using a No 11 blade knife. The stoma in the trachea should be the size of the tube to be used. The tube is then inserted through the stoma. Suction should be available to remove the secretions from the trachea. If no suction is available, the head should be lowered once the trachea has been loosely opened. The skin incision is loosely closed with interrupted sutures to avoid surgical emphysema.

Where there is extreme urgency and the operator lacks experience or assistance, laryngotomy should be performed. By finger palpation the thyroid cartilage is located and just below this a smaller protruberance is felt; this is the cricoid cartilage, the space betweent the cricoid and thyroid cartilage is avascular. A transverse incision is made in this space and the tracheal lumen is readily entered. A rubber or plastic tube can be placed through this opening and held in place by suturing it to the skin. In the absence of tubing, a clamp can be used as a temporary measure to keep the incision open.

CHAPTER 24

Cold injury

Introduction

The prevention, recognition and treatment of cold injury conserves manpower. Local cold injury should not occur in any army, given proper equipment, good training and rigid discipline.

Prevention

a *Trench foot* Keep the feet dry and clean; use foot powder. Frequent changes of clean dry socks. Suitable footwear; use of insoles. Maintain good circulation in lower limbs by exercise, correct posture, massage and avoidance of constriction. Drainage of ground; use of duck boards. Personal health discipline.

b *Frost bite* Correct use of suitable clothing, especially in regard to insulation, wind-proofing and avoidance of damp. Shelter from wind whenever possible; improvisation. Keep equipment as dry as possible, especially sleeping bags. Do not touch metal with bare hands. Work in pairs and watch each other for early signs of frost bite; revive affected parts without delay. Hot food and hot drinks; avoid alcohol. Personal health discipline.

The conditions under which lesions due to cold readily occur are:

a *A DRY COLD climate* Snow and ice are usually present and the temperature seldom rises above 0 °C (32 °F.) Exposure is conducive to frost bite.

b *A WET COLD climate* with rain, sleet and mud. It can be found on land or sea and is typical of winter in so-called temperate zones where the temperature ranges from 10 °C (50 °F) to – 12 °C (10 °F). On land these conditions predispose to frost bite and trench foot. Immersion foot, which etiologically resembles trench foot, may occur on exposure to sea water while total body immersion causes general hypothermia. Both the above climates can be found at HIGH ALTITUDES. In all such environments the hazards are aggravated by WIND.

Previous injury from cold increases an individual's susceptibility to cold lesions.

Pathogenesis

Causative factors

a *General exposure*   With body cooling, the temperature, humidity, wind and altitude lead to, or increase, body heat loss. Cold, wet, windy conditions are treacherous.

b *Local chilling*   This varies with the degree and rate of heat loss which is accelerated by direct exposure, wetness, wind and contact with a cold surface.

Below freezing point

a *The initial reaction*   Tissue chilling leads to arteriolar contraction to reduce further heat loss. If moderate, only a slowing of capillary blood flow occurs. If intense, blood flow ceases, and unless momentary, a degree of injury proportional to the duration of ischaemia results. Tissue contact with a frozen object leads to freezing of the superficial tissues to a depth proportional to the temperature and duration of contact. This may be instantaneous.

b *The chilling reaction*   Deep to the frozen tissue zone, chilling leads to an increase in blood viscosity which augments the effect of arteriolar spasm in producing stasis. This extends the depth of the injury to tissues above freezing point. Prompt re-warming limits this effect.

c *Arterio-venous shunts*   Capillary stasis, in the absence of re-warming, leads to by-passing of the affected area by direct communications between arterioles and venules. The shunts are intermittent and lead to alternate warming and chilling of the affected area, with an overall effect of continuing inadequately compensated body heat loss and a falling core temperature, as cooled venous blood returns to the heart. At a 'danger point' in the core temperature the shunts cease and freezing of the part commences and extends with general body cooling unless urgently treated.

d *Hypovolaemic shock*   Blood loss produced by other injuries decreases the blood volume and depletes the peripheral circulation, accelerating the cold injury.

e *Physical factors*   The progress of vascular spasm and statsis to freezing is accompanied by the formation of ice crystals in the extra-cellular fluid. This increases its tonicity and produces cellular dehydration. Intensive freezing may produce intra-cellular ice formation. Either of these factors disrupts the normal metabolic processes of the cell. Tissues vary in their

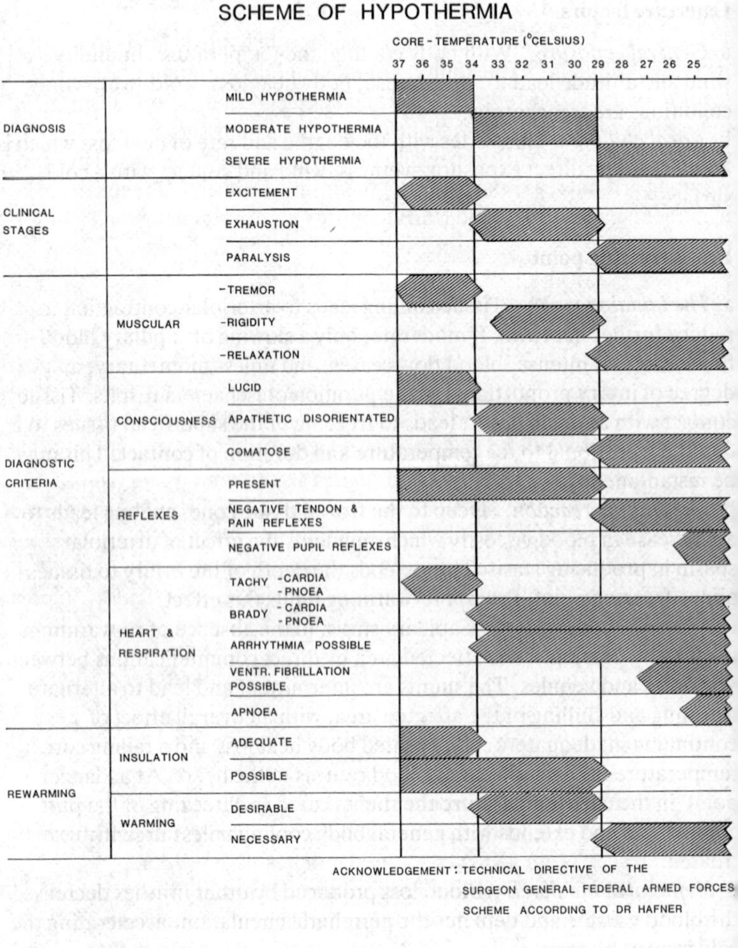

Figure 20   Scheme of hypothermia

susceptibility to cold – most easily injured are skin and blood vessels, then nerves and muscles, progressing to the relatively resistant structure of tendon and bone.

f *Thawing*   Vascular endothelial damage from hypoxia leads to increased capillary permeability. On thawing, the resultant plasma leak leads to oedema, blister formation and haemoconcentration, again increasing stasis and hypoxia. The effect of this on tissues whose metabolic requirements, especially for oxygen, have been raised by warming is to increase the extent of the injury. Associated reactive hyperaemia adds to this and leads to more extensive oedema and blistering.

Above freezing point

Serious injury may result from arteriolar spasm with persisting hypoxia and deficient cell nutrition, resembling the area around frozen tissue. Prolonged exposure can produce this in a temperature as high as 10 °C (50 °F). This occurs in trench foot and immersion foot after long periods in cold, wet clothing or immersion in cold water. The tissue damage may equal that of freezing. The oedema, blistering, muscle and nerve damage produced may be reversible, depending on the severity of the exposure and adequacy of the circulation. Tissue loss is often minimal. Cold, by reducing the metabolic needs of a tissue, reduces its sensitivity to hypoxia and so, to a limited extent, is protective.

Clinical features of cold injury

a. *General hypothermia*

(1)   Acute heat loss, as occurs in immersion in icy sea water (about −2 °C or −28 °F), leads to a rapid fall in core temperature which can be fatal if rescue is not achieved in three minutes. Even at core temperature of 35 °C there is reduced mental capacity with reduced initiative and inability to make proper judgements, followed by increased blurring of the mind down to 31 °C (88 °F) where there may be total unconsciousness. Shivering begins, but ceases at 30 °C (86 °F) and then body heat loss becomes proportional to the body-environment temperature difference. Muscle spasm flexes the body and impairs respiration. Voluntary muscle power is lost, particularly of the digits. Death from cardiac arrest – or more often ventricular fibrillation, may

occur – quite often but not always within the interval 28 °C – 22 °C. Below 22 °C cardiac arrhythmias are rare. Re-warming through this range should be done under cardiac monitoring.

(2)   Less acute heat loss, as occurs in arctic conditions on land with exposure and severe fatigue, gives rise to progressive deterioration in central nervous function. Initially an ataxic gait and fatigue progress to disturbed cerebration, drowsiness and unconsciousness which is not influenced by violent shivering.

At 30 °C (86 °F) patients are unconscious and often pulseless, but tendon and pupillary reflexes persist. The diagnosis of death is difficult and failure to revive on re-warming is the only real criterion.
Respiration is not recognizable, but is sufficient as there is shifting of the dissociation curve and a great decrease in oxygen consumption.
27 °C (78 °F) is regarded as dangerous, with death from cardiac arrest in ventricular fibrillation.

(3)   Pulmonary damage may follow hyperventilation after strenous exertion, eg at cold, high altitudes. Haemoptysis and bronchospasm occur.

b. Local cold injury

Frost bite   Frost bite is caused by temperatures below freezing and is confined to extremities and exposed areas of the body. Numbness of exposed parts followed by tingling and redness after warming, and sometimes later desquamation, does not constitute frost bite as no real tissue damage occurs.

The true extent of frost bite is difficult to assess, but fortunately the treatment of all degrees is the same. Speed of onset, degree of cold and duration of freezing are pointers in the history. Rapid surface freezing is followed by slower freezing of deeper tissues.

Superficial frost bite – the skin and immediately underlying tissues only are involved.

Initially   The very first stage, frostnip, is the 'white spot', most often seen in the face or on the ears. This is the stage where a local frost bite should be recognized and re-warmed by the skin to skin method. In the next stage the injured area has a marbled, white, frozen appearance and is insensitive. It feels cold and firm, but is resilient to gentle pressure and moves freely over underlying bony points.

After re-warming mild cases are at first numb and assume a mottled blue-red colour. Swelling occurs, accompanied by stinging and burning fo some time. No blisters form. In more severe cases blisters appear in 24 – 36 hours and become hard and black in about two weeks. Oedema settles with complete bed rest but throbbing and burning pain persists for several weeks. Redness, tenderness and sensitivity to even mild cold persist for variable periods after healing has occurred. Excessive sweating may continue for some time.

Deep frost bite   Penetration occurs through skin and subcutaneous tissues into deeper structures.

Initially the frozen surface is pallid, yellowish and waxy. It feels cold and solid and will not move over bony prominences. In warm atmosphere condensation occurs on the skin.

After re-warming it becomes cyanotic and bluish. Extensive oedema affects the whole extremity, may last more than a month and may be accompanied by stiffness of the digits. Aching and throbbing after about two days is associated with shooting pains lasting two to eight weeks. Huge blisters appear in the first week, then blacken and dry. Later they are sloughed off, sometimes as the complete cast of a digit. Parts which fail to blister will probably fail to survive. The resulting, underlying thin, red sensitive skin takes many months to return to normal. It may itch and perspire profusely. Normal sensitivity to cold may never be recovered. Hypoxia deep to the frozen tissues is the probable cause.

Extreme cases which are not rapidly re-warmed result in loss of tissue. The skin becomes grey and remains cold due to vascular thrombosis. Blisters, with proximal oedema, may mark the line of demarcation. Dry gangrene follows in one or two weeks with adequate care, and the tip of the area becomes black and mummified. Reliable definition of the line of demarcation takes about 10 weeks. Earlier assessment is misleading as much viable tissue may underlie the black eschar.

Moist gangrene, the result of added infection, extends the tissue damage. The part is wet, soft and inflamed. The whole limb is painful and swollen. Even in patients where the skin circulation recovers without gangrene there may be damage to nerves, nerve endings, muscle fibres and sweat glands which leads to hyperaesthesia, pain, hyperhidrosis and finally fibrosis of the peri-articular tissue, tendon sheaths and muscles.

c   Non-freezing cold injury

1)   *Trench foot and immersion foot*   This commonly affects the lower limbs and is the result of immobility, often in a dependent position, in cold, wet conditions. It gives rise to a feeling of coldness, numbness and tingling.

(a) Pre-hyperaemic phase.   This lasts 6 – 24 hours. The feet are white, cold, painful and heavy. The affected foot may be mottled, red and blue. The toes and ankles are stiff. Walking is difficult. Local tendon jerks and deep muscle sensation may be lost and a stocking type of sensory loss develops. Peripheral arterial pulses may be impalpable. Before thawing (unlike frost bite), the tissues feel resilient, but after thawing this distinction disappears and the history may be the only guide to differentiation. Re-warming can result in severe swelling up to the knees.

(b) Hyperaemic phase.   This may last for two months. The feet become flushed with bounding peripheral pulses. Swelling increases with blisters, ecchymoses and petechiae. Gangrene will occur in distal parts which fail to become warm. Infection results in extension of the gangrenous area. The line of demarcation is marked by intensified hyperaemia and blistering. After a few days the hyperaemia and swelling subside and the feet become pale, but remain warm. Areas of necrosis usually superficial become more clearly defined. Pain is initially continuous and diffuse, but after 7 – 10 days it becomes stabbing and is aggravated by movement or heat. Shooting pains spread from the centre of the foot to the toes, last for weeks, and gradually recede. Anaesthesia recovers slowly. Wasting of the intrinsic muscles leads ultimately to flat foot and clawing of the toes may occur. X-rays show marked osteoporosis.

(c) Post-hyperaemic phase.   Chronic disability may result. The foot may become permanently cold with an exaggerated sensitivity to cold. Pain on warming and hyperhidrosis may be features.

(2) *Chilblains*   A mild local reaction to dry cold. In the acute stage there is swelling and the skin is red, hot, tender and itches. Between active periods the skin is red and rough. There is no tissue loss.

Treatment

General hypothermia

a Of short duration (ie with an active core circulation) – *rapid re-warming* aims to restore body heat without the risk of paradoxical cooling. On removal from cold water further heat loss occurs by conduction from the body core to the chilled exterior shell. This induces a further call in the deep body core temperature of 4 °C (7 °F) ('after drop') which may be fatal. Immersion in hot water prevents this by simultaneously heating the surface tissues.

When the body appears practically dead attempts should be made to raise the dangerous level of body temperatures as quickly as possible. Resuscitation by mouth to mouth respiration with alternate chest compression should be carried out, though muscle spasm may make this impossible.

When there are many casualties (eg ship-wreck) the unconscious, whether breathing or not, should be treated first. As an emergency measure, while preparations are made, warm water should be thrown over the casualties.

Method Remove wet clothing, then place the patient in a tub with water between 41 °C – 45 °C (106 °F – 113 °F) until the rectal temperature rises above 35 °C (95 °F) or shivering stops. Once shivering stops and consciousness returns external warming can cease. Body heat should be restored before the rapid re-warming of frozen limbs is attempted, and the limbs should be left out of the bath for this reason.

b After prolonged exposure and extensive deep freezing (ie with a sluggish core circulation), *slow re-warming* without added external heat is better. Paradoxical cooling and imperfect blood oxygenation are caused by warming the superficial tissues while the heart and lungs are still cold. Peritoneal lavage with a sterile solution at 37 °C can be used with good effect.

In hypothermia, danger occurs during re-warming when the patient's thermoregulatory centre causes shivering with an increase in body temperature. This increases tissue oxygen demand and overloads the heart and lungs, already hypoxic from a sluggish core circulation. At this stage shivering can be prevented by the application of external heat. Remove the patient when the core temperature reaches 33 °C to avoid hyperpyrexia.

Babies require slow re-warming. They tolerate sudden temperature changes poorly.

Ventricular fibrillation may respond to procaine amide injection.

c When no facilities exist for warming in a bath, warmth should be provided by a change into dry clothes under shelter, placing the patient in a sleeping bag, using the bodily warmth of comrades, and by hot drinks and food, as soon as the patient is able to swallow.

Frost bite

Alcohol mistakenly taken for prevention, predisposes to cold injury by producing peripheral vasodilation and interfering with heat regulation.

First aid Sudden blanching or cessation of cold discomfort, often followed by a feeling of warmth in the affected part, can be effectively treated by locally applied warmth until a normal colour returns. Examples are – the firm pressure of a warm hand; warm breath, shielded by cupped hands; frost nipped finger tips in a warm armpit; toes or heels on the abdomen of a companion; followed by dry socks and loosely laced boots. Friction and rubbing of any kind increases tissue damage and is contra-indicated.

Evacuation Evacuation should be to hospital as soon as possible. In the event of staging becoming necessary during evacuation, support can be given by a unit where the patient can be kept in comfort in an even room temperature and at complete rest until final transfer can be affected.

A strong patient can walk on frozen feet, but NOT after thawing or re-freezing as serious tissue loss occurs with an increased susceptibility to infection. Stretcher transport is then essential. A man with a frozen foot is not a stretcher case unless otherwise injured. He may save his own and his companions lives by remaining ambulant. Tissue loss after several days walking may be nil or negligible, but there must be no constricting clothing above the affected area. Immediate rapid re-warming and aseptic care in a hospital or suitable unit minimizes serious tissue loss. If stretcher borne, general measures to maintain whole body heat and minimize heat loss are necessary as the patient is seldom able to maintain his own body heat in extreme cold. Hot fluids, warming between two warm bodies in a dry, warm sleeping bag, and the use of a sleeping bag to prevent further heat loss are desirable measures.

General management in a major unit

Rapid re-warming followed by aseptic, conservative management summarises treatment. Further damage is prevented by extreme care and gentleness at all stages, together with the prevention of infection.

Method All cold, wet clothing is removed gently. Warm water may facilitate the removal of frozen clothing. The frozen part is then immersed in a warm bath, ideally at 44 °C (112 °F). Repeated temperature checks close to the frozen limb, by a thermometer or uninjured hand (which cannot normally bear a temperature in excess of 47 °C (116 °F), are essential.

A whirlpool bath containing hexachlorophane is ideal, but to ensure thawing of the deeper tissues the water must not be allowed to cool below 42 °C (108 °F). This necessitates the continual and repeated addition of water to the bath, never above 46 °C (115 °F) and away from the frozen part.

If a bath is not available the part should be wrapped in towels and warm water at 44 °C (112 °F) poured over it continuously.

Re-warming should last about 20 minutes or until the nail beds flush. A purplish colour is an ominous sign. After thawing, the part should be mopped dry with great care. In the elderly, thawing may depress cardiac function and myocardial oxygenation may become critical.

Other methods. Dry heat If liquid re-warming is impossible, warm hands, axilla or abdomen, warm air, loose warm clothes or blankets can be used. Careful wrapping with sterile bandages minimizes the slightest friction. These measures must be continuous and take three to four times as long as immersion.

DO NOT try to re-warm by exercising the frozen part. Damage is increased.

DO NOT rub a frozen part at all.

DO NOT expose it to an open fire, really hot water or other intense heat.

The partly or totally anaesthetic limb is unable to react to further injury.

General measures

a The disturbing appearance of the frost-bitten parts calls for *reassurance* by those in medical and nursing attendance.

b A *high calorie, high protein diet* with vitamin supplements is required.

c *Sleep and rest* should be encouraged. After the first 10 minutes of re-warming pain increases, but does not become unbearable. Older patients with a poor circulation suffer more pain.

Aspirin tablets (600 mg) will not mask other injuries or depress respiration. It is useful throughout treatment. Pethidine 25–50 mg half an hour before re-warming may be given if the patient's condition is good. An alcoholic hot drink, in warm surroundings, is a potent peripheral vasodilator and gives some sedation. Tranquillizers are useful to calm nervous patients. Narcotics should be used with caution because of the risk of addiction in long term use.

d A booster dose of *tetanus toxoid* is given.

e An orally administered broad spectrum *antibiotic,* eg tetracycline, should be administered as soon as possible.

f *Physiotherapy* Active movements are encouraged at least twice a day or more from the start, with the avoidance of all friction. Finger movements for 10 minutes every hour are carried out through a full range. Buergers exercises are carried out four times a day. A warm bath greatly assists exercises.

g *Contra-indicated* are:
Smoking
Anti-coagulants
All local applications.

h Where facilities exist the *benefit of an oxygen chamber* should be considered.

Surgical intervention should in general be avoided. It damages marginally viable tissues and increases the risk of infection. Encircling tight eschars on digits may be split after two to three weeks to free joints. Amputation has a place only many months after injury when complete demarcation of the mummified part has occurred. Premature amputation sacrifices viable deep tissue. Wound closure should be partial and followed by intensive aseptic whirlpool treatment. Infected gangrene may require surgery to limit spreading cellulitis, but this is unusual. Complete rest, asepsis and antibiotics may, however, affect auto-amputation with maximum preservation of tissue.

Prognosis Reheated tissue requires oxygen for survival. The core of a limb on which the skin depends for its circulation may take 24 hours to thaw. Proportionately, the more slender digits unfreeze more quickly. Assessment of the degree of freezing and hence the prognosis is extremely difficult.

Trench foot immersion foot

This is treated in a warm bath at 35.5 °C–37 °C (96 °F–98 °F) to relieve pain. Men whose feet have been damaged short of freezing should not walk more than is absolutely necessary. The injured limb is elevated and never allowed to dangle. In the hyperaemic phase, a cool temperature, not below 18 °C (65 °F), lessens pain. Watch should be kept for signs of pneumonia and renal damage. The appearance of the limb in the first week may be alarming and swelling is likely on getting out of bed. Sympathectomy has no place in the treatment of the acute phase of cold injury.

Management of the wounded in a cold climate

First aid The prevention of heat loss and maintenance of the peripheral circulation is of primary importance. Warmth is the first essential to the immobile, stretcher borne patient. Treatment of the wound is secondary unless blood loss threatens to impair the circulation.

Bleeding should be controlled by pressure and elevation to save life. Encircling bandages and dressings should be avoided, but profuse bleeding may necessitate a shell dressing bandaged firmly over clothing. *Tourniquets are dangerous* and risk the loss of the limb from frost bite.

Wounds should be covered by loose, sterile dressings to protect them from injury and infection during evacuation.

Fractures Missile injuries of limbs require adequate splintage: the lower limb a Thomas splint. Particular attention must be paid to the circulation and temperature using extra covering, preferably furs and, whenever possible, as is used in Scandinavia, an external source of heat. A boot must always be removed below a sprain or fracture and replaced by warm coverings. Boots constrict and are poor insulators.

Morphine: should be carried by the medical officer in warm body clothing to prevent freezing. It can be used even after thawing. Multiple injuries may necessitate its use and, as intravenous administration may be difficult, it can be given orally in larger doses. Cold delays the absorption and action and increases the toxicity of injected drugs, especially narcotics. As dosage is cumulative, it should be reduced and given at increased time intervals.

Antibiotics should be given orally as a prophylactic measure. Sedatives are dangerous as they may suppress shivering and induce hypothermia.

Smoking causes peripheral vasoconstriction and may tip the scale against the survival of a limb.

The main aim is to prevent chilling. Place the patient in a sleeping bag and evacuate immediately.

General management

Remove wet clothing gently. Hot drinks should be given. Keep the affected extremities at room temperature and the body warm. Shock with multiple injuries and freezing must be treated vigorously by elevation of the feet, oxygen and transfusion with blood, plasma or dextran to restore the blood volume.

Treatment following thawing

Treatment after thawing is as important as rapid re-warming. Full aseptic technique is essential. Frost-bitten parts are carefully cleansed by gentle toilet without rubbing, using hexachlorophane, cholorohexidine or another benign surgical soap solution. Alcoholic solutions damage the tissues and cause pain. Sterile cotton wool pledglets between the digits prevent maceration and rupture of blisters. Blisters should not be snipped or removed, but left to dry up.

The injured part is treated by exposure so long as it remains warm and dry and nothing touches it. Sterile sheets and cradles are important. After re-warming, it is maintained at normal body heat: if cover proves necessary, loose, soft, dry dressing are used. A pillow behind the calf keeps a foot off the sheet. Even light pressure from sheets or tight dressings can increase tissue loss. Whether in a hospital bed or sleeping bag, pressure must always be avoided. The part should be left undisturbed except when soiled dressings require changing. Bed rest continues until all swelling has subsided and all blisters and raw areas have dried up. The injured part is kept horizontal. Raw areas and oozing blisters are occasionally cleaned with mild, non-alcoholic antiseptic preparations.

It is better to avoid all tampering if possible. Antibiotics are indicated to combat infection. If available, a whirlpool bath should be used for 20 minutes twice a day with hexachlorophane.

A man whose feet or hands have been damaged by cold should not be returned to a fighting unit in a cold climate.

CHAPTER 25

Surgery in the tropics and tropical diseases of surgical significance

Tropical diseases are seen in soldiers serving overseas or in the UK in those recently returned from service in a tropical climate. Their recognition in endemic areas need not present any difficulty provided a careful history is taken, but may not be easy in a non-endemic area. The Handbook of Army Health and the health precis for the areas prepared by the Royal Army Medical College should be consulted as a guide.

General principles

a *Air conditioning* Air conditioning of wards and some theatres is some protection against post-operative complications. Elective surgery should be avoided in severe hot weather, when heatstroke may prove fatal after a relatively simple surgical procedure.

b *Correction of dehydration* In emergency surgery in tropical conditions the dehydrated patient must have his fluid loss made good before being subjected to even a minor operation. Fluid loss before, during and for some days after the operation must be restored and that from over-sweating prevented – bulky dressings and too many bedclothes should be avoided: pyjama trousers and a single sheet, as a rule, are all that can be tolerated. Careful attention must be paid to fluid balance: intake and output must be carefully recorded.

c *Prevention of urinary calculi* Because epidemiological studies have shown an increased incidence of stone formation in the tropics, the subject of urinary calculi is best dealt with in this section. Urinary calculi may be classified as primary or secondary. The latter are most commonly associated with urinary stasis and subsequent infection by organisms liable to render the urine alkaline, such as B proteus or Staphylococcus aureus. It is well recognized that patients immobilized for long periods have a considerable increase in urine calcium excretion as a result of mobilization of calcium from the bones. These patients are therefore particularly liable to stone formation. Patients who require catheterization, or periods of indwelling catheterization, are especially at risk and the greatest care must be taken not to introduce infection into the urinary tract during catheterization. Careful attention should be paid to the reaction of the urine, which should be tested twice daily. Acidifying agents such as mandelamine may be indicated where the urine is consistently alkaline. Infection must also be excluded by regular urine microscopy and culture, and the appropriate therapy prescribed where indicated.

Urinary calculi

Primary stones seen in military practice are generally idiopathic and found subsequently to be associated with idiopathic hypercalciuria. The association of excessive sweating, more concentrated urine and an increased incidence of urinary calculi is well documented. Recent Army research has suggested that ultraviolet light by stimulating vitamin D production in the skin increases the urinary calcium excretion. In the prevention of primary stones therefore an adequate fluid intake of at least five litres per day in the tropics is required, and a limited exposure to sunlight would seem mandatory.

Diagnosis   The classical intermittent or colicky loin pain which radiates to the groin or testis should be supported by the presence of red blood cells in the urine and by radiology. Where possible emergency intravenous urography should be performed before treatment is commenced. This will differentiate right sided pain from appendicitis or cholecystitis and will demonstrate the severity of the obstruction. As many stones are too small to be seen on a plain X-ray, the spasmodic effect they have on the ureteric muscle may be demonstrated if serial films are taken over the course of many hours. Contrast medium secreted by the glomerulus and tubules will ultimately mix with the obstructed urine distally and 'point' to the site of the stone. This obviates the need for ascending pyelography later.

Management   Pethidine 100 mg (± buscopan 20 mg) may be given on admission. The pethidine is more effective if half the dose is given intravenously. Parenteral fluids may be required: a fluid balance chart should be initiated and all urine examined for the presence of stones.

An elevated temperature suggests superadded infection in an obstructed kidney and is an indication for ampicillin or septrin. If the fever is not controlled within hours, surgical intervention is indicated to preserve the kidney from irreparable damage by pyelonephritis.

Most stones are ultimately passed, but the luxury of waiting indefinitely is denied to military practitioners.

The principal indications for surgery:

a *In the acute phase:*

(1) Presence or subsequent development of infection in an obstructed kidney.

(2) Absence or non-function of the contralateral kidney causing calculous anuria.

(3) Intractable pain.

(4) Small calculi in the region of a ureteric orifice which may be released by meatotomy.

b *In the chronic phase:*

(1) Recurrent infection.

(2) Evidence of increasing obstruction.

(3) Stone remaining in: Renal Pelvis (or pelvi-ureteric junction). Upper ureter. or at the pelvic brim or ureteric orifice, ie sites of ureteric narrowing.

(4) Stone 0.5 cm diameter.

(5) Personal commitments of patient (exigencies of the service).

(6) Patience of patient and medical attendant exhausted.

Surgical procedures All approaches to the ureter must be extraperitoneal. A longitudinal ureteric incision should be made over the stone. A ureteric catheter should be passed proximally and distally to exclude other obstruction. A splint when the ureter is grossly thickened may reduce the risk of stenosis. An intra and extravesical approach may be required when the calculus is impacted in the intramural portion of the ureter. All wounds must be drained. Persistent leakage after 12 days may be due to debris in the distal ureter which the passage of a ureteric catheter endoscopically may remove.

The patient must be X-rayed at the last possible moment before surgery in case the stone has moved or been passed.

Stones salvaged from the urine or removed at operation must be sent for analysis. All patients must be referred for calcium studies to exclude hypercalciuria or hyperparathyroidism. Subsequent follow-up is mandatory as long term studies have shown a 75 per cent recurrence rate in males. But, as the average time to recurrence is 9.5 years, a patient should not be automatically downgraded unless some abnormality in his calcium metabolism is identified.

Modifications of surgical methods in the tropics

Recognized surgical methods have to be modified to suit conditions. In the treatment of severe burns in heat-stroke conditions the unburned area of skin and its freedom to function is of more importance than the burn.

Exposure treatment is essential and the burns may be sealed quickly by the use of Nobecutane. A sterile mosquito net, a fan and fly spray are of great value.

In under-developed areas service surgeons will often be involved in 'hearts and minds' treatment, as the natives in the tropics usually suffer from malnutrition and live in squalor and poverty. There may, at times, be a marked racial difference in reaction to injury or disease, related to religious beliefs and lack of understanding. A patient in fact may recover from an operation of the greatest magnitude or succumb to one which is not thought to be serious. He may also recover complete function in an apparently hopelessly damaged limb or refuse ever again to bend his knees after a menisectomy, correctly performed. Given the opportunity he may well forcibly remove a plaster jacket, and operation dressing, or any drainage tube. This only underlines the necessity of strict nursing supervision.

By the same token the availability of an artificial limb post-operatively should be taken into account in planning an amputation. A Syme's amputation, for example, may be a better proposition in some countries than a below knee amputation at the site of election. A warm climate will in fact be more favourable to an amputation stump than the cold and wet of a more northerly clime.

Diagnostic difficulties

For the newcomer to the tropics difficulties in diagnosis abound. A disease apparently surgical may prove purely medical and a medical disease may have a surgical complication. Not infrequently two diseases are present. The history is of great importance and any disturbance of the usual sequential pattern should be viewed with suspicion. In suspected appendicitis, for example, vomiting before pain is often of significance and diarrhoea perhaps indicative of dysentery rather than inflammation in the pelvis. Acute appendicitis in the dysentery ward is always a possibility.

The blood picture is often a useful aid to diagnosis and should be routinely examined in all abdominal cases, for malaria may account for some of the symptoms.

The white cell count may also provide useful collateral information. A figure of 6000 in the tropics suggests a medical fever, of 12 000 acute appendicitis with a gangrenous appendix and of 20 000 a liver abscess.

A stained blood film should also be examined, if in doubt, for malarial parasites which in the thin film are intracellular.

TROPICAL DISEASES OF SURGICAL SIGNIFICANCE

The risk of tropical disease in an endemic area will be recognized, but the occasional occurrence of such diseases in temperate areas requires some knowledge of tropical conditions and emphasizes the need for careful histories.

Tropical diseases can mimic or complicate surgical conditions, and frequently influence diagnosis and treatment. An example is provided by an old aphorism: when confronted with an acute abdomen suggestive of acute appendicitis, the surgeon in the tropics should consider the possibility of malaria, dysentery (amoebic or bacillary), roundworm or an acute sickle-cell crisis.

Malaria

Malaria is diagnosed by the examination of suitably stained blood films. A negative film does not exclude the diagnosis, and examinations may have to be repeated until the diagnosis is not in doubt.

Falciparum malaria A common presentation is fever (which need not show 'tertian' periodicity), headache and nausea, with hepatosplenomegaly, anaemia and jaundice depending on the duration of the disease.

But there is little that is typical about 'malignant' malaria, and its presentation can be confusing. A quiet onset can rapidly deteriorate into one of the dramatic manifestations where treatment may be of no avail. Occlusion of the microcirculation may lead to infarction of any organ producing a localized and misleading picture.

Plasmodium falciparum causes a rapidly progressive infection in non-immune persons, and tends to kill. Deaths from malaria in the UK have all been due to P falciparum acquired in Africa, and have occurred within 10 days of leaving Africa. In each case diagnosis was delayed for at least a week.

Recrudescences may occur up to two years (usually one year) after the first attack. A history of residence, however brief, in an endemic area, must not be overlooked.

Malaria is curable, and deaths usually avoidable. In endemic areas, blood films on every acute admission are justifiable.

Treatment Chloroquin is still the standard drug in the treatment of malaria, but chloroquin-resistant falciparum malaria has spread through South East Asia, and parts of Central and South America. It is wise to assume chloroquin resistance in patients from these areas.

Chloroquin may be given orally in a dose of 600 mg (base) followed in six hours by 300 mg and 300 mg again on each of the following two days. If there is actual or potential vomiting, the initial dose at least must be given IV (200 mg base by slow injection or in 500 ml saline in 30 minutes). The drug should also be given IV if the patient is seriously ill or if complications are present. If chloroquin resistance is suspected 500 mg quinine should be administered by slow IV injection or in 500 ml saline. It is rarely necessary to repeat these IV doses (of either drug) more than once, and never within eight hours.

Other forms of malaria (P vivax, ovale, malariae) These 'benign' forms of malaria are rarely lethal, but are prone to chronicity and relapse with the maturation and release of asexual forms of the parasites. Relapses may occur up to five years (10 years with P malariae) after exposure. The taking of prophylactic drugs in endemic areas reduces but does not eliminate these relapses.

After an initial period of remittent fever, the pattern of a rigor recurring every second or third day is established. Splenomegaly, anaemia and jaundice may be present in persistent cases. Serious complications are rare.

Treatment Radical cure requires destruction of erythrocytic and tissue forms of the parasite. A three day course of oral chloroquin as detailed above is combined with primaquine 7.5 mg twice a day for 14 days.

Amoebiasis

Infestation with Entamoeba histolytica has been found world-wide. In the majority of cases it is a harmless commensal, and the presence of cysts in faeces is not an indication for treatment. In the warmer regions, including parts of southern Europe, the organism may invade the bowel wall or migrate to other organs, especially the liver. The latent period varies from a few days to many years, so that clinical amoebiasis can present in temperate regions in patients exposed elsewhere. The invasive disease is very rare indeed in northern Europeans who have never been abroad to the tropics or sub tropics.

Intestinal amoebiasis Presentation may vary from mild, intermittent diarrhoea lasting for months or even years, to acute severe dysentery progressing rapidly to peritonitis and death. In its various forms differential diagnosis will include bacillary dysentery, schistosomiasis, ulcerative colitis, Crohn's disease and carcinoma of the colon or rectum.

Diagnosis is made by the identification of the actively motile trophozoite usually containing ingested red blood cells in unstained preparations from fresh stools or in material obtained at sigmoidoscopy. In most cases, single or multiple ulcers can be seen in the rectum or lower colon, and scrapings of the exudate from the floor or biopsy from the edge of such ulcers can be examined for parasites.

Except in the fulminant or complicated case fever and constitutional signs are not present. Blood investigations are often not helpful, but serological tests (eg amoebic fluorescent antibody titre) may be useful with any degree of tissue invasion.

Treatment Metronidazole 800 mg three times a day for five days will cure 95 per cent of patients and involves no problems of serious drug toxicity. Ill patients should also receive emetine 60 mg IM daily for five to ten days. Emetine is a general tissue toxin with particular effect on the heart, and it is necessary to keep the patient in bed under supervision during treatment. Dosage should be reduced if demanded by the condition of the patient.

Complications

a *Perforation and peritonitis* Most cases will recover on treatment with emetine and antibiotics together with the usual supportive therapy. If surgery cannot be avoided, it should be limited to the minimum necessary.
b *Amoeboma* Granulomas present as single or multiple tender masses, usually in the caecal region. They respond to medical treatment. The mortality following surgery is over 50 per cent.
c *Haemorrhage* Profuse bleeding due to erosion of a vessel in the bowel

wall should be treated with blood transfusion, emetine and metronidazole. Surgery may be necessary, but involves a poor prognosis.

Hepatic amoebiasis

Evidence of concomitant bowel invasion is very unusual in hepatic amoebiasis, so diagnosis by identification of the parasite is impossible. The clinical picture seen in British service personnel consists of fever, pain and tenderness in the hepatic region, and enlargement of the liver, which is usually palpable below the costal margin. The majority of abscesses occur in the upper part of the right lobe, and an elevated, immobile diaphragm can be detected by clinical and X-ray examination. There is a moderate neutrophilia and a raised erythrocyte sedimentation rate (ESR). If available, serological tests are reliable and helpful and liver scanning can be used to localize abscesses. In their absence, a therapeutic trial with emetine, chloroquin or metronidazole may produce a definite, but not necessarily dramatic, response over a few days.

More florid forms of the disease, often of considerable duration, may be seen in indigenous populations.

Different diagnosis Primary and secondary carcinoma, pyogenic abscess and infected hydatid cyst.

Treatment Metronidazole is an all-purpose drug in amoebiasis. It can be supplemented with emetine 60 mg for ten days or chloroquin 150 mg bd for four weeks. Resolution of small liver abscesses can be expected, but others may require aspiration if they are large or palpable, or if symptoms do not remit on drug therapy. Open drainage and such procedures as marsupialization lead to complications, and are never appropriate. Indiscriminate needling for diagnostic or therapeutic purposes is unnecessary with modern diagnostic aids and effective therapy.

Complications Extension of an abscess into adjacent structures is not uncommon. Empyema, basal pneumonia, lung abscess and the production of amoebic pus in the sputum indicate spread through the diaphragm. Peritonitis and pericarditis can also occur. Appropriate drug therapy may have to be augmented by surgical treatment.

Schistosomiasis

Worms of the *Genus Schistosoma,* measuring up to 2 cm in length, live in the portal vein and its tributaries. Gravid females migrate to the pelvic plexuses. The eggs with terminal or lateral spines, reach the mucosal lining of the bladder and intestine, where they produce a local inflammatory response. Some are passed in the urine or faeces. They are infective only to snails.

Hepatic fibrosis, with enlargement of the liver and spleen, is common in all forms of established schistosomiasis.

S Haematobium   Various parts of Africa and Middle East. This species mainly selects the vesical plexus, producing urinary symptoms. The eggs may be found in the urine, traditionally in the terminal part of the midday specimen. Others are calcified, and surgeons in endemic areas become very familiar with the 'sandy-patch' appearance of the bladder wall on cystoscopy. Papillomata, containing many eggs, may develop, and are potentially malignant. Haematuria is the common presenting symptom, often with frequency and dysuria. The urethra, seminal vesicles and ureters may all be involved.

S Mansoni   Africa and South America. In this type, females move to the haemorrhoidal plexus, and the eggs reach the wall of the lower bowel, causing dysentery or at least blood stained stools. Polyps and rectal prolapse are seen in chronic cases but portal hypertension due to hepatic fibrosis tends to dominate the late clinical picture.

The eggs may be identified in faeces, or from rectal biopsies taken at proctoscopy. In the absence of a visible lesion, biopsies can be taken from an area above the level of haemorrhoidal veins. The material is examined as a fresh wet preparation under low magnification.

S Japonicum   China, Japan, Phillipines. Adult worms inhabit the small veins of the large intestine, mainly the haemorrhoidal plexus, but also the gastric and mesenteric veins. Its pathogenicity resembles that of S Mansoni, but its effects tend to be more severe.

Treatment of schistosomiasis   Niridazole (Ambilhar) 25 mg per kilo body weight in two divided doses daily for five to seven days. Toxic effects can be troublesome, and any complicated case, especially if there is evidence of liver involvement, should be treated in hospital, preferably by a physician with experience of the problem.

Leishmaniasis

The Leishmania protozoa are widely distributed through the tropics and sub tropics as natural parasites of rodents. The vector is the sandfly which flies feebly for short distances at a modest altitude, so the disease is often limited to specific localities.

a In *Visceral Leishmaniasis L Donovani* parasites are found in the entire reticulo endothelial system. Fever may be conspicuous, but other constitutional symptoms may be few, and the disease can continue for months. Enlargement of the liver, spleen and lymph glands develops, with some wasting and generalized pigmentation (kala-azar = black sickness). There are typical changes in the blood counts, ESR and serum proteins. The disease is diagnosed by recognition of Leishman-Donovan bodies in material obtained by biopsy from lymph glands, bonemarrow, liver or spleen, in that order of preference.

b *Glandular Leishmaniasis* A chronic, painless adenitis without systemic disturbance has been reported in British servicemen in the Mediterranean area. It is regarded as an arrested form of visceral Leishmaniasis, and is distinguished from the other causes of lymphadenopathy by the finding of Leishman-Donovan bodies in glands removed at biopsy.

Treatment Sodium antimony gluconate (Pentostam) by injection.

c *Dermal Leishmaniasis* Moist or ulcerated, and dry indurated forms are recognized, depending on strain variations of the parasite, L tropica. The lesions occur on any exposed surface, and may be multiple. The dry form begins as a papule which grows and may ulcerate centrally, but scabs over. It tends to heal spontaneously in several months, leaving an atrophic scar. The wet form is more destructive but also heals eventually, producing a disfiguring, depressed scar.

The diagnosis is made by recognizing Leishman Donovan bodies in tissue fluid obtained by aspiration or by biopsy.

Treatment with Pentostam may be necessary for multiple lesions, or for ulcers in areas of functional or cosmetic importance.

d *Espundia* Muco-cutaneous Leishmaniasis found only in Central and South America. The nose and mouth may be extensively damaged by granulomatous ulceration.

Leprosy

Not strictly a tropical disease, but the vast majority of cases occur in tropical and sub-tropical countries, especially in Africa and the Indian sub-continent. No case has been contracted in the United Kingdom for about 50 years.

Clinical presentation is very variable, depending largely on the immune status of the patient. The diagnosis may be overlooked unless a history of prolonged domicile in an endemic area is obtained. The disease affects the skin and peripheral nerves.

A chronic skin condition with altered or absent sensation, with associated depigmentation and rash, but without irritation, may suggest the diagnosis. Thickened peripheral nerves with damage to sensory and motor fibres may be seen with a variety of palsies, deformities, neuropathic ulceration, absorption of phalanges, and painless trauma.

The diagnosis is confirmed by the examination of dermal material from ear lobe or from the active edge of a lesion, in which Mycobacterium leprae may be seen in a suitably stained preparation.

Cutaneous larva migrans

Caused by the infective larvae of various dog hookworms. These penetrate the skin and move around in the epidermis for weeks, causing itching and an urticarilal track. The condition is most commonly seen in the feet of children, and is cured by freezing the advancing end of the track, or by inunction of thiabendazole ointment.

CHAPTER 26

The medical management of mass casualties

Mass casualties may occur in peace – for instance in underdeveloped areas in time of natural disasters – or as the sequel of nuclear warfare. The senior medical officer at the scene should declare that because of limited medical resources 'mass casualty conditions' prevail.

Definition A mass casualty situation is one in which an overwhelming number of seriously injured or otherwise incapacitated individuals, within a limited area or multiple areas and a brief period of time are placed upon locally available medical facilities quite unable to supply medical care for them (NATO Glossary AAP6 (2)).

In these circumstances the aim of the medical services must be to assume care to the greatest benefit of the largest number.

Assistance of other services

Other agencies must assist:
a By providing specialist support.
b By taking over tasks to free all medically trained personnel to use their medical skills to best advantage.
In particular assistance would be required from:
a Headquarter staff to afford command and control facilities, direct other specialist services and organize general duty personnel assistance.
b Transport agencies to provide traffic control and information services.
d Signals to provide emergency communications.
e All arms to provide general duty personnel to free medical personnel for their primary task.

Preparation and training

In considering the medical response three types of situation may be contemplated:
Situation A is one in which mass casualties occur where no medical unit is immediately available and initial action is in the hands of regimental personnel with or without medical officers. Clearly here the accent will be

on first aid and rapid evacuation, and no pre-planned organization can be used. Medical personnel will be few and the need for all soldiers of all arms to be proficient in first aid is therefore obvious, while regimental or RAMC medical assistants will be required to perform more skilled tasks including minor procedures normally reserved to the medically qualified. Those medical officers present will be fully engaged in organizing the total medical effort, triage and treatment of high priority cases. Medical equipment may be in short supply and a series of medical emergency packs have been devised to be held in garrisons against such an emergency. These are described in Annex A.

Situation B is where a field medical unit is at hand but has no potential for definitive surgery; an example is a field ambulance without field surgical team support. The emphasis in this instance will again be on first aid and evacuation but the unit may be able to hold and treat low priority cases. Plans must be made to organize the unit in a way similar to that suggested in Annex A and, even though no formal surgical support is present, a progressive care organization similar to that in a hospital is adopted.

Standing operating procedures (SOPs) should be practised regularly, at least annually, in unit exercises and should include:

a the organization of the unit and deployment of personnel to deal with mass casualties;

b training of individual personnel in their role;

c optimum use of available assistance from other service agencies;

d criteria for categorization and management of casualties;

e control and use of critical items of medical supply;

f liaison with civilian authorities where and when applicable;

g disposal of dead.

In Situation C a medical establishment with surgical potential, a field or general hospital, is overwhelmed by mass casualties. Here the emphasis lies in using all available manpower as economically as possible and providing smooth organization for the rapid reception and categorization of casualties. Again SOPs are required along the lines suggested above and these must be practised regularly.

Much therefore can be accomplished by individual and collective training to prepare to meet such emergencies and, having a standing field medical organization, the Army Medical Services are uniquely placed to respond to such situations in the most effective way.

Triage

Conventional triage must be abandoned under these conditions. Casualties must be classified by type and severity of injury and to take account of the likelihood of good quality survival. Many variable factors make it impossible to lay down firm rules that are generally applicable. However, the following guidelines with examples of each group make a framework for categorization:

a *IMMEDIATE treatment group T1*

This group includes those patients who require some form of first aid surgery to save life or limb. The procedure should not be time consuming and should concern only those in whom the chances of good quality survival are high. Allotment to such a group assumes the presence of a forward surgical team which can be reached with minimal evacuation. Respiratory obstruction. Accessible haemorrhage. First aid amputations. Open fractures.

b *DELAYED treatment group T2*

This group comprises those patients fit for evacuation, who need time consuming surgical treatment, but whose lives will not be unduly endangered by delay. The amount of delay imposed will often be critical, but its effects may be minimized by the use of antibiotics, intravenous fluids and nasogastric suction when applicable. Closed fractures of large bones. Burns of up to 30 per cent (roughly estimated). Large muscle wounds. Abdominal injuries. Thoraco-abdominal injuries. Head or spinal injuries.

c *MINIMAL treatment group T3*

This is likely to constitute a very large group and may account for more than a third of the injured. It includes all those patients with a relatively minor injury who can be effectively dealt with when first seen by the medical officer or other medical attendant and subsequently care for themselves or be helped by untrained personnel. Small lacerations or abrasions. Closed fractures of small bones. Small burns (10 per cent unless face and hands).

d *EXPECTANT treatment group T4*

This comprises those patients who are the victims of serious and often multiple injury and whose treatment would be difficult, time consuming and complicated. They are often not fit to move along hazardous evacuation routes, and, if fully treated, make heavy demands on medical manpower and supples. They should not be allowed to enter and encumber the evacuation routes, but should receive appropriate supportive treatment locally. The extent of treatment will depend on available supplies and manpower and may involve the use of large doses of narcotic analgesics. These patients should not be abandoned, but every effort should be devoted to their comfort and the possiblility of survival with even the most alarming injuries always kept in mind. Burns of more than 30 per cent. Multiple injuries. Severe head or spinal injuries. High and lethal doses of radiation.

Association of irradiation and conventional injury on mass casualty category

If a casualty has received a combination of irradiation and conventional injury his mass casualty categorization may be varied according to the following table:

Serial	Conventional injury mass casualty category	Irradiation dosage received		
		150 rads	150-400 rads	400 rads
(a)	(b)	(c)	(d)	(e)
1	Purely irradiated with no other injury	T3	T2	T4
2	MINIMAL T3	T3	T2	T4
3	IMMEDIATE T1	T1	T2	T4
4	DELAYED T2	T2	T2	T4
5	EXPECTANT T4	T4	T4	T4

It may not always be possible to determine the dosage of irradiation which a casualty has received. In these cases reliance must be placed on clinical symptoms and a categorization on clinical symptoms is suggested as follows:

a Headache   – T3
b Headache and nausea   – T2
c Diarrhoea, vomiting and other symptoms   – T4

An early categorization of T4 may be changed at a later stage depending on the progress made by the casualty.

It is essential to recognize that casualty sorting is a dynamic and not static process. Many factors affect a decision. A significant alteration in one of them may allow the patient to be placed in a new category.

Evacuation

The order of evacuation of casualties to the nearest surgical facility will clearly be T1, T2, T4, T3. The critical decision will be which casualties to categorize T1. This will depend upon the time to be taken to reach a surgical centre. The shorter the time, the greater number of casualties will benefit from immediate treatment and thus be in category T1.

Management at a medical establishment

Reception   It is in reception where most use can be made of pre-planned organization and team work. The main need for a reception area is a large empty space to facilitate movement of casualties and communication between working teams. Depending upon manpower available and the numbers of casualties, the reception staff should then be organized into a series of filters shown diagrammatically in Annex A.

a *Monitoring and cleansing team(s)*   The task of these teams will be to decontaminate casualties if a nuclear or chemical environment exists.

b *Primary filter(s)*   These personnel will rapidly sort obvious T1 and T3 cases from the rest. No formal examination or documentation is carried out at this stage.

c *Preliminary examination team(s)*   The task of these teams is to ease subsequent definitive medical officer triage by initiating documentation, loosening clothing and carrying out superficial examination which should follow a set pattern.

d *Medical officer team(s)*   At this stage final decisions on categorization are made on clinical grounds. It is essential that the most experienced medical officer available should supervise this work.

Treatment

For treatment purposes the unit should be organized into separate areas for high, medium and minor care, each of which should be staffed and equipped accordingly. Casualties will pass from reception into these areas depending on the category to which they have been allotted. While selection for high and minor care areas is less difficult to define, the mix of patients in medium care will cause the greatest concern. Alteration in the condition of casualties in this area may change them from delayed (T2) to either immediate or expectant category.

The grievously injured expectant cases (T4) will require to be made as comfortable as possible. It would be callous to mix them with the minimal cases in the minor care area and equally wasteful of medical resources to send them to the high care area. A diagrammatic scheme of the reception and treatment of mass casualties is in Annex A.

Conclusion

The senior medical officer must be constantly aware that the situation is a finite one, and be prepared to return to conventional methods as soon as possible. For the same reason those responsible for triage must remember that it is a continuous process and the need for constant reassessment of the individual's category is paramount.

ANNEX A to CHAPTER 26

Scheme for triage in a medical establishment receiving Mass Casualties

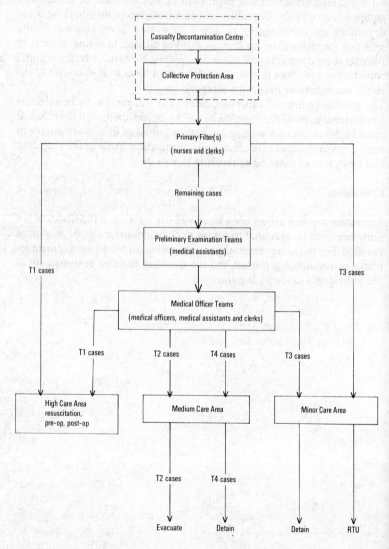

MEDICAL EMERGENCY PACKS

Medical emergency packs to be used in mass casualty situations should be designed to meet the following requirements:

Treatment is to be confined at least to:

a The treatment of shock

b The establishment and maintenance of a free airway

c The control of haemorrhage

d The relief of pain

e The application of sterile wound dressings

f The immobilization of fractures, etc

g The control of infection

h The emergency care of injuries which require priority in treatment, eg the closing of sucking chest wounds, chest tube drainage

j Basic nursing.

The contents of the packs should be limited to those items indispensable in carrying out these measures, bearing in mind that in most cases the first aid will be given by persons other than trained medical personnel.

The medical emergency packs should be considered as a supplement to existing assemblies and regularly stored medical material, designed primarily for first aid to mass casualties. The packs should be kept as simple and practical as possible.

The packs may be grouped as follows:

Type I – for use by non-medical personnel

Type II – for use by trained medical personnel

Type III – for basic nursing purposes

If desirable, another type could be supplied including splint sets, litters (stretchers), blankets, etc.

Another way of grouping may divide the above mentioned indisposable items in:

Phase I – for use by non-medical personnel

Phase II – for use by trained medical personnel.

Method of packing

Weight, size and shape of packs should be such as to enable one person to carry them.

Packing should permit quick orientation and easy access to the different items. Each type of pack will have one stock number, as a single issue item, to facilitate re-supply and cross-servicing. Each pack will contain a printed list of items by functional characteristics.

CONTENTS OF MEDICAL PACKS

The medical emergency packs are to contain the following items listed in general terms by their functional characteristics:

a *Dressings:*
  (1) Field dressings, first aid, large medium and small (sterile).
  (2) Burns dressings (sterile)
  (3) Bandages, gauze (sterile)
  (4) Pads, gauze, surgical (sterile)
  (5) Adhesive plaster
  (6) Cotton wool
  (7) Bandages (sling) triangular
  (8) Eye dressings

b *Drugs, blood substitutes, chemicals:*
  (1) Injectable, strong analgesic, syrettes (morphine or substitute).
  (2) Analgesic, oral
  (3) Tranquillisers
  (4) Anti-emetics and intestinal sedatives (for radiation sickness)
  (5) Ophthalmic analgesic
  (6) Blood substitutes, IV electrolytes
  (7) Salt tablets, oral (for Rosenthal method)
  (8) Water purification tablets
  (9) Cortisone injections
  (10) Anaesthetics
  (11) Antibiotics (broad spectrum)
  (12) Tetanus toxoid, tetanus anti-toxin
  (13) Liquid antiseptic
  (14) Soap, surgical
  (15) Plaster of Paris materials including emergency splint packs
  (16) Splints, wire, ladder and cutter
  (17) Lubricant, surgical

c *Miscellaneous material:*
  (1) Scissors, bandage
  (2) Airways, pharyngeal
  (3) Pins, safety
  (4) Tourniquets

(5) Surgical instruments, set for haemostasis, excision, suture, chest drainage, tracheostomy; needles and suture, unabsorbable
(6) Syringes and needles
(7) Sterilizer, with reserve spirit container
(8) Naso-gastric tubes
(9) Catheters, urethral, plastic
(10) Field cards with pencils
(11) Pencil, skin marking, and plaster marking

d *Nursing equipment:*
   (1) Kidney dishes
   (2) Urine bottles
   (3) Bed pans
   (4) Cups, plates, cutlery, kettles
   (5) Candles, matches

CHAPTER 27

Rehabilitation

Aim

Rehabilitation aims at the restoration of health and function, and the return to duty in the shortest possible time of those who have become unfit by injury or disease.

This objective should be clearly borne in mind and from the earliest possible stage the 'rehabilitative approach' should govern all medical and surgical treatment. The consequent improvement in morale and the preservation of confidence in their future will be of incalculable benefit to patients.

Organization

Rehabilitation must be planned and in addition to the specific medical or surgical treatment, its main components are:

a *Physiotherapy* to restore mobility to joints, strength to muscles and co-ordinated movement to limbs or other affected parts. Exercises both remedial (ie specifically directed to the affected part) and general, form the essential basis of the treatment, and are aided as required by other forms of physiotherapy.

b *Occupational therapy*   This is divided into two types:

(1)   Remedial or specific occupational therapy. This type is designed to provide involuntary exercising of the injured part whilst it is engaged in a creative handicraft. The method is of particular value in restoring mobility and co-ordinated function to injured hands.

(2)   Diversional or general occupational therapy, as its name implies, is designed to provide mental stimulation and prevent boredom. An infinite variety of hobbies, handicrafts and entertainments can readily be provided at all stages in a patient's treatment.

c *Organized outdoor games* for the later stages.

d *Vocational retraining*   In the final stages the soldier is prepared for a return to duty by drill, marches, etc, and tradesmen develop their particular skills in the workshops of the Occupational Therapy Department.

Stages in rehabilitation

a *At military hospitals* Restoration of function begins in bed as soon as any existing danger to life or limb has been eliminated. The medical and nursing staff should at all times bear in mind the rehabilitative approach. Physiotherapists, remedial gymnasts, occupational therapists, BRCS workers and the RAEC are there to provide all facilities. The fullest use should be made of their services.

b *At Joint Services Medical Rehabilitation Units* These specially equipped and staffed units are designed to continue and complete the rehabilitation of the long term or major case. These will in the main be patients who have sustained major trauma of the locomotor system or who have suffered from illness with muscle paresis, or who are recovering from major orthopaedic operations. When fit to become ambulant such patients will still be significantly disabled and will require intensive and specific rehabilitative treatment on the lines indicated above. It is important that as soon as they are fit to be up all day they be transferred from the dependent atmosphere of the hospital to the more purposeful, positive and active regime at the Medical Rehabilitation Unit (MRU).

INDEX

Tarsorrhaphy   242
Tetanus   57–9
– immunization   57, 58
Third echelon, field hospital   15
Thoraco-abdominal wounds   202
Tracheostomy   30, 59, 245, 288
– technique   262
Transfusion – intra-arterial   46
– rapid aids to   45–6
– reactions to   47
Trench foot   265, 269, 274–5
Turning frames, Stryker,
   Emesay, improvised   190–1
Tympanic membrane, rupture
   of   256–7

Urethra, injuries of   226–7
Urinary calculi, prevention
   of   277–8

Uveitis   238

Vascular injury   140
Vaso-vagal shock   34
Ventilation, pulmonary
   stabilization of   19
– controlled   116
Ventriculitis   180
V-Y advancement   133

Water depletion   73
Wound missile, distribution   5

Yaw   3

Z-Plasty   133

Printed in England for Her Majesty's Stationery Office
by Linneys of Mansfield
Dd. 698726   K40   4/81

NOTES

NOTES

NOTES

NOTES

NOTES